Teacher Inquiry

The research teachers carry out into their own professional practice and environment is increasingly recognized as highly relevant and valuable. As well as being an exciting and fulfilling kind of research to carry out, it informs both policy and practice in education, constitutes a key resource for teachers, teacher educators and policymakers and is important for professional development.

Bringing together accounts of teacher research projects from all over the world and from all sectors of education *Teacher Inquiry: Living the Research in Everyday Practice* covers:

- The practicalities of initiating and conducting teacher research;
- The different models and methodologies available to teacher researchers;
- The issues surrounding, and emerging from, teacher research.

The editors' introduction provides insight into the reasons for undertaking teacher inquiry, its valuable role in contemporary education and what new directions this form of research might take in the future. The collection reflects the incredible diversity of teacher research, and is a rich source of both information and inspiration for any teacher embarking on, or thinking of conducting, research into their own professional context.

Anthony Clarke is Associate Professor and **Gaalen Erickson** a Professor at the University of British Columbia's Centre for the study of Teacher Education.

Teacher Inquiry

Living the research in everyday practice

Edited by Anthony Clarke and Gaalen Erickson

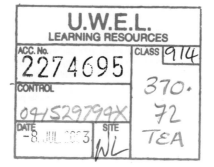

RoutledgeFalmer
Taylor & Francis Group

LONDON AND NEW YORK

First published 2003
by RoutledgeFalmer
11 New Fetter Lane, London EC4P 4EE

Simultaneously published in the USA and Canada
by RoutledgeFalmer
29 West 35th Street, New York, NY 10001

RoutledgeFalmer is an imprint of the Taylor & Francis Group

© 2003 Edited by Anthony Clarke and Gaalen Erickson

Typeset in Palatino by
HWA Text and Data Management Ltd
Printed and bound in Great Britain by
Antony Rowe Ltd, Chippenham, Wiltshire

British Library Cataloguing in Publication Data
A catalogue record for this book is available from the British Library

Library of Congress Cataloging in Publication Data
A catalog record for this book has been requested

ISBN 0–415–29794–X (hbk)
ISBN 0–415–29795–8 (pbk)

For
Isobel and George
Anne and Melvin

Contents

List of contributors

Vinnie E. Acklin is the Project G.O. teacher at Randolph Elementary School, Arlington, Virginia. A teacher-researcher, as well as a writing consultant of the Northern Virginia Writing Project of George Mason University, Vinnie's interests also include reading and elementary math.

Ron Avery is a teacher at General Currie Elementary School, Richmond, British Columbia. He seeks to teach what a caring human should know.

Gillian Bickerton is an experienced elementary teacher who values the teacher researcher role for its contribution to understanding her practice. She has a doctorate in Educational Psychology and Special Education. Her doctoral study focused on the development of children's understanding of buoyancy.

Robin Bright is a Professor of Education at the University of Lethbridge in Alberta. She teaches courses in English Language Arts, Early Childhood Education, Writing and Gender. She is the author of several books and articles on literacy and family literacy in Canada and abroad.

Marina Carter teaches French, history and English at Charles E. London Secondary in Richmond, British Columbia. Her interests include travelling, cooking, and reading. One day Marina hopes to write a book about her experiences as an educator.

Cynthia Chambers teaches curriculum studies, English/Language Arts and First Nations education at the University of Lethbridge. In conjunction with the Literacy Research Centre housed at the University of Lethbridge, she is currently undertaking a project on traditional pre-contact aboriginal literacy.

Anthony Clarke is a teacher educator at the University of British Columbia with an interest in teacher education, student teaching and advisory practices.

Miriam Cooley is an art educator in the Department of Elementary Education of the Faculty of Education at the University of Alberta. She previously taught at Acadia University in Nova Scotia. Her work in teacher education is grounded in experience as an art specialist in elementary, middle years, and secondary classrooms, in post-secondary studio and art education programs, and as an artist/researcher in photography, video and film.

Jacqueline D. Delong is Superintendent of Education responsible for Program Services for the Grand Erie District School Board, a board of 31,000 students in southwestern Ontario, Canada. Her PhD thesis asks and answers the question, "How can I improve my practice as a superintendent of schools and create my own living educational theory?" She is president of the Ontario Educational Research Council, co-creator and editor of *The Ontario Action Researcher* electronic journal and a fervent supporter of practitioner-researchers in her board and province.

Sukhy Dhillon is an elementary school teacher in Delta, British Columbia. Sukhy has taught adult education, English as a second language at the high school and primary levels, primary learning assistance and physical education. Her interests are in parental involvement, particularly of Indo-Canadian parents in Canada and in India (comparative studies) as well as the role of mothers in their children's education.

Kim Douillard co-directs the San Diego Area Writing Project (SDAWP) and is the coordinator of the SDAWP Teacher Research Group. As a multiage teacher at Cardiff Elementary School in Cardiff-by-the-Sea, California, Kim values inquiry and writing as tools for learning for both students and teachers.

Gaalen Erickson is the Director of the Centre for the Study of Teacher Education at the University of British Columbia. His interests embrace the areas of student and teacher learning specifically in the fields of science education and more generally in teacher education.

Sarah Fletcher is a lecturer in Education at the University of Bath. She taught in schools for over twenty years and now works with teachers as they create their own professional knowledge to improve teaching and learning in their classrooms. Her passion for this "research mentoring" and disseminating teachers' knowledge is evidenced by her website at www.teacherresearch.net.

Leah Fowler teaches undergraduate pre-service teachers and graduate students at the University of Lethbridge. Her research focuses on difficulty in teaching and narrative research methods in curriculum studies and language arts. She is at work on a new book related to her research interests. Her new book (in review) is called *A Curriculum of Difficulty: Narrative Research and the Practice of Teaching*.

Rosamar Garcia is an intermediate grades elementary school teacher in Richmond, British Columbia. Rosamar has been the lead teacher for the *Learning through the Arts* program at her school and is keenly interested in understanding creative thought in math, science and art.

Peter Gouzouasis is an Associate Professor and Coordinator for Music Education in the Department of Curriculum Studies at the University of British Columbia. A lifelong teacher-learner for the past 25 years, his cutting edge work at UBC enabled him to establish the FAME cohort in 2000. His interests include arts-based applications of traditional and digital media across the curriculum, and arts-based research from a musician's perspective.

Kit Grauer is the Deputy Head and Coordinator of Art Education for the Department of Curriculum Studies at the University of British Columbia. Kit's interests include arts-based and image-based research as well as teacher education.

Amanda Nicole Gulla is an elementary school staff developer at the Professional Development Center on the Lower East Side of New York City. A poet and a writer, she is also a teacher-consultant for the New York City Writing Project, and an instructor at New York University and Bank Street College. She is currently writing her doctoral dissertation on the use of story in teachers' learning processes.

Erika Hasebe-Ludt teaches curriculum studies, literacy and culture, and English as a second/other language in connection with teacher education at the University of Lethbridge, Alberta. Her research focuses on auto/ biographical writing in between languages and cultures.

Donelda Henderson is a primary teacher in Richmond, British Columbia. She has taught kindergarten and combined early primary grades for 31 years. Her undergraduate focus was in Early Childhood and Integrated Curriculum Planning. She is currently completing a Master of Education in Language and Literacy at the University of British Columbia.

Garry Hoban is a senior lecturer at the University of Wollongong, NSW, Australia. He encourages pre-service teachers to research how they learn in university classes in order to deduce insights into ways of teaching. He has been using the World Wide Web as a way of sharing insights in teacher research.

Elizabeth Jordan was a secondary science teacher for 11 years before moving to the University of British Columbia 14 years ago. Her interests include problem-based learning, constructivism, learning, problem solving, and an active involvement in pre-service teacher education.

Elizabeth Kreuger was a program coordinator for the Nunavut Department of Education at the time of authorship. She currently lives in the Eastern

Townships of Quebec, where she teaches elementary school and lectures at Bishop's University.

Jim Kreuger is a program coordinator for the Department of Education in Nunavut Territory, Canada, where he has lived with his wife and two children since 1993. His professional interests lie at the intersection of Curriculum Development, Community Development, and Teacher Professional Development. He collaborated with his sister, Elizabeth, on the study presented here.

Kathy Lavery is a teacher at General Currie Elementary School, Richmond, British Columbia. She is interested in developing, within students, an attitude of respect: for oneself, one's peers, one's environment, through a program that transcends the classroom walls.

Carl Leggo is a poet and associate professor in the Department of Language and Literacy Education at the University of British Columbia where he teaches courses in writing and narrative inquiry. His research interests include autobiography, living poetically, and pedagogy of the heart.

Barbara Leigh, co-founder of the FAME cohort, was recently appointed Vice Principal with the North Vancouver School District. She has been an elementary classroom school teacher for 27 years, including work as a specialist in dance, music and technology. For the past 6 years she was a faculty advisor and instructor in Teacher Education at the University of British Columbia.

John Loughran works in the Faculty of Education at Monash University Melbourne. He has been actively involved in teacher education for the past decade. His research interests include teacher-as-researcher, reflective practice, science education, and teaching and learning. Recent publications include *Developing Reflective Practice, Opening the Classroom Door* (Loughran and Northfield), *Teaching about Teaching, Improving Teacher Education Practices Through Self-Study* (Loughran and Russell) and *Researching Teaching* (Falmer Press).

Chris Lugar teaches senior high English and drama at Northeast Kings Education Centre in Canning, Nova Scotia. His interests in developmental drama have led him from provincial curriculum development and implementation to research into the effect that developmental arts experiences have on adolescents as well as the mentally ill. This work has led him to a master's degree focusing partially on the development of "self" in secondary drama experiences.

Judith McBride is a special educator at Macdonald-Cartier High School in St Hubert, Quebec. She has a particular interest in the social/academic experience of the learning disabled adolescent. Judith is a doctoral candidate and part-time lecturer in the department of Educational

Psychology at McGill University and the focus of her work may be found in adult learning theory as it may support the stories of the teacher-researcher. As a teacher-researcher herself, she strives to bring the two interests together.

Danan McNamara is a teacher-researcher with the San Diego Area Writing Project at the University of California, San Diego. A multiage teacher at Cardiff Elementary School in Cardiff-by-the-Sea, California, Danan believes teacher-research is an essential component to teaching and learning as it promotes advocacy for teachers, students and quality education.

Jean McNiff is an independent researcher. She is also Adjunct Professor at the University of Limerick, and a Visiting Fellow at the University of the West of England. She has written widely about issues of professional development, using action research approaches.

Ian Mitchell, now a senior lecturer at Monash University, Melbourne, has spent 23 years teaching secondary science. For the last 14 years, his work has been split between his school and his university. He has a long involvement in teacher-research, both as a teacher and as an academic friend.

Donna F. Nelson is a kindergarten teacher at Mosinee Elementary School in Mosinee, Wisconsin. She resides in Mosinee with her husband, Kurt, and children, Chris (20) and Nikki (16). Her previous action research interests have included: inclusion of special needs students, teacher burnout and ethics in education.

Louise Panziera is an intermediate teacher in Richmond, British Columbia. Although she enjoys teaching all subjects, her passion is Language Arts. When she is not teaching reading and writing, she is doing it herself at home while her baby takes his naps.

Michael Pollard is an Associate Professor in the Faculty of Education at the University of Lethbridge. His interests include children's literature, writing, the role of story in the learning process, learning styles and holistic approaches to education.

Marion Porath is a Professor in the Department of Educational and Counselling Psychology, and Special Education at the University of British Columbia. Marion has taught at the elementary and university levels. Her interests include social development, advanced development, constructivist theory and problem-based learning.

Sharon Shockley Lee is Associate Professor of Education at Southern Illinois University, Edwardsville. Following Paulo Freire, her goal is rigorous and joyful learning and teaching. She uses qualitative methods for self-study and to investigate the practice of other educators. Sharon is particularly interested in social justice and ethical issues in education.

Henry St. Maurice is Director of Field Experiences and Professor at the University of Wisconsin – Stevens Point. He has also taught in elementary, secondary and rehabilitation programs. His research interests include rhetorical, philosophical, and historical studies of teacher education.

Kay Strouse graduated from the University of Illinois, Champaign-Urbana, Illinois, with a BA in Speech Communication. She earned education credits for teacher licensing from Illinois State University, Normal, Illinois and an MS in Education from the University of Wisconsin – Stevens Point, Wisconsin. Currently, she teaches writing at Stevens Point Area Senior High and serves the school district as the Assistant Language Arts Coordinator.

Owen van den Berg is a native of South Africa, and has published in the fields of action research, curriculum, politics of education, history teaching and early childhood education. Since 1995 he has been living in St Louis, Missouri, where his major work has focused on supporting teachers doing action research. He is currently Associate Professor in the National College of Education at National-Louis University.

Christine Waechter is a teacher of fourth grade in Stevens Point, Wisconsin. Her research interests include the importance of writing as a means of reflection on life experiences.

Susan Walsh is a PhD candidate in the Department of Secondary Education at the University of Alberta. She has taught English Language Arts, drama, and French in public schools as well as dance and fitness in the community. She currently works and plays in the areas of teacher education and poetry.

Jack Whitehead has been a lecturer in the Department of Education of the University of Bath since 1973. He is a former President of the British Educational Research Association and a Distinguished Scholar in Residence at Westminster College. Original ideas from his self-study research include the inclusion of "I" as a living contradiction in educational enquiries of the kind, "how do I improve what I am doing?" His award winning website, http://www.actionresearch.net, contains his doctoral research on the creation of a new disciplines approach to educational theory together with the living theory doctoral research of practitioner-researchers associated with the University of Bath.

Pamela Winsor is an Associate Professor at the University of Lethbridge where she teaches courses in language arts education and supervises

student teachers. Her research interests include professional development through portfolios, implications of technology for reading
instruction, and teacher education programs in economically developing
countries.

Acknowledgements

An edited book of this nature requires the cooperation and support of a number of people. We would like to acknowledge them here.

Many of the chapters in this book had their origin in a very successful annual meeting of the International Conference for Teacher Research held in Richmond, British Columbia in April 2001. We want to thank the following people who were members of the organizing committee for this conference: Elaine Decker, Betty Eades, Nancy Everett, Pam George, Stephanie Hardman, Sabina Harpe, Larry Hurst, Christine Massot-Simpson, Kathy Pantaleo, Janet Powell, Al Sakai, Margie Savigny, Marcie Timmins, Janet White, and Jessica Williams.

We wish to acknowledge the excellent support and work of Hywel Evans, our working editor with RoutledgeFalmer. He responded to all of our many queries with dispatch and grace. Finally we owe a great debt to our local editorial assistant, Judy Paley. She was indispensable in terms of keeping the project on schedule, anticipating potential issues, proofreading and generally overseeing the many different tasks associated with a collaborative effort which brings together forty-five different authors.

Chapter 1

Teacher inquiry
A defining feature of professional practice

Anthony Clarke and Gaalen Erickson

Tony and a colleague recently submitted a self-study manuscript (an analysis of two faculty members inquiring into their use of technology) to a journal that was recommended as a viable outlet for their research. After almost a year, the manuscript was returned with an invitation to resubmit with revisions. Although the editor did not indicate any difficulty he had with self-study manuscripts, the reviewers certainly did; for example, one wrote:

> These experiences are very individualistic and may or may not be generalizable to broader populations of teacher educators. (Manuscript review, personal communication, April 15, 2002)

This refrain, familiar perhaps to others who inquire into their own practice and seek to share those inquiries with a wider audience, represents a range of issues that confront those who engage in teacher inquiry. While some of our colleagues find it difficult to appreciate teacher inquiry as a legitimate form of research, this form of inquiry is increasingly being recognized by a broad spectrum of educators who constitute our professional communities (Clarke 2001). Teacher inquiry – or teacher research as it is sometimes known – has made significant inroads at local, national, and international levels. Indeed, one such forum, the International Conference on Teacher Research, now in its tenth year, was the impetus for the collection of papers that appear in this text. The emergence of a vibrant and extensive teacher inquiry literature not only attests to its importance for understanding the complex world of schooling but supports our contention that it is one of the defining features that distinguishes teaching as a form of professional practice and not as labour or technical work.

What is professional practice?

There are many definitions of professional practice. Key dimensions common to all definitions include: specialized knowledge, intensive preparation, a code of conduct, an emphasis on continued learning, and the rendering of a public service (Brown 2001; Sachs 1997; Sykes 1990). Only in recent times has the practice of teaching been considered a profession. Important to our discussion here is the concept of "continued learning" and its emergence in teaching.

Hargreaves (2000) charts four distinct phases over the past 100 years that illuminate the development of teaching as a profession: pre-professional, autonomous professional, collaborative professional, and the post-modern professional. In the first two phases teachers are primarily technicians in the classroom. In the first phase teachers follow system-wide directives about particular teaching practices, and in the second phase, although given greater authority to select from among particular pedagogical strategies, teacher practices are carefully prescribed by those in positions of higher authority (superintendents of instruction, etc.). In both instances curriculum is "a given" with little discretionary license on the part of the teacher to negotiate or modify it.

In phases three and four we witness the emergence of teacher inquiry as an element of teaching practice where recognition of personal practical knowledge (Connelly and Clandinin 1985) signals a shift in our appreciation of how teachers continue to learn about their practice and the role that inquiry plays in curricula and pedagogical decisions: "teachers often learn best in their own professional communities ... on-site, built into ongoing relationships ... ." (Hargreaves 2000: 165) In the third phase, collaboration among teachers enables authentic professional communities to develop in schools that investigate and respond to local problems and issues. In the fourth phase, the post-modern phase characterized by a recognition of complexity and uncertainty, Hargreaves argues that now more than ever it is imperative for teachers to engage in systematic and sustained inquiry that "lifts teachers out of the pre-professional prejudice that only practice makes perfect." (p. 167) Failure to do this, Hargreaves cautions, will result in deprofessionalization forces wresting control of curricula and pedagogical practices from teachers (witness recent calls for "centralized curricula, and testing regimes," Hargreaves 2000: 168).

While Hargreaves warns of the political agenda that underlies any formalized standards for a profession, nonetheless, there is almost universal agreement that inquiry and reflection in and on practice are essential elements of the teaching profession. For example, in the United States, the National Board for Professional Teaching Standards defines a teacher as one who is able to "analyze classroom interactions, student work products, their own actions and plans in order to reflect on their practice and continually renew and reconstruct their goals and strategies." (NBPTS 2002) In England, the General Teaching Council regards professional teachers as those who "continually reflect on their own practice, improve their skills, and deepen their knowledge." (GTC 2002) The Australian College of Educators argues that it is incumbent upon members of the teaching profession to be "reflective practitioners ... committed to their own professional development: seeking to deepen their knowledge, sharpen their judgment, expand their teaching repertoire, and to adapt their teaching to educationally sound developments arising from authentic research and scholarship." (Brock 2000: 11)

In short, for teaching to assume the mantle of a profession a central tenet of that practice is the ability and willingness of its members to inquire into their own practice; into ways of improving and developing their practice consistent with the unique contexts in which they work and with an appreciation of current trends in education. Most of the chapters in this book, particularly in the first section on Enacting Teacher Research in Practice Settings, exemplify this focus on the improvement of practice through systematic inquiry – a focus strongly supported by Bullough and Pinnegar (2001).

What is teacher inquiry?

Teacher inquiry is ... a generally agreed upon set of insider research practices that promote teachers taking a close, critical look at their teaching and the academic and social development of their students. ... Although known by many names – teacher research, action research, practitioner research, insider research – teacher inquiry involves classroom teachers in a cycle of inquiry, reflection, and action. In this cycle, teachers question common practice, approach problems from new perspectives, consider research and evidence to propose new solutions, implement these solutions, and evaluate the results, starting the cycle anew. (Lewison, in press)

As Lewison (in press) indicates, teacher inquiry is *research*. We emphasize the word research to deliberately signal that self-study in teaching is a systematic and rigorous process designed to explore and extend teacher knowledge (Cochran-Smith and Lytle 1993). The word research here is consistent with the type of activities that Hargreaves uses to delineate between the pre-professional and professional phases in the history of teaching.

As the chapters in this text reveal, teacher inquiry takes on many forms and includes practitioners at all levels of the educational system. Underlying all forms, is the analysis of one's own practice with all the attendant challenges and celebrations associated with such scrutiny. It is encouraging to see these issues, prominent in the current literature, for example, Pritchard's (2002) and Zeni's (2001) analyses of ethical issues in teacher inquiry, taken up in a variety of forms by the authors within this text. Teacher inquiry is also an active enterprise with outcomes more often represented as *teacher knowing* (learning that is in a state of evolution) rather than *teacher knowledge* (implying learning that is more fixed and stable). This shift represents a further movement towards Hargreaves' post-modern professional. It is no coincidence that paralleling the emergence of teacher inquiry as a legitimate form of research, is the development of richer and more varied representational forms that capture the essence of teacher inquiries; forms that were unheard of in the educational literature 25 years ago. This text captures a sampling of those forms, some more established and others more exploratory. In fact, some of these forms, drawing upon the uses of new digital tools and media, are extremely difficult to represent in a text format.

Mindful of Cochran-Smith and Lytle's (1993) admonishment against shuttered insularity within teacher inquiry communities, this text also provides an opportunity for comparison and cross-referencing by present-ing cases, methods, models, and emergent issues from an international community of educators. This comparative dimension is particularly important as teacher inquiry – largely a case-study literature – requires peer review, commentary, and critique to ensure substantive development and contribution for those engaged in the investigations and for the members of the broader professional community to which they belong. As announced at the beginning of this chapter, the issues surrounding the public credibility and publishing of this work remain problematic. A crucial aspect of this public credibility is negotiating the tension between one's own practice and the more public understanding of that practice. Bullough and Pinnegar (2001), in their important article on establishing quality criteria or guidelines in self-study research, nicely capture this tension:

> Quality self-study research requires that the researcher negotiate a particularly sensitive balance between biography and history ... such study does not focus on the self per se but on the space between self and the practice engaged in. There is always a tension between those two elements, self and the arena of practice, between self in relation to practice and the others who share the practice setting.
>
> (Bullough and Pinnegar 2001: 15)

Inquiry is embedded in *professional* practice

Some authors highlighting the interesting tension that exists between practice and inquiry suggest that the former sometimes constrains the latter. For example, Sachs (1997) acknowledges that teacher inquiry is a hallmark of professional practice but, following Fullan (1993), worries that at times teachers become so preoccupied with pupil learning that they often neglect their own learning and therefore diminish their standing as professionals:

One of the hallmarks of being identified externally as a professional is to continue learning throughout a career, deepening knowledge, skill judgment, staying abreast of important developments in the field and experimenting with innovations that promise improvements in practice (Sykes, 1990). Here lies one of the paradoxes for teacher professionalism for as Fullan (1993) notes, as a profession, we are not a learning profession. While student learning is a goal, often the continuing learning of teachers is overlooked. While continuous learning and the improvement of our practice should be at the core of teacher professionalism in many instances this is not so. (Sachs 1997: 7)

We share this concern but believe there is an important distinction between a preoccupation with "student learning" (which includes class scheduling, record keeping, and report writing) and a preoccupation with "how students learn." Schön (1988), among others, argues that the latter is the cornerstone of professional practice. Further, a preoccupation with how students learn is a necessary precursor to being curious about one's own practice. When reframed in terms of "how students learn," inquiry is embedded in practice and teacher learning as a natural (unavoidable?) outcome. This is an important distinction for us. In contrast, we suggest that when a teacher ceases to be inquisitive about his or her practice – inquisitive about how students learn – then his or her practice ceases to be professional. Without inquiry practice becomes perfunctory and routinized.

In the chapters that follow, the authors demonstrate how inquiry is embedded in professional practice. They share insights about how their inquiries are enacted, the methods and models they use, and the issues that emerge from their inquiries. Teacher inquiry is carried out in the "indeterminate, swampy zones of practice" (Schön 1987: 3) and benefits from the support of colleagues engaged in similar enterprises and the scrutiny of the wider educational community. The accounts confirm Hamilton and Pinnegar's (1998) observation that "the multilayered, critically imbued, reality-laden world is the text of the self-study scholars." (Hamilton and Pinnegar 1998: 235) At times provocative, and at other times contemplative, this collection of writing provides an important resource for the teaching profession and illustrates the level of scholarship that this genre of inquiry generates and sustains within our profession.

Bibliography

Brock, P. (2000) Standards of Professional Practice for Accomplished Teaching in Australian Classrooms: A National Discussion Paper. Australian College of Education, Australian Curriculum Studies Association and Australian Association for Research in Education. Available online: http://www.austcolled.com.au/dispaper.pdf.

Brown, J. (2001) *The Definition of a Profession,* Princeton: University Press.

Bullough, R. and Pinnegar, S. (2001) "Guidelines for quality in autobiographical forms of self-study research," *Educational Researcher*, 30, 3: 13–21.

Clarke, A. (2001) "The landscape of teacher education: critical points and possible conjectures" *Teaching and Teacher Education*, 17,5: 599–611.

Cochran-Smith, M. and Lytle, S. (1993) *Inside/outside: Teacher Research and Knowledge,* New York: Teachers College Press.

Connelly, F. M. and Clandinin, D. J. (1985) "Personal practical knowledge and the modes of knowing: relevance for teaching and learning," in E. Eisner (Ed.) *Learning and Teaching the Ways of Knowing* (pp. 174–98), National Society for the Study of Education Yearbook, Chicago: University of Chicago Press.

Fullan, M. (1993) *Change Forces,* London: Falmer Press.

General Teaching Council: Professional Standards (2002) Professional Standards. Available online: http://www.gtce.org.uk/gtcinfo/code.asp.

Hamilton, M. and Pinnegar, S. (1998) "The value and promise of self-study," in M. Hamilton (Ed.) *Reconceptualizing Teaching Practice* (pp. 235–46), London: Falmer Press.

Hargreaves, A. (2000) "Four ages of professionalism and professional learning", *Teachers and Teaching: History and Practice*, 6, 2: 151–82.

Lewison, M. (in press) "Teacher inquiry," in E. P. St John, S. A. Loescher and J. S. Bardzell (Eds) *Improving Early Reading and Literacy in Grades 1–5: A Resource Guide for Programs that Work*, Thousand Oaks, CA: Corwin Press, Inc.

National Board for Professional Teaching Standards (2002) National Board Certification. Available online: http://www.nbpts.org/nat_board_certification/.

Pritchard, I. (2002) "Travelers and trolls: practitioner research and institutional review boards," *Educational Researcher*, 31, 3: 3–13.

Sachs, J. (1997) "Reclaiming the agenda of teacher professionalism: an Australian experience," *Journal of Education for Teaching*, 23, 3: 264–77.

Schön, D. (1983) *The Reflective Practitioner: How Professionals Think in Action*, New York: Basic Books.

Schön, D. (1987) *Educating the Reflective Practitioner: Towards a New Design for Teaching in the Professions*, San Francisco: Jossey-Bass.

Schön, D. (1988) "Coaching reflective teaching," in P. Grimmett and G. Erickson (Eds) *Reflection in Teacher Education* (pp. 19–29), New York: Teachers College Press.

Sykes, G. (1990) "Fostering teacher professionalism in schools," in: R. Elmore (Ed.) *Restructuring Schools: The Next Generation of Educational Reform* (pp. 59–96), San Francisco: Jossey Bass.

Zeni, J. (2001) "A guide to ethical decision making for insider research," in J. Zeni (Ed.) *Ethical Issues in Practitioner Research* (pp. 153–66), New York: Teachers College Press.

Part I

Enacting teacher research in practice settings

Chapter 2

Writing matters

Exploring the relationship between writing instruction and assessment

Kim Douillard

Beginnings of district-wide writing assessment

During the 2000–1 school year, our small coastal school district of fewer than 1,000 students decided to implement a standards-based writing assessment for our K-6 students (approximately 5–12 year-olds). I responded to this new development with mixed feelings. One part of me welcomed the attention to writing that a new writing assessment would bring to our district. Another part of me feared the limitations of this assessment and the prospect of writing instruction becoming another "teaching to the test" opportunity. I didn't want writing to become formulaic with the writing assessment as the sole focus. I still wanted writing to be creative, explorative, and meaningful to students. Instead of complaining, resisting, or passively acquiescing, I decided to use this as an opportunity for inquiry. As a teacher-researcher and a teacher with a strong interest in writing, I became involved in the development of our district prompted writing assessment and researched its effect on my students. Specifically, my research focused on my desire to understand the relationship between classroom writing instruction and district-wide prompted writing assessment.

As a small district, we often wait to implement new assessments and curriculum mandates until bigger districts and our County Office of Education develop their own versions. Our school year began with a binder containing the writing assessment prompts developed by the San Diego County Office of Education. From the beginning these were only a template, a starting place, and open to change to suit the needs of our students and our learning community. As a positive, these prompts were process-based, including time for brainstorming, drafting, editing and recopying. The time limits were generous and included opportunities for whole class modeling. As a negative, many of the prompts were contrived and limiting. The third grade prompt, write a letter to a student (that you have never met) who is coming to your classroom, is a writing situation that narrows student writing. First, combining the format of the friendly letter with the expectation of narrative description confounds the issue. Third grade students often write "chatty" friendly letters ("Hi, how are you?") filled with the informality of peer-to-peer conversation. I wondered, is the purpose of the prompt to test letter format (a convention) or to assess narrative description? In addition, writing to an imaginary student contributes to the contrived nature of the prompt.

Since teacher research means looking closely at my own practice, examining student work, and analyzing the relationship between the two I needed to establish a baseline of student writing in my own classroom. A first day writing sample, an unprompted piece of the student's choice, established a starting place for student writing for the school year. I continued to collect data during the school year including samples of student writing both in response to the assessment and from other writing opportunities, anecdotal records of student reactions and interactions, notes on my own process and that of the other teachers I work with, and "official" results from scoring papers. With the support of my colleagues in the San Diego Area Writing Project (SDAWP) Teacher Research Group, a group of educators from all over San Diego County who teach a variety of grade levels, I analyzed the data, asked new questions, and returned to my multiage class of first, second, and third grade students for more information throughout my inquiry.

With my first day writing samples collected, I set to work revising the writing assessment prompts for my district. My challenge was revising the third grade prompt. In our two-school district the third grade is divided between the schools. With separate administrators and staff, communication between the schools can be a challenge. One example of this communication gap is the fact that the third grade at our other school began their year with the friendly letter prompt without communicating their process with our site. Meanwhile, I researched the standards, looked to a variety of sources for definitions of writing genres, consulted teachers from other districts, and also learned more about the new writing assessment to be given to fourth grade students statewide. My investigation led me to believe that the friendly letter would not be our ideal format for assessment of writing content. Instead a focus on narrative description would better prepare our students who would soon be taking the statewide fourth grade writing assessment, which is a response to literature. After much thought and many revisions I came up with the prompt:

> Think of a place you know well. While this place may be real or imaginary, it should be a place you are familiar with. In your writing describe the place. Include how it looks, what you do there, and how it makes you feel. Use details that will allow your reader to visit this place with you.

First attempts

I tried the prompt out with my own students to see what kind of writing they were able to produce. The initial trial in November, a set of papers that would not be assessed formally, greatly informed me about the nature of the assessment and about instructional opportunities I could utilize to help my students. From this data I learned that my students were eager writers. They approached the writing assessment with their usual confidence, many students looking at it as an opportunity to try something new with their writing. I also learned that my students value and depend on peer response. They wanted to read their drafts to another student for input and advice, a process that is usual in my classroom.

My students were annoyed that I could not "adult edit" their pieces. They knew that errors existed – errors that they were not able to correct on their own, in spite of being allowed to use any non-electronic resources in the room. Following this prompted writing I took advantage of the student frustrations to teach them more explicitly about the resources in the room: dictionaries, spellers, thesauruses, and grammar books. We discussed the purposes of assessment and came to an understanding that assessment is really not the time for experimentation in writing. As much as I learned from the students, I was not prepared for what I would learn from the scoring sessions yet to come.

After the development of the prompt, third grade teachers and administrators from both sites met to negotiate and agree on a prompt to be used by both schools. Referring to the writing standards for third grade and consulting with fourth grade teachers about the kind of writing students should be producing as they enter fourth grade, narrative description seemed a more appropriate focus for third grade writing. Influenced by the demands of the upcoming fourth grade assessment, both sites agreed to teach the friendly letter as part of their writing curriculum but to use the narrative description as the third grade writing prompt.

Scoring

In February, first through third grade students were given the revised writing assessments. These papers would be used to allow teachers the opportunity to test the prompts, score papers by grade level, and establish anchor papers to illustrate what writing that meets standards looks like. Our first obstacle was reading student papers in February and imagining what they should be in June. Our next problem was using a rubric (Table 2.1) that did not provide enough information to differentiate between meeting and not meeting standards.

In addition, as a staff we had to negotiate whether "standard" meant the minimum acceptable level for that grade level or what we hoped to

Table 2.1 Third grade writing Rubric

		Grade 3 *A place I know*
Scoring	**(Content)**	1 = seldom, not yet evident 2 = sometimes evident, does not meet standards 3 = evident, meets standards 4 = very evident, above standards
(Conventions)		+ = above standards √ = meets standards – = below standards
Traits	**(Content)**	Writing is personal and interesting Describes a place in one well-developed paragraph Uses descriptive language
(Conventions)		Writes legibly Writes complete sentences Uses correct verb tense Uses correct capitalization and punctuation Spells third grade high frequency words correctly

achieve (our ideal). We spent some time calibrating ourselves by reading papers and discussing the elements that would make a paper a "3" or a "2", and established what we thought would be baselines to help us score the papers.

The conversations were rich and informing. We learned about what mattered to the teachers and how they perceived their students as writers. Some teachers began the scoring process with a disclaimer, cautioning the scorers that students were not good writers. Variations among teachers were tremendous and many complained about not knowing how to teach writing. Some teachers focused mostly on correctness and found it difficult to evaluate writing separately for content and correctness. Other teachers were looking for a more formulaic approach to the prompt. They wanted the first sentence to introduce the place and each following sentence to develop the details in a linear fashion.

We left our first scoring sessions feeling unsettled. Teachers questioned the difference between a "2" paper and a "3" paper. I was frustrated with many of the scores awarded by other teachers, not understanding why student writing was scored the way it was. I had students who were strong writers scored below standard for reasons I couldn't understand, and saw papers written less effectively in my opinion scored higher. Using the numbers 1–4 for content and +, √, – for conventions didn't inform my teaching or help me understand my students' strengths and weaknesses as writers. I wanted specifics. Which of my students used description effectively, breathing life into the writing? Which students rambled, losing meaning as they drowned in a sea of words? Who wrote well but didn't know when or how to stop? Which of these elements caused the score to be a "2" rather than a "3"?

Terry's writing

Terry's writing assessment (see below) is an example of my frustration. Terry is a strong writer who writes with confidence, detail, and voice. She constructed a multi-paragraph piece describing her experience skiing in Lake Tahoe. In this piece she described the run, her own activities and the way she felt about the experience. She began with a strong lead but didn't quite end her piece. Terry's piece received a score of 2√ by two different scorers (third grade teachers in our district). When I asked for clarification of the score, I was told that her writing was "off topic" and "too descriptive." Terry's writing score shocked me. I saw her writing as engaging and interesting. Clearly Terry was able to describe her experience, even if at times she tended toward excessive description. Her writing was organized and developed, and in my experience was an example of an accomplished third grade writer. Terry's wasn't the only student's assessment score that bothered me, and I wasn't the only third grade teacher in the district feeling frustrated about district-wide writing assessment and scoring.

Terry's February writing assessment

Skiing in Lake Tahoe

Crunch! As I ski down the lower waterfall run I can hear the sound of cracking as I break the chunks of snow in half and form "S" shapes in the snow. Sky's with purple and a mixture of white and light blue sag over tiped chair lifts hanging from the sky's edge as polls for chair lifts stamp a circle in the snow. They icey snow is the shape of a splotch of paint that plopped right off a painting easl. The bumpy hills remind me of a pillow stufed with billions of white feathers that pop out. And the mountian reminds me of popcorn popping out of a bag you get at the Movie Theaters.

As I slowly weave my way through the bumps. My right ski skids in front of my left ski and I slide into the splits. For a while I slide down on my butt until I gradually push my self back up. I have a few more bumps to go than the rest of the hill is flat like a pancake and steep like the Splash Mountian ride at Disneyland.

I race to the bottom of the hill and stick my polls behind my back and slide my ski's together parallel like a racer. I can hear my knees crack as I bend down so my bottom is almost touching the back of my ski boots and my shins feel like somebody kicked me supper hard with a soccer ball.

When I slide to the bottom I feel like I could plop on the couch and immediately close my eyes. Little white spots appear through my cherry red cheeks from exhaust while spots look like French vanelia paches that got zigzagged soed on to red overalls.

My coach Thomas sneaks my class through a secret way through trees that we didn't know of. So we couldn't see the black dimond sign. The black dimond runs are the hardest runs on the mountain. They are steeper, bumper, and I had to make a lot more turns than I did on blue and green runs.

New questions

Thinking about the writing assessment, writing instruction in my classroom, and writing standards took me through a myriad of emotions. I found myself doubting my writing program, my own version of a writing workshop that I have had success with over the last several years. I found myself doubting my students and their ability to express themselves in writing.

I began to look closely again at the writing assessment: what it told me, what it didn't tell me, and what I still wanted to know. I understood that my students were fluent writers who could get their ideas on paper. I knew that they were aware of errors in conventions that they were unable to fix alone. I saw that responses to their writing from their peers were an important tool for revision. The assessment didn't tell me specifically what my students were doing well and it didn't point out ways I could make my teaching more effective. For me, assessment that doesn't impact instruction is meaningless. As a teacher-researcher I wanted to examine the data – students' work – to find ways to make instruction more effective. As a teacher, I need to use what I know about my students' strengths and weaknesses to guide my instruction. If my students are not achieving I want to know why and what I can do in the classroom to improve learning.

Once again I began to research my questions. I spoke to teachers from all over the county, from elementary to university level. I also went to my teacher research group. I asked them what they saw when they read my students' writing assessments. I asked them about rubric scores and rubric development. As they described what they saw when they read my students' writing I paid attention. I also looked closely at my students' writing. I noted their strengths and the areas that still needed development. I looked at the features found in published writing and asked myself, "What makes writing good?" I turned to experts in the field of writing, Ralph Fletcher (1993), Donald Graves (1994), Lucy Calkins (1986, 1994), and

Shelley Harwayne (1992), and asked the same question as I reread their books. In addition, I began to think about how I might communicate to administrators, parents, and students about the results of our district writing assessment.

My conversations with other teachers helped me see that I needed to articulate clearly what I saw when I looked at my students' writing. Instead of classifying the writing as "strong," I needed to specify exactly what I saw when I read the writing that made it strong. I began to develop a tool for myself that I could use to articulate the specifics of my students' writing. I knew that the tool had to be easy to use and give me information about what students did well in addition to pointing out areas where students still needed instruction and/or practice.

Dimensions of writing

With the help of my teaching partner, Jan Hamilton, I created a tool I call "Dimensions of Writing" (Table 2.2). I listed what I thought was important to effective writing and she helped me format it in a way that it could be used easily with a highlighter pen. I used the Dimensions of Writing to evaluate the same writing assessments that had been scored by the third grade teachers. I also asked several other teachers at my school site to use the Dimensions of Writing on their students' papers. I asked them to let me know if it was helpful, what needed to be changed to make it more effective, and whether anything was missing. With my initial use I decided to compare what I had learned from the rubric scoring to what I learned by using Dimensions of Writing. From the results of the February rubric scoring, I could see that most of my students did not meet standards in either content or conventions, but I could not see what they were able to do or in what areas they needed help. Using my original draft of the Dimensions of Writing, I was able to see more clearly both what students were able to do and what areas they still needed to develop. My students were able to use description and detail and develop their writing with some organization. They needed to focus more on topic development, and endings were a challenge for many of my students.

From the teachers who tried out the Dimensions of Writing I learned that two choices for conventions (mostly correct, minimal/not present) did not allow them to separate students who clearly were competent from those who still needed more instruction and practice with their language mechanics and spelling. Further discussion with other teachers led me to reorganize the order of the items, making it easier to use, and to add a space for prompt response since some students write well but do not directly address the prompt in an assessment situation. Continued revision has led me to the current working version illustrated in Table 2.2.

Table 2.2 Dimensions of writing

Dimensions of Writing			
Craft:			
Lead	effective beginning	some attempt	no beginning
Active Verbs	obvious throughout	sometimes used	seldom used
Adjectives/Adverbs	obvious throughout	sometimes used	seldom used
Specific Nouns	obvious throughout	sometimes used	seldom used
Vocabulary	advanced	age/grade appropriate	limited
Sentence Variation	significant variation	some variation	no variation
Simile/Metaphor	used effectively	attempted/overused	not attempted
Sensory Imagery	effective	some	minimal
Dialogue	effective	appropriate	not present/ineffective
Originality (a surprise, different perspective)	fresh and different	attempted something new	nothing unusual
Ending	effective ending	some attempt	no ending
Organizational Elements:			
Organization	organized	somewhat organized	unorganized
Topic Development	well developed	some development	undeveloped/off topic
Coherence	easy to understand	makes sense	hard to follow
Prompt Response (if applicable)	effectively addresses prompt	addresses part of prompt	does not address prompt
Conventions:			
Punctuation	mostly correct	errors of risk	minimal or not present
Capitalization	mostly correct	inconsistent use	minimal or not present
Spelling	spells grade level words correctly	does not interfere with understanding	interferes with understanding
Handwriting	legible/neat	spacing/proportion problem	difficult to read
Sentence Structure	complex	complete	run on/fragments
Grammatical Construction	mostly correct	subject/verb agreement	verb tense errors
Writing Behaviors: (scored by classroom teacher)			
Willingness to Write	writes willingly	writes with support	resists writing
Risk Taking (trying something new)	daring	some experimentation	stays with the known

Comments:

Another scoring

The end of the school year brought another opportunity for students to complete the writing assessment and for teachers to score the writing. Because of the Dimensions of Writing, third grade teachers at my school site continued our discussion about writing and qualities we wanted to see in our students' writing. Unfortunately, the end-of-school crunch of activities prevented third grade teachers from the two school sites from getting together to score student writing. Instead each site scored student papers separately. This situation limited discussion between third grade teachers, preventing the sharing of new understandings gained since the February scoring. In some ways it also made scoring easier. The third grade teachers at our site share lunch and meet regularly both formally and informally offering many opportunities to talk about students and exchange teaching strategies.

This scoring session proceeded smoothly. A revised rubric, based on a close examination of state standards for the third grade, clarified some of the questions raised in February. There were fewer teachers scoring and the writing was better. Students had experienced prompted writing assessment before, as had teachers. All of the teachers scoring the third grade writing at our site had used and commented on the Dimensions of Writing prior to the scoring session. We had a common language for talking about the relative strengths and weaknesses of particular papers. It was also June. We knew what our students were producing – rather than imagining what they might achieve over the next couple of months. While we still had questions and differences of opinion, we had clearly made progress in our use of the prompted assessment and the rubric scoring.

Reporting to parents and students

I made a conscious decision not to directly share the results of the writing assessment with parents and students. I had too many questions and reservations about the integrity of the results to report those numbers. This one-time assessment was not representative of my students as writers; it was merely one piece of the puzzle. I wanted my students to continue to love to write and to see themselves as writers rather than label them as below standard or meeting standards. Instead, I took a close look at writing instruction in my own classroom. I used what I learned from the Dimensions of Writing to focus writing instruction on areas of weakness I noticed in the class as a whole. We worked on developing ideas and on endings. We talked about the prompt and what it asked for. But more than anything else, we continued to write. We wrote poetry and paragraphs, letters and descriptions. We wrote to think, to explore, and to explain. We wrote daily. We wrote for ourselves, for our classmates, for our families. We wrote drafts and published after much revision. We displayed our writing on the walls of our classroom, bound it in books, and recited it at a public reading.

Terry's June prompted writing assessment (see below) was scored at 4√ by two teachers during the end of the year scoring process. While this piece of writing was clearly more focused and included a more defined ending than her February piece, what struck me most was how many similarities there were between the two pieces. It's hard to know whether the difference in scoring was strictly because of her improvement or because teachers became more experienced at identifying effective writing. Terry chose a different topic, maybe one more suited to the prompt than her choice in February. Her writing was still descriptive – in fact her voice clearly rings through both pieces. Once again she described an experience and took her reader with her. For Terry, the distance between a "2" and "4" on the rubric was small.

Terry's June writing assessment

My Temptation and Desision

I search, looking at all the flavors and toppings, reading the labels. I touch the smooth glass covering the ice cream and toppings trying to deside which flavor to get. Chocolate, mint chip, pepper mint, bubble gum, blue rassberry, strawberry chesecake, and vanilla. I finally chose a flavor of ice cream, mint chip. I feel anxious watching the other adults and kids slowly lick their ice cream as I wait for my dessert to arrive. I hold my temptation in and start reading all the posters and signs.

I look back at the same kids and see that they are now licking their lips and saying yum! Now my temptation is growing. I feel like there is a hole marching band in my stomach that's saying feed me! feed me! I can hear my stomach growling and my stomach feels holow like a log. I feel like it has been a hole hour now! Soon the ice cream lady come's and I cross my fingers hoping that it is my ice cream. "Here you go" the ice cream lady said. "Thanks" I replied. As soon as I got my ice cream I gobbled it down and after that I felt perfectly full!

A new school year

Our beginning of the year writing assessment took place this year in October instead of February. We have teachers new to the third grade and a whole new group of students to assess. Still, our experiences from last year inform our scoring. Once again I have decided not to share the beginning of the year rubric scores with parents and students. The information is simply not specific enough to guide students' progress. Instead, this year I completed a Dimensions of Writing checklist for each student's writing assessment and shared that information with parents and students at conference time. This gave me specific information to explain to students and parents about the writing. Whether or not the student had already "met standards" according to the rubric score, I could highlight both strengths and areas for improvement for all of my students.

Lasting lessons

Examining both the prompted writing assessment and scoring process and the role that the assessment process plays in the classroom helps me to improve my practice and to be a better teacher of writing. I have learned what writing assessment does and does not tell me about writing in the classroom. I have a better understanding of how the prompts themselves help and hinder writers. I understand the purpose of rubrics for district-wide assessment and I know the limitations of reducing student writing to a number with a symbol.

Writing is a complex process. Attempts to reduce it to a number disregard the multifaceted nature of the work. Teaching and learning are also complex processes. It is important to appreciate this complexity, especially in an educational climate that strives to reduce learning to test scores and teaching to scripted performances.

I am still working to both expand my understanding of writing and the writing process and to articulate my understanding to my colleagues, parents and students. Teacher research allows me to examine mandates and expectations in education instead of resorting to complaints or feeling demoralized by the educational and political system. Teacher research serves as powerful and meaningful professional development. Instead of a "one size fits all" inservice, my own inquiry led me to new knowledge that helps me improve my teaching and the learning that takes place in my classroom. My research sent me searching for answers, questioning how assessments are structured and why particular prompts are constructed. By problematizing the assessment process, my understanding increased. I created a tool that helped me teach and communicate with parents and students. With the understanding gained through my teacher research I am able to advocate for students and for myself as a teacher. Teacher research helps keep me focused on what really matters, my students and their learning.

Bibliography

Calkins, L. (1986, 1994) *The Art of Teaching Writing*, Portsmouth, NH: Heinemann.
Fletcher, R. (1993) *What a Writer Needs*, Portsmouth, NH: Heinemann.
Graves, D. (1994) *A Fresh Look At Writing*, Portsmouth, NH: Heinemann.
Harwayne, S. (1992) *Lasting Impressions: Weaving Literature into the Writing Workshop*, Portsmouth, NH: Heinemann.

Chapter 3

Play(ing) > < living
Researching creative growth

Miriam Cooley and Chris Lugar

Miriam:

Across the circle, a hand went up. "I'd like to see what you guys did at that conference. Can't you do it for us too?"

Chris and I looked at one another. The question was not at all unexpected. Knowing these students as we did, and in light of the up front honest atmosphere in the classroom, we could expect to be called to "put our money where our mouth was." These tenth grade students had welcomed me, the university researcher, into their class on a regular, often daily basis, and Chris and I had been forthright about our research project and about our conference presentation the week before. They knew that we had started our conference session with a short improv of two high school students meeting in the cafeteria and discussing the merits and issues of Chris's drama program and of participating in a research project. Of course they wanted to know how we had represented them to those far away strangers.

So Chris borrowed a toque and pulled it down around his ears. I fished some barrettes out of my purse and slipped one into my hair on each side of my head. We pulled a table into the edge of the circle – and we were on!

That was the moment of truth for two teacher-researchers. For five years Chris as a high school drama teacher, and I as a university visual art educator have been pursuing a collaborative, school-based, research project in Chris's tenth grade developmental drama class. Our research was an exploration of the creative process in teaching, art making, and researching. We focused on the role visual arts and drama programs play in assisting adolescents in expressing their understanding of personal, cultural, and educational experiences. The veracity of whatever claims we made about what students learned through the drama program, and the contribution that a visual arts component could make to such a program, were tested by the most discerning of authorities: the students themselves. To my great relief we passed with flying colours.

Our collaboration came about more by serendipity than design when I voiced an interest in teacher-research in arts education and my new colleagues introduced me to Chris. Although he had not thought of it as "research," Chris had many questions about drama education that he wanted to pursue. We had much in common and we easily established an enduring collegial partnership. Both of us had many years of high school teaching experience and shared a respect and enthusiasm for the creative energy that adolescents radiate. We had witnessed the self-reflection, growing self-confidence, divergent thinking, and critical awareness, as well as development of particular art making skills, that occur when students engage in creative artistic work. We wanted to better understand the teaching practices that promote that development, to explore the dynamics of integrating two art forms, and to strengthen students' understanding of drama and art as meaningful avenues to learning about themselves and their world. In order to understand how students and teachers create together one has to witness the process as it unfolds in the classroom, even though the presence of a stranger in the room may alter the environment for teacher and students.

The dynamics of collaborative research/teaching practices were a mutual concern. Regardless of the growing popularity of integrating the arts into the teaching of everything from reading to physics, in my experience current interdisciplinary practices in arts curricula tend to be superficial flourishes rather than lasting curriculum development. Equally, considering the proliferation of programs that involve professional artists in classrooms, we had concerns about how such artist/teacher collaborations could happen and could promote real change in ongoing teaching practice. We set out as reflective practitioner researchers (Taylor 1996) to explore the dynamics of what we expected would be a profitable collaboration; to observe and document and reflect upon our own teaching and researching practice, always with careful attention to the responses of students.

Chris:

When our research began the drama program was expanding due to popularity and the Department of Education requirement that all high school students take a fine arts credit. Having taught the drama program for eight years, I was at the point where I was wondering why some things worked and others did not. It was apparent that most students benefited from the program as they developed their self-esteem and confidence. Others found an appreciation for the arts that they had been reluctant to pursue prior to their involvement in drama. Most students enjoyed the level of comfort that they felt as the course developed. While these were certainly desirable and intended outcomes, I found that I wanted to know more about why and how these things were happening.

When Miriam approached me to begin a project, I was interested but a little cautious. I was concerned about how my students would perceive the inclusion of a researcher in the classroom. Most of my drama classes develop a positive atmosphere but I have learned that it has a precarious balance that can be disturbed by unexpected events. We began by asking permission of the students to include her after they had been fully informed of the project. Predictably, most of them had little or no concern and were generally enthusiastic about being the "guinea pigs." Throughout the term Miriam attended as many classes as possible and took an active role in the class activities rather than being a quiet observer in the corner. This proved relatively successful in the first year and even more so in the subsequent years.

So we began. We chose to proceed with an exploration format where we would use our own observation, the reflection journals of students and student interviews, photographs and videotape to record and document our work.

Miriam:
Our research relationship profited greatly from the time that Chris and I spent getting to know each other prior to my arrival in the class, talking about our teaching experience and our philosophies of life and learning. Trust and respect are fundamental requirements in a developmental drama class and equally so with our research collaboration since it was the only basis upon which I could be involved in the class. It is an invaluable element of our work together.

Although our research methodology encompassed aspects of established research practices, we proceeded in a manner that we understood at first as "organic" in the sense discussed by Schechty and Whitford (1988), and then as reflective practitioners. We both valued the other's wealth of knowledge and skill in their particular art form and although we were aware of our differing institutional expectations, our shared quest was "for a better state of things for those we teach and for the world we all share" (Greene 1995: 1). We shared the conviction that creative artistic experiences are essential to holistic, critical education. We did not attempt to pre-determine the integration of the visual arts aspects, but we were prepared to let the project unfold in its own time. We had faith that when the opportunity presented itself we would know what would be appropriate.

Unwittingly we had taken up the stance of reflective practitioner researchers who "not only draw on an intuitive knowledge base as a way of dealing with these [professional] challenges ... they utilize reflection-in-action as a means of directing their own and others' behaviour" (Taylor 1996: 27–8). Reflection-in-action is the complex inner dialogue of on-the-spot decisions embedded in the unpredictability of the pedagogical moment, reflection that "not only happens before and after the performed event but informs the very event itself" (Taylor 1996: 30). Taylor points out that this approach is attractive to arts educators because "it honours the intuitive and emergent processes that inform artistic meaning-making" (Taylor 1996: 28–9) and we seem to have intuitively assumed this approach. We understood art making as meaning making and therefore assumed that our research as meaning making would proceed in a similar manner.

Chris:
The first issue was acceptance of a researcher as part of the group. In the first year, Miriam joined the class in the second term. The group had already bonded and had found its footing as a reasonably cohesive group. As we began the activities, Miriam willingly participated in the activities and the students, especially the boys, readily accepted her. Some, however, were upset with the changes. As researchers we learned a valuable lesson about the delicate balance that exists in a developmental drama class. Despite the relative strength of connections that already exist, any change will ultimately influence the dynamics of relationships in the group. The established sustaining patterns of behaviour and relationships within the group had not been destroyed but it had changed. I suspect that the students who had difficulty felt that their place of safety had been intruded upon and that in itself would have been upsetting.

In subsequent years Miriam joined the group right from the initial classes when everyone is getting used to each other. What we discovered, although predictable, was profound in its simplicity: Miriam simply became part of the mix. She was accepted because her presence was an established norm in the classroom. The students easily included her in the introductory activities as well as the more involved drama activities that occurred later. Over time, she became more of an observer and with the art-based projects, a resource and activity leader. But, even with this shift in identity, the students have proved to be more accepting than our initial group.

Miriam:
As the class progressed I watched for situations where I felt that some aspect of visual art would make a contribution to the drama process. This came as Chris was working to engage students in dramatized storytelling and to develop students' ability to respond to their peers' presentations. Both concerns were addressed by engaging students in a process of aesthetic response (Cooley 1991; Horner 1990) to reproductions of art works. They were encouraged to formulate personal responses to the works, to discuss their ideas with others who may have quite different impressions of the same work, and to work collaboratively to generate new stories, tableaux, and scenes based on those responses, to which they again were encouraged to respond. These activities promoted students' confidence in expressing their ideas, helped break down the notion of externally imposed "right" answers, and freed students to play intellectually and dramatically with the stories that they generated themselves. To encourage attention to concerns for self-identity we asked them to create a three-dimensional self-portrait, at home, using any materials that they felt were appropriate and to bring it "under wraps" to class. Once the Art Gallery was set up students entered to view the sculptures, to write down a response to each work, and to guess the artist. Later Chris read out the responses and guesses for each

one and the creator had an opportunity to comment and answer questions. These poignant works, many on the concept of the "outer Me" that the world sees and the "real Me" that I hide, revealed insight, sensitivity, and remarkable trust in Chris and their peers.

Taylor's assertion that "at the heart of the artistic act is a willingness by both the art's makers and spectators, to transcend the boundaries of fixed realities and enter virtual ones" (Taylor 1996: 29) underlies drama and visual art experiences. To engage in creative inquiry as students or as artists is to tolerate and value *metaxis*: the state of holding the real and the "as if" simultaneously in experience (Boal 1995: 43), or as Winnicott (1971) would say, "a paradox is involved which needs to be accepted, tolerated, and not resolved" (p. 53). We, along with the students, engaged in a lively process of generating ideas, trying them out, assessing, proposing new possibilities, questioning, and responding to each other's efforts, permeated with the dialogic conversations of reflection-in-action.

Reflection-in-action proved to be a research methodology amenable to inquiry in the lively, highly mobile nature of the drama classroom. Art and drama teachers frequently constitute a single person department so our ongoing dialogue of observations and questions at points throughout the lesson were unique opportunities to assess the subtle, fragile, profound, or exuberant learning that we saw unfolding before us in each class. We generally managed a few minutes of conversation after each class to reflect on the day's events and consider the next innovation before I went off to write my journal, but the real reflection-in-action was as Chris moulded a dynamic and creative community from a diverse grouping of students. His ability to "read" the mood of the class and to draw from his repertoire of activities the ones to help them focus, develop trust, stay in character, or overcome lethargy as the situation required was remarkable. On many occasions we conferred briefly and either carried the activity on longer, posed an additional question for them to explore, or initiated a different activity altogether. One such occasion was with respect to the written responses to the three-dimensional self-portraits. We originally asked them to describe the work but the responses were simply, "Awesome!" or "Cool!" When we rephrased the question to ask students to complete the sentences, "This piece makes me feel …" and, "I think the person who made this is …," the responses were much more thoughtful. They provided a list of compelling ideas from which to develop ongoing dramatic works.

We understand drama, artistic work, and our own research practice as a creative process that transcends the constraints of reality, and engages the practices of play. D. W. Winnicott asserted that "in playing and perhaps only in playing, the child or adult is free to be creative" (Winnicott 1971: 53) and that "it is only in being creative that the individual discovers the self" (p. 54). For Winnicott play is the foundation of all creative cultural endeavours – art, literature, religion, etc. His proposals were grounded in observations of the young child's early engagement with an object outside her/himself as foundational to our sense of agency and as the avenue to the imagination. We accept children's early engagement with the objective world as play, but our culture and certainly our educational institutions are hesitant to accept that there is educational value in playing. Nonetheless, drama and art educators have long contended that to create a work of art is to play in a very serious way and to pursue "a type of problem solving behaviour that integrates 'private meanings' into a product of social value" (Kris, in Courtney 1968: 106). Our students demonstrated this repeatedly. Dramatic play generates knowledge and we contend that research into creative practice requires research approaches that are themselves playful and creative.

Chris:

Throughout our research I was curious about the place of "fun." I agree with those who say that they learn better when they are having fun but I wondered what it meant. I was particularly curious about the high level of comfort and ease students develop with each other and with the activities. Initially, many students profess that they cannot "act" and I tell them that it is not necessary and that many people do not "act" very well, even some of those that are paid to do so. To overcome this natural tendency to be anxious about one's own artistic skills, there is an effort to develop a positive class environment through a series of foundational activities. Curiously, while many students consider these initial activities fun, this sense of fun extends to later, more challenging activities. By calling it fun, I understood that they meant there was a sense of enjoyment, but I felt it went deeper than that.

At the beginning, the drama activities are designed so that everyone can find a sense of comfort and enjoyment. By enjoying themselves together, trust, a sense of place, and success as a working group develop. As they build on their successes, the threshold of their collective success rises. A high level of mutual concern for the development of all the participants encourages individuals to be more at ease with new and challenging events. Or, it can be called fun. According to Kris (Kris, in Courtney 1968), a sense of fun accompanies the emerging mastery of a new skill or ability. This is not the sort of fun that is considered frivolous. Rather, it is the full-bodied sense of accomplishment that accompanies true growth. This important part of self-knowledge develops largely because of the fun inherent in the activities.

The use of the term play has become important to understanding the value of fun. While "play" is loaded with a great deal of meaning for the general population as a description for recreation, it is also useful when trying to understand what is going on in a creative arts classroom. Many activities in a developmental drama environment take the form of a game, challenge, or "try it and see." In this atmosphere, participants achieve a degree of success simply by attempting the activities with a positive attitude rather than being obliged to master a specified set of skills. The student her/himself determines the relative success of that attempt, as opposed to an external observer. Young people seem to have a natural sense for the importance of fun in an event. They do not have an annoying need for all moments to be productive. They know when something has greater meaning, even if it seems frivolous. In other words they know how to have *important* fun and learning becomes more organic through this process of meaningful play.

This aspect of meaningful play involves agency, engagement and ultimately, coming to a greater understanding of self. Agency refers to students' ability to provide their own directions for the curriculum. They effectively develop their skills in drama as they pursue activities and topics of their own interest. This approach supports the natural need for students to develop a sense of power and control over their own lives. They are doing more than just fulfilling a teacher's directives; they are sorting out important issues of self along the way. Engagement is that level of concentration that is reached when an activity becomes important to the participant beyond external motivation – when it develops its own intrinsic motivation. Winnicott (1971) refers to this phenomenon, associating it with the same sort of state of concentration reached with older children and adults when they pursue an activity that holds great meaning. One can extrapolate that as a person learns more about this natural ability through play, the ability to access that state develops more effectively. We continued to observe their growing sense of confidence and self-identity as we increasingly understood, valued, and fostered an environment where students are able to experiment (play) with different possibilities.

For example, an activity I use called *Worlds Apart*, is a simulation game where the class is split into two groups to form two distinct alien cultures that encounter one another. One group visits the other to complete a mission while the hosts try to lead the visitors through a welcoming ceremony. Both groups are told that they are peaceful societies but neither group knows that the other was told this. Predictably the meeting is a messy affair. Both groups try to advance their ideas at the same time, leading to chaos. Eventually, they begin to sort things out. Throughout the whole activity, there is always a great deal of laughter. Initially, there is nervous laughter but often very funny things happen as each group encounters the bizarre and seemingly meaningless sounds and gestures of the other group. At the same time, there is a great deal of interpretation and adaptation as they try to accomplish everything that is expected of them. Thoughtful groups spend a lot of time negotiating. Many groups quickly assume that the other group is aggressive and they try to force their own agenda, which ironically only reinforces the behaviour from both groups. Years later students have commented that it was a lot of fun and one of the most memorable activities they did throughout the course. Many say it is the event where they felt they had learned the most. As one student commented as she left the class that day, "I could just feel my brain working!"

Like this one, many other developmental drama activities ask students to redefine the circumstances of their lives. These activities are rich with educational experiences ranging from group dynamics to interpretation of other cultures, to finding one's place within a group and carrying out the group mission. But it is all make-believe ... or play. By consciously creating certain factors of identity in your imagined existence, you organically begin to question the real issues in your own life. Students often realize the power of communicative devices when they mistakenly but repeatedly return to familiar ones to make their points during the exercise. Although a sense of fun is the vehicle, the learning takes place later, as students critically consider the experience. Deeper meanings are realized once students are able to clearly recall and articulate their feelings and ideas.

The conclusion of this project prompted renewed reflection and insight as we considered how to present our experiences. We had much to convey about what we had experienced and learned but we were unsure about appropriate format. We had integrated so much of our learning with that of my students that it didn't seem to work for us to simply relate the experience to a group of adults a continent away. To be true to the spirit of our project we decided to take the participants through a Cook's tour of a few of the activities we had used with the students so that individual meaning would be developed by the participants in a similar fashion to the students.

Miriam:

Just as creative experience promotes learning on many levels, our research promoted insights into students' personal and artistic development, integrated arts curricula, and processes of collaborative classroom-based research. As reflective practitioner researchers we were able to recognize the vitality of the community of learners that we had become. All of us, including the students, inhabited the roles of student, teacher, artist, and researcher at some point, often simultaneously. I find the *Worlds Apart* activity is a fitting metaphor for the initial encounter of student/teacher/researcher in a classroom. The codes of each role are mysterious to the others, necessitating thoughtful negotiation if communication and understanding are to develop. As we "played" we also revelled in the dialogic conversations of reflection-in-action that sparked our individual and collective self-reflection. The fields of visual art and drama are particularly amenable to "playing" and through our work we understand not only the students' creative work, but also research as necessarily grounded in the open, engaged aesthetics of play. We all want to "feel our brain working."

Bibliography

Boal, A. (1995) *The Rainbow of Desire: The Boal Method of Theatre and Therapy*, New York: Routledge.

Cooley, Miriam (1991) "Changing parts, changing hearts, changing me? An investigation into my response to video art," unpublished MA thesis, Concordia University, Montreal.

Courtney, R. (1968) *Play, Drama and Thought*, London: Cassell & Company Ltd.

Greene, Maxine (1995) *Releasing the Imagination: Essays on Education, the Arts, and Social Change*, San Francisco: Jossey-Bass Publishers.

Horner, S. (1990) "Responding to art: 2D and not 3D, that is not a question," *NSCAD Papers in Art Education*, 5: 31–46.

Schechty, P. and Whitford, B. (1988) "Shared problems and shared visions: organic collaboration," in K. A. Sirotnik and J. I. Goodlad (Eds) *School – University Partnerships in Action; Concepts, Cases, and Concerns* (pp. 191–204), New York: Teachers College Press.

Taylor, P. (1996) "Doing reflective practitioner research in arts education," in P. Taylor (Ed.) *Researching Drama and Arts Education: Paradigms and Possibilities* (pp. 25–58), Washington: Falmer Press.

Winnicott, D. W. (1971) *Playing and Reality*, London: Tavistock Publications.

Chapter 4

Learning through sketching

Danan McNamara

"We're going to the garden!" my students yell, as I walk out to the play-ground to pick them up after recess. They spot their yellow sketchbooks and blue sketch pencils in wicker baskets. Heading across the blacktop, past the equipment of caterpillar crawlers, swings, pirate ladders and more, we meet the soccer field and our garden is in sight just beyond the fence. Some walk and talk, others run and skip, 5, 6, 7, 8 and 9-year-olds gather at the metal-checkered fence to receive their sketching supplies. Once in hand, we all walk outside the school grounds down the path and into another world. Here they have planted seeds and starters (seedlings) and have done pest control by carefully looking through the leaves for other life to be moved, gently, to the empty lot next door.

It is within this space that they settle. Some on the sides of raised garden beds, others on paths of mulch. Still others nestle in dirt, exploring and getting close to what has captured their attention. It is a two-way street. Just as this aged leaf has captured Ben's eye, Ben too has captured this leaf. Using his eye to guide his hand he creates the twisted stem, the jagged edges, the cracks and sprinkling of dirt. His eye wanders and his hand follows (Figure 4.1).

Figure 4.1

Figure 4.2

Child: Do you know what I'm sketching?

And to me, who sits beside this child, it is obvious.

Teacher: You've sketched the second vine [Figure 4.2]. See? There's the first, second and third leaf. You've sketched the second vine.
Child: Yep! You're right.
Teacher: I could tell. You captured the curve, the leaves and the vines. It's amazing!
Child: Contour drawing does that.
Teacher: Does what?
Child: It helps you see.

In the spring of 2000 I had the pleasure of listening to and meeting Joni Chancer, author of *Moon Journals*. As she shared the voices of her students as well as her own voice, both personal and professional, I found that woven through it all was an underlying sense of wonder and excitement towards the world in which we live. She told us how she and her students sketched everyday and as she spoke I realized that sketching was going to be my next scaffolding technique to support my students' writing and at the same time allow me the opportunity to be the adult or one of the adults, in the lives of my students that Rachel Carson spoke of in her book, *The Sense Of Wonder* "If a child is to keep alive his inborn sense of wonder ... he needs the companionship of at least one adult who can share it, rediscovering with him the joy, excitement and mystery of the world we live in" (Carson 1956: 55). I've found sketching to be the perfect metaphor for teacher research and it is this relationship that I'd like to illustrate for you.

There are two types of sketching techniques that my students and I use daily in my multiage class of first, second and third graders. One is contour sketching, the other is blind contour. During a contour sketch you look closely, go slowly, capturing on paper what you are focusing on. When sketching using the blind contour style, you sketch as you do during a contour, except you ignore your drawing hand and the paper you are drawing on, you do not peek. Realize that your sketch may look like scribbles. It's all right. Both art forms help to develop the relationship between the hand and the eyes. They also allow you to utilize your other senses too, particularly the sense of touch. While doing a blind contour sketch, the sense of touch comes into play as you feel your hand glide along the paper, giving you reference to space and placement on the page. Regardless of the style being used, each form helps to maintain your focus on the object you've chosen as you try to capture it.

As a teacher-researcher, contour sketching illustrates those moments, when as a professional, I've had the opportunity to visit other classrooms and peek inside to see children learning. Having seen something like Writer's Workshop, I then have an image to work with to help me incorporate these practices into my classroom. Blind contour sketching portrays those times when I've read or heard of learning that I'd like to try with my students, but I'm unable to observe it when it's happening. In cases such as these, I need to use my other senses, especially when I implement these ideas in my own classroom. When beginning something new with my students, besides looking closely, I need to listen, and feel it out by listening to my inner voice, noticing how the students are responding, are they comfortable or are they anxious? I also have to remind myself that this new experience, this sketch if you will, won't look exactly like the one I saw or heard. I may see some familiarity, a line, a curve, but the sketch

Figure 4.3

itself will be different, because it's mine. Carissa's blind contour of her foot illustrates this idea (Figure 4.3). It is clear she was drawing her foot. She noted how she tried to do a heel, but instead she got something else, an ear. In the end, she can see glimmers of her foot but she can also see so many other things from her sketching experience. That is teacher research. Taking part in looking closely and by taking the time to notice, seeing so many other parts to learning and teaching.

The objects my students and I sketch and write about relate to our area of study. So when we were studying oceanography we sketched sea stars. On one day, Chloe, a second grader, wrote:

> My sea star is as rough as sand paper on the bottom. When I put a magna-find-glass on it I saw light! But when I put the smaller circle, it was just a hole on the top where I saw a flower.

When Chloe shared her writing with me it was clear she was looking closely at her object and was very focused. She had made some interesting observations and was doing a nice job describing what she observed. I invited her to look again at her sea star. When she returned after some time she had written the following:

> That's when I gasped. I was amazed of what I was seeing! Of a sea-star that had light and holes together at first I thought my eyes were tricking me. It's also dirty. I thought that when we where using charcoal. That … someone sketched on the sea star.

Chloe's piece illustrates so perfectly how sketching helps one to look closely, focus, make observations and look again only to see something we hadn't seen before. As a teacher-researcher this happened to me with a student I once had, Rebecca. She began kindergarten spelling only her name. She soon learned words such as "cat" and "mom." She incorporated these CVC (consonant, vowel, consonant) words into her writing, but at the same time squiggle writing, called syllabic hypothesis (Martens 1996), also represented writing to her. In her book, *I already know how to read: A Child's View of Literacy*, Prisca Martens explains how

> Emilia Ferreiro (1984; Ferreiro and Teberosky 1982) refers to this "matching" of oral words or syllables with written marks as the syllabic hypothesis. The syllabic hypothesis is a "guess" children invent for how to relate the language they speak and hear with the language they read and write in texts.
>
> (Prisca Martens 1996: 34)

For Rebecca, her syllabic hypotheses were her stories and they were physically longer in length. As I looked over her writing samples, I observed she knew directionality. Her words and squiggles moved left to right and from the top to the bottom of the page. However, it wasn't until a colleague at my school site, another teacher-researcher, invited me to look again at the data I had gathered on Rebecca that I saw something new. I collected her writing samples and xeroxed copies from her notebook, and literally laid them chronologically on the floor in front of me. It was then that I saw something I had never seen before! Just like Chloe, I gasped! I noticed, for the very first time, that every syllabic hypothesis story Rebecca wrote began with a capital "R" and a lower case "b," the first and third letters of her first name. I was amazed! I had never witnessed this about her writing despite the numerous times I had read and looked closely at her work or shared it with other colleagues and teacher-researchers. In addition to this new finding, her use of capital and lower case letters gave me insight into her understanding of the use of these structures. She knew names and sentences began with capital letters and were followed by lower case letters and this was evident in her writing. These anecdotal notes and findings supported me as I read professional literature regarding young children's development, and how children at her age and literacy development often use letters of their name or other important words when learning how to write using conventional letters. As I read, I connected personal observations of my student's learning with the authors' work. This in turn helped me educate my students' parents about their child's learning and development.

Daily sketching with tangible objects such as leaves, shells or other items that relate to our area of study, provides my students with the opportunity to make detailed observations using their senses. Noticing the way something looks, feels, smells, tastes and sounds is a natural invitation for children to make complex interpretations. These insights become quite elaborate over the course of time as sketching provides support for all my students, regardless of ability or age, including my second language learners. This was evident in my first grade student Max, an English as a second language learner. Sketching taught him how to look closely and by learning to look, Max developed the ability to utilize his environment to further his understanding. Learning how to look through sketching and applying this technique of looking closely helped Max express himself more clearly in writing. If he or another student needed a word, Max would be able to find it in the room, be it in a song, poem or book. In addition, his vocabulary developed as children shared their ideas orally after sketching as well as during our daily author's chair. As others shared, Max was introduced to new words. This allowed him to familiarize himself with the English language and as a result articulate his thinking more precisely.

The scaffolding Max has received through sketching is identical to the support teacher research has given me. It has taught me how to be more observant. And like Max, I've learned to utilize my environment more fully to inform my teaching practice. My writing too has become clearer. And like Max, if I am looking for support to help me articulate my thinking, I can find the word or words I need through the voices of authors who can scaffold me until I am ready to be on my own.

Before we move on to our writing, the students and I do a quick share of our sketch, explaining what we noticed with others at our table. Having this time built in at the end of sketching time is essential. The students welcome the opportunity to share their work and hear the ideas of their peers. It provides an intimate setting to speak to a small group, practice listening, and inform our understanding. Through this process of sharing we learn how each of us looks at the world differently, and by sharing, we are given the opportunity to see the world in new and exciting ways.

These same qualities that are found when my students and I share in our classroom are also found within my teacher research group through the San Diego Area Writing Project at the University of California, San Diego. The dynamics that take place in our monthly meetings, through dialogue, sharing data, student samples, writings of our own as well as others, provide a system of support unlike any other professional development that I've been involved in throughout my professional career. Just as sketching has scaffolded my students at their various levels, teacher research supports and informs me as I grow in the teaching profession.

The observations made by way of sketching become a starting point for my students' writing. In addition to being a starting point, sketching welcomes revisiting through multiple sketches of a single object. It is through this re-acquaintance that observations become intricate and detailed, just like when teacher-researchers revisit their practice.

The following are the sketches and observations of a third grader. Figure 4.4 is a blind contour and Figure 4.5 is a contour.

> One part of my sketch looks like a snake's upper jaw. My real foot tastes and smells like rotten eggs (Figure 4.4). This is a contour of my right foot. It looks like piranhas and barracudas attacked it (Figure 4.5).

I find these sketches interesting because the results are so different. In addition to the sketches, Chris made observations about his foot that, on both occasions, are unique and offer a place to begin writing as well as expand on ideas by asking "Why?" It is this question that pushes Chris forward that also pushes me with regards to teacher research and my practice. By asking myself "Why?" I am asking myself to see the relevance and value of what is being observed.

When sketching feathers, Carissa, a third grader, wrote the following pieces:

Figure 4.4

Figure 4.5

A fether functions like a leaf because the fether pretects the bird like a leaf pretects the tree buy shading the roots like a leaf boat. The fether is like a surf board because the surf board can float and balance. The fether is made like that so it can cover up the bird. [A feather functions like a leaf because the feather protects the bird like a leaf protects the tree by shading the roots like a leaf boat. The feather is like a surfboard because the surfboard can float and balance. The feather is made like that so it can cover up the bird.]

While sketching another feather she wrote:

It also functions like a leaf because if you drop the fether it glids down, and if a leaf falls from a tree it glides down. The fether is like a surf board because they are both sleik so it can glide throu the air. The surf board is sliek so it can glid throu the water. [It also functions like a leaf because if you drop the feather it glides down, and if a leaf falls from a tree it glides down. The feather is like a surfboard because they are both sleek so it can glide through the air. The surfboard is sleek so it can glide through the water.]

Carissa is taking her observations further by finding out how her object, a feather, functions like other objects, surfboards and leaves, those objects that remind her of her feather. This is a complex task. Her first statement: "A feather functions like a leaf because the feather protects the bird like a leaf protects the tree by shading the roots like a leaf boat," is so rich. Her mind just seems to be overflowing with ideas and connections of which she is trying to make sense. She is relating a feather to a leaf then makes reference to a leaf boat! One might wonder, "boat?" Yet her next sentence takes us to water: "The feather is like a surfboard because the surfboard can float and balance." Her third statement: "The feather is made like that so it can cover up the bird" isn't clearly related to the previous statement, but she is trying to make sense of abstract relationships forming in her mind. Her observations about form and function regarding another feather she sketched are most clearly stated in her last three statements:

> It also functions like a leaf because if you drop the feather it glides down, and if a leaf falls from a tree it glides down. The feather is like a surfboard because they are both sleek so it can glide through the air. The surfboard is sleek so it can glide through the water.

These abstract connections are due to her having been asked to stretch her thinking further by examining the relationship between form and function through writing and sharing her thoughts. I find it relates to the concept that author Eleanor Duckworth speaks of in her book *The Having of Wonderful Ideas: and Other Essays on Teaching and Learning*. Eleanor wrote:

> Intelligence cannot develop without matter to think about. Making new connections depends on knowing enough about something in the first place to provide a basis for thinking of other things to do – of other questions to ask – that demand more complex connections in order to make sense. The more ideas about something people already have at their disposal, the more new ideas occur and the more they can coordinate to build up still more complicated schemes. [Simply stated,] Wonderful ideas do not spring out of nothing. They build on a foundation of other ideas.
>
> (Duckworth 1987: 14, 6)

Teacher research supports and encourages the having of wonderful ideas. As Eleanor Duckworth (1987: 5) wrote, "Having confidence in one's ideas does not mean 'I know my ideas are right,' it means 'I am willing to try out my ideas.'" And it is the trying of ideas that I feel is crucial to teaching. Teacher research provides us with knowledge at our fingertips that we can use to best meet the needs of our students. It supports us as the expert in the classroom who knows what is best for our students and learning.

Seeing the growth my students have made as writers, artists and thinkers from having incorporated sketching into our day has been exciting. My student, Tyler, summed it up well when she wrote that sketching helps her to think. If working with the concrete and sketching those observations helps children to think in more complex and abstract ways, then it will help them express themselves orally and in writing. This in turn builds fluency and helps my students look at writing as a process instead of a product.

While sketching in the garden one day, a child asked for an eraser. Yoko responded saying the child didn't need an eraser and then added, "That's what's great about sketching; you can turn mistakes into something you like." Teacher research and sketching are resources for my students and me. The more I see, the more resources I have, so that I may, as Yoko stated, "turn mistakes into something [I] like." and create a learning environment for all my students to thrive in. For it is my desire for my students and myself to be life-long learners. As Eve Merriam wrote in 1991 "... to be curious – to take the time to look closely, to use all [our] senses to see and touch and taste and smell and hear. To keep on wandering and wondering." Sketching and teacher research are the tools to help me accomplish my goals. They invite me to look at the world in various ways, the bottom, the top, the side and the front, like Ben's sketch of his shoe (Figure 4.6). And I feel it is this approach to looking that will help me and my students keep alive our curiosity and excitement towards the world we live in and nurture all of our wonderful ideas.

Figure 4.6

Bibliography

Carson, Rachel (1956) *The Sense Of Wonder*, New York: HarperCollins Publishers.

Chancer, Joni and Rester-Zodrow, Gina (1997) "Moon journals: writing, art and inquiry through focused nature study," Portsmouth, NH: Heinemann.

Duckworth, Eleanor (1987) *The Having of Wonderful Ideas: and Other Essays on Teaching and Learning*, New York: Teachers College Press.

Martens, Prisca (1996) *I Already Know How to Read: A Child's View of Literacy*, Portsmouth, NH: Heinemann.

Merriam, Eve (1991) *The Wise Woman and Her Secret*, illustrated by Linda Dockey Graves. New York: Simon & Schuster.

Chapter 5

Shall we dance?

Researching the way we match student teachers with school advisors

Peter Gouzouasis and Barbara Leigh

One cannot understate the power of the metaphor to "translate" experience. Marshall McLuhan was keenly aware of this fact when he stated, "All media are active metaphors in their power to translate experience into new forms" (McLuhan 1994: 57). Without metaphors, as translators that we generally refer to as media, it would be difficult for teacher educators to design educational programs, facilitate learning, interpret various teaching and learning events, or express ideas about learning and teaching. Moreover, without metaphors artists would be hard pressed to describe their artistic compositions with "vocal symbols" (McLuhan 1994: 57), to "carry over" ideas from one medium (e.g. a music composition or dance) to another (e.g., language). As we work in an Arts context, with Arts content, meta-phors rooted in the Arts help us explain how students with Arts backgrounds form relationships with teachers who possess a keen interest in integrating the Arts across the curriculum. In short, as art(ist) educators, metaphor is the medium through which many of our activities are expressed, composed, elaborated, and clarified.

"Will you, won't you, will you, won't you, will you join the dance?"
Lewis Carroll, Alice's Adventures in Wonderland, 1865

The FAME cohort attracted highly creative, innovative student teachers – with academic backgrounds from both the Arts and Sciences – who possess exciting ideas for the future of Canadian education, to this trailblazing project (Gouzouasis 2000, 2001). Another important theme in our cohort is the relationship between play, imagination, and creativity (Singer and Singer 1990). As many academics – including Brian Sutton-Smith, Mihalyi Csikszentmihalyi, Brian Vandenberg, and Michael Lewis – have proposed, "play is just plain fun" (Milne 1939: 40). In over twenty years of combined teaching experience in university teacher education programs, we observed through music education methods classes that many students were not having fun in elementary teacher education. In keeping with Einstein's notion that "imagination is more powerful than knowledge" (Viereck 1929: 17), part of the impetus for designing a cohort such as FAME was rooted in our beliefs that we needed to (re)introduce play, creativity, and imagination into teacher education and to infuse those principles across the entire curriculum. Influenced by that theme, traditional teaching, learning, curricular and pedagogical principles and communication concepts were taught exclusively through arts-based activities, enabling student teachers to make concrete connections between theory and practice in a playful, creative environment. We just didn't talk about play, we lived and modeled it in our classroom at the university – a typical lifeless lecture room was transformed into a vibrant, living classroom space by the thirty-five student teachers and their team instructors over the course of six months.

"A teacher in search of his/her own freedom may be the only kind of teacher who can arouse young persons to go in search of their own."
Maxine Greene, *The Dialiectic of Freedom*, 1988

One of the most important connections between the university and the schools in teacher education is made in the student teaching practicum experience. Teaching and learning are human experiences. As such, human relations, communications, and interpersonal interactions are perhaps the most important aspects of teaching and learning. That, as well as exploring notions of what it means to enter the profession of teaching and "becoming" a professional, was a recurring theme during the first six months of classroom interactions with the FAME cohort. Based on those perspectives, our research question was to determine the extent to which student teacher and sponsor teacher input on practicum pairing or "matching" would impact upon the success of the FAME student teaching experience. We applied the conceptual FAME outlined above to an examination of this question.

"Learning to dance and joining together in the same set helps to give a group of people, no matter what their background, a feeling of cooperation and oneness."
Richard G. Kraus, *Square Dancing of Today*, 1950

For the first month of our "extended" short practicum, we started off by "playing." Our student teachers were rotated through at least two different classrooms, with different grade levels, each Tuesday morning at different schools. During this incubation period, each student teacher had the opportunity to meet eight teachers in four different schools during the morning sessions. That in and of itself was an amazing exposure to diversity in cultural and socio-economic contexts, and to teaching and learning environments, issues, and strategies. For example, whereas one of our schools is considered as an "inner city" school, another places its local community among the highest in socio-economic backgrounds (e.g. household income levels) in all of Canada. Our afternoon sessions were composed of a rotation of debriefings and discussions, as well as creative applications of New Media workshops at the local district centre – the Leo Marshall Curriculum Centre. The district curriculum centre houses a state-of-the-art computer laboratory that contains ten PCs and ten iMac computers as well as an instructor's workstation and state-of-the-art projection system. A primary focus of this first play experience was for our student teachers to observe all they could about the classrooms and teaching processes, discover what grade(s) they would prefer to teach, and talk to children to see what they thought about notions of "school" and "their teachers." Thus, all thirty-five students noted a "weekly tip" that was collected and disseminated to the entire group in an organized binder when they returned to campus.

**"We dance round in a ring and suppose.
But the secret sits in the middle and knows."**

Robert Frost, *The Secret Sits*, 1942

There is much that we can share about our rationale and philosophical reasoning for this approach to organizing our short practicum, which totaled two weeks in length (Fall 2000). In the second month of our academic year, student teachers were assigned in pods to one of our eight practicum schools. Initial assignments were based on the student teacher's (1) background, (2) expertise in Fine Arts and New Media, (3) gender (with only seven male student teachers we placed each in separate schools), (4) interpersonal skills, (5) leadership skills, and (6) weekly reflections (i.e. reviews). Through this process, we attempted to create well-balanced (i.e. in terms of life skills and academic, cultural and social interests and expertise) school communities of student teachers. During the four full day visits, students continued to rotate through at least two classrooms per day, as they continued making detailed written observations on practice and its relationship to theory, and continued to engage with teachers and children in the schools.

At the end of the full day rotations, both student teachers and sponsor teachers were provided with selection forms. Also, to help sponsor teachers make their final selection decisions, detailed student teacher profiles were provided. Those profiles included information ranging from professional interests, special interests (including hobbies and talents), willingness to be involved with extracurricular activities and outdoor experiences, and initiatives (willingness and abilities to take on leadership roles within the group and school). The selection instructions were simple and sincere. Student teachers were to rank every sponsor teacher and/or classroom and provide positive comments on what they would learn from a placement in that environment. Sponsor teachers were to rank their choice(s) of student teacher(s) and present their choice(s) based solely upon positive reasoning and constructive observations.

"Creative dance, for both children and teacher, starts from the known"
Joyce Boorman, *Creative Dance in Grades Four to Six*, 1971

Upon collection of the selection forms, and prior to the full week introductory practicum, the co-team leaders met with principals at each school, and confidentially discussed the sponsor teacher/student teacher choices. This was the first step – as a square dance begins with two people choosing each other as partners, we matched student teachers to school advisors to form new classroom partnerships. With the exception of one student teacher move – based on a student dropping out of the cohort when she came to the realization that she was interested in secondary, not elementary, education – the sponsor teacher/student teacher matches have become the cornerstone for practicum success in our cohort. It was evident that student teachers were interested in commenting on their choice of sponsor teacher, classroom and school. In four schools, we had a perfect correlation between student and sponsor teacher desires for partnerships. In two of those four schools, it was clear from our analysis that students had "pre-selected" their sponsor teachers based on their own "negotiations." We found this to be disturbing on at least two levels. First, it was evident that strong personalities within student teacher groupings seemed to manipulate the selection process. Second, the point of this exercise was to allow students to positively reflect upon diversity in teaching. It is worrisome that many student teachers seem to hold very strong beliefs and biases about education and teaching (Bolin 1990; Paine 1989). While these notions were not revealed in the written commentaries, we were uncertain as to whether student teacher choices were made either (1) on sound, philosophical and praxial grounds or (2) on some other basis. Although one may consider that many student teachers come into the profession with rich life experiences and solid academic backgrounds, emotional "baggage" and unfounded biases about what "should" be in a classroom and how a classroom "should" be run may interfere with sound assessments of educational situations and settings. Certainly, student teachers are not "blank slates" to be molded by master teachers. However, through numerous activities rooted in play, imagination, and creativity we strove to emphasize the importance of open mindedness and respect for various teaching styles and techniques, and encouraged a sense of wonderment and awe in observing teaching processes and children's learning. We encouraged the student teachers to bring this philosophical approach to their choice process in the selection of school advisor and classroom.

"Where there is an open mind, there will always be a frontier."

Charles Kettering

In one school we experienced some interesting interplay between the principal and teachers in the negotiations regarding who would be matched with one, highly desirable student teacher. In that school, one particular teacher wrote both positive and negative comments about two students. The principal suggested it would be better to match that teacher with their first choice. We attempted to match student and sponsor teachers based on student choice, however, the sponsor teacher threatened to remove themselves from the project unless their demands for a particular student were met. Moreover, the student teacher of choice also skewed their positive comments toward an assignment with that same teacher making negative comments regarding other teachers in the school. That was the only student teacher that did not follow our explicit directions. At another school, one sponsor teacher felt that they could not work with a particular student teacher so we also honored that request. In stark contrast with those relatively few scenarios, in two particular schools, sponsor teachers were highly pleased with the overall quality and character of all the student teachers, and the sponsor teachers were willing to allow us to make the assignments. In our two other schools, because the teachers liked and felt comfortable with all the student teachers in their school, they left assignment decisions to the university cohort leaders and school principals.

We concluded the Fall 2000 term with a five-day teaching experience (i.e. the final week of our two week practicum). The Holiday season is an exciting time to be working in elementary schools, and our foresight in planning made this a wonderful scenario of observational and teaching opportunities. Students started the week with fifteen minute, micro teaching lessons (e.g. calendar and book reading activities) and gradually increased to a total of sixty minutes by week's end. The focus of micro teaching lessons was the related British Columbia Ministry of Education prescribed learning outcomes. The results have been quite amazing, in many ways, for both sponsor teachers and student teachers. One common sponsor teacher remark has been on the strong curriculum knowledge base that the student teachers now possess. As one person remarked, "They know the new curriculum better than we do; we're all going to learn this year."

**"On with the dance! Let joy be unconfined;
No sleep till morn, when Youth and Pleasure meet
To chase the glowing Hours with flying feet."**
Lord Byron, *Childe Harold's Pilgrimage*, 1812–18

At the end of the full week practicum, teacher and student teacher feedback was incredibly positive. In the words of one teacher, "If more teachers knew that this is how student teachers were placed, more of us would be willing to take student teachers into our classrooms." In fact, what has emerged in at least one school is such an intense feeling of "security" and bonding that the sponsor teachers are reluctant to share their student teachers across classrooms and schools. In a broad sense, that limits the practicum experience for both them and the student teachers as we look ahead. Not surprisingly, anecdotal comments regarding the selection process continued throughout the school year. During one conversation regarding a student teacher's remarkable progress, the sponsor teacher proudly remarked, "I wanted to work with her from the very first day."

**Honor your partner. Honor your corner. All hands
round and circle left.**
A popular square dance call

Interestingly, the narrative data revealed that all the sponsor teachers and administrators were very happy with the quality of the student teachers on both interpersonal and academic levels. That was still evident in most, but not all, situations as we began the second week of the thirteen week, final practicum. While this paper focuses on the impact of this process on sponsor teachers and student teachers, there were other, additional benefits. Primarily, our selection process enabled cohort leaders to meet with teachers and administrators in all the schools, enabling communications and trust early on in our working relationships. We were able to share our visions and knowledge freely and openly. Moreover, we were able to express concerns and successes very openly. There was a sense that the FAME project will be welcomed into these same schools in future years. Due to scheduling issues, all but one of the 2000–1 practicum schools is working with the FAME cohort in 2001–2. As we choreographed the final dance, the extended practicum, we were aware of the challenges facing our student teachers. Many found that their vision of what practicum should look like was not the reality of what actually happens in a school. However, most sponsor teachers, student teachers, and faculty advisors developed a strong sense of trust, unity and teamwork that is crucial in the lifelong dance(s) we encounter in the teaching profession.

> The state of the mind which enables our actions to promote growth and generate awareness is so bound up with the flux of the moment that it is hard to analyze. The bond between the teacher and the taught, and the dancer and the dance, is at once intimate and tenuous, ever changing, ever bonding, and always new.
>
> It is hoped that this sense of flow has not been lost in pinning down the "why's and wherefore's" and technical format for teaching. It is hoped that the dancing spirit of the child [or in our case – student teacher] has prevailed through all the rhyme and the reason.
>
> Moira Morningstar, *Growing with Dance*, 1986

Six of our thirty-six students experienced various forms of difficulties during the final practicum. Of the six, two did not complete the final dance. One withdrew herself from the final practicum after coming to the decision that she did not want to teach; that left her sponsor teacher heartbroken – the teacher both lost her dance partner and felt that she had not done enough to encourage her partner to stay in the dance. Another had difficulties with classroom management and curriculum delivery and was pulled from the classroom for reassignment in the Fall of 2001 and successfully completed the repeat (i.e. makeup) practicum. One of the six students was assigned to a different classroom when it became apparent that he wanted to "boogaloo" and the sponsor teacher wanted him to do a traditional waltz. The remaining three were able to work through their difficulties and successfully complete their "recitals." All six were exemplars of the fact that choosing dance partners and building working relationships are not easy tasks.

The process of allowing input from school advisor and student teacher prior to matching partners for practicum was a very successful one. What we discovered was that first impressions of one's dance partner may change for many reasons. Some may be "external" to the partnership (e.g. job share situations and lack of school advisors who volunteer), and others may be "internal" to either the sponsor teacher (e.g. a sponsor teacher's lack of experience; a sponsor teacher's previous teaching and learning experiences, including their own practicum) or student teacher (e.g. a student teacher's maturity level, a lack of skills to apply theory into practice, skills to cope with and handle stress, skills to discover self, and skills to learn through making mistakes).

"The most important single ingredient in the formula of success is knowing how to get along with people."

Theodore Roosevelt

From at least one perspective, learning how to teach is learning how to collaborate. That collaboration takes the form of a dance between numerous partnerships created in the dynamics of a classroom. University advisors, sponsor teachers, student teachers, and students work closely together to choreograph the dance. There are times when one needs to learn basic skills, practice steps, and practice dance patterns individually. Then there are times when we need to dialogue and listen to each other, to think about the dance, and to feel our bodies move in harmony and in contrast – to work together.

"Each collaborator brings to the work a different set of strengths and resistances. We provide both irritation and inspiration for each other – the grist for each other's pearl making."

Stephen Nachmanovich, *Free Play:
Improvisation in Life and The Arts*, 1989

Through it all, the support role of a university faculty advisor is best elaborated in a song, "I Hope You Dance," performed by Leann Womack (lyrics and music by Mark D. Sanders and Tia Sillers), that encompasses the metaphoric theme used in FAME and applied in the analysis of our experience in matching student teachers and sponsor teachers.

> I hope you never lose your sense of wonder,
> You get your fill to eat but always keep that hunger.
> May you never take one single breath for granted.
> God forbid love ever leave you empty handed.
> I hope you still feel small when you stand beside the ocean,
> Whenever one door closes I hope one more opens.
> Promise me that you'll give faith a fighting chance.
> And when you get the choice to sit it out or dance,
> I hope you dance,
> I hope you dance.

Face the music and dance

Considering the broad base of literature regarding student teacher supervision, it is imperative that researchers explore new learning strategies to facilitate critical stages of the practicum and pre-service teacher development. St. Maurice (2001, 2002) adroitly provides a broad rationale for self-study of supervisory practices, and it is within that realm that the present research is situated. In a broad sense our focus has been on the avoidance of practicum termination. Moreover, for the writers, the philosophical tenet of viewing change as a constant within a pragmatist's world view is superseded by an organismic research program (Overton 1984) where change is not only a constant, but change is inevitable. Change is development, and the notion of "becoming," and the process of becoming a teacher, is central to the heuristic.

It is through metaphorically applied quotations, that are interspersed throughout the text, and song lyrics that our notions of matching student teachers with sponsor teachers were developed and continue to be nurtured. We believe that our matching approach can work well in numerous student teaching contexts, but we realize that not everyone likes to dance and not everyone can dance. Those are but some of the many issues we will continue to explore as we learn the new dances of the second year of student teachers of the FAME cohort. Once one comes onto the dance floor, a dance may be interpretative and free form in nature. A teacher may need to tap dance at times, then use ballet skills to develop control and model their strengths. They may do a bit of jazz dance to spice up the room, and add personal flair with a few steps of flamenco.

One never knows until the final dance begins what dance repertoires will be more valuable and will be needed in each situation. Depending on the dance at hand, dance partners may change and frequently exchange. Dance partners develop complex relationships. True, partnerships fail for various reasons, but a focus on open communications, trust, and relationship building is the foundation to any successful human enterprise. For us, these issues are what makes teaching, learning, and *dancing* such exciting life experiences.

Bibliography

Bolin, F. S. (1990) "Helping student teachers think about teaching: another look at Lou," *Journal of Teacher Education*, 41, 1: 10–19.

Boorman, Joyce (1971) *Creative Dance in Grades Four to Six*, Don Mills, ON: Academic Press Canada Limited.

Carroll, L. (1865) *Alice's Adventures in Wonderland*. http://www.online-literature.com/carroll/alice/.

Frost, R. (1942) *A Witness Tree*, New York: Henry Holt and Company.

Gouzouasis, P. (2000) "Understanding music media: digital (re)genesis or cultural meltdown in the 21st century," in B. Hanley and B. A. Roberts (Eds) *Looking Forward: Challenges to Canadian Music Education* (pp. 225–50), Victoria: CMEA Publications.

Gouzouasis, P. (2001) "The role of the arts and new media in Canadian education for the 21st century," *Education Canada*, 41, 2: 20–3.

Greene, M. (1988) *The Dialectic of Freedom*, New York: Teachers College Press.

Kraus, R. G. (1950) *Square Dancing of Today*, New York: A. S. Barnes and Co.

McLuhan, M. (1994) *Understanding Media: The Extensions of Man*, Cambridge, MA: MIT Press.

Milne, A. A. (1939) *Autobiography*, New York: Dutton Publishing Co.

Morningstar, M. (1986) *Growing With Dance*, Heriot Bay, BC: Windborne Publications.

Nachmanovich, S. (1989) *Free Play: Improvisation in Life and The Arts*, New York: Jeremy P. Tarcher/Penguin-Putnam Publishing.

Overton, W. (1984) "World views and their influence on psychological theory and research: Kuhn-Lakatos-Laudan," in *Advances in Child Development and Behavior, 18* (pp. 191–226), New York: Academic Press.

Paine, L. (1989) *Orientations Toward Diversity: What do Prospective Teachers Bring?* (Report) East Lansing, MI: National Center for Research on Teacher Education.

Singer, D. G. and Singer, J. L. (1990) *The House of Make-Believe: Children's Play and the Developing Imagination*, Cambridge, MA: Harvard University Press.

St. Maurice, H. (2001) "Supervising unsuccessful student teaching assignments: two terminators' tales," *The Educational Forum*, 65, 4: 376–86.

St. Maurice, H. (2002) "Self-study of supervisory practices in beginning teacher terminations," *International Journal of Leadership in Education*, 5, 1: 61–75.

Viereck, G. S. (1929) "What life means to Einstein: an interview," *The Saturday Evening Post*, 26 October, 202, 17.

Chapter 6

One teacher-researcher's continued quest to improve her students' vocabulary to boost their achievement in reading

Vinnie E. Acklin

Context and background

Randolph Elementary School is a neighborhood school with a population of over 500 students from many ethnic groups that speak over twenty different languages. The largest group of students is Hispanic, and African-Americans comprise the second largest group. Due to their economic status, the majority of the students are eligible to receive reduced or free lunch. During the 2000–1 year, I focused on accelerating or enriching the reading achievement of my second and third graders. I was the reading extension teacher for thirty-one students in four small groups from two homerooms. My four groups included twenty-two girls and nine boys. Similar to the diversity at Randolph, there were fifteen Hispanic girls, six Hispanic boys, four African-American girls, two African-American boys, one Caucasian boy, and three Asian girls. My students had academic abilities that ranged from below average to average. Their reading abilities ranged from students who read one year below grade level to students whose reading was on grade level. To teach reading, the classroom teachers used an anthology, and I taught the key vocabulary words of the reading selections in the anthology. The students and I shared the reading of chapter books, and we developed their test-taking strategies. Both the classroom teachers and I taught our students for forty-five minutes.

My main goal was to help my students read with greater ease. I believe that being able to read and being able to comprehend what is read are two of the main keys to success in any subject in school. My research was focused on the improvement of my students' vocabulary because I believe that if I can improve their vocabulary, I can improve their achievement in reading. My students, their parents and my colleagues were informed that I was doing a teacher-research project during which I would continue to monitor the impact of my instructional techniques on my students' learning. They were told that if my findings indicated that I needed to modify those techniques, I would do so. They were also informed that the guiding question for my research was: "What instructional strategies can I use to improve my students' vocabulary that will improve their achievement in reading?"

Procedures

Assessment strategies

To assess my students' academic ability, I administered two standardized tests. The DRP (Degrees of Reading Power) Test was used as a pre- and post-test. It was given in September of 2000 and in May of 2001. It is an untimed, multiple-choice test with non-fiction passages whose length and level of difficulty increase. This test uses the cloze procedure, which requires the students to use context clues to select words to complete a series of blank or incomplete sentences within passages. There were twenty-eight blanks on the second grade DRP and forty-two blanks on the third grade DRP. A gain of ten DRP units is equivalent to one year of growth in reading. The DWM (Degrees of Word Meaning) Test was also administered to all students in November of 2000 and in May of 2001. Similar to the DRP, the DWM is an untimed, multiple-choice test with forty bold-faced words in context. It was used to track the growth of my students' estimated range of words. To take the test, the students selected the synonym of a word from one of eight possible choices.

Teaching strategies

In addition to the tests administered, I used several innovative teaching strategies. Two vocabulary programs on CDs that are produced by Visions Technology in Education were used. The three activities that I used are the vocabulary flash cards, the scrambled word activity and the crossword puzzle. These programs were used to help my students study the key vocabulary words of the literary selections that were taught. In November of 2001, the students were permitted to take the flash cards with the key words of several selections home to play concentration. The next day they wrote a journal entry about their experiences.

In addition to the CD programs listed above, my students selected one of the key words from one of our literary selections, used a sheet of paper to record the word and its definition, used the word in an original sentence, and drew a picture to illustrate its meaning. While doing the first vocabulary project, the third graders presented their words in class; then they presented these words to another class. After that, they wrote a journal entry about these experiences. Figure 6.1 shows one of my students' creations.

Periodically, I used a game that I created; it is called Acklin's ESP (Extra Sensory Perception/Awareness). I used it to review key words and key concepts in reading. It was adapted from a TV game called *Password*. It

Figure 6.1

motivated most of my students to participate in class more actively. When I first taught my students how to play this game, I wrote, acted out or signaled a clue to a key word or concept. Then I showed the students how to raise their hands to participate. The first student that raised his/her hand was recognized. If a student gave the correct response, his/her name was recorded on the board. If this student's response was incorrect, I gave another clue. After I exhausted the clues, I told the students the correct response. The game was continued after a clue to another key word or concept was given.

As indicated in the first paragraph of this paper, the students in my second and third grade reading extension groups had a range of reading abilities. Most of them read on grade level; however, there were several students in two of my four groups that read six months below grade level. However, the majority of my students improved in their performance on the DWM (Degrees of Word Meaning) and the DRP (Degrees of Reading Power) Tests (Refer to Tables 6.1–6.4.).

According to the results shown in Table 6.1, six second graders progressed satisfactorily because they gained more than ten units of growth on the DRP. Four students only needed one or two units of growth to gain one year of growth in reading. Three students did not experience any growth, one student's score declined, and one student's growth could not

Table 6.1 Scores on the second grade DRP (Degrees of Reading Power) Test for the 2000–1 year

Student	Pre (Fall)	Post (Spring)	DRP Units
A	15–	31	+16
B	15–	29	+14
C	15–	29	+14
D	19	33	+14
E	33	42	+9
F	27	21	–6
G	19	31	+12
H	33	42	+9
I	29	51	+22
J	27	36	+9
K	19	27	+8
L	Not enrolled	42	–
M	15–	15–	+0
N	15–	15–	+0
O	33	33	+0

Table 6.2 Scores on third grade DRP (Degrees of Reading Power) Test for the 2000–1 year

Student	Pre (Fall)	Post (Spring)	DRP Units
A	30	32	+2
B	23	25	+2
C	25	35	+10
D	33	40	+7
E	32	31	–1
F	38	41	+3
G	29	34	+5
H	31	31	+0
I	41	53	+12
J	34	42	+8
K	23	35	+12
L	34	26	–8
M	35	44	+9
N	37	43	+6
O	31	43	+12
P	34	29	–5

be calculated because the student was not enrolled early enough to take the pre-test.

Meanwhile, on the third grade DRP, four students' scores matched or exceeded the ten units of growth. Three students only missed the recommended growth by one to three points; five students made some progress, but they did not make the expected gain, one student did not experience any growth, and three students' scores declined (Table 6.2).

An analysis of the second graders' performance on the DWM in Table 6.3 showed that the estimated range of twelve students' knowledge of words grew from 50 to 400 words. One student did not show any growth, and two students' scores could not be calculated, because they were not enrolled early enough in the fall.

A study of the third graders' performance on the DWM show that the estimated range of the words that eleven students knew grew from 50 to 800 words. Two students scores did not show any growth; two students' scores declined, and one student's score could not be calculated because the student was not enrolled early enough in the fall (Table 6.4).

Findings of the study

The findings of my study as exemplified in the data from Tables 6.1 to 6.4, and in my classroom observations, are summarized in point form below:

1   With practice and positive feedback, a reluctant reader can begin to read with increased fluency and improved comprehension.
2   A student's performance on the vocabulary part of the end-of-the-unit test might improve while his/her performance on other parts of the test, such as sequencing, might not improve.
3   Students respond more positively to the use of vocabulary activities that require their input/involvement.
4   To help a student to improve his/her performance on a standardized test such as the DRP and the DWM, it is important to teach the student how to understand the cloze procedure during which context clues are used to select words to complete a series of blank sentences within passages.
5   Innovative ideas can also become commonplace.
6   Many students like to draw and tell about their drawings.

Implications

Based on my experience in this study, I would put forward the following recommendations and implications for teaching practice:

1   Numerous opportunities for practice with positive feedback need to be provided to help reluctant readers to become fluent readers.
2   Teach vocabulary strategies, but do not neglect the teaching of other reading comprehension skills.
3   The use of original visual illustrations and oral presentations can help a student to internalize the meaning of key words.
4   Teach the cloze procedure.

Table 6.3 Scores – estimated number of words known – on the DWM (Degrees of Word Meaning) Test for second grade reading extension students for the 2000–1 year

Student	Pre (Fall)	Post (Spring)	Estimated range	Gain
A	1,350–1,650	2,400–2,900	300–500	+200
B	Not enrolled	1,100–1,350	Not enrolled	
C	630–810	1,200–1,500	180–300	+120
D	630–810	2,650–3,150	180–500	+320
E	2,400–2,900	2,400–2,900	0	+0
F	380–480	2,200–2,650	100–450	+350
G	1,200–1,500	2,900–3,450	300–550	+250
H	1,350–1,650	4,050–4,750	300–700	+400
I	1,800–2,200	3,450–4,050	400–600	+200
J	2,650–3,150	3,450–4,050	500–600	+100
K	900–1,100	1,650–2,000	200–350	+150
L	Not enrolled	1,100–1,350	Not enrolled	
M	100 or fewer	480–630	100–150	+50
N	280–340	630–810	60–180	+120
O	2,000–2,400	3,450–4,050	400–600	+200

Table 6.4 Scores – estimated number of words known – on the DWM (Degrees of Word Meaning) Test for third grade reading extension students for the 2000–1 year

Student	Pre (Fall)	Post (Spring)	Estimated range	Gain
A	1,100–1,350	2,000–2,400	250–400	+150
B	2,000–2,400	2,000–2,400	0	+0
C	900–1,100	1,800–2,200	200–400	+200
D	4,750–5,500	5,900–6,850	750–950	+200
E	810–1,000	630–810	190–180	–10
F	6,850–7,850	6,850–7,850	0	+0
G	2,000–2,400	2,650–3,150	400–500	+100
H	2,900–3,450	4,750–5,500	550–750	+200
I	5,100–5,900	9,050–10,350	800–1,300	+500
J	1,100–1,200	5,500–6,350	100–850	+750
K	900–1,100	1,100–1,350	200–250	+50
L	1,650–2,000	1,200–1,500	350–300	–50
M	2,650–3,150	9,700 –11,000	500–1,300	+800
N	2,200–2,650	4,750–5,500	450–750	+300
O	2,200–2,650	4,750–5,500	450–750	+300
P	Not enrolled	2,400–2,900	Not enrolled	

5   Vary the approaches used to teach vocabulary strategies.
6   Students' positive reactions to drawing and talking about their drawings can be used to help to improve their reading achievement.

Conclusion

Although this is the final year that vocabulary will be the topic of my teacher-research project, I will continue to use the most productive vocabulary strategies and lessons that I discovered. In my effort to improve my students' vocabulary to boost their achievement in reading, I noted several improvements in their academic performance. In addition, I noticed that I obtained more student-generated input (charts, surveys, written and/or verbal responses). Also, I made several modifications in my teaching strategies. I am more aware of my students' reactions (verbal, non-verbal and written) to my instructional strategies. Throughout the 2001–2 year, my students' feedback (verbal and non-verbal) motivated me to modify or change my teaching strategies. Elementary teachers as well as secondary teachers can use the findings and implications of this research to help them to deliberately plan and teach vocabulary lessons in innovative ways so that their students will be motivated to internalize the meaning of their key vocabulary words. To keep their lessons exciting and challenging, they can also use my findings to continue to locate and use a variety of approaches to teach these words.

Bibliography

Frasier, D. (2000) *Miss Alaineus: A Vocabulary Disaster*, New York: Harcourt, Inc.

MacLean, M. S. and Mohr, M. (1999) *Teacher-Researchers at Work*, Berkeley, CA: National Writing Project.

Pavelka, P. (1997) *Making the Connection: Learning Skills Through Literature 3–6*, Peterborough, NH: Crystal Spring Books.

Uretsky, B. and Leader, B. (1999) *Crossword Companion Elementary*, Eugene, OR: Visions Technology in Education.

Uretsky, B. and Leader, B. (1999) *Vocabulary Companion Elementary*, Eugene, OR: Visions Technology in Education.

Chapter 7

Teaching from the inside out

An image-based case study of teacher development in *Learning through the Arts*

Kit Grauer and Rosamar Garcia

Introduction

In this chapter we examine the beliefs and practices of a teacher involved
in a particular artists-in-the-schools program called *Learning through the
Arts*. This program is sponsored by the Royal Conservatory of Music
(Toronto, Canada) and is designed to be a professional development model
for teachers wishing to learn how to integrate the arts into all subject areas
within the curriculum. The program brings different artists into a school
to work with all of the teachers at a particular grade level. Over three years,
the school takes on an arts-infused curriculum model. Much of this model
is dependent upon a variety of factors such as: teacher, and artist, beliefs
around art and teaching; the time and energy needed to plan an appropriate
curriculum together; and an inquiry-based process of understanding what
it means to learn *through* the arts. The case presented here is part of a much
larger study that follows artists and teachers over a three-year period and
is meant as a window into both the world of the teacher and researcher as
they use an image-based research methodology.

We are attempting to continue the work of Bresler (1993) in understanding teachers' and artists' knowledge of the arts and pedagogy by
drawing on phenomenology, case study and action research. During the
1970s and 1980s, artists-in-residence programs grew and became an
important feature of education (e.g. Nash 1979). During the 1990s and
beyond, programs such as these continued to flourish and in some instances
became recognized as important additions to school programs witnessing
reduced or eliminated programs in the arts. In other instances, these
programs were viewed as important additions to already strong programs
in the arts or were created to enhance school reform efforts across the core
subjects, while promoting the arts as essential subjects whenever possible.
Many of these programs were brought forward as ways to enrich the overall
curriculum. In Canada, many of these programs were brought in just as
elementary classroom generalists were replacing specialists in the arts. Even
then, the programs were often justified on the basis of their effect on non-

arts subjects rather than their importance to human understanding through the arts.

According to Doyle (1990), research in teaching and teacher education has always been seen as a pragmatic enterprise intended to improve teaching and teacher education rather than to simply describe or to understand it. While this is not the type of study that offers generalizations, it does point to some powerful ideas that resonate with other experiences in artist-in-schools programs. If teachers are to have a voice in their own education it is important that opportunities are available to hear those voices and understand the impact of this type of innovative program on teacher development.

Burnaford, Aprill and Weiss (2001) have noted that the arts open up dialogue among educators. They discuss the idea of finding "the elegant fit" (p. 25). An elegant fit implies the separate pieces of the curriculum have been brought together to produce a new and more satisfying whole. The elegant fit occurs when teachers find the right forms and processes to deliver ideas and when students, teachers and artists are actively engaged in the learning process.

It is essential to establish that the case presented here is a part of a much larger study. What it provides is an initial window into one of the classrooms and the interaction between the artist and teacher as interpreted through the teacher-researcher's self-reflection and the university researcher's images of the event and responses. Several strategies are employed as ways to nurture our thinking as image-based educational researchers. Digitized images, taken during each session, are used as a source of images to prompt our reflections, interpretations and analysis. The technique of photo elucidation (Collier 1967; Harper 1998) is based on the simple idea of inserting a photograph into a research interview. The difference between interviews using images and text, and interviews using words alone, lies in the way we respond to these two forms of symbolic representation. We find, as does Harper (2002), that images evoke deeper levels of human consciousness than do words. At our debriefing sessions, the researcher shows the digitized images taken during our observations of the artists and teachers working together in the classrooms. As the researcher, artist and/or teacher interpret the image, a dialogue is created in which the typical research roles are reversed and our resulting dialogues suggest a more collaborative method for research.

In the original presentation of this dialogue, the teacher, Rosamar, the artist, Richard; and the university researcher, Kit, discussed a much larger set of images in front of the audience at the International Conference on Teacher Research (ICTR) 2001, *A Calling of Circles – Living the Research in Everyday Practice*. A primary purpose of this presentation was to demonstrate the power of photo elucidation for reflection and analysis. In this chapter, Rosamar and Kit decided to present a shorter version of that session, concentrating on responding to each other and the images as they triggered important junctures in our own understanding of the values associated with this experience and this type of program. In this way images (Prosser 1998) become central to our work. Images are a part of our methodology and part of our presentation. We have also decided to integrate text fonts that will give the reader a chance to imagine voice. In this chapter "Palatino" is the font of academic writing, and Rosamar and Kit's reflections are represented by different fonts: Rosamar in *Lucida Handwriting* and Kit in *Textile*. In this way, we are pursuing image-based educational research, as a way of presenting our findings in artistic forms that we hope will enhance understanding of both the methodology and the area of research.

Opening the window

Richard Tetrault is a visual artist whose work includes making community-based murals. He was the visual artist chosen to participate at the Grade Five level and it was his first year in the *Learning through the Arts* program. Rosamar, as a Grade Five teacher, had been introduced to Richard through the LTTA program. The first image is of the open page of the artist biography that was sitting on Rosamar's desk when Richard first came into her classroom. Although the image is of a simple artifact present in the classroom, in the responses it is obvious that it signified more to both Kit and Rosamar. It was the springboard into exploring the presuppositions we both brought into the initial encounter with the collaboration between this artist and this teacher.

Contemplating the View

The case study presented here resonates with many of the themes that we are encountering in our larger study (Grauer *et al.* 2001). In particular, several themes emerge when viewed through the lens of our research questions on artists' and teachers' beliefs about learning and teaching and understanding of pedagogical content knowledge.

Beliefs about teaching and learning

Teacher reform over the last decade has emphasized teaching as an intellectual rather than a technical enterprise. In fact, there has been a tremendous move toward the creation of intellectual communities of teachers, students and teacher educators (Nelson and Hammerman 1996). The schools electing to be a part of the LTTA program clearly see themselves as sites for professional development in the arts. Rosamar, as the lead teacher in her school, epitomized that view. She saw Richard's visit not

I had the advantage of knowing a bit about Richard and Rosamar prior to watching their relationship develop. Richard had been the artist involved in an international children's art mural project I was acquainted with and so I knew his amazing capacity to bring out the best artistic response in children. Rosamar was a teacher who had always impressed me with her professionalism and capacities as a teacher and a learner. I saw this image as an example of her willingness to learn more about the artist and prepare for the session.

When I read this bio, it was no more than a collection of facts, like something you read about an actor before a play or a musician before she comes on stage. And then I met Richard.

Learning through the Arts hasn't been just any pilot. For me it's been an opportunity to peek through a window and watch the artist at work, then experience the wonder of being invited to co-create and share the magic with the students in my class.

Figure 7.1

only as a worthwhile opportunity for her students, but also a chance for her to begin to understand how to think like an artist.

Although Shulman's (1986) idea of pedagogical content knowledge has been developed substantially since it was first voiced, it falls short of adequately describing a construct useful for elementary generalist teachers engaged in art education. Research and writings in the area of pedagogical content knowledge are predominantly situated around secondary teaching in the traditional core academic disciplines. Pedagogical content knowledge presupposes both knowledge and beliefs about subject matter that form the basis of what Shulman (1992) entitles, "wisdom of practitioners." It is a term that implies that the pedagogical understandings are built upon prior subject matter knowledge.

Rosamar entered the Learning through the Arts program in the best possible way as a full participant with her classes. Her active involvement with the program enriched her own learning in a multitude of ways. Her own questions about thinking like an artist helped open up rich avenues of learning for herself and her students. Even her choice of words like "opportunity, experience, wonder, co-create and magic" demonstrates the types of thinking that underlie her teaching. The images of her and Richard are ones of full engagement.

Rosamar was extremely at ease interacting in a team teaching way with Richard. Sometimes she followed his lead and, at other times, she brought the class focus back to her own curriculum goals. It was an "elegant fit."

Figure 7.2

Rosamar's comments support the observation made throughout the literature, see for example McCoubrey (2000), that elementary generalist teachers do not possess subject matter knowledge in art. Their beliefs toward art are not based on knowledge but on personal or school-acculturated experience. A fresh understanding of the subject of art by working with an artist can have a transforming effect on the pedagogical understandings and beliefs teachers hold toward the content to be taught. The concept of discipline-based pedagogy (Grauer 1998) more closely approximates the reality of the elementary generalist teacher. Discipline-based pedagogy extends our understanding of the relationship of subject matter and pedagogy when subject matter knowledge appears to be lacking. In Rosamar's words, "Teaching from the inside out means knowing

Richard's comfortable manner with the kids was evident the minute he walked into the room. He had obviously done this activity a million times before. But I needed to know more about his process. What was it about his thinking as an artist that set him apart from me as a teacher? If I was going to develop expertise as an art teacher, I had to do more than just learn a technique from the master himself, I had to get to know his way of thinking, his way of looking at and responding to the environment around him.

Figure 7.3

While the kids drew, I tried to listen to the comments he made as he walked around and chatted with each of the students.

I noticed that he wasn't critical. No comments about "adding more color or detail or filling up the space," comments I might have made. He described what it was that he saw in each child's picture, or said nothing at all.

Figure 7.4

But he had a plan and through the format of a triptych and by selecting the colors himself, he almost guaranteed that the end results would be aesthetically appealing. If I was going to be able to guide students this skillfully, I realized that I would need to develop more expertise in the discipline of art.

Rosamar also had a plan. Her class had spent a week at the Vancouver Aquarium and she wanted this mural-making activity to be more than an art project but also a chance to work with the ideas of integrated curriculum. She was able to work with Richard's proficiency and her own goals to develop a worthwhile project. The pedagogical skill and expertise that Rosamar brought formed a strong bond with the discipline-based knowledge that Richard had to share. At every opportunity, she made this connection.

Figure 7.5

the discipline well enough that, in fact, you actually belong to the club. It is cultural apprenticeship at its best."

The nature of collaboration between artist and teacher

Although the structure of this program usually works against the time needed for substantive collaboration between artists and teachers, Rosamar and Richard were able to engage in reflection-in-action and formed a team teaching situation that was collaborative. The artists in LTTA were in over

Rosamar not only made the connections for herself, she was also continuously attempting to make connections for the children to similarities between the writing process or by scribing Richard's words and ideas on the board.

Something that struck me about Richard was his different sense of time. Whenever he worked with the students, he never seemed constrained by any time factors. This was a very interesting idea and something I wanted to think more about: time and its relationship to the creative process.

Figure 7.6

The students felt a strong sense of ownership when working on these banners. And I did too. I couldn't help but dabble a sponge here and there, mix a color or two. I felt pulled in by the intensity of the activity and soon lost track of time myself. This chance to observe my own process was invaluable, as ultimately I will have to stand in my own shoes as an art teacher.

Figure 7.7

twenty classrooms in a seven-week period and barely could know the names of the teachers, let alone their curriculum and instructional objectives. However, for Richard and Rosamar, they designed a unit of instruction that built on the best of each of their expertise and made the most of their time together. Rosamar had already developed a strong

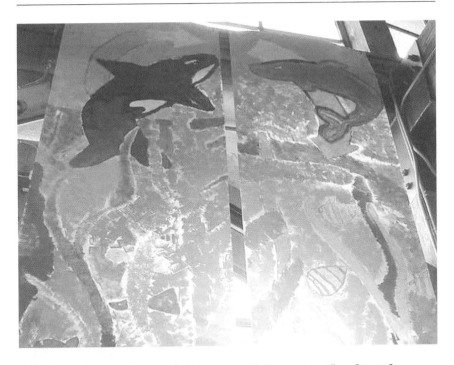

Teaching from the inside out means knowing the discipline well enough that, in fact, you actually belong to the club. It is cultural apprenticeship at its best.

Apprenticeship has had a long tradition in the arts and both Richard and Rosamar grew from their experiences working together. Both process and product were honoured throughout the experience leaving everyone proud of their involvement.

Figure 7.8

ecology unit at the Vancouver Aquarium, and she was excited to see how the mural making could bring the children's understandings together in different ways. Richard was a master at bringing out artistic representations from a community of learners. Together, they were able to work from and learn from each other's strengths and provide a rich learning environment for the students and each other. The level of active participation suggested in the images was typical of their collaborative manner. Rosamar continuously made links between Richard's teaching and other aspects of the curriculum and Richard used his expertise to extend the students' understanding of both the science objectives and the artistic process. This partnership echoed the "elegant fit" described by Burnaford, Aprill and Weiss (2001).

The response of the children in shaping beliefs

For most teachers there was no greater incentive to positively view the arts' place in learning than to see successful responses from the students in their classrooms. In the image-based interviews, teachers invariably discussed the engagement that they saw pictured on the faces of the children involved in the arts experiences. Motivation, expressiveness and accomplishment are categories that teachers attribute to engagement with the arts. For Rosamar, this was clearly the case. She comments on the ownership of the children as a result of their engagement with the murals and her own resulting pride in what they have accomplished. She was encouraged that children could represent their thinking in different ways and that some children who were not successful in other academic activities could be successful through the arts. In many instances, throughout the LTTA program, the level of work that the children accomplished was far beyond the expectations of the teachers and caused the teachers to reassess their own beliefs about teaching and learning in and through the arts.

The role of the researchers and image-based methodology in affecting beliefs

The use of a digital camera did not seem to affect the responses of the children to the sessions with the artist and teacher. When the researcher entered, the children seemed oblivious to another adult presence in the class. This was apparent in taking images with the digital camera; there was seldom any concern or even acknowledgement from the children that they were being observed. In the case of Rosamar and Richard, the images shown are from a much larger set of over 100 images. The use of image-based research methods seems to have some exciting possibilities for a greater involvement of the participants, especially as it was used in this school. Beyond what was evident from the sample of Rosamar and Richard, many of the other teachers used their images of the classes interacting with each artist with the children as reminders of what they had learned and as ways of reflecting on the experience. A computer-generated slide show was produced for the school's Open House and was another example where teachers' beliefs about the importance of the arts were positively affected by putting together and watching this show. It was encouraging to see students and parents engaged in dialogue about the artist visits. The image-based interviews with the teachers allowed glimpses into interactions of which they were not previously aware and allowed the teachers and artists to re-examine the artists' visits in ways that enhanced understanding (Grauer *et al*. 2001). As suggested by Harper (1998), photo elucidation techniques did blur the distinctions between researcher and participant. This also extended Bresler's notions of case study and action research as powerful tools in understanding artists' and teachers' knowledge of the arts and pedagogy.

The particularities of each artist and each classroom are bringing sets of questions that are exciting to pursue across classrooms and across time. Given the rising interest in artist-in-residence programs across Canada, and particularly the *Learning through the Arts* programs across Canada and internationally, this image-based educational research contributes insights into the beliefs, practices, and issues surrounding such programs. The view from the window into this classroom demonstrates that for Rosamar, teachers can work collaboratively with artists to gain access to the clubs that will allow them positive learning experiences for themselves and for the children in their classrooms.

Acknowledgment

The research reported here was supported, in part, by the Social Sciences and Humanities Research Council of Canada. We would also like to thank the UBC research team of Rita Irwin, Sylvia Wilson and Alex de Cosson for their contribution to this project.

Bibliography

Bresler, L. (1993) "Teacher knowledge and scholarly discourse in the visual arts: Drawing on phenomenology, case study, and action research," *Visual Arts Research*, 19, 1: 30–46.

Burnaford, G., Aprill, A. and Weiss, C. (2001) *Renaissance in the Classroom: Arts Integration and Meaningful Learning*, Mahwah, NJ: Lawrence Erlbaum Associates.

Collier, J. Jr. (1967) *Visual Anthropology: Photography as a Research Method*, New York: Holt, Rinehart and Winston.

Doyle, W. (1990) "Themes in teacher education," in W. R. Houston (Ed.) *Handbook of Research on Teacher Education* (pp. 3–24), New York: Macmillan.

Grauer, K. (1998) "Beliefs of pre-service teacher education," *Studies in Art Education*, 39, 4: 350–70.

Grauer, K., Irwin, R. L., de Cosson, A. and Wilson, S. (2001) "Images for understanding: snapshots of *Learning through the Arts*," *International Journal of Education and the Arts*. Online. Available: http://ijea.asu.edu/v2n9/.

Harper, D. (1998) "An argument for visual sociology," in J. Prosser, (Ed.) *Image-based Research: A Sourcebook for Qualitative Researchers*, London: Falmer Press.

Harper, D. (2002) "All about pictures: a case for photo elucidation," *Visual Studies*, 17, 9: 28–33.

McCoubrey, S. (2000) "But I'm not an artist: beginning elementary generalist teachers constructing art teaching practices from beliefs about ability to create art," unpublished doctoral dissertation, University of British Columbia, Vancouver.

Nash, L. (1979) "Improving the arts in your school," *Thrust for Educational Leadership*, 8, 3: 14–16.

Nelson, S. N. and Hammerman, J. K. (1996) "Reconceptualizing teaching: moving toward the creation of intellectual communities of students, teachers, and teacher educators," in M. W. McLaughlin and I. Oberman (Eds) *Teacher Learning: New Policies, New Practices*, New York: Teachers College Press.

Prosser, J. (Ed.) (1998) *Image-based Research: A Sourcebook for Qualitative Researchers*, London: Falmer Press.

Shulman, L. S. (1986) "Those who understand: knowledge growth in teaching," *Educational Researcher*, 15, 2: 4–14.

Shulman, L. S. (1992) "Renewing the pedagogy of teacher education: the impact of subject-specific conceptions of teaching," paper presented at the First International Conference on Subject Specific Teaching Methods in Teacher Education, University of Santiago de Compostela, Spain.

Chapter 8

Tunngavik homework helpers

An action research project exploring a northern school–family partnership

Elizabeth Kreuger and Jim Kreuger

Introduction[1]

The purpose of this study was to document the development and evaluation of the Tunngavik Homework Helpers program, from the vantage points of the program coordinators, teachers, and parents who actively collaborated in its planning, development, and implementation. A critical perspective of teaching/curriculum development as research was adopted. The authors, who worked as program coordinators for the Regional School Operations (RSO) office, acted as two members of the facilitation team developing and implementing the program; reflection on facilitation forms part of the critical analysis contained herein. Teachers, likewise, became researchers as throughout the study they reflected on their practices. Parents gained access to and experienced demystification of the process of curriculum development as the Tunngavik Homework Helpers program evolved. The study was carried out in a small community in the Nunavut territory of Canada.

Coghlan and Brannick (2001: 3, 4) maintain that "[a]ction research has traditionally been defined as an approach to research that is based on a collaborative problem-solving relationship between the researcher and client which aims at both solving a problem and generating new knowledge." Fischer (2001) identifies curricular innovations as an area suitable for teacher action research. Wason-Ellam, Ward, and Williamson (1999) demonstrate that through action research intercultural teachers can collaborate and develop common understandings. Hall (1978) identifies participatory action research as a way in which communities can break the monopoly of knowledge and thus empower themselves. This study incorporates elements of teacher action research with community (parental) empowerment in the area of homework and home–school relations.

Rationale

There is a commonly held belief that parental involvement in the schooling of children positively correlates to the success of those children in school. However, Friedel contends that "although many educational researchers have validated the relationship between parental involvement and student achievement, they have not investigated these issues from the perspective of Native parents" (Friedel 1999: 139). The very acceptance of the relationship between parental involvement and student achievement has marginalized Aboriginal families in two ways. First, through their non-participation, Aboriginal parents are held partly responsible for Aboriginal education's negative statistics. Second, their participation is often arbitrarily assigned rather than defined by the community.

In Nunavut, there is a general tendency for parents to become less active in the formal schooling of their children after the early years. MacKay and Myles (1995: 166) report that lack of Aboriginal parental participation may be related to the parents' intimidation by, alienation from, and ambivalence toward the education system. Another possible reason for parents' withdrawal, speculated here, could be related to confidence – i.e. more a case of "not knowing how to help" than "not wanting to help." Whatever the reason, it is this withdrawal that is distressing, as it gradually weakens the child's primary support network and creates an ever-growing gap between home and school.

Taking into account Lipka's (1989) suggestion that educational projects should deal with issues that the community can rally around, homework was proposed by RSO as such an issue. The purpose of the project was to co-develop a homework program with parents and teachers which would encourage and support parents in participating in the formal schooling of their children and which would increase communication between home and school.

Development of the Tunngavik homework helpers program

The approach used in Tunngavik Homework Helpers is based on a South African series of grade-specific homework books that focus on numeracy and literacy skills (*Parent Assisted Learning Program* 1999). The notion of sharing the curricular goals with the parents and asking for their assistance in reaching these goals was a fresh idea for the RSO staff and they were interested in the community's reception of such an approach. Many of the elementary school staff agreed to participate as co-investigators.

A well-attended community meeting solicited parents' feelings toward the issue of homework and gauged their interest in the development of a homework program. Two statements formed the foundation from which the discussion progressed: (1) parents love their children and want them to succeed; and (2) teachers care for their students and want them to succeed. During the course of the meeting community members voiced overwhelming support for school homework and worked together to develop four belief statements:

1   We believe that homework should be challenging, interesting, skills-based, and fun if possible.
2   We believe that homework should be a regularly scheduled activity.
3   We believe that our children need our support with homework activities.
4   We believe that the school must provide support to the parents regarding homework.

The belief statements served as the vision which guided a parent-teacher steering committee in overseeing a team of teachers and RSO program coordinators in the development of Tunngavik Homework Helpers for the grade three Inuktitut and English language streams. The pilot program consisted of Inuktitut and English language workbooks with eight weekly assignments in first language reading and writing, second language reading, and mathematics. Participating students received all the necessary school supplies, including a book bag, while participating classrooms were provided with reading books, manipulatives, and educational games for lending to participating families.

Implementation phase

The first eight-week module of the program was ready to implement in October 2000. Two Parent/Student Orientation evenings, one for each language stream, were scheduled, and grade three students took home special invitations to their parents or guardians. The objectives for the evenings were to generate excitement for the program, to familiarize the parents/students with the program, and to gather initial feedback from stakeholders. The evening was organized so that each parent would move with his/her child through a series of four centers, each focused on a specific homework component (first language reading and writing, second language reading and writing, or math). In addition, in order to make the evening festive, several games were added to the agenda and refreshments were served. Following the orientation, the pilot period ran from October until December 2000.

Data collection

Data were collected before and after the implementation of the first module. Pre-implementation data were collected using a Parent/Student Homework Component Questionnaire (completed during the Orientation evenings), as well as the facilitators' reflections recorded in a guided journal. Expectation Surveys were also filled out by the stakeholders on the first day of implementation. Post-implementation data were collected from an analysis of the completed homework books, pilot teacher interviews, a Parent/Student Homework Questionnaire, and the authors' reflections.

Evaluation results – pre-implementation

Parent/student homework component evaluations

Five themes emerged from both language streams' Parent/Student Homework Component Evaluations, filled out at the Orientation evenings. The most common theme was one the researchers labeled "Student Enjoyment." Students' most common written response was, "It was fun;" and while parents' responses varied, "fun" was still the most common sentiment. In addition, over 80 per cent of the students circled the happy face on the evaluation to describe each of the activities.

"Level of Difficulty" was the second most common theme. The vast majority of comments indicated that the task was easy or at a level at which the child could be successful. Written responses included, "The book she was reading was nice and easy for her;" and "Well done, engaging activity." There were, however, some comments that indicated that the child found the task difficult or that the child needed extra practice, such as, "Karen had a hard time reading but I think this is going to help her and us."

The third most frequent comments revolved around the theme of "Positive Learning Experience for Parents." Many parents commented on the fact that the activity was helpful and that it was actually a learning experience for them. "This evening was a learning experience for me as a parent" and "I have to learn more because I didn't finish school but I hope my daughter will learn better than I," are examples of parents' written responses that fell under this theme.

"Enjoyment of Working Together" was the fourth most frequent theme. It was obvious that parents enjoyed the experience of working with their children while children enjoyed the attention they received. Parents' comments included, "Tonight's math activity was fun tonight. Both parent and kid had to work together" and "I really enjoyed listening to my child reading."

The last theme to emerge was "Parent's Awareness of Child's Abilities." Through the Tunngavik activities, the parents developed an understanding of their children's strengths and weaknesses. Comments such as "I enjoyed it, it helps me to better understand where my daughter stands" and "She still gets her 'p' and 'd' mixed up, other than that she seems to know the short 'a' and 'e' words" are examples of parents' recognition of their children's abilities.

Facilitators' reflections

Members of the parent-teacher steering committee as well as RSO program coordinators facilitated the evening and shared their reflections afterwards. There was strong evidence of the orientation's success both in terms of turnout and enjoyment. Twenty-five of the twenty-seven English stream children were accompanied by at least one parent or guardian while thirteen of the seventeen Inuktitut stream students attended the Inuktitut orientation. This, in itself, showed that parents are very interested in helping their children in school and that they are willing to work toward this end. In addition, there was an overwhelming optimism for the future of the program and a real commitment to make the program responsive to the needs of the children and their parents. Comments such as "I am very motivated and enthusiastic about the program" and "I felt the evening was a great success! The turn-out showed a wellspring of parental concern for helping their children to succeed in school" are examples of the facilitators' written comments.

Expectations survey

On the first day of the pilot, teachers, parents, and students filled in an Expectation Survey, the results of which showed that all three groups had high expectations and were confident and excited about beginning the program. Overall, they indicated that they thought the program would improve students' academic skills, communication between the home and the school, and parents' knowledge about what their children do in school. "At times some parents can't make it to school because of other duties. This will really help" and "Yes, I feel it's going to help my child improve more" are characteristic comments from the survey.

Evaluation results – post-implementation

Workbook analysis

The pilot phase was completed just before Christmas, at which time the student workbooks were collected and analyzed. Distinct differences in the data between the language streams emerged. For this reason, the findings are presented separately. It should also be noted that the demographics of both the Inuktitut and English language streams were very similar – the Inuktitut language stream was comprised solely of Inuit students while in the English stream, all but three students were Inuit.

Twenty-five of the twenty-seven students in the English stream completed the eight-week module. Parents communicated to the teacher through the "homework log" on average more than two out of a possible three times per week. In addition, students indicated an overall enjoyment of the activities and parents' comments reinforced the original five themes from the pre-implementation evaluation (student enjoyment, level of difficulty, positive learning experience for the parents, enjoyment of working together, parent's awareness of child's abilities).

In the Inuktitut stream, students completed only the first two weeks of the program. A discussion with the classroom teacher provided insights. She thought that the parents had trouble reading Inuktitut syllabics (writing system) and because the workbooks were unilingual Inuktitut, the parents could not understand the activities. She also felt that the instructions to the parents were too long and they were written at too high a level. For the most part, she felt that the homework assignments were more like lessons, involving too much teaching on the part of the parents. Finally, the parents failed to mark the assignments and since the teacher felt it was their responsibility to do so, the marking was not done. After two weeks of the workbooks being returned unmarked, the classroom teacher decided to suspend the program.

The authors' reaction to the workbook analysis was mixed. The results of the English stream were exciting for several reasons. First of all, to have the vast majority complete the first module was certainly something to celebrate, especially in a school system where homework is not the norm. The two incomplete workbooks were determined to be directly related to non-attendance at the initial orientation. The fact that the parents were communicating with the teacher regularly each week through the workbooks certainly demonstrated an interest in their children's participation in the program. The researchers were also encouraged to see that the students still seemed to enjoy the activities and that the same five positive themes were found in their parents' comments.

Although disappointed with the results of the Inuktitut stream, the authors were not discouraged, as, with any action research, it is often the unexpected detours and outcomes that are the most revealing. Even though the classroom teacher's perspective on the reasons for its failure were already relayed, it was still disappointing that she had not felt comfortable enough to inform the other researchers before she suspended the program. If her insights had proved valid, some form of adjustments might have been possible so that the parents and students could have completed the program. In order to pinpoint the necessary adjustments or edits, the researchers would certainly have provided an opportunity for the parents and the students to voice their feelings.

Student/parent post-implementation questionnaires

At the end of the pilot phase, celebration evenings were held separately for each language stream's students and their parents/guardians, serving to honor and evaluate the program's completion. The importance of this feedback was especially critical for the Inuktitut language stream as the program was in need of extensive changes.

Data collection at this phase of the project took a similar form as in the orientation. Once again, the parents and students filled out questionnaires at each of four centers. In addition, each of the facilitators kept notes on the discussions that took place at his/her center.

Four major findings surfaced from this data. First of all, the student responses were more positive than were the parent responses in both language streams. In general, the students thought the homework tasks were shorter, easier, and more enjoyable than did the parents.

Second, the parents of both language streams struggled with understanding the Inuktitut syllabics in the workbooks and the majority showed a definite preference for reading in English. In addition, parents in the Inuktitut stream wanted bilingual workbooks, whereas most parents in the English stream did not. Initially, the Inuktitut stream teacher thought that bilingual workbooks would defeat the purpose of learning Inuktitut but, after much thought, she decided that bilingual parental instructions would be a possible solution.

The third finding revealed distinct differences between the parents of the English and the Inuktitut language stream students. Once again, the parents in the English stream reaffirmed the original five themes of student enjoyment, level of difficulty, positive learning experience for the parents, enjoyment of working together, and parent's awareness of child's abilities. The parents in the Inuktitut stream, however, did not reaffirm the original five themes; rather, three new themes emerged: (1) difficulty in reading Inuktitut syllabics, (2) dialectical differences, and (3) assignments were too long.

All three of the new themes seem to be related to the parents' difficulty in reading syllabics. Most of these parents took their own schooling in English and did not develop a strong foundation in written Inuktitut. As well, written Inuktitut was introduced in the 1950s and, thus, many of the parents' parents were not in a position to teach it at home. This, compounded by the dearth of written Inuktitut materials, possibly accounts for the fact that many parents cannot read or have difficulty reading Inuktitut. In addition, if the reader is struggling with the syllabics, then dialectic differences could add another level of frustration to reading. Difficulty in reading would also lengthen the amount of time needed to complete the nightly homework assignment and certainly it is recognized that writing in syllabics is more labor intensive. Combined, this reading difficulty and longer writing time could account for the third new theme – assignments are too long.

The final finding in this data was that the Inuktitut language stream did not complete volume one, whereas the English stream did. With this in mind, the researchers were very excited when the actual attendance at the Inuktitut Stream Celebration was higher than it had been for the Orientation. It was obvious that even though the students and parents did not complete the volume, they were very interested in collaborating to refine the program in order to make it more appropriate.

Pilot teacher interviews

Both of the piloting teachers thought the program was valuable and would like to repeat it in the following year with another grade three class. The

Inuktitut stream teacher was interested in helping to improve the Inuktitut program. The English stream teacher has been transferred to grade one but she is interested in developing a homework program for that grade.

Both of the teachers felt that Tunngavik Homework Helpers improved the communication between the home and school. Although the Inuktitut stream only participated for two weeks, the teacher thought that the workshops had a positive effect on the parents' expectations of home–school communications. The English stream teacher felt that home–school communication was strong throughout the pilot. Parents indicated to her, during parent-teacher interviews, that they felt the same. Both piloting teachers also felt that their students enjoyed the program while they were in it.

Problems arose for both teachers in regard to the marking of assignments. The Inuktitut stream teacher strongly believed that marking was the parents' responsibility and she suspended the program after two weeks when marking was not done. The English stream teacher decided to mark the assignments to ensure that the program continued. Although it meant more work for her, she felt that having the teacher mark the assignments signaled to the home that the program was important.

When asked what they thought worked especially well, the Inuktitut stream teacher reiterated that she thought the workshops were very valuable. The other teacher's feedback was more specific to the program. She liked the workbook format and thought that the homework bags and pencil cases were well taken care of. The English stream teacher also liked the weekend games and added that the class homework chart and stickers seemed to work for her class.

The pilot teachers had different suggestions for improvements. The Inuktitut stream teacher wanted to see the parent instructions written bilingually and in shorter, simpler Inuktitut. In addition, she wanted to see more use of the local dialect wherever possible. The English stream teacher's suggestions focused on ways that she could improve the delivery and administration of the program. She wanted to incorporate the homework themes more into her classroom planning. In addition, she thought it was necessary to keep her classroom instruction ahead of the homework or make adjustments to the homework when she fell behind. Her last suggestion centered on the selection of appropriate books to meet the students' needs and interests. She felt that many of the books provided by RSO were unsuitable.

Conclusions and reflections

The authors learned many things, both anticipated and surprising, from this study. First of all, related to the success of the Tunngavik Homework Helpers program, they learned that parents and teachers can collaborate to develop a homework program and that such a program can:

- improve communication between home and school,
- give parents a first-hand look at their children's strengths/weaknesses and likes/dislikes regarding school work,
- give parents a better understanding of the skills and knowledge that are being taught at school,
- be enjoyable for students when they get support from home and school, and
- depend on students to manage and transport their homework between home and school.

The study also established that even a coordinated homework program creates extra work for the participating teachers.

Unexpected results of the study were related to language. Parents of both streams preferred to read in English. The low literacy levels in Inuktitut restrict the parents' abilities to support their children with an Inuktitut homework program. In addition, there is a real resistance among parents to accept educational materials written in other dialects of Inuktitut. This becomes a serious problem because of the dearth of published Inuktitut materials in the pilot community's dialect.

Based on what the researchers learned about parents' literacy levels in Inuktitut, the results seem to cry out for community-based adult literacy or family literacy programs. The initial tenet that parents, if given the proper support, could and would help their children with homework tasks could be flipped around so that tasks are designed at the literacy level of the children. The children would then become the teachers, demonstrating their learning each night to their parents. The children, themselves, would facilitate the learning process. Certainly, developing a skill so that they could use it to help their families would have a high intrinsic motivation value for parents and students alike.

Upon reflection, two weaknesses in the project made themselves apparent to the authors. First, the starting point of the project was the RSO office and although the curriculum conception, planning, and development stages were community collaborations, ownership of the evaluation remained close to the RSO office. This narrow locus of ownership limited the power and control that parents and teachers could experience and exercise. Finally, student success was never defined in the study. The assumption was made that success for both parents and teachers meant success with the school curriculum. This made the curriculum sacrosanct and did not allow for parents or teachers to question its value.

This study has certainly met Coghlan and Brannick's (2001) criteria for action research. Collaboration was fundamental, problem solving was the approach, and new knowledge was generated. Action reasearch which involves parents and teachers in issues of mutual concern has great potential to transform education at the community level. Future studies can benefit from both the strengths and limitations of this study.

Note

1   We would like to thank all the participants in this study, the community, the school, the parents, Kivalliq School Operations and especially the pilot teachers and their students. In addition, we would like to thank Laurel Kreuger for her feedback and editorial comments.

Bibliography

Coghlan, D. and Brannick, T. (2001) *Doing Action Research in Your Own Organization*, London: Sage Publications.

Fischer, J. (2001) "Action research rationale and planning: developing a framework for teacher inquiry," in G. Burnaford, J. Fischer and D. Hobson (Eds) *Teachers Doing Research: The Power of Action Through Inquiry*, London: Lawrence Erlbaum Associates.

Friedel, T. (1999) "The role of Aboriginal parents in public education: barriers to change in an urban setting," *Canadian Journal of Native Education*, 23, 2: 139–57.

Hall, B. (1978) "Breaking the monopoly of knowledge: research methods, participation and development," in B. Hall and R. Kidd (Eds) *Adult Learning: A Design for Action*, Toronto: Pergamon Press.

Lipka, J. (1989) "A cautionary tale of curriculum development in Yup'ik Eskimo communities," *Anthropology and Education Quarterly*, 20: 216–31.

MacKay, R. and Myles, L. (1995) "A major challenge for the education system: Aboriginal retention and dropouts," in M. Battiste and J. Barman (Eds) *First Nations Education in Canada: The Circle Unfolds*, Vancouver, BC: University of British Columbia Press.

Parent Assisted Learning Program (1999) Cape Town, South Africa: Maskew Miller Longman (Pty).

Wason-Ellam, L., Ward, A. and Williamson, K. (1999) "Giving voice to intercultural teachers: finding common ground through action research." Retrieved March 20, 2001. Available online: http://www.stf.sk.ca/mcdowell/research/projects/project45.html.

Chapter 9

Circles of caring: living curriculum in the classroom

A performance presentation

Ron Avery, Marina Carter, Sukhy Dhillon, Donelda Henderson, Kathy Lavery and Louise Panziera, mentored by Dr Carl Leggo

[Drumbeats]

Marina:
Welcome. The drum calls us together to listen, to listen with our hearts as well as our heads.

Kathy:
From January to April, 2001, thirty-six teachers met in a course titled "Living the Research in Everyday Practice." The course was initiated by the organizing committee for ICTR in order to provide Richmond teachers with opportunities to research their everyday experiences. The teachers researched their practice and shared stories through poetry, performance, art, narrative, and journal writing. As the stories were shared, a thread of caring for students and ourselves emerged, weaving a tapestry of incredible texture and beauty. The prose and poetry in this work are fragments of this tapestry. There are bright and dark colours. Threads of caring, sharing and laughing are woven in with judging, doubt, tears and guilt.

Marina:
Symphony of Voices
I really do want to be a transformational teacher. You know the kind that breathes, eats and digests chalk dust. The kind that you swear has a sleeping cot at the school in order to transform the learning centers by the next morning. The kind that's in sync with the trendiest educational gurus and can mutate her lesson plans according to the latest paradigm shift. Just when I think that I'm there, that my moment of glory has come, I'm really not. Either because the paradigm shift has shifted once again or because something or someone is always beckoning, calling and summoning me to life. Now you might say what do you mean? Is someone calling you on the phone? Well let me explain, it's a little more complicated than the phone. The calling is more like surround sound. In my head there's a whole

orchestra and a symphony of voices bellowing and strumming, mainly out of tune. In the soprano section the children are badgering, the marking is summoning and so are the dusting, the ring around the toilet, the dentist, the big bad wolf, God, and the third Kraft dinner this week. The alto section crows that the rolls on my stomach are lamenting, along with the jammed printer, the ever speedy e-mails, the late birthday cards, my bank statement, yesterday's newspapers, the missing button on my husband's shirt, the movie that had to be returned last week, the third ring around the toilet, my high cholesterol, the Christmas decorations from last year, the expired KFC coupons, and the mold in the fridge singing the Ode to Joy. Booming basses remind me about the application for summer camp that has missed its deadline, the second letter from the mammography clinic and ten years worth of pictures still waiting to be put in that elusive album.

Oh yeah, I forgot about the misplaced library book, the internet that we are paying for and not using, the new Martha Stewart project that will transform me into a craft queen, the dry cleaning Nazi who continues to insist that we did not bring the jacket to his establishment, the Victoria's Secret catalog that lied about ... and last but not least the Safeway card that every loyal customer has except for me. Well to tell you the truth, I really have one but it's always in my other purse.

I really do have aspirations to be a great teacher. However, the symphony of callers in my brain has reached a crescendo and the only tune it continually plays is the William Tell Overture. The brass section seems to be especially loud, bellowing that there's been no sex for a week, while the wind instruments are singing the praises of fiber, Metamucil and hormone replacement therapy. Each instrument, each note, each accompaniment, each pitch and inflection plays around, against, over and through me and I relate to each rhythm in tongues.

Louise:
Duane Huebner writes:

> Feelings of doubt, inadequacy, fallibility, possible incompetency, are endemic to teaching. I would go so far as to wonder whether a teacher who lacks such doubt can be a good teacher
>
> (Huebner 1999: 307).

Taken from the writing of a prominent educational psychologist, and primary age children, a found poem by Donnie Henderson:

Psychologist:	All Reading in 540 Days:
	Recommended Kindergarten Assessment Schedule
Teacher:	*Mid-Year?*
Psychologist:	Letter Naming Fluency Onset Recognition Fluency
Teacher:	*End of Year?*

Child:	**I want to go near animals and draw about it.**
Psychologist:	Phoneme Segmentation Fluency
	Nonsense Word Fluency
Teacher:	*Nonsense!*
	Kindergarten Benchmark Goals?
Child:	**I wish I could learn about plants.**
Psychologist:	Established Initial Sounds Phonological Awareness by Winter
	If you hit 25–35 correct on Onset Recognition Fluency
Teacher:	*ORF?*
Psychologist:	In winter of Kindergarten, the odds are in your favor to reach 35–45 correct on Phoneme Segmentation Fluency
Teacher:	*PSF?*
Child:	**I wish I could learn about making desserts.**
Psychologist:	Established Phonological Awareness by Spring
	If you hit 35–45 correct on Phoneme Segmentation Fluency
Teacher:	*PSF?*
Psychologist:	In spring of Kindergarten/fall of first grade, the odds are in your favor to hit 40 or more correct on Nonsense Word Fluency
Teacher:	*NWF?*
	Nonsense!
Child:	I want to learn about rats.
Psychologist:	If you hit 40 or more correct on Nonsense Word Fluency
Teacher:	*NWF?*
	Nonsense!
Psychologist:	In winter of first grade, the odds are in your favor to hit 40 or more correct on Curriculum-Based Measurement
Teacher:	*CBM?*
Child:	I wish Ashley will play with me.
Psychologist:	If you hit 40 or more correct on Curriculum-Based Measurement
Teacher:	*CBM?*
Psychologist:	Reading in spring of first grade
Teacher:	*You are an established reader?*
Child:	I like to learn about bees and space.

The child's voice fades under the pressure of the mandated curriculum and the teacher's questions are ignored.

Louise:
David Jardine writes:

> The problem with technical-scientific discourse is not some indigenous evil or surreptitious intent; rather it is found in the way in which such

discourse has come to pervade the possibility of raising questions about our lives and the lives of children.

(Jardine 1992a: 118)

Marina:
Krista Ediger, a secondary teacher, writes:

How Does a Little Education Sound?

Everything is labeled with a thick black marker: computers, desks, chairs, books, audio-visual equipment, and even the posters that adorn the walls. The insignificant, serviceable carpet and the glow of the artificial lighting complete the decor of the institution. The room is cluttered with such a variety of objects, completely unrelated to one another, that they all become indistinct and unimportant, especially once the voice begins to speak, interrupting the incessant murmur that has originally dominated the sounds of the room. Reluctantly, the murmur is reduced to a faint but persistent level of background accompaniment, as the voice takes center stage, amid the loud cracks of three-ring binders, the constant zipping and unzipping of pencil cases and the click click click of mechanical pencils.

For a while, the audience, clothed in the latest fashion, with name brands prominently displayed, scratches furiously, brightly coloured and patterned nails drifting from left to right across a page. The whisper of a grating pencil, the muted tapping of a ball-point pen, dotting i's and crossing t's, and the occasional swish of a felt-tip pen, sliding effortlessly from one word to the next, replace the initial clamour. At the request of the voice, someone jumps onto a nearby counter to open the window. The musty air needs to be refreshed; however, the open window seems to have a negative effect on the energy level in the room. Someone yawns. Someone else pulls out an elastic and proceeds to run her fingers through her hair, straightening and pulling it back into a tighter, neater ponytail. When she has finished, she takes the elastic in one hand and stretches it around the ponytail three times in order to secure it in place. Someone else gets up and moves to the other side of the room to throw something into the garbage. On his way back, he stops at a desk to whisper something in his friend's ear. They both laugh.

The inattentiveness is contagious. Soon the room is filled with distracting movements, not conducive to concentrated focus. All hands are kept busy with numerous types of fidgeting. The left to right direction of the pen or pencil across the page becomes focused in a single area. Writing utensils create sounds that become increasingly pronounced as note-taking is replaced by shading, colouring and darkening designs in the upper left-hand corner of lined paper. Some abandon their binders completely in favour of planning their schedules, organizing their responsibilities and amending their telephone directories in their agendas. Others work on perfecting the pen trick where a pen is woven through all five fingers first one way and then the other, until a continuous pattern is established. Not everyone is an expert at this. An occasional dropped pen or pencil cracks on the surface of a desk or metal geometry case. Undaunted, the culprit picks up the magic wand and begins again.

After exhausting the more engrossing and taxing forms of wasting time, the students resort to holding their pens or pencils between their first and second fingers at the second knuckle and moving the writing tools back and forth faster and faster. If done with enough speed, the illusion of a butterfly is achieved. Or they play with their hands: adjust their watches, twirl their rings around their fingers and tap their fingers one immediately after the other, in a manner generally associated with impatience and boredom. Feet move every which way, at times banging against the legs of chairs and desks, at times rubbing together the soles of shoes, at times clapping down onto the carpeted floor. Sleeves are unrolled and then rolled up and then are unrolled and then rolled up until the roll is satisfactory. Earrings are taken out, in order to clean away the wax build-up with the sharp tip of a pencil, and then put back in again. Fingers comb through bangs and the ponytail needs fixing yet again.

The focus of the attention then switches from hands to mouths, which have to endure the hard, gritty texture of fingernails, plastic pen caps, and the wood that surrounds the lead of HB pencils along with the smoother textures of skin from around fingernails, material from a scrunchie, and the orange paint that surrounds the wood of HB pencils. Those who have continued to or have reverted to paying attention to the voice often bite their lips in thoughtfulness, sometimes carefully removing the first layer of skin that covers their upper lips. Some are more gentle to their taste buds and opt for the traditional stick of gum or candy, or settle for simply running their tongues along their teeth, or trying to remove that bit of food stuck between their teeth that has been bothering them since lunchtime.

While the mouth seems to be the body part of choice at this point, other parts of the body are not ignored. One student decides to clean his ear without the aid of a Q-tip, sticking his little finger painfully down his ear canal. He collects the wax from his finger onto his thumbnail and dives deeply once again into his ear. After completing the same process on his other ear, he flicks the resulting wax ball onto the floor as discreetly as possible, under his desk towards the outside of the room. Someone else does the same with the dirt she has gathered from under her fingernails with the tip of her mechanical pencil. Others check for sleep in the corners of their eyes amid the coughing, the sniffling, and the clearing of throats that puncture the incessant din that reigns in the classroom.

Comfort gains importance as time goes on. Hands drop what pens and pencils they are still holding and move to neck muscles and temples where they begin the deliberate movements of a massage. Afterwards, they move from massaging to supporting chins or foreheads. Soon two heads fall from this position to laying in the nook created by a bent elbow on a desk.

Kathy:
Andy Hargreaves writes:

> A key challenge for teachers is whether they can live with or even actively encourage full-blown cooperative classrooms, that are charged with spontaneity, unpredictability, danger and desire; or whether they will opt for safe simulations of these things that are controlled, contrived and ultimately superficial in character.
>
> (Hargreaves 1994: 174)

Ron:
Only experts create knowledge

Information everywhere, and not a bit to bite
The children are lethargic, they've been up half the night.
They have found the mother lode, the source of endless facts
They have got their download file, filled right up to the max

They can pick and choose, and go where they desire.
Some will pick sublime and true, and some will pick the mire.
But each and every one of them, call them quick or slow,
Know now how to do it, where to click and go

Digital delivery, of all there is to know
Turns conduits of expertise, into a pointless boring show
Were servants of a system, that claims to know the truth
All who say they don't agree, well they're just uncouth

Only experts create knowledge? never was it true
As many people in the world, as many points of view
To prop up that old paradigm, you have to stretch the skin
Of arguments of knowledge, until they're paper thin.

The industrial model system, of info for the masses
Is making us poor teachers, look like horses asses
The time has come to say, what we should have said before
Nothing is known for certain, but we're filled with love and lore.

Kathy:

Henry Giroux writes:

> While pedagogy is deeply implicated in the production of power/ knowledge relationships and the construction of values and desires, its theoretical center of gravity begins not with a particular claim to new knowledge, but with real people articulating and rewriting their lived experiences within rather than outside of history.
>
> (Giroux 1994: 284)

Sukhy:

Janet Powell writes,

Taking Care of the Bully

In a recent letter to the editor of the Richmond Review Newspaper the writer complained bitterly about the way schools are dealing with bullying. He blamed schools for the ongoing problem and bemoaned the fact that teachers aren't "taking care" of the bullying situation in a sufficiently swift and harsh manner. He wrote of "simple solutions" like suspension, expulsion and criminal prosecution.

While I appreciate the writer's concern for the well-being of children being bullied on school grounds, I think that he has forgotten one very important thing. The bullies are children too. He said that the schools don't care. On the contrary, we do care very deeply. We care about all students entrusted to us including, and perhaps particularly, the bullies, who are very likely to be children who have been bullied themselves and know no other way of asserting power and feeling in control.

The shortsighted solution when dealing with bullies is simply to punish them. Send them home to, perhaps, the very situation which taught them to be bullies in the first place. The solution is easy if we are willing to write off our young bullies and give up on them; however, if we don't believe that any of our children are disposable then solutions become a little more complex.

Yes, schools need to do everything in their power to protect children from bullying. They also need to do everything in their power to love and care for the bullies, to build up their feelings of worth and control in the world so that they don't need to take their pain and frustration out on others smaller and weaker than they. So to the writer of the letter I say, we care for all of the children at school. Effective solutions are far from simple but we will continue to "take care" of the bullying situation by "taking care" of the bullies.

Louise:

Max Van Manan writes:

> ... educators need to show that in order to stand up for the welfare of children, one must be prepared to stand out and be criticized.
>
> (Van Manan 1991: 47)

Donnie:

The Tone of Teaching
Forever questioning the way life is to be lived,
Thoughtfully,
Thoughtfulness, a special kind of knowledge,
To enter into the world of a child,
Hopefully,
Hope,
Live with hope,
Experience children as hope.
Hope strengthens, builds.
To hope is to believe in possibilities,
Experiencing the possible
Body and spirit, thoughtfully connected,
Life forever questions about the way it is to be lived.

Ron:

Michael Fullan writes:

"Success lies in the creative activity of making new maps. The combination of heart and head is crucial for effectiveness." (Fullan 1993: 43)

Louise:

Comrade in Arms
6:00 pm – waiting for my last report card conference.
It would be a good way to end two marathon evenings.
Cecil had come a long way – in his own way.
Making Cecil walk two inches taller was the goal and
I was sure his mom would be pleased.

Cecil joined Division One in October.
I remember his baggy windbreaker and oversized pants,
The way he carried a skateboard under his arm like a security
    blanket.
Cecil never moves; he always jolts, bounds, or sprints, in fact
There are times when he seems to be miming track and field events
    around the room,

He doesn't talk about dad much because
he lives with his three older sisters and mom.
Oh, and he loves to dance.
Reading, writing, math? Not so much. But dancing, yes.

One day when I was reading
A book about a boy who always
Gets in trouble because he can't keep still
Cecil shouts **"That's me, that always happens to me."**
The next chapter explains how Joey Pigza feels like
A shaken up can of coke ready to explode
"Me too!" bounces up Cecil with a big smile on that freckled face
Finally, he's found a comrade
Cecil borrows the book after school

6:10 pm – Cecil and mom walk in,
"I just want to warn you right now
My kids are driving me nuts
And I'm in a pissy mood."
Sympathy? She hasn't earned it yet.
Anger? A little, this conference may not work out like I planned.
Suddenly a mere two inches became a huge challenge.
I wanted Cecil to feel good about tonight,
"Well, Cecil isn't driving me nuts, in fact
He's doing so much better, and I really love
The energy he brings to class."
Mom raises an eyebrow.
The conference continues and I
Realize it will be a balance of conference
And counseling session for mom.
She vents,
We listen.
I stick up for Cecil.
Now things are going the way they should.

Until,
I'm at the other side of the room
Looking for some examples of
Magazines Cecil seems to enjoy reading
When I hear **"Speaking of magazines, where's that**
Latest Sports Illustrated, Cecil?" his Mom inquires.
Oh no!
She came up from behind,
Out of nowhere,

And Cecil and I were not prepared.
I had taken the Sports Illustrated Swimsuit issue from Cecil
At recess, and it was still sitting in my filing cabinet.
A magazine filled with beautiful women, and even though all the models
In this forty page magazine are posing with swimsuits, there isn't more
Than two yards of fabric among them.

I didn't want to get him in more trouble,
Yet I hoped he would do the right thing and be honest with his mom.
I pretended to still be searching for the other magazines.
"Which one?"
**"The one you wanted to take to Soccer Practice
But I said not to, where is it?"**
"Oh well it's in my room somewhere"
"Sure?"
"Yep."
She seems to believe him.
We end on a positive note as I diplomatically
Bully mom into staying quiet so Cecil and I
Can get down to what's important, to
Him.

That night I felt slightly guilty for my silent complicity in his lie.
A line had been drawn.
The right thing to do, versus the right thing to do for Cecil
At that time and place.
Which lesson is to be learned?
To a young boy that honesty is the best policy,
Or to myself, that at times, the choices we make as teachers are not so black and White.
I end up having a pretty good sleep.

Next day Cecil walks into class,
Skateboard under his arm,
Comes up and says,
"Thanks, Mrs P."
"For what?"
"You know," he smiles and makes his
Way to his desk.
He's found another comrade.

Ron:
David Jardine writes:

> How are we to do justice to this particular episode that happened to a particular teacher at a particular time and place, while at once respecting the undeniable kinship we experience in hearing this teacher's tale?
>
> (Jardine 1992b: 51).

Ron:
As soon as she saw me she smiled and headed over to see me. It was Pia, one of the nicest students I have ever had the privilege to know, now in grade eleven. In grade seven, she was unfailingly kind to everyone. When someone has that quality along with intelligence, athleticism and beauty, it is hard not to hold such a student as a favourite in one's private being. Her older brother Tony was similarly gifted. I had taught him a few years before when he was in grade seven. He had been popular, athletic, happy-go-lucky. An important member of our basketball team, his silky quick moves were a big part of our success. Days before the season-ending tournament he sprained his ankle very badly. We would have to play without him. By day three of the tournament we were in the finals, but we were in a desperate losing battle late in the game. Tony pressed forward; he insisted he could play. I relented; it had been five days since his sprain occurred. On the court though it was immediately obvious his ankle was still badly damaged; every step he took contained a limp, and when he ran you could see him hold in the pain. It was a heartbreaking sight, a young person willing to suffer so for his team. I quickly pulled him out of the game and life went on, of course, despite our loss.

So when Pia came over to see me as I sat in the bleachers watching this year's players in their big tournament at the local high school, history held us together. She approached with her arms open and gave me a big hug; wonderful and sincere. "Pia, how are you doing; it's so good to see you." It was delightful to be in the presence of such youthful goodness. "And how is Tony?"

She hesitated, and then: "Well he's OK, but last Thanksgiving … he tried to kill himself." Shock. Disbelief. And then unexpectedly a deep sadness completely incongruous with the elation of the moment before. How could one so young and gifted suffer that much? Tears welled up into my eyes. I had a psychic glimpse of a young man whom I had cared for, being horribly, miserably unhappy, and I wept, in the gym, at the basketball game. "Well tell him I was asking about him," was the only thing I could manage further to say. Pia nodded, I will, gave me another hug, and left.

Louise:
bell hooks writes:

Teachers who love students and are loved by them are still "suspect" in the academy. Some of the suspicion is that the presence of feelings, of passions, may not allow for objective consideration of each student's merit. But this very notion is based on the false assumption that education is neutral, that there is some even emotional ground that we stand on that enables us to treat everyone equally, dispassionately.

(hooks 1994: 198)

Kathy:

Teaching and Caring

We arrived bundled in the back of three rattle trap trucks, packed together and somewhat sleepy-eyed. It was hot already and the dust rose up to meet us on the bumpy road. We were 20 Richmond High School students and 4 teachers from a Global Perspectives course in the Dominican Republic to build a school extension desperately needed at Loma Baijia, a small mountain hamlet. The school had 400 students in three classrooms, half the size of ours, with no books, one pencil each, and perhaps in the older grades a notebook; all on less than an acre of dirt.

Caring is visibly present here. The Dominicans care deeply about each other as human beings, and the children come to their school with great smiles on their faces and hugs and kisses for their teachers, their fellow students and their guests. They have little material wealth, but are rich in joy. The Richmond students also care greatly about their world and those far away – enough to work hard all year fund-raising money for bricks, cement, and paint. They care enough to labour long hours in the baking heat and humidity, mixing heavy sloppy cement by hand and hauling cement blocks up ladders in chain gangs, day after day after day. They comfort and care for children and adults alike as six or eight teeth are extracted by our accompanying dentists. They learn about themselves, and their capacity to care for others.

This is a story about teachers caring too. Caring about broadening the lives of as many students as possible and making for better understandings in this world. It's about teachers who are willing to go without a break midway through the year and donate their time and money to what they believe is a good cause and important curriculum in a young person's life. It is a story about Dominican teachers caring enough to teach every day, with no supplies, as well as cook meals for the students and workers and help with the construction so the job can be done and more students can come to the school. It is about them humbly asking for help from the community for special students like Miliagro, a brilliant 9-year-old who must be carried a kilometer up a steep dirt road to the school because she has spina bifida and can't walk.

The tears and smiles and the working together of a kaleidoscope of nationalities, cultures, colours, heritages, religions, personalities; the working together in one common mission so that more young people can become educated, and have a better life, plainly demonstrates the deep-set art of caring in the quest for understanding others, ourselves and the world.

Donnie:
David Jardine writes:

> The old pedagogies will no longer do in the face of the ecologies of flesh and bone and the Earth's dear torn heart
>
> (Jardine 1994: 63).

Kathy: If we are to survive we need creative problem-solvers.
Donnie: We need thinkers who will find ways to mend the holes in the ozone layer,
Ron: to stop the burning of the rain forest and clean up the oceans,
Sukhy: to care enough to make sacrifices for the millions who live in abject poverty.
Louise: Multiple choice questions are not going to mend the Earth's torn heart.
Marina: We will have a much better chance with caring and creative problem-solvers.
Donnie: It will take courageous teaching to achieve this.
Kathy: It will take teachers who are brave enough to buck the system,
Ron: to refuse to teach to artificial tests,
Sukhy: to offer instead authentic, integrated opportunities for students to interact in the world.
Louise: It will take the creation of schools which are loving and connected communities.
Marina: Communities willing to protect and nurture, where the consistency of caring is far more important than the consistency of rules.
All: It **is** possible.
Donnie: To conclude, a song by Joyce Poley: *Hands of the Heart*. (All stand, join hands, and sing together.)

Hands of the Heart
(Deep In Our Soul)
Words and music by Joyce Poley

Deep in our soul lie feelings and plans
Waiting to dance into life through our hands
The poet writes sonnets, the artist paints dreams
And all of our world becomes more than it seems.

Chorus:

And we touch one another
in our own special way
In a letter of love
or a sculpture of clay
In the squeeze of a hand
or a gentle caress
And the more we reach out
the more we are blessed.

For each of us shares who we are through our hands
In playing concertos or tilling the land
In a doll stitched with care or a great work of art
Our hands are the tools that speak for the heart.

SONGSTYLE MUSIC (SLOCAN)
Kennedy Heights PO Box 84570
Delta, BC V4C 8G1
email: jpoley@istar.ca

Bibliography

Ediger, K. "How does a little education sound?" unpublished work.

Fullan, M. (1993) *Change Forces*, London: Falmer.

Giroux, H. A. (1994) "Doing cultural studies: youth and the challenge of pedagogy," *Harvard Educational Review*, 64, 3: 278–308.

Hargreaves, A. (1994) *Changing Teachers, Changing Times: Teacher's Work and Culture in the Postmodern Age*, Toronto: The Ontario Institute for Studies in Education Press.

hooks, b. (1994) *Teaching to Transgress: Education as the Practice of Freedom*, New York and London, Routledge.

Huebner, D. E. (1999) *The Lure of the Transcendent: Collected Essays by Duane E. Huebner*, (Ed.) Hillis, V., Mahwah, NJ: Lawrence Erlbaum Publishers.

Jardine, D. W. (1992a) "Reflections on education, hermeneutics, and ambiguity," in *Understanding Curriculum as Phenomenological and Deconstructed Text* (pp. 116–27), New York: Teachers College Press.

Jardine, D. W. (1992b) "The fecundity of the individual case: considerations of the pedagogic heart of interpretive work," *Journal of Philosophy of Education*, 26, 1: 51–60.

Jardine, D. W. (1994) "Hermeneutics and the ecological imagination," in P. Lang (Ed.) *To Dwell with a Boundless Heart: Essays in Curriculum Theory*, New York: Peter Lang.

Powell, J. "Taking care of the bully," unpublished work.

Van Manan, M. (1991) *The Tact of Teaching: The Meaning of Pedagogical Thoughtfulness*, Albany: SUNY Press.

Chapter 10

Ethical obligations in teacher research

Sharon Shockley Lee and Owen van den Berg

The overarching ethical issue in teacher research involves the relationship between researchers and subjects. Academic literature about research ethics tends to make "protection" of "human subjects" its central focus. Traditionally, researchers have met ethical standards by obtaining informed consent, guaranteeing anonymity, and allowing subjects to opt out of investigations (Eisner 1991; Smith 1990; Lincoln 1990). Much of the debate that continues is not so much about the appropriateness of "privacy, anonymity and confidentiality," as Lincoln (1990: 279) terms them, but about the difficulty of attaining them, particularly as the goals and foci of teacher research are likely to change as the work progresses.

This line of reasoning – that research ethics is a matter of "protecting human subjects" – we argue, is too conveniently innocent of existing power relations within most research settings. Researchers' unilateral decision to "protect human subjects" without even consulting them reflects the arrogance of privilege. In this paper we consider two approaches to research ethics – "protection of human subjects" vs. "ethical obligation" – by providing brief vignettes from our own research experiences.

First, we distinguish between "outsider," "insider," and "insider–outsider" teacher research. In the case of "outsider" teacher research, a teacher studies other educators for the fundamental purposes of understanding and improving educational practice generally. In the case of "insider" teacher research, teachers investigate themselves to improve their own practice. Often referred to as action research, practitioner inquiry, or reflective practice (Cochran-Smith and Lytle 1999), the researcher is both investigator and pedagogical actor. "Insider-outsider" research involves collaborative self-study. Practitioners and other researchers seek to accomplish both purposes: understanding and improving one's own practice and informing and improving the practice of others. (See, for example, Smith and Geoffrey 1968.)

In the vignettes that follow, Owen will briefly tell the tales of two ("insider") investigations into his own practice. Sharon will recount stories of two studies of school principals: one example of "outsider" and one example of "insider–outsider" research. In the final section of the paper, we analyze the ethical issues that emerge from these cases.

Cases of "insider" teacher research: Owen's attempts at "reporting back"

In 1987 I set up a Master's program in Action Research in the University of the Western Cape in Cape Town, South Africa. The University was in the forefront of the resistance to the apartheid regime, and the program was launched explicitly to promote educational and political transformation in South Africa. This "structured" program offered a year of coursework to a cohort group of students, followed by a "mini-thesis" involving action research in the students' classrooms. In 1992 I decided to write a research report on the program as part of my PhD research. The major focus of the study was my role as innovator within a university context. In writing the story of the "Class of '87" I followed these procedures (for fuller accounts see van den Berg 1994; van den Berg 2001b).

1   During 1987 I made extensive notes on what was occurring, and had frequent sessions with the group about "how things were going." Students completed an end-of-year evaluation of the program that I used extensively in preparing an end-of-year report to the Faculty (School) of Education.

2   I kept records of my meetings, as thesis supervisor, with each of the students as they moved towards degree completion.

3   In 1994, when I began to write a "history" of the "Class of '87," I reread the students' completed theses, taking note of comments they had made about (a) the course, (b) changes in their educational practice, and (c) how they viewed action research.

4   I shared the draft chapter with members of my PhD committee (in the USA), consolidated feedback comments onto a single copy of the text, and then shared this with key non-students who were involved with the process, including external program and dissertation examiners.

5   I convened a meeting of the eight program graduates, telephoning them and then sending a letter and the draft chapter. I asked them to write comments on the draft and return it to me at the meeting, along with additional comments; to bring with them notes or artifacts of their experience relevant to my writing; and to answer questions about whether the course and thesis experience had made any permanent difference in the way they did their work, and what they felt about the supervision they had received during the thesis phase.

6   The group meeting, June 9, 1993, was attended by all but one student. All provided their copy of the draft chapter, comments, and responses to the questions. I chaired the meeting, and had an "outsider" record

its proceedings. I circulated those minutes to all who had attended; all approved the minutes.

Regarding my role in the meeting, I wrote the following:

> I ... did not see myself as a "passive interviewer," just capturing their views. My sense of accountability, and the process we developed in the course, made me want to explain certain things to them ... and to argue certain matters with them. ... [I]t was set up as a form of "triangulation" – first they were asked to write comments on the text, then to discuss these with the group (on the idea that often one has views, but these might be changed based on ... reasoned argument ...) ... This is a complex and time-consuming process, but justified on ... democratic and epistemological grounds ...
>
> (van den Berg 1994: 219)

The students stated that my chapter "was a fair representation of the events of that year" and that "the group was in agreement that the meeting was conducted to their satisfaction."

7   Subsequently I reworked the chapter to incorporate all students' feedback. Since most students were Afrikaans speaking, I also submitted my translations to them to ensure that I had captured their views accurately in translation. All names mentioned in my text were individuals' real names; all read and approved the text, including their names.

In 1997, I took an appointment in the Department of Educational Studies at St Louis University. I was to teach an undergraduate cultural diversity course. Expecting my students to come from fairly undiverse backgrounds, I encouraged them to explore their own cultures related to key issues – race, gender, social class, language, disadvantage and giftedness, and so on (for a fuller account, see van den Berg 2001a).

I wanted students to understand that as teachers their classrooms would develop distinctive cultures, and that engaging in action research would help them understand their classroom culture. A reflective practitioner, I investigated my own teaching and respected my students as partners in that endeavor; because I expected students to trust me and do significant personal sharing, I had to risk modeling an action research investigation with my students.

I wrote regular reflections on the course and invited anonymous written course evaluations from the students. Near the end of the course I wrote a long analysis of the course as a whole; students read it and added written responses. I then edited student comments into my original text, presented it for classroom discussion, and finalized the text. Students decided if the final text would include their real names.

In these two studies, I had two purposes: to provide an account of what happened and to improve my practice. Recognizing my obligation to my students helped me work toward both these goals.

From the conference table to the kitchen table: Sharon's ethical dilemmas

When Owen was setting up graduate programs in South Africa, I was working on my dissertation (1992), an ethnography of an urban elementary school principal, not far from home in St Louis, Missouri, USA.

"Alvin Haines" (pseudonym) had been principal of Roosevelt School, located south of a small river known as the "Mason–Dixon Line." Below this line, schools served primarily poor and working-class children of African descent. He established a strong reputation as a "white knight" who rescued troubled schools. Haines was being reassigned to Washington School. I might have the chance to study the "white knight" principal as he began improving another troubled school.

While negotiating permission to conduct the study, I relied on established ethical practices: informed consent, anonymity, and non-intervention. Commitment to these practices satisfied my dissertation committee and the university's internal review board – men who made decisions around conference tables in the relative safety of the university.

When Haines and I first met, I promised to protect the anonymity of participants by using pseudonyms for all proper names. I also guaranteed not to intervene in the school. My role would be observing and interpreting events as they naturally occurred. He indicated these were adequate safeguards and agreed to the study.

I had to obtain and maintain Haines' approval for access to the school. As we began the study, he did not ask nor did I consider inviting him to critique and approve drafts. During the first year of the study, Haines casually mentioned that when the research was complete he would like a copy of the final report and copies of all my data. I explained that he would receive a copy of the dissertation, but I could not share field notes or transcripts of interviews without violating the confidentiality I had guaranteed other informants. Haines never again mentioned access to data.

My subject appeared not to need protection. He was at the apex of his administrative career; I was a doctoral student. The "white knight" principal appeared powerful, well armored, privileged, proud – more likely to exploit than to be exploited.

Informed consent, anonymity, and non-intervention soon proved inadequate to guide my actions as researcher. In the second month of the two-year study, I observed Haines paddle children, and I became aware of conflicting ethical obligations.

Haines ... tapped the paddle twice on the surface of his desk. Andre ... leaned over to place his hands where the paddle touched the desk. Haines ... struck five sharp swats ... Haines placed the paddle under [Andre's] chin and lifted his face until their eyes met. The man towered over the boy. My mind began to juxtapose images of Haines and Andre with scenes of masters and slaves.

(Lee 1992: 99–100)

I was disturbed by the data I collected. During the two years he was principal of Washington School, Haines reported paddling students 218 times. I found this particularly troubling since Haines regularly under-reported his use of corporal punishment. I uncovered evidence of other illegal and unethical behaviors including child abuse and sexual harassment.

I struggled with the public's right to know, the community's right to hold public employees accountable, and the children's rights to safety. But I adhered to the commitments I had made and meticulously protected the anonymity of Haines and other participants.

I had also committed to non-intervention, to simply observe as events naturally unfolded. I wanted to stop Haines. Instead, I stood by silently collecting data. I felt the angst of conducting "inaction research" (Gentile 1994), fiddling while Rome burned.

When confronted with the dissymmetry of power between Haines, teachers, and children, I wanted to side with the least advantaged (Rawls 1971), "to look at the world through the eyes of its victims" (West 1993: 133), the students. I had promised confidentiality and non-intervention. I kept my promise, but I am convinced that some form of action to protect the less powerful, children and teachers, would have been more ethical.

After his assistant principal verified its accuracy, I mailed a draft of the dissertation to Haines. He threatened to sue, but fortunately did not follow through on his threat. I regret that my study caused him pain, but I take solace in knowing that my research revealed that people like Haines work in schools, that they are not adequately supervised or held accountable, and that they harm those who are less powerful.

I am currently collaborating with Margaret Andrews and Dorothy James (pseudonyms) on an ethnography of a female elementary principal (Andrews, Lee and James, 2002). Margaret is a university professor. Dorothy is the principal. She is not research subject, informant, participant (Lee 2000) or inhabitant (van den Berg 2001b). She is colleague, collaborator, and co-author. This is a fundamentally different relationship than I had with Haines. The reader "heard" the white knight's words only in my "voice." Haines never spoke for himself. I spoke for him.

In our current principal ethnography, we found that reporting our collaborative research in unison tended to distort Dorothy's voice. We developed a new approach to (re)present our findings that we term *counterpoint trio*. Our musical metaphor is best represented in the compositions of J. S. Bach, perhaps the greatest composer of contrapuntal music. His three-part inventions or *sinfonia* are excellent examples of three-part counterpoint. In these compositions, Bach wove three melodies together rather than making one melodic voice predominant with subordinate voices as supporting harmony. In reporting our collaborative research, each of us shares her experiences from her own perspective in her own voice. The counterpoint trio expresses a "loving epistemology" (Young and Laible 2000): independent and collaborative reflection; a deep and enduring respect for each other's uniqueness and common humanity; and a fundamental obligation to one another.

The three of us struggle to envision and conduct collaborative research that is more ethical, less hurtful and more healing for others and ourselves. Our actions and relationships counter Capper's (2000: 695) view that "research on or with anyone is unethical." Our deliberations occur, not at a conference table at the university, but at Margaret's kitchen table. The kitchen table has become the "center of gravity" for our study.

Sarah Lawrence-Lightfoot (1994) described the dining room table as the "center of gravity" in her family home. Family and friends, members of the black intelligentsia, gathered there.

> ... these men were "the brotherhood," with bonds that were deep, language that was fascinating, laughter that was infectious, and conversation that I only half understood. I could feel how much they needed and loved one another in their charged and fiery dialogues, in their siblinglike rivalries, in the ways their ideas danced in and out of one another. Coming to the table, they looked forward to a comfort and camaraderie that they could never fully achieve in the university settings where each was usually the token Negro and often the first of his race to set foot in the place.
>
> (Lawrence-Lightfoot 1994: 4)

Around Margaret's kitchen table, Dorothy, Margaret and I grapple with fundamental epistemological and ethical issues. We also bake bread; edit drafts; commiserate; formulate outlines; laugh; offer critical and analytical feedback; check in with husbands and children; pose challenging questions; tell stories; enjoy camaraderie; make discoveries; drink coffee; construct new theories; generate new possibilities; confront one another; respect each other; support each other; care for each other; and try to develop a "loving epistemology" (Young and Laible 2000). The mutual, reciprocal obligations of the kitchen table bring us closer to ethical research.

Discussion: how can teacher-researchers fulfill ethical obligations?

The opening section of this chapter described the traditional view of research ethics, focusing on the protection of human subjects. We argued that a central ethical issue in teacher research is the relationship between researchers and subjects. In fact, both Owen and Sharon have chosen not to use the term "subject." Owen prefers the notion of research "inhabitants," and Sharon refers to "collaborators" and "co-researchers."

What can we learn from the ethical decisions we made when conducting these four studies? First, Sharon's study of the white knight principal belies the assumption that the researcher is usually more powerful than the subject. So, researchers are not always in positions of power – but often they are. In those circumstances, we argue that researchers are obligated to respect "research subjects," not just protect them.

Owen was the "subject" of both of his studies described here. His students might be viewed as informants or participants. Students, although less powerful than Owen in the research process, influenced the direction of his studies.

Second, can researchers safeguard themselves and their subjects by coming to clear understandings at the start of the research? Both Owen and Sharon attempted to be open and honest about the purposes of their research with varying degrees of success. Eisner (1991) warns that it is problematic for researchers to ensure that subjects' understanding of a project is the same as researchers'. Researchers spend long periods of time wrestling with ethical issues in research that may be unfamiliar to subjects. What is more, "the concept of informed consent implies that the researcher knows before the event that is to be observed what the event will be and its possible effects. Just how does one get that knowledge?" (Eisner 1991: 214).

Sharon seemed to have an agreement with Alvin Haines that would safeguard against problems. But she began to be uncomfortable with what she witnessed. Committed to non-intervention, what was she to do? Which of Sharon's subjects did she protect – Alvin Haines or his "victims?" If this were not dissertation research, would she have dealt with these dilemmas differently?

In Sharon's other narrative, she speaks of the "loving epistemology" between herself, Margaret and Dorothy. This is not "outsider research" with Sharon acting as "non-interventionist," but as critical friend who openly tries to influence the principal's actions. The three co-researchers invested considerable time in building relationships and clarifying purposes, not just one brief meeting to "size up" the others. And the kitchen table offers a safe setting where equals interact. Still, this "loving epistemology" could sour, and no amount of advance negotiation can prevent that possibility. And the voices of Sharon, Dorothy and Margaret are heard much differently in the counterpoint trio than the voices in the Haines research.

The stark reality of teacher research may be that when relationships between research participants remain positive, there is no need for "human subject protection," but when those relationships deteriorate, no amount of advance negotiation will prevent a meltdown, recrimination and even legal action.

We now turn to a third critical point. Teacher research involves investigating socially complex phenomena – it is therefore epistemologically and ethically essential that the research involve fully what Fullan (1991: 65) terms the "process of coming to grips with the multiple realities of people who are the main participants." If we, as researchers, are not responsible to the inhabitants of our study, our research is likely to reflect the dominant perspective and voice of the researcher, not the multiplicity of views and the cacophony of voices of lived realities.

A major ethical issue for us, then, is why should anyone believe that a researcher's version of the story and interpretation of events has credence? Clifford captures the central ethical concern in teacher research:

> ... how is unruly experience transformed into an authoritative written account? How, precisely, is a garrulous, overdetermined cross-cultural encounter shot through with power relations and personal cross-purposes circumscribed as an adequate version of a more or less discrete "other world" composed by an individual author?
>
> (Clifford 1988: 25)

In both his studies reported here, Owen held a position of institutional power. Why should a reader consider the final version of his stories to reflect anything other than his biases and preoccupations? His answer would be, "Well, the same question can be asked of any research, including so-called 'objective' studies which appear to be 'objective' because they successfully embed and reify the researchers' biases and preoccupations." Owen argues that he has "invited others into his text" and let them disagree with him. His text shows evidence of constructive negotiation.

Ultimately, the text is his, and he is entitled to his position. Ethically, Owen has attempted to account for the multitude of other voices in his text, by referring it back to all the players, building their comments into the text, and by detailing the methodology he followed to produce his texts. But Owen claims the right to say that nobody holds veto power over the publication of his research.

In Sharon's studies described in this paper, she made commitments hoping to ensure ethical research. In the study of the white knight principal, she found traditional ethical strategies inadequate.

In the insider-outsider study of the female principal, Sharon and her colleagues practice other safeguards. The research is collaborative, and the principal herself is co-researcher. Co-authors write narrative and interpretation as counterpoint trio, honoring the voice and perspective of each co-researcher. Kitchen table conversations center the research. Perhaps Sharon and her colleagues move closer to ethical research through mutual respect and undominated discourse (McKerrow 2000).

In this chapter, we have reflected on various strategies we have tried to help us practice *more* ethical research. We continue to pursue the possibility of research that is safe for all involved; research that offers participants free and equal voice; research without power inequities.

As teacher-researchers, we work toward minimizing the injuries we do to ourselves, and others, but we have not been able to eliminate hurt. We seek ways to heal and support and challenge each other along the way. We appreciate the differences in the ethical questions we raise, the ethical issues we confront, and the ethical commitments we make. We respect that one view is not necessarily better or worse than another. As teacher-researchers we simply reflect, "This is what works for me at this time and why," and, "This is how I will do it next time." As teacher-researchers and as people, we may never be fully loving, compassionate, or just, but we can always do better.

Bibliography

Andrews, M. (pseudonym), Lee, S. S. and James, D. (pseudonym) (2002). "The man in the principal's office (re)visited by a woman," in G. Perreault and F. Lunenberg (Eds) *The Changing World of School Administration* (pp. 267–81), Lanham, MD: Scarecrow Press.

Capper, C. (2000) "Life lessons and a loving epistemology: a response to Julie Laible's loving epistemology," *Qualitative Studies in Education*, 13, 6: 693–8.

Clifford, J. (1988) *The Predicament of Culture: Twentieth-Century Ethnography, Literature, and Art*, Cambridge, MA: Harvard University Press.

Cochran-Smith, M. and Lytle, S. (1999) "Relationships of knowledge and practice: teacher learning in communities," in A. Iran-Nejad and P. Pearson (Eds) *Review of Research in Education* (pp. 249–306), Washington, DC: American Educational Research Association.

Eisner, E. (1991) *The Enlightened Eye*, New York: Macmillan.

Fullan, M. J. (1991) *The New Meaning of Educational Change*, New York: Teachers College Press.

Gentile, J. (1994) "Inaction research: a superior and cheaper alternative for education researchers," *Educational Researcher*, 22, 5: 30–2.

Lawrence-Lightfoot, S. (1994) *I've Known Rivers: Lives of Loss and Liberation*, Reading, MA: Addison-Wesley.

Lee, S. (1992) *Hegemony in an Elementary School: The Principal as Organic Intellectual*, doctoral dissertation, University of Missouri, St Louis, Dissertation Abstracts International, 53 (04), 1008A (University Microfilms No. 92–24760).

Lee, S. (2000) "'A root out of a dry ground': resolving the researcher/researched dilemma," in J. Zeni (Ed.) *Ethical Issues in Practitioner Research* (pp. 61–71), New York: Teachers College Press.

Lincoln, Y. (1990) "Toward a categorical imperative for qualitative research," in E. Eisner and A. Peshkin (Eds) *Qualitative Inquiry in Education* (pp. 277–95), New York: Teachers College Press.

McKerrow, K. K. (2000) "Postmodern angst, public education, and professional ethics," paper presented at the 54th Summer Meeting of the National Council of Professors of Educational Administration, 21st Century Challenges to Educational Administration, Ypsilanti, MI.

Rawls, J. (1971) *Theory of Justice*, Cambridge, MA: Harvard University Press.

Smith, L. (1990) "Ethics in qualitative field research: an individual perspective," in E. Eisner and A. Peshkin (Eds) *Qualitative Inquiry in Education* (pp. 258–76), New York: Teachers College Press.

Smith, L. and Geoffrey, R. (1968) *Complexities of an Urban Classroom: An Analysis Toward a General Theory of Teaching*, New York: Holt, Rinehart and Winston.

van den Berg, O. (1994) *Innovation under Apartheid: Collaborative Action Research in a South African University*, doctoral dissertation, Washington University, St Louis, MO. Dissertation Astracts International, 55 (08), 2351A (University Microfilms No. 94–33549).

van den Berg, O. (2001a) "Affirming difference while building a nation: teaching diversity in neo-apartheid America," in W. Goodman (Ed.) *Living and Teaching in an Unjust World* (pp. 150–61), Portsmouth, NH: Heinemann.

van den Berg, O. (2001b) "The ethics of accountability in action research," in J. Zeni (Ed.) *Ethical Issues in Practitioner Research* (pp. 83–91), New York: Teachers College Press.

West, C. (1993) *Keeping Faith: Philosophy and Race in America*, New York: Routledge.

Chapter 11

What are the new literacies?

Writing and teaching and living with the questions

Erika Hasebe-Ludt, Robin Bright,
Cynthia Chambers, Leah Fowler,
Michael Pollard and Pamela Winsor

> ... so before all beginning, and I want to beg you, as much as I can, dear sir, to be patient toward all that is unsolved in your heart and to try to love the *questions themselves* like locked rooms and like books that are written in a very foreign tongue. Do not now seek the answers, which cannot be given you because you would not be able to live them. And the point is, to live everything. *Live* the questions now. Perhaps you will then gradually, without noticing it, live along some distant day into the answer.
>
> (Rilke 1934)

> To reach an understanding with one's partner in a dialogue is not merely a matter of total self-expression and the successful assertion of one's point of view, but a transformation into a communion, in which we do not remain what we were.
>
> (Gadamer 1975)

Introduction

Literacy as decoding written text and the literate person as one fluent with high culture has given way to the complexities of new, multifaceted literacies that include the traditional concepts of decoding and exegesis, as well as orality and numeracy, technological and media literacy (Ong 1982; McLuhan 1962). These new literacies also encompass broader notions of what constitutes text (action, media, speech, hypertext, symbols, cultural signs, as well as writing); increasingly sophisticated ways of creating, interpreting, disseminating, and evaluating such texts; and an increasingly complex understanding of the pedagogy appropriate to such multiple literacies (Graff 1986; Willinsky 1990). These changes have profound implications for curriculum and pedagogy from the public schools to teacher preparation in the university, to graduate education for practicing teachers (Readance and Barone 2000). They also make contradictory and conflicting textual demands upon teachers and learners. In a world of local and global changes, students and their teachers are all now required to read and write the word as well as the world (Freire and Macedo 1987; Barnes and Duncan 1992).

Research process and procedures

In order to consider these literacy demands, a group of six researchers at the University of Lethbridge, Alberta, has begun a longitudinal study of the implications of the new literacies for teacher education. Their key research questions are: What are the new and important literacies and what are the implications of these for teacher education and society? What are significant literacy events? What makes living well pedagogically with/in these literacies possible, and what makes it difficult? Researching these questions is part of an action research process situated in the "practice-as-inquiry" form of this tradition (Schön 1983; Carr and Kemmis 1986) which examines theories, practices, and policies with the intention of creating new knowledge to effect social change. By employing this particular type of action research, the researchers are focusing on questions about professional practice, requiring participants to articulate and analyze existing literacy and pedagogical practices, to search collectively for alternatives where appropriate, and to reflect on the implications of these. The data presented here are part of this ongoing reflective cycle after the first year of living with the research questions (Patterson *et al.* 1993; Carson and Sumara 1996).

Through a series of multi-site research projects in Southern Alberta, teachers and learners – children in schools, students in teacher preparation programs, practicing teachers, and teachers pursuing graduate education – are engaging with the questions from a wide range of backgrounds and interests, such as the following: examining student teachers' writing portfolios and their perceptions of themselves as writers; collecting and analyzing written and oral narrations of what it means to be a literate person and a teacher living and teaching in aboriginal communities; discussing literacy issues in light of what beginning and experienced secondary teachers now should know and be able to do; establishing writing groups as significant literacy events for teachers; collaboratively studying *The Courage to Teach* (Palmer 1998); developing a working definition of literacy as it pertains to children in the early grades.

During this initial phase of the project, samples of the texts that teachers and students read and generated were assembled as artifacts in response to the questions. From these artifacts, the researchers first created a readers' theatre script for a conference, then the following textual collage that selectively brings together and juxtaposes the voices of participants from across the various projects, as a way to portray samples of the images and texts in a mixed, non-linear intertext. The voices range from those of teachers participating in writing groups and supervisors of student teachers in K-12 classrooms (age group 5–17) to those of young students themselves. We hope these texts create small openings into the dialogues about literacy and the sites of living pedagogy (Aoki 2000).

Dialogues about literacy and pedagogy

We enter these dialogues with a reflection by one of the researchers involved in collaborative action research on young students' literacies (Hiebert and Raphael 1998).

> As I have watched young children use their growing capacities to use technological tools to make sense of their worlds, I am convinced that their voyage into literacy is one of sharp contrasts to that of the generation teaching them. Symbol-making has long been recognized as significant to literacy.
>
> Jennifer and Julia were working together to collect the information they needed to complete their social studies assignment. They were to write at least three days of Martin Frobisher's journal, one before he set off, one or more while on the journey, and a final entry after the voyage. The girls discovered discrepancy between the website and the printed information they were using as references. Just how many ships were there? The website says three, the text says two. They turned to their teacher for assistance and thus began a conversation that addressed far more than the fact that one ship sank early in the voyage and thus had been summarily dismissed by one author.
>
> "Why do you suppose that the information is different?"
>
> "cause somebody didn't do their research to find out."
>
> "How could you find out which is correct?"
>
> "We could look at another site."
>
> "Or find another book."
>
> "Do you remember when we talked about using the Internet for information that we said anyone can post information and that no one checks many sites?"
>
> "It looks like no one checked here."
>
> After reading from another site, the girls resolved that their position was that three ships began the voyage. The girls sought truth in their sources and were alarmed to discover contradiction. They did, however, have opportunities for meaningful learning about principles that

guide research. Their dilemma is a reminder that new literacies require new forms of critical thinking and reasoning. Students must be helped to become "healthy skeptics" (Leu 1997: 65), learning critical reading skills that have not always been necessary within an environment of traditional classroom texts.

Much of my inquiry has involved participant observation in elementary classrooms where children are using technology. I am doing this as one way of coming to better understand what it means for those children to be literate. At the same time, I am seeking to learn what their teachers believe it means for children to be literate. It is my belief that teachers' perceptions of what it means for children to be literate influence their teaching.

In a writing group, teachers reflected on the necessity to become more critical and more public with their voices, expressing both the fear and the exhilaration that come with sharing writing as part of their professional obligation. One teacher talked about the struggle involved when searching for voices that have been made silent following the rules while growing up:

> This frustrates me because I know how hard I work with my own writing. Students need to hear their own voices, but they are so quickly and sometimes permanently squelched. A writing group is a political place, a place of finding voice and asking the tough questions. It's about the grammar and the word choice and the development of ideas and all of that, but writing is about thinking. One cannot write what one has not thought about. This is political. In an age of Wal-Marts and McDonalds a critical thinker is not common, desired or wanted.

Another teacher spoke about the false safety that comes with hiding one's voice for fear of facing the tough questions

> and the secrets hidden like the cockroaches that find safety in the dark.
>
> Keep the lights off and you can pretend there is no such thing as cockroaches. You can pretend that they are not crawling over your bare feet. This writing group holds the promise of killing the cockroaches. That's why I keep coming. I hate the cockroaches but I am just as afraid of what I have to do to kill them.
>
> Yesterday, there was another school shooting. Yesterday, I spoke to you about writing about silence, memory, me, and the other school shooting …Writing hurts, sometimes later, it seems to heal, but the hurting is constant and the healing is very slow. Sometimes, I think I am writing in circles, twirling, twirling … Writing is a dangerous thing. Do you remember telling me no one would die if I gave voice to those

hidden things? The adult knows, but the little girl is terrified. What other loss will this voice incur?

In this writing group, which met twice a month, listening to other writers reading their work, exploring memories, and the places they write from (Neilson 1998), teachers slowly gathered the courage to allow their writing to become a public and political act:

> I am profoundly aware of how their writing affects me, my body's tension, my heartbeat, my breathing. The richness of listening has made me aware of the movement of words and the struggle to allow the words to be present.

For the facilitator of the group, this building of a community of inquiry constitutes a hopeful act, one that she sees as crucial for creating a new and different way of living and writing in the academy and in schools, a vibrant act that is vulnerable and unpredictable in its outcome but also necessary to create a new ethos of pedagogy: "I envision a strengthening of our voices, a growing trust in the work, in the writing and rewriting of our lives."

> The task of human life in general is to find free spaces and learn to move therein. In research this means finding the question, the genuine question … to finally arrive at the point where one finds the truly open questions and therefore the possibilities that exist … and thereby possible ways of shaping our own lives … to create with one another new solidarities.
>
> (Gadamer 1986: 59)

In another writing group, the struggle to bring forth personal stories was evident. The group reluctantly shared from an intellectual safety that kept everyone distant and removed from a real discussion and exchange. One of the participants wrote:

> Our group has come together for the second time. After a first meeting to talk about the project, distribute the text and some general talk about where we are and why we're here, I go away enthused and excited about the journey we have agreed to take together. But now the second meeting is here and the feelings are quite different. We have each read the first chapter in *The Courage to Teach* on identity and integrity in teaching. I feel my tentativeness as we discuss how we will share our work. I'm reluctant to step forward, reluctant to share my inner most thoughts and feelings. I remind myself: It's a big first topic: our strengths and potentials, our shadows and limits, our wounds and fears. Any

and all of the above, just lay it out there for all to see. Robert Frost's poem jumps into my mind:

We dance round in a ring and suppose
But the Secret sits in the middle and knows.
                              (Frost 1967)

What is the secret that sits in the middle of this group this evening?

A university supervisor working with pre-service teachers reflected on the difficulty and complexity of attending to the personal as part of the professional when writing new wor(l)ds of pedagogical identities:

> The rules of engagement are changing, so who is the self that teaches – a centered stable writing persona with a pre-set curriculum or a co-constructed, generative ever-changing self? As an individual teaching human being, I watch apprenticing teachers struggle with the high school English Language Arts curriculum. It is still an elastic bastion which holds the tensions between democracy and colonial rule, between Grand Narrative canons and counternarrative Petit Recits, between a text and its reader, between a message and its author. And that requires me, and it requires language arts teachers to be writers and readers and viewers and speakers and listeners and representers. The teaching self is a shape shifter with no stable place in the world. Perhaps that forces us to attend to the spaces between.

In this context, student teachers' voices reflected on the process of becoming writers and being asked to engage in personal writing over time:

> I felt I would never be able to teach children about writing. I was quite overwhelmed.
>
> I have regained confidence in my writing abilities.
>
> I realized the importance of being a writer along with my students.
>
> I realized that I should try to make my writing real and honest.
>
> I feel that I can write more from my heart than before.
>
> I realized that I don't have to write a story all the time – writing comes in many forms. I realized that I actually like writing.
>
> I don't have to be ashamed of my writing.

Writing from a place of cultural and linguistic difference, coming from Indonesia to pursue graduate interdisciplinary studies in dance and education, a teacher gradually realized the power of poetic writing and journaling in a new language, discovering a love of writing, and the importance of being present in this creative act of shaping and moving into a new identity in a new world:

> Sometimes I am writing in my head. What I mean is when I am walking I start writing. The writing just comes to me ... Then I just sit down, and start writing from that moment, because I have lost the moment that has passed ... It passed through me just as the wind blowing through my head, my body ... I could not touch it anymore ... It is gone. What can I do – I am just able to write what comes in each moment of my life ... I love writing and writing is becoming part of myself. It is just like the wind blowing away, and I try to reach it, but it's gone already.

> *When you practice walking meditation, you go for a stroll.*
> Thich Nhat Hanh

> The same is true for a journal. When you write in a journal, you go for a stroll, without purpose or direction, without a travel plan. You start now, and you walk for a while, write for a while, then you stop. What you have is a fragment. What you have is a record of your awareness. The next day you do it again. And perhaps the next day, and the next. What you have is many fragments – of yourself, of your mind, of your awareness of the world.

> (Holzer 1994: 2)

Across another curricular and pedagogical site, a teacher wrote about her experiences with her Grade 11 English students, and how most of the students don't think of themselves as writers and as creative at all. She talked about school buildings that are hollow, both physically and spiritually and otherwise, where creativity starves. Once, she remembered, the students formed a circle when she had to step out of the classroom, a writers' circle that spontaneously emerged out of a craving for community, a need for creativity. She commented on how circles are significant in all that she does, how important it is to model writing that touches creative minds and nurtures them, so that, slowly, a response happens, a trust in spontaneous authentic expression, an opening to that place where creativity can ignite, live, and be affirmed.

> ... Which brings me back to Thich Nhat Hanh who wrote, "The purpose of walking meditation is walking meditation itself. Going is important, not arriving." ... The same is true for journal writing. When you are in the flow of creation, you are here – going, walking, writing, but always here.

> (Holzer 1994: 4)

A researcher working with issues of aboriginal literacy told the story of a First Nations teacher for whom writing became both an expression of life's original difficulty and a site for survival and re-creation of the self:

Muskwachees College sits across the railroad tracks on the Samson Reserve. The College is a set of old ATCO trailers, and walking down the hallway to the staff room, I trip on the linoleum which once held the trailers together. Now the ground has shifted and cracks appear between the units. It's four o'clock and I am here to recruit teachers and administrators from the four band schools at Hobbema – Ermineskin, Montana, Samson, and Louis Bull – to a master's of education program through the University of Lethbridge. I am not really looking for business: Ron Buffalo has invited me. He shows me into a small classroom, crowded with tables and chairs. We make coffee and arrange donuts, the standard nutritional fare for teacher meetings. Filtered water is available, a minor concession to changing times.

A few men and women enter slowly and I try to greet each one. One woman seems familiar and mentally I am whizzing through the filing cabinets of my memory to retrieve her file. Ah yes, Yvonne Buffalo.

"Hello. How are the kids?" Yvonne is a teacher in her early thirties, a single parent of seven children all of whom live at home. In 1997, she enrolled in a Curriculum Studies course I was teaching at Hobbema, part of an earlier attempt to offer an M.Ed. in conjunction with Muskwachees College.

After the session is done, Yvonne watches while I answer the inevitable questions people have, ones that need to be asked in private. "What if my GPA is lower than 3.0?"

Conscious of her waiting, I pull away from the small group and turn to Yvonne standing by the chalkboard. "I want you to know that the writing we did in that class changed my life," she says. "I have never stopped writing, and that writing has saved my life. I just want you to know that." She hugs me, she is crying. I return her hug, and over her shoulder I can see that the donuts were not eaten. I remember one of the stories she wrote in that class.

After three years attending primary school on the reserve, Yvonne starts grade four at the public school in Ponoka. One day she brings a yellow cake for a classroom party. She had saved her money for the cake mix, borrowed cake pans from her aunt, and decorated the cake with colored icing. The next day her grade four classmates refused to eat her cake, because "an Indian had made it."

Another teacher, writer, and researcher of aboriginal literacy in his school on one of the local reserves, recounted the following dialogue:

My three-year-old son told me that he doesn't like Indians. "You are part Indian," I said. "No, I'm not," he replied, "Indians are bad guys." The irony of this situation is not lost on me. Here I am – a Métis, who has been attempting to uncover my father's family history – a history clouded in shame, alcoholism, and "passing for white." At the same time I am working in the field of Native education and doing my best to understand the impact that the history of colonialism has had on the students I teach and the community I work in. Then suddenly, my son has an attitude.

I want to give her the courage to say the next hard thing, without fear of ridicule or expulsion if she strays across the borders of good taste, good sense or good judgment demarcated by a tradition she has had no part in forming. I want her to do the same for me. This is what we can all do to nourish and strengthen one another; listen to one another very hard, ask hard questions, too, send one another away to work again, and laugh in all the right places.

(Mair 1994: 25)

Courage comes in different ways. Coming back to the writing group, M. shared his thoughts and feelings about the recent death of his son in response to a group question about vulnerability. He wanted the members of his group to listen and be with him in the silence that honours the text.

Where am I vulnerable? Dealing with my own grief over Robert's death is a place where I am vulnerable and a place where I avoid talking and acting and acknowledging the sadness I feel and the pain of what I have lost. I appreciated Angela speaking about the drug problems at the Junior High. I immediately thought of Robert. That's where his long struggle with drug addiction began.

The day after our meeting I called the Vancouver coroner's office. I had been delaying this call for several weeks. Dr Robinson apologized for not sending me her final report on the cause of Robert's death and she said she would fax it to me immediately. I tried to discourage her, saying snail mail would be OK but realized I was avoiding once again, so I gave her our faculty fax number and said send it.

I retrieved her report before anyone else might see it and sat in my office to read what she had to say. It's one of the most difficult things I've ever had to do. There in black and white was her account of the last day and night of my son's life with the detailed description of what killed him. All matter of fact and to the point without any sense of what I, as his father for 29 years, had had to deal with, work through, affirm, deny and finally acknowledge. "Death ends a life but not a relationship." He is still my son and I am still his father.

I come back to my teaching, to working with the Division One teachers yesterday and enjoying what opened up for people as we read and wrote, spoke and listened to each other and to the artists who write and sing and draw. My balance comes from these encounters; from these opportunities to share my love for stories and how they affirm and elevate experience, allowing me to take my next step on my journey toward wholeness.

> We dance round in a ring and suppose
> But the Secret sits in the middle and knows.
>
> (Frost 1967)

The voices of the writers, their questions, meditations, and compositions, began to speak with a new solidarity and courage, a new way of addressing the world. They struggled with moving their writing from diary to journal writing – secret writing that was not for anybody's eyes/ears – to public writing. They struggled with choosing excerpts from their writing and with how to say things in ethical ways. They came to writing new worlds and new selves in and outside of classrooms, facing memories that before were too painful, too secret to face, addressing how they were becoming part of different communities in their work/lives, sitting in dialogue with each other, witnessing each other's engagements as learners in a chorus of original voices that work creatively with the difficulties of becoming literate in new ways:

> In the writing group we may not find any answers to our questions. In fact if we did, I would be a bit skeptical of them. But it is in the asking of questions, in the searching out in our writing, in the sifting through the debris of media and other sources of messages and in locating resonances with insights from various messages that, as David Smith suggests, we can claim territory. We can know what we think and in this knowing we are liberated but also made into agents of thoughts in action.
>
> What do we kill in teaching? I live into the questions because there is much unsolved in my heart: What do we need to learn about one another? How can I live well in teaching? What is it to teach literacy now? Whose stories need to be heard? What do stories do? There is a genuine puzzlement as I see school teaching changing before my eyes and ask what is the teaching place? What is the real work in teaching? And while I ask these over and over I must resist easy answers. But some new literacies seem connected to qualities of relationships, cultural difference, technology, inner government, narrative, ethics, and identity striving to live generatively, with authenticity. I face the possibility that I will not find answers and have to live with hard mortal mysteries.

Perhaps to live well in teaching is to develop a literacy of sempiternal hope amid knots and tangles.

These glimpses into the writing processes and products of the various research groups illustrate the complex ways in which the worlds of teachers and students interact. Writing and living and teaching with the questions, in both dangerous and empowering ways, allows each of us the opportunity to grow and develop as teachers, students, colleagues, and friends. Writing and living and teaching with the questions reflects the increasing tensions between local and global literacies which continue as part of the action research cycle.

The agency surfacing in the acts of writing and reading calls for literacy as a social, autobiographical, political, and cultural movement (Pinar 2000). Documenting the everyday movements of literacy realities in specific sites, questioning how we speak with each other, asking what it is we are talking about, what it is that we are saying, remains a challenging process for us as researchers, teachers, and teacher educators. Writing and re-writing our words and worlds in these ways, we continue to search for new solidarities, ask hard questions, listen to each other, and invite our readers to extend these dialogues with others.

The only aim of writing is life …

(Deleuze and Parnet 1986: 6)

Acknowledgment

We thank all the participants in this study, in particular Michelle Bertie-Holthe, Constance Blomgren, Dwayne Donald, Maria Darmaningsih, and Ashelyn Redman. We also gratefully acknowledge the support of this research through a University of Lethbridge Research Excellence Envelope Grant and a Social Sciences and Humanities of Canada Research Initiative Grant.

Bibliography

Aoki, T. T. (2000, April) "Locating living pedagogy in teacher 'research': five metonymic moments," keynote address given at the International Teacher Research Conference, Baton Rouge, Louisiana.

Barnes, T. J. and Duncan, J. S. (Eds) (1992) *Writing Worlds: Discourse, Text, and Metaphor in the Representation of Landscape*, London: Routledge.

Carr, W. and Kemmis, S. (1986) *Becoming Critical: Education, Knowledge and Action Research*, Victoria, Australia: Deakin University Press.

Carson, T. and Sumara, D. (Eds) (1996) *Exploring Collaborative Action Research*, New York: Peter Lang.

Deleuze, G. and Parnet, C. (1986) *Dialogues* (Trans. H. Tomlinson and B. Habberjam), New York: Columbia University Press.

Freire, P. and Macedo, D. (1987) *Literacy: Reading the Word and Reading the World*, New York: Bergin & Garvey.

Frost, R. (1967) *The Complete Poems of Robert Frost*, New York: Holt.

Gadamer, H.-G. (1975/85) *Truth and Method*, New York: Crossroad.

Gadamer, H.-G. (1986) "The idea of the university: yesterday, today, tomorrow," in D. Misgeld and G. Nicholson (Eds) *Hans-Georg Gadamer on Education, Poetry, and History* (pp. 47–59), Frankfurt: Suhrkamp.

Graff, H. J. (1986) *The Labyrinths of Literacy: Reflections on Literacy Past and Present*, London: Falmer Press.

Hiebert, E. and Raphael, T. (1998) *Early Literacy Instruction*, Orlando, FL: Holt, Rinehart & Winston.

Holzer, B. N. (1994) *A Walk Between Heaven and Earth: A Personal Journal on Writing and the Creative Process*, New York: Bell Tower.

Leu, D. (1997) "Caity's question," *The Reading Teacher*, 51, 1, 62–7.

Mair, N. (1994) *Voice Lessons: On Becoming a (Woman) Writer*, Boston: Beacon Press.

McLuhan, M. (1962) *The Gutenberg Galaxy: The Making of Typographic Man*, Toronto: University of Toronto Press.

Neilson, L. (1998) *Knowing Her Place: Research Literacies and Feminist Occasions*, San Francisco: Caddo Gap Press.

Ong, W. J. (1982) *Orality and Literacy: The Technologizing of the World*, London: Methuen.

Palmer, P. (1998) *The Courage to Teach*, San Francisco: Jossey-Bass.

Patterson, L., Santa, C. M., Short, K. and Smith, K. (Eds) (1993) *Teachers are Researchers: Reflection and Renewal*, Newark: International Reading Association.

Pinar, W. F. (2000) "Strange fruit: race, sex, and an autobiographics of alterity," in P. Trifonas (Ed.) *Revolutionary Pedagogies: Cultural Politics, Instituting Education, and the Discourse of Theory* (pp. 30–46), New York: Routledge.

Readance, J. E. and Barone, D. M. (Eds) (2000) "Envisioning the future of literacy," *Reading Research Quarterly Special Issue*, 35, 1, 312–443.

Rilke, R. M. (1934/93) *Letters to a Young Poet* (Trans. M. D. Herter Norton), New York: W. W. Norton.

Schön, D. (1983) *The Reflective Practitioner: How Professionals Think in Action*, New York: Basic Books.

Smith, D. G. (2000) "Preface", in D. Jardine, *Under the Tough Old Stars: Ecopedagogical Essay* (pp. ix–x), Brandon, VT: The Foundation for Educational Renewal/ Solomon Press.

Willinsky, J. (1990) *The New Literacy: Redefining Reading and Writing in the Schools*, New York: Routledge.

Chapter 12

How we have grown

Reflections on professional development

Donna F. Nelson, Kay Strouse,
Christine Waechter and Henry St. Maurice

Our group has met informally and presented our research at conferences for many years. We chose 2001 as an occasion to reflect on our professional development over the past five years. We also conducted our action research as a response to our state's new rules for teacher licensure, mandating five-year professional development plans (Wisconsin DPI 2000). As recent reviews of changes in teacher preparation and licensure suggest, teaching careers are varied, complex and not easily summarized in uniform standards, plans and portfolios (Cochran-Smith and Fries 2001; Darling-Hammond 2001; Peske *et al.* 2001). In our research, we asked about how we have learned to teach and, by implication, how our careers would have been assessed according to current and proposed standards for teaching. We gathered data, discussed and wrote about the following thematic questions:

- Professional Development: What route, if any, did we follow in learning about teaching over the past five or more years? Were there benchmarks by which we assessed our goals and accomplishments?
- Ethics: What moral standards did we apply to our practice? In specific cases, what were the results of our decisions to abide by those standards?
- Reflection: How does reflective writing affect our practice? Are there benefits to documenting and reflecting on teaching practices? Does reflection aid in reducing stress, or can it be another stressor?

In tracing patterns in our professional development, we collected and analyzed various data in response to these and related questions. The next three sections are first-person narratives of findings by individual group members, after which we will draw some implications to hopefully help our own and others research and reflection on teaching as a profession.

Donna Nelson
Public use of private writing: an ethical issue

In reflecting on my years as a kindergarten teacher, many life lessons come to mind. The lessons I would like to share are the result of two action research projects I have done on ethics and professional development. In a particular divorce case five years ago, a custody suit was brought over a student in my classroom. I found that my private documentation and private classroom journal writing were subpoenaed as evidence of the child's parental care. Last year, another custody dispute was brought by the State of Wisconsin against a parent seeking to remove a child from home. I was again subpoenaed. I have been a strong supporter of journal writing for classroom documentation, in appropriate ways and for the right reasons. My experiences in court, however, have scared some of my colleagues away from writing about their practices, especially documenting the lives of children in their classes. By sharing my stories, I mean to tell teachers about the risks and the benefits.

It was in a third case, in which a parent was taken to court over a child's custody, that the stakes became much higher. I had contacted social service workers several times to report incidents, as mandated by state law. Not only did I have to produce my documentation and reflective writing in court, but I also made a strong personal statement of what I believed was right for this child. One day, a lawyer came to school to talk to me. I was not sure what was happening, but had been assured they had permission to talk to me and that I had to talk to them. Normally, I would avoid talking to anyone for any reason about these matters, but when I got this far into the legal system, it was scary.

Following this meeting, I assumed that the matter had been settled. I was told that the child would no longer be left alone at home. Soon, however, the child was found left alone again, locked out of her home, so her case returned to court. The mother was extremely upset that they were trying to take her child away, and she blamed me for it. I feared for my family's and my safety. I knew I had to do the right thing, but asked, "At what cost?"

I learned that, when we teachers think we have confidential information, we should know that nothing is really confidential. If someone in the legal system wants to look at something or talk to someone, they will find a way. It seems to me that we should know it is possible and decide for ourselves whether it is ethical or not to use our private writings in public. When we keep documentation, we have to also keep in mind that if some-one does want it, they will get it. After this past experience, I changed the way I think and write as an advocate for children. I believe that I always wrote appropriately and did not make too many judgments, but now I am even more careful with my writing. It is still the right thing to do, for a lot of reasons, but it must be done correctly to protect also one's self as well as to protect children.

Over the years I have seen increases in the needs of children in my classes. I have seen family situations changing: more children are given care in extended families, agencies and programs. I believe that educators must be advocates for children in spite of situations that sometimes seem overwhelming. We need to remember why we became teachers in the first place, and we need to take care of ourselves or we will not be well enough to care for the children. I have found that by focusing my writings and reflections on children and their families, I have renewed my faith in my work.

Kay Strouse
The long and winding road less taken

In reflecting on our past five years of professional development through action research, it becomes difficult to narrow to just those five years without reflecting on my entire career, because each step of my career has followed decisions and foundations made before it. Looking back over twenty-five years of professional development, I can identify three major elements: articulation, networking and adaptation.

Action research has permitted me to reflect upon my practice in profound ways that I find gratifying, sustaining and affirming. Still, the recursive nature of the learning process always brings my students and me full circle to return to basic questions about why and how and what we do, only to swing out in new directions, new angles, new circles creating new paths and then returning to the comfort of familiar surroundings to reflect upon the experience.

How lucky I was, as a first year English and speech teacher in a small rural community in north central Illinois, to make connections with another first year teacher in the same field. We sought out one another in order to engage in discussion about our difficulties and successes in our classrooms. We were in a building with many veteran teachers marching their way toward retirement and an administration that let us know that no one had ever been fired except for being a weak teacher. We asked, "How is 'weak' defined?" It seemed that sending problem students to the office and not taking care of classroom management issues provided the best definition of "weak." Not only were we mentors for one another, we also directed all of the speech and drama activities: the one act play contest, forensics, debate, radio club and spring musical. With so much work, it was hard to believe that any time was left for reflecting.

Nonetheless, I noticed that my grade nine students, who had graduated from several different grade schools, came to my school with exceedingly disparate preparations for high school. I campaigned with my administrator for an articulation committee with the eighth grade English teachers to discuss curriculum and objectives for incoming students so that I could adjust my lessons accordingly. This was a novel idea for a community where each small grade school maintained its own separate district with managing board.

During the three years at that school, I often questioned why I had gone into teaching. I had graduated with a BA in speech communication from the University of Illinois, never expecting to teach, in fact resisting the notion. I believed that a host of companies were just waiting to add me to their rosters of trainees, but when I found that I seemed qualified only for their receptionist positions, I was insulted at the prospect of using a college diploma to answer telephones. I realized that I'd have to return to school to get a piece of paper saying I could do something, but what? I fondly remembered long lazy summer days life-guarding at local country clubs where tennis and golf-playing moms dropped children off for morning swimming lessons. My decision to teach, therefore came primarily from my success at teaching willing youngsters to swim. Thus, when I entered a teacher-training program at Illinois State University, all I knew was that I could finish in two semesters. After thirty credits and student teaching, the state of Illinois licensed me to teach speech, English and psychology.

My student teaching experience exhilarated me. I worked with two cooperating teachers in the school where I also signed my first teaching contract, in a town thirty miles from my rural home community, in a building with a librarian who had been one of my high school English teachers and with a superintendent who was a golfing buddy of my dad. My cooperating teachers gave me complete autonomy in the American Literature, drama and two speech classes. Both of them resigned at the end of the school year. I interviewed and accepted a contract offer from the superintendent at a beach telephone that summer.

Unfortunately, after three rather frustrating years in that district, even with the friendship and mentorship of my colleagues, even with the endeavors to articulate with the eighth grade teachers, even with the autonomy to adapt my curriculum to the needs of my students, I felt restless, ineffective and frustrated with a school that allowed mediocrity and complacency to overshadow real and effectual learning. The football coach had even tried to coerce me into passing a starting player. Although graduate school in theater arts attracted me, I opted to marry my college sweetheart and move to what I had heard was, the progressive state of Wisconsin, the place just north of the Illinois border where I had vacationed with my family as a child.

It was September, not the best time to be seeking a teaching position, but I found a position as a speech and debate teacher in Stevens Point, a small city in central Wisconsin whose kindergarten through 12th grade district supported a three-year comprehensive secondary school of 2,000 rural and suburban students. Pleased to learn that their speech program used the same book I had ordered in Illinois, I felt comfortable with a required semester speech course, except for the film unit taught during the last six weeks and using titles already ordered on 16 mm reels of movies I had not seen. Fortunately, a veteran teacher supplied me with mimeographed background materials and set up the movie projector on an AV cart for me each Monday morning. Debate, on the other hand, provided more of a challenge. I was scheduled to teach two sections that had been taught by a non-content certified teacher and a college freshman who had been on the school's state winning team during the previous season. We struggled for power throughout the semester – the students, some of whom were third year debaters and expecting a repeat of the state title, the college student/coach, the principal who came to evaluate me on the day of a test where students up and left, slamming doors, angry at me for giving a test at all, to go the library to do some real work, and me, the young teacher.

By the second semester, the department chairperson assigned new courses to me, one of which included two sections of a twelfth grade literature elective at the end of the school day. In a state where the legal drinking age – still at eighteen – provided liquid lunch-time opportunities, my students told me I should be happy they even bothered to come back to class regardless of their condition. The principal disbanded one of my speech classes because it was too small. This sent me to a supervision position in the commons area for student dining and study. After we had spent several weeks developing a classroom community, the students unhappily became members of convenient new classes and then stormed the office protesting against the principal's decision. He was not amused and accused me of conspiring with the students.

After seven years I had begun to burn out: my health was failing. My career had begun to stabilize, but I also felt that I was starting to stagnate. I knew that I would have to do something different if I was going to stay sane. Suddenly, one afternoon I saw an interesting posting on the bulletin board of the teachers' mailroom for a liaison teacher to coordinate pre-service education majors from the local university within our district's classrooms. Although it looked somewhat interesting, I must have been too busy to follow up on the position until I saw it once again printed in our local teachers' association's monthly newsletter. After that second sign, I called our district's personnel office to inquire about the position. I wrote an application letter but did not hear back until the day after I had casually mentioned my interest to my principal and learned that I was to come to the district office the next day for an interview. This interview, conducted by the personnel director and the university's director of field experiences, included both of the two candidates: me and the high school hockey coach. The following day the secretary in the personnel office called to tell me I had the job. This new situation would include working with an intern teacher who would be licensed and could legally take my place in the classroom when I needed to be out of the building at district elementary and junior high schools as well as the university.

My first intern had been one of my favorite students while she was in my tenth grade writing class some eight years before. We also had been classmates in a combined undergrad/grad English course at the university. Her father had been one of my professors for a coaching debate and forensics course; her mother was a colleague in one of the junior high English departments; her older sister had debated for me; and her younger sister had made a positive and lasting impression on me also in that tenth grade writing course. My goodness – we were practically related! Our semester together could not have been more invigorating for me professionally. Because two of us could coordinate class lessons, we could schedule special activities and events for our students that would have been difficult alone: the university's theater director came to an arranged two-hour block for two of our classes to share slides of Anne Frank's house in Amsterdam during our Jewish Literature unit; we dressed up as Emily Grierson and William Faulkner for a reading of "A Rose for Emily;" she photographed our students reading to second graders at a local elementary school.

My next few years of teaching brought exciting continued work placing university students in district classrooms, along with managing classes with different interns, each of whom kindled new growth and dimension in my professional development. I was also doing more speaking at conferences and learning about a new way to reflect on my practice: action research.

As a writing teacher, I believed in the importance of modeling for my students. Each time I asked students to write, I wrote along with them and shared both my triumphs and failures. Action research allowed me to write in a new way along with my students. Each semester notebook pages filled with my musings about my classes, and patterns began to emerge from year to year. Questions and concerns that arose one semester might reappear again during another. I could use the journal to investigate possible causes, effects, and solutions before I would jump to a conclusion about an issue. Encouraged by a group of talented teachers, we began writing about our experiences and sharing our findings. Our writings became more focused, and our journals answered important questions in our individual professional lives. We had the occasions to speak about our writing to other professionals who we encouraged to begin by "just writing."

When several years ago the reading coordinator asked me to assist her in the district's reading office, I used my journal to answer an envious colleague's question, "Just what are you doing when you're in the reading office?" My journal provided insight into the important work we did in order to assist teachers in helping students in all levels of language arts. Then one year, frustrated with having to grade twelfth grade literature projects, I journaled to find a new way to assess their work by helping them be more self-reflective about the time and effort they had committed to the projects. This year's topic allowed me to write about my career as a story, not simply lines beginning with action verbs on a résumé. I could finally give credit to some of those individuals who have had such a powerful influence in shaping the professional I am today.

Although I am beyond mid-career, I have been fortunate to have encountered good and talented professionals who have helped me along the way to see old patterns with new eyes and remember the words of one of my mom's dearest friends, a kindergarten teacher in our small rural Illinois community, who told me early in my career, "Times will change. New techniques, philosophies and materials will come and go, but nothing replaces a good teacher." I circle back to the words and deeds of those people who have supported, directed and influenced my teaching so that I may continue to create and reflect.

Christine Waechter
My inner voice

In each of us there is an inner voice, the one that questions us and reaffirms our practices. Using this inner voice for professional development is a powerful tool for seeing one's self and practices. Reflections on the inner voice are stepping stones into the future.

I found this inner voice many years ago when I was a child. Like many young children, I was given a diary. In my diaries I wrote about secrets, wishes, and daily happenings. I remember reading my diaries later and would laugh over what I once thought was important. As I grew, I kept writing, in the borders of my class notes and in my letters to a special person in my life. These writings captured my thoughts and questions about what I was doing and why I was making choices. I have since packed away these important documents until my golden years, but a few years ago I did take the time to re-read them again. I was impressed that I did reach the goals I set in those long-ago years and have since built new goals.

I began my teaching career in 1968. As a new teacher I set out to change the world. I had learned through my experiences as a student teacher that I was ready for anything. I quickly learned that, although my professional training had been excellent, it didn't prepare me for all that I experienced in my classrooms. The pages of my first lesson plan books soon became places for me to write the questions and reflections of the day.

In the nine years I spent in my first district, I taught third, fourth, seventh and eighth grade English, science and art, as well as art for all of grades, kindergarten through eight. Each of these changes came with a great deal of soul searching over what I was doing and what directions I wanted to take next. I searched for ways to improve as a professional. As I look back over those years, I wish I was a more reflective writer, so that I could read what I thought about the decisions I made.

When I started my family, the reflections I had made about learners helped me think about my work as a full-time mother. The years I spent at home didn't end my professional development, as I read, thought and wrote about what I wanted to do in the future. I have always felt that my two children provided me with the greatest understanding of my role as an educator.

After six years of my work as a parent at home, our family moved to central Wisconsin. This change made a major impact on my life. I soon realized that I needed to return to the profession I loved: I needed to return to teaching in a classroom. I was hired for part-time teaching assignment at a Lutheran school. As soon as I began this new position, I reflected on where I was as an educator and where I wanted to go. It seemed to me that the profession had moved past me. So, back to school I went, to the University of Wisconsin – Stevens Point. I was eager to again become a student.

At the same time, I left my part-time position and returned to a full-time position in the public school system. When the idea of working toward a Master's degree first came to me, I put it on the back burner, thinking, how could I be a good mom and teacher while working on a Master's program? I continued to take classes that were relevant to my teaching whenever I found time in my busy schedule. One evening my oldest son asked me why I didn't have a Master's degree. I thought about that question, and realized that I really had no reasons why I hadn't finished the degree. This wonderful child challenged me to obtain my Master's degree by the time he finished high school. I thought I could do it in three years, but as it turned out I had only two and a half years because he planned to seek early graduation. Somehow by the end of that short time period, we both had diplomas in our hands.

As a direct result of my son's challenge, I took a course at the university that changed my professional development in ways I could never have imagined. Seven years ago, I began an intensive process of reflective journal writing in a course I was taking at the University of Wisconsin – Stevens Point. I was given the opportunity to write reflectively about the class I was taking. I was encouraged to question what the professor was doing in his class. After the class came to an end, we were encouraged to take this practice of reflective journal writing into our classrooms in the fall, and I did just that. The impact was overwhelming.

My journey through reflective journaling began with a teaching situation I had with a new arrival room for students learning English as a second language. The learners I had in this room came from refugee camps. They had little or no experience with the English language and American customs. My job was to get them ready for a regular academic classroom. It was frustrating in so many ways that I needed to vent my frustrations. Writing was a way that I thought would be beneficial to all. I began by recording the events of each day, including comments I was hearing in the halls, the behaviors the learners were displaying each time they had to leave their safe classroom, and my feelings about how each day progressed.

By the time the second semester began, I started reviewing what I had been writing. I found my writings to be full of questions. This led me to the second step of my reflective practice, using writing for solving problems. I decided to share my journal with its questions and reflections with my principal. This was a very difficult decision that demanded a great deal of trust in my principal. I needed to be sure my writing would not be used as evidence for judgment about my work, but rather an instrument to help me make decisions and changes in my teaching.

Through many conversations and continued writing, my principal and I developed plans for the following year. My classroom would be paired with a classroom of native English speakers, so that the students in both rooms could become learning partners. Again, through the next year I wrote again about what I was seeing and hearing in and out of the classroom. My colleague became my partner in this research. She was also encouraged to write and reflect on each day's events. Reflective writing was a new challenge for her. She was near retirement and reluctant to start using a journal for documentation and reflection. At times I simply placed our dialogue journal on her desk and said, "Write!"

In addition to improving my own practices and those of my peers, the process of reflective journal writing has also helped me as a mentor of student teachers. My journal is a resource for recording a student teacher's professional growth while in my class, especially when things are not going well. It has been my practice to keep a dialogue journal with my student teachers. I can say things that cannot be shared while teaching and that can be reflected on afterwards. For some student teachers the idea of a shared journal is threatening. I have found that there must be a rapport between both the participants, or it doesn't work.

A number of volunteers have come to me from the University to work in my classroom. They bring with them new talents and insights. I developed a form for them to complete before they leave after each day. I ask them to reflect in writing on what they have seen and done during their time in my classroom. This writing has brought some very valuable information to my attention. As a professional I find I can too easily be distracted in the flow of my day. I don't always have the opportunity to work closely one on one with each student in my class for an extended amount of time. These volunteers do get those opportunities, and their insights have given me many new ways of looking at my learners.

Reflective journal writing helped me as I went through a change in my assigned grades and schools. As I reviewed my writings about my transfer, I found they focused on the physical conditions of my new classroom. They were filled with negative comments about all the things I missed from my previous school. These negative reflections were not helping me accept change. From the time I re-read them, I started to look at the good the change had brought. Later in the year, my writing again focused on what I wanted to improve for the next year. I asked, "What can I do to make my classroom better? Where do I want to go professionally?" These questions helped me look closely at my professionalism.

My reflective journaling played a great role in my personal life when I experienced difficulty with my teenaged son. I knew he was not telling me what I needed to know about his life. I began the process of active listening and then recording the things he would talk about with me. We actually set a time each day when he and I could sit down together. Then when I read those entries at the end of each week, I realized that he was telling me a lot about his life, only it was in bits and pieces. Through the weeks, I was able to keep track of what he was doing and who he was doing it with. I admit that I was scared and worried.

Finally, one evening he came to talk to me as I was writing and he discovered what I was keeping in my journal. He asked why I was keeping this information and I told him I was concerned about him and wanted to keep track of his life. I promised him the journal would become his after he had his first child. My journal now took on a deeper meaning, because my son would ask that certain things he told me be added to my journal. In two cases, these written records were evidence that kept him out of trouble when his friends made poor decisions in his absence.

This personal reflective journal allowed me to record my feelings and questions about my child. But, more importantly, it allowed me to keep my personal life separate from my professional life. I am now more convinced than ever that when I write about my daily trials, they become more manageable. My reflective journal writing has become a powerful tool for my professional and personal development. I am more aware of my everyday surroundings and my thoughts and feelings. My years of keeping and using reflective journals have helped me avoid feeling stagnant, because I am always thinking about how I can do things differently. Through this process I have become more able to take charge of my life. I sometimes wish my high school English teacher could see me now. I still struggle, but in high school I was an unwilling and inept writer. She once told me there wasn't enough red ink in her pen to mark my paper.

As I read through our group's sections in this chapter, I reflected on our group's writing. To me, it is like a web: each thread touches another. Each thread is different in some way, yet no thread in the web is unimportant. We each find our own purposes in our writings for professional and personal growth. We cannot separate our teaching and home lives in our writings. We write to vent, reflect and make decisions. In finding, recording, analyzing and sharing our inner voices over the years, we have become more thoughtful and strong.

Implications

Our action research showed us that we could not have foreseen the challenges we encountered in our careers. No five-year plan would have sufficed, although we might have liked to have the clarity of generally agreed standards, benchmarks and rubrics. Knowing that hindsight is always more informative than foresight, we find that the most important implication of our action research is that skills for documenting practices and supporting reflection deserve more emphasis in pre-service and in-service teacher education.

In the midst of a contentious debate over which inputs, processes or results are most important in assuring teacher quality, our findings imply that reflection-in-action should be a major component of professional development at all stages in all professions (Schön 1991; Zeichner and Liston 1996). Despite the presence of reflection in standard #9 in the Wisconsin and US Interstate Standards for Teaching ("The teacher is a reflective practitioner who continually evaluates the effect of his or her choices and actions on pupils, parents, professionals in the learning community and others, and who actively seeks out opportunities to grow professionally."), it should have greater prominence.

We also believe that our research shows the importance of cohesive cohort groups in facilitating reflection. We have built our own learning community of fewer than ten members, along lines suggested by recent studies in social psychology and sociology of communities (Putnam 2000), which state that successful groups are small enough to bond their members closely together, but also open to connect to other communities. Our group of professional teachers has built strong bonds of common experiences, forming a circle of support, and in encountering other circles of teacher-researchers, we have built bridges to mutual understanding and widened support. Our professional development may be summarized as circles upon circles, a dynamic process that is still beyond the range of any standardized test or generalized form.

In conclusion, our professional and personal lives have grown, and will grow, in circles. The spiral model of practitioner research (Zeichner and Noffke 2001) describes our work and the way that we have studied it. We look forward to more years of teaching, research and sharing, and trust that this chapter and this volume will inspire others to form circles that help them understand, explain and enrich both our profession and the lives of the students and communities we all serve.

Bibliography

Cochran-Smith, M. and Fries, M. (2001). "Sticks, stones and ideology: the discourse of reform in teacher education," *Educational Researcher*, 30, 8, 3–15.

Darling-Hammond, L. (2001) "Standard setting in teaching: changes in licensing, certification and assessment," in V. Richardson (Ed.) *Handbook of Research on Teaching* (4th edn) (pp. 751–76), Washington, DC: American Educational Research Association.

Peske, K., Liu, E., Moore Johnson, S., Kauffman, D. and Kardos, S. (2001) "The next generation of teachers: changing conceptions of a career in teaching," *Phi Delta Kappan*, 83, 4, 304–11.

Putnam, R. (2000) *Bowling Alone: The Collapse and Revival of American Community*, New York: Simon & Schuster.

Schön, D. A. (1991) *The Reflective Turn: Case Studies in and on Educational Practice*, New York: Teachers College Press.

Wisconsin Department of Public Instruction (2000) *Rules for Teacher Education*, Madison, WI: Wisconsin Department of Public Instructions. Available online: http://www.dpi.state.wi.us/dpi/dlsis/tel/newrules.html.

Zeichner, K. and Liston, D. (1996) *Reflective Teaching: An Introduction*, Mahwah, NJ: L. Erlbaum Associates.

Zeichner, K. and Noffke, S. (2001) "Practitioner research," in V. Richardson (Ed.) *Handbook of Research on Teaching* (4th edn) (pp. 298–330), Washington, DC: American Educational Research Association.

Part II

Methods and models in teacher research

Chapter 13

Using the World Wide Web for researching teaching–learning relationships

Garry Hoban

Gaining an understanding of teaching and learning as a dynamic relationship is one of the important insights a teacher at any level – elementary, secondary or tertiary – can develop (Hoban 2000). This means thinking about a classroom as an interactive context rather than as a static environment. For example, classroom contexts are always changing because of the interactions from numerous interrelated influences such as the type of teaching, curriculum and variety of children with a range of experience, intelligence, gender, culture and ethnicity. It is for this reason that teachers need to conduct teacher research on their own practice to develop an understanding of the complexity of classroom interactions and to respond with the most appropriate type of instruction.

One way to develop such an understanding is for pre-service students *and* their instructor to conduct research on their own classroom interactions at university. This type of teacher research has two purposes. First, it is a form of teacher research for me as I systematically study my own practice and reflect upon how my teaching influences the learning of my pre-service teachers. Second, my own tutorials at university are used as an opportunity for the pre-service teachers to conduct research on how they learn in light of my teaching. The outcome for pre-service students is that they can theorize from their experiences as learners to develop a metaphor that represents the relationships in a real classroom. This type of teacher/pre-service student research is symbiotic and is consistent with what Cochran-Smith and Lytle call "teacher research as ways of knowing in communities" (Cochran-Smith and Lytle 1999: 18). In this respect, teachers and students in a classroom are joint inquirers about classroom interactions:

> This work pays particular attention to the discourse of learning communities, the conjoined efforts of teachers and students as inquirers, and the role of inquiry in the fields of literacy and curriculum. The emphasis here is on blurring the boundaries of research and practice and on conceptualizing practice as a critical and theory-building process. The larger goal is to create classrooms and schools where rich

learning opportunities increase students' life chances and to alter the cultures of teaching by altering the relations of power in schools and universities.

(Cochran-Smith and Lytle 1999: 18)

During their university education, pre-service students are exposed to a wide range of content and teaching strategies as well as interacting with a variety of students. This context provides a wonderful opportunity for students to study how they learn in an authentic classroom setting. Encouraging students to study their experiences as learners at university, therefore, personalizes their understanding of themselves and of learning processes as well as providing data for the teacher-researcher who is their instructor.

A teacher research framework for studying classroom relationships

Over the last four years, I have developed a framework to support pre-service teachers in researching themselves as learners in university classes which also provides me with data on my teaching (Hoban 1998, 2000). This framework promotes reflective practice, encouraging each pre-service teacher to be "a researcher in the practice context" (Schön 1983: 68) with the context being their own university classes. There are three phases in the proposed research framework which encourages students to conduct a "systematic inquiry that is collective, collaborative, self-reflective, critical, and undertaken by participants of the inquiry ... [for] the understanding of practice and the articulation of a rationale or philosophy of practice" (McCutcheon and Jung 1990: 148). The first phase, analyzing class experiences, occurs weekly during the course and the second and third phases, synthesis and theorizing, are completed by students towards the end of the course when students deduce a metaphor to represent the relationships in their classroom learning.

In 1999, a World Wide Web (WWW) site was designed with a FileMaker Pro database as a tool to help pre-service students use the research framework. In previous courses the pre-service students used a pencil and paper method to document in a journal what they learned and how they learned. But often students were unsure what to write about and how to theorize from their research to develop their own metaphors for learning. The WWW site was designed with the intention of minimizing the cognitive load on students when reflecting by using a screen design with cues to "promote understanding by allowing the reader to focus on new information rather than devoting time and energy to variations for format" (El-Tigi and Marbe Branch 1997: 25). In addition, the web site assisted students in sharing their experiences and theorizing about their research to deduce a metaphor as a representation of the complexities of how they learn.

Phase 1 – Analysis

Using this research framework, learning is considered as an individual process of knowledge construction which is supported by social interactions with the outside world (Duffy and Cunningham 1996). After each three-hour class, pre-service students log onto a WWW site with four categories focusing on personal, social (teaching and peer) and contextual influences on learning for students to document their research. This includes:

1   *personal* factors attributed to the individual student, such as prior knowledge, feelings, self-esteem and motivation;
2   *teaching* factors attributed to the instructor/lecturer/tutor such as instructional strategies used, class organization, goals, rapport;
3   *peer* factors attributed to other students, such as how they encourage each other, share ideas and cooperate in tasks; and
4   *contextual* factors attributed to the task, setting and environment.

Pre-service students document factors on the template of the web site which enhance or inhibit their learning according to these four categories. The web site also provides each student with access to other students' data about their analysis of their learning experiences.

Phase 2 – Synthesis

Towards the end of the course, the database collates each student's weekly documentation of the factors using the four categories identified in Phase 1. For example, they can collate the teaching factors for all weeks onto one page to help them deduce the main teaching factors which influence their learning. After completing their collations, they synthesize the factors, resulting in the identification of several key factors for each of the four categories. They present this synthesis in a table called a "Learning Profile."

Phase 3 – Theorizing

Each pre-service student considers the key enhancing factors identified in his/her Learning Profile and theorizes to develop a metaphor (Lakoff and Johnson 1980) which represents relationships in an optimal learning environment for their university class. Students use the key factors from their Learning Profile to label their metaphor as an example of theorizing to explain "*plausible* relationships proposed among *concepts* and *sets of concepts*" (Strauss and Corbin 1994: 278, italics in original). Finally, students are expected to use their insights into how they learn to deduce implications for their future role as teachers. This three-phase research framework can be used in any teacher education course and my students used it in their undergraduate science methods course.

Examples of student use of the research framework

This study reports on the teacher research of 25 pre-service students who used the research framework in a 13-week science methods course as part of a Bachelor of Teaching (Elementary) program in 1999. The purpose of the course was for students to study different ways of designing a unit of work for use in an elementary science classroom and to develop a metaphor as a representation of a relationship between teaching and learning. The students had a one-hour lecture and a two-hour hands-on practical (laboratory) class each week. The one-hour lecture explained aspects of the science content followed by a two-hour practical class for students to experiment with hands-on activities related to the particular science topic addressed in the lecture. Various teaching strategies were used throughout the course to provide students with a range of teaching experiences to study.

After each weekly class, the students used the WWW site for their teacher research to analyze their experiences in the course. First, students documented *what* they learned from the class using pencil and paper, which included writing about the background knowledge related to the topic. For example, when doing a topic such as "Floating and Sinking" the students wrote about the activities attempted such as designing and making model boats as well as follow-up information about buoyancy and why different boats float. Second, the students documented *how* they learned on the web using four fields to identify the personal, social (teaching and peer) and contextual influences on their learning. All 25 students in the course used the research framework on the WWW and excerpts from the documentation of one of the students is now provided.

Phase 1 – Analysis

An example from Taryn's research of the weekly analysis of factors which influenced her learning in week two, which was on the topic of "Electricity," is shown below.

Personal factors

INHIBITING

- lack of *prior knowledge*. I don't know much about electricity at all and I am *not very confident* in my abilities to conduct experiments successfully. I guess I was told a bit in high school that I wasn't the top of the class with things like that;
- *lacked confidence* in my abilities. I am a good student but I don't trust that enough;
- *rushed* in the activities and not enough time;

- *tired*, up late reading;
- thinking of other things such as my learning journal so that I am too busy to concentrate fully on the task at hand;
- *confused* with the topic of electricity.

ENHANCING

- *interested* to learn about something that I didn't know a great deal about;
- *good mood*;
- *motivated*, ready and wanted to learn;
- *reflecting* on new ideas and making a decision on how I wanted to attempt activities.

Teaching factors – lecturer

INHIBITING

- *no explanation* on electricity. I felt that I was left stranded and that I didn't know anything and I still only know what I picked up along the way during the lesson;
- I felt that I was *rushed* to finish when I was having some trouble;
- I needed *more help* and I didn't get it so I stayed confused.

ENHANCING

- *encouragement* in feedback;
- *lack of criticism* increased my self-esteem and I wanted to have a go;
- clear and detailed *explanations of expectations* for our journal. Of all the journals I have had to write at university this is the first time I have had a clear understanding of my direction. This has helped to motivate me and keep me interested. Thank you. I don't feel that I am writing nonsense;
- *genuine interest* in our comments and concerns;
- good to give us some *freedom* to explore;
- *enthusiasm* motivated me to learn more.

Peer factors – students

INHIBITING

- still *not comfortable* with the class as I don't know them all very well;
- I get annoyed when *people don't listen* to all information and ask dumb questions;
- group tried to work together but did *not work very well*.

ENHANCING

- great group;
- fun, lots of laughs;
- encouragement to try;
- enthusiasm;
- supportive;
- good class size;
- comfortable atmosphere.

Contextual Factors

INHIBITING

- uncomfortable stools;
- cold room;
- couldn't readily find the equipment we wanted;
- time.

ENHANCING

- doing real activities
- time to muck around.

It should be noted that she identified both enhancing and inhibiting factors for each of the four categories on a weekly basis. For example, in week two she identified five personal factors which inhibited her learning (lack of prior knowledge, lack of confidence, rushing, tired and confusion) and four personal factors which enhanced her learning (interested, good mood, motivated and reflection). She also identified enhancing and inhibiting teaching, peer and contextual factors. She did this on a weekly basis for ten weeks until the end of the subject.

Phase 2 – Synthesis

Taryn used the database on the web site to collate all of her weekly reflections towards the end of the subject according to the four categories, and synthesized her reflections to deduce key factors for each of the four categories for her Learning Profile, as shown in Table 13.1.

Phase 3 – Theorizing

From her theorizing on her data, Taryn deduced a metaphor of a "Playground" to represent her classroom learning, as shown in Figure 13.1. She chose this metaphor because a playground represented the relationship

Table 13.1 Taryn's learning profile for the course

Influences	Positive/enhancing factors	Negative/inhibiting factors
Personal Factors (Me – the student)	Prior knowledge and experiences Personal reflection Motivation for topic Interest Confidence	Lack of prior knowledge Tired Bored Lack of control
Teaching Factors (You – the lecturer)	Structure in lessons Clear explanation Fun atmosphere Encouragement by lecturer Questions answered Guidance	Talked too much Unclear explanations Sidetracked Rushed activities
Peer Factors (Other students)	Collaboration with group Interaction with others Encouragement by group members	Others not listening Interrupting others Dumb questions Know-all students
Contextual Factors	Time Range of activities Enough equipment Freedom to be an active learner	Uncomfortable stools Lack of time Lack of equipment Need more hands-on activities

that linked factors for an optimal learning environment in a class involving "structured lessons, fun and interaction." The key enhancing factors identified in her Learning Profile in Table 13.1 were used to label the diagram. She explained how the house in the centre of the playground represented a combination of the *personal* and *teaching* factors which influenced her learning, providing "structure in lessons, prior knowledge, experience and guidance" which were the fundamental conditions for her "growth, exploration, reflection and hard work." The sandpit provided a place for additional *peer* interactions such as "collaboration, discussion with others, freedom to explore and space to create personal meaning." The swing represented time for reflection and growth in her knowledge. The roundabout represented the influence of negative factors on her learning when she goes round and around but does not get anywhere. The monkey bars represented her continual effort to learn and finally the whole playground needed to be in a relaxed and enjoyable atmosphere. Importantly, a feature of her metaphor are the two-way arrows used throughout which show the dynamic interactions between teaching and learning in the classroom.

Taryn concluded her research by deducing two main implications for her teaching based on the analysis of her learning experiences in the course. First, she thought that it was important for her future role as a teacher to

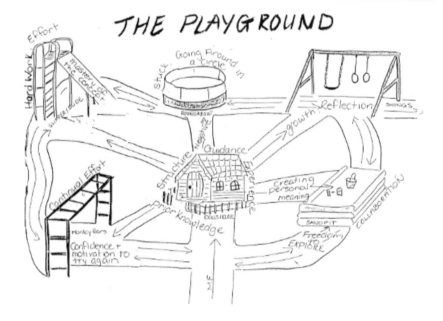

Figure 13.1

provide "structure and guidance" in lessons because this was consistent with the way that she learned. She explained that the guidance and structure in a lesson comes from a clear explanation from the teacher and her own active interest in the topic. Second, she realized that "not everyone learns as I do and I forget this and tend to get frustrated with those who do not need the structure and guidance that I do." The main implication was that in a classroom situation she needed to use a "diversity of teaching strategies and activities for the students in my classroom."

Summary of metaphors from other students

The other 23 students in the course also used the research framework to deduce metaphors to represent relationships between teaching and learning. Some of these metaphors included a game of baseball, launching a rocket into space, an elevator in a building, a playground, a ski lift, a garden with a range of plants and a game of golf. The students labeled these metaphors with key factors identified in their Learning Profiles and all of these metaphors showed the dynamic relationships between personal, social and contextual influences on learning.

Implications for my own teacher research practices

By monitoring the pre-service teachers' data from their use of the research framework, I gained a better understanding of my students' learning which informed my teaching. For my own teacher research, the data from Taryn discussed in the previous section was different from some of the other students in the class. Whereas some of the students were comfortable with the topic of "electricity" and learned from the activities, Taryn was confused and felt "stranded" by my teaching of the topic. She blamed her lack of understanding on her own personal lack of prior knowledge, the lack of clear explanations from me and her discomfort with the social aspect of being with other students that she did not know very well. For each weekly data set, I quickly became aware that it was not unusual to get a range of student responses to my teaching. Some of my insights into teaching as a result of this research are shown in Table 13.2.

Discussion and conclusion

Trainee teachers spend over 300 hours each year in university classes and I believe that some of this time should be spent on researching and theorizing about their own experiences as learners. The teacher research framework presented in this chapter provides a guide for students to study classroom relationships by focusing on personal, social and contextual influences on their own learning. The outcome is that all of the metaphors produced by the pre-service students had a combination of influences and many were connected with multiple arrows to represent the dynamics of classroom learning. It is clear from this study that the research framework encourages students to reflect upon teaching and learning as a relationship rather than as separate entities, which is so common in teacher education programs.

There are extra benefits for pre-service students when they use the WWW for the research framework. One benefit is that the web site helps students to document their research by using a template with fields for each of the four categories of factors – personal, teaching, peer and contextual – which act as cues to identify influences on their learning. Also the database has been designed to collate the weekly data which makes it easier for students to compare and contrast the factors to deduce their Learning Profile. These key factors are then used to label their metaphor. What is quintessential here is that pre-service students realize that it is always a *combination* of factors that influence classroom learning. Also, placing their data on the WWW allows students to share their learning experiences and helps them to understand that in any class there will always be different perspectives on the interactions that occur. It is the consideration of these different perspectives that enables a class to begin to act as a learning community.

There are, however, ethical considerations when pre-service students use this teacher research framework. When pre-service teachers study their own experiences as learners in university classes, they analyze real life relationships between teaching and learning. In this process, teacher educators like me expose their practice to critique from their own students.

Table 13.2 Insights from the student research with implications for my teaching

Insights from student research	Implications for my own teaching
• students do not experience the same learning in any tutorial	• try to interact with each student to monitor their learning
• students like a clear purpose for the lesson	• begin a lecture or tutorial with an advanced organizer in the form of points to be covered or a concept map
• students have different levels of prior knowledge about topics	• try different strategies to ascertain students' prior knowledge at the beginning of lessons
• students like to have a connection made between lectures and tutorial experiences	• ask students at the beginning of each tutorial about the main points from the lecture and what was confusing
• **students like me to know them as a person**	• take time to know each student personally and find out their interests
• learning does not happen in an instant and can be non-linear	• try to interact with students as much as possible and revisit ideas in different ways
• **use humor to build a relationship with the students in a class**	• tell anecdotes to illustrate points about teaching and try to relate to students' experiences
• students like to explore their own ideas	• encourage students to try out their ideas and learn from mistakes
• I cannot assume how students are thinking in my classes	• tap into students' ideas by listening to their feedback and be prepared to modify my teaching
• students like me to "practice what I preach"	• model different ways of teaching and justify why I teach the way I do
• students like a summary at the end of a class session	• conclude each class with a revision of "what did I learn"

Some teacher educators may be uncomfortable when making themselves vulnerable to criticism from their own students. But this models an understanding of the problematic nature of teaching and the importance of studying your own teaching practices (Hamilton and Pinnegar 1998). Some students, however, may not be comfortable in analyzing the teaching of their instructors for fear of some form of retribution. These students must have the right not to participate in these forms of self-research. Hence a level of trust needs to be generated between instructors and pre-service students if they are to be open about researching the relationship between teaching and learning.

I am the only person who saw all of the students' metaphors in the course as I marked their research. It would be valuable for the students to also share their metaphors by giving group presentations or by putting their diagrams and explanations on the World Wide Web. This would give students an opportunity to critique each other's metaphors to identify their strengths and limitations as well as demonstrating how there are always different interpretations of the same learning experience. Also, the web site currently does not have a field for me to make comments on my interpretation of my teaching and this will be added to the next version. Finally, it is my hope that the teacher research framework proposed in this paper will support students in better understanding Schön's (1983) metaphor of education as a "swamp." In this respect, I want pre-service students to think about classrooms as multi-dimensional contexts and "map the state of the swamp, and not just the anatomy of its alligators" (Biggs 1993: 74) to appreciate the complexity of classroom learning.

Acknowledgment

I am very grateful to my pre-service student, Taryn Conway, who gave me permission to use material from her research in this chapter.

Bibliography

Biggs, J. (1993) "From theory to practice: a cognitive systems approach," *Higher Education Research and Development*, 12, 1: 73–85.

Cochran-Smith, M. and Lytle, S. L. (1999) "The teacher research movement: a decade later," *Educational Researcher*, 28, 7: 15–25.

Duffy, T. M. and Cunningham, D. J. (1996) "Constructivism: implications for the design and delivery of instruction," in D. H. Jonassen (Ed.) *Handbook of Research for Educational Communications and Technology* (pp. 170–98), New York: Macmillan.

El-Tigi, M. and Marbe Branch, R. (1997) "Designing for interaction, learner control, and feedback during web-based learning," *Educational Technology*, 37, 3: 23–9.

Hamilton, M. L. and Pinnegar, S. (1998) *Reconceptualizing Teaching Practice: Self-study in Teacher Education*, London: The Falmer Press.

Hoban, G. F. (1998) "Reciprocating self-study: a reflective framework for conceptualising teaching-learning relationships," paper presented at the annual meeting of the American Educational Research Association, San Diego (ERIC Document Reproduction Service No. ED 423 216).

Hoban, G. F. (2000) "Using a reflective framework to study teaching-learning relationships," *Reflective Practice*, 2, 1: 165–83.

Lakoff, G. and Johnson, M. (1980) *Metaphors We Live By*, Chicago, IL: University of Chicago Press.

McCutcheon, G. and Jung, B. (1990) "Alternative perspectives on action research," *Theory into Practice*, 29, 3: 144–51.

Schön, D. A. (1983) *The Reflective Practitioner: How Professionals Think in Action*, New York: Basic Books.

Strauss, A. and Corbin, J. (1994) "Grounded theory methodology: an overview," in N. K. Denzin and Y. S. Lincoln (Eds) *Handbook of Qualitative Research* (pp. 273–85), London: Sage Publications.

Chapter 14

Problem-based learning as a research tool for teachers

Elizabeth Jordan, Marion Porath and Gillian Bickerton

Introduction

The roles of teacher and researcher can be very difficult to combine in the classroom. The main role of the teacher traditionally has been one of guiding, encouraging and challenging learners while at the same time juggling the logistics of a typical classroom situation. The notion of research within that tradition was one of collecting assignments and materials after students experienced certain learning conditions and then analyzing the resultant learning. Analyses of student learning were thus done *after* the process of learning had occurred. Assumptions then had to be made about what happened *during* the learning process.

A learning strategy called *Problem-Based Learning* (PBL) provides classroom teachers with the opportunity to take the two unique roles of teacher and researcher and merge them into a technique where the teacher-researcher becomes actively involved in the learning process itself. In many ways PBL validates and supports the type of role most good teachers demonstrate; that is, an effective teacher presents a problem, listens to the students, evaluates, and then provides feedback in an appropriate form. In this familiar classroom role there is active engagement between teacher and learner in the learning process, as well as in the outcome.

Definition of problem-based learning

Problem-based learning is a focused learning strategy based on real world problems where conditions and parameters vary; that is, the problem itself is ill-structured. Working together, students form problem solving groups that discuss the problem, generate hypotheses, identify learning issues, gather information, discuss topics and issues, negotiate understanding among themselves and find plausible solutions (Barrows and Myers 1993). When the problem is designed as one that is specifically engaging to the learners, as well as reflecting curricular goals and objectives, it makes the students stakeholders in their own learning. The learning environment shifts to one where the teacher takes on roles more in line with coaching, diagnosing and questioning rather than disseminating knowledge. By guiding students, basic knowledge is worked and reworked into higher levels of thinking for the student. In this way problem-based learning becomes multi-functional or flexible pedagogy.

For teacher-researchers the PBL technique provides a format requiring few shifts in philosophy or practice. However, while PBL validates and supports much of the work done by teachers in classrooms and provides a useful tool for teacher research, there is a critical shift in the role of the teacher that should be highlighted. The teacher moves from "delivering" or "covering" the curriculum to "setting the stage" for students to find and solve problems relevant to the topics in the curriculum and to themselves as learners. Before we present background on PBL and discuss its suitability for teacher research, it may be helpful to consider models of mind that underlie different teaching approaches (Bruner 1996) as a useful framework for thinking about the critical shift in the role of the teacher. How we conceptualize others' minds has incredible implications for how we teach (Bruner 1996).

- If we think of learners as needing to acquire skills via teacher demonstration and subsequent practice, we have a model of mind as imitative. The teaching focus is on skill sets, not understanding.
- If we think that once learners know the facts, they will be able to apply them effectively, we conceive of the learner's mind as a tabula rasa (blank slate) waiting to be filled with facts dispensed by teachers, books, and/or other knowledge sources.
- If we see children as *thinkers*, then we teach in a way that reflects our curiosity about children's understanding of the curriculum and schooling. This model of mind assumes the child's capacity to reason and engage in discussion. Teachers who possess this model of mind make an effort to understand how children think, how they reflect on their thinking, and how they remember and organize knowledge and learning.
- If we see children as needing to distinguish their own knowledge from the objective knowledge in their culture, then we teach in a way that unites the previous model of mind – children as *thinkers* – with study of the past. We help children to understand what distinguishes "personal knowledge" from cultural knowledge. We also strive to utilize children's ways of knowing in our instruction. We help them to build bridges between their own conceptions of knowledge and those of the culture.

The last model of mind best describes a problem-based approach to learning, teaching, and teacher research, and is consistent with the theoretical underpinnings of PBL.

Theoretical framework

Problem-based learning has its foundation in Constructivism. This theoretical framework concerns our understanding of how individuals construct knowledge, or how learning occurs, based on each individual's personal understandings and shared experiences. Within this theory, the learning process is:

> Viewed as a self-regulatory process of struggling with the conflict between existing personal models of the world and discrepant new insights, constructing new representations and models of reality as a human meaning-making venture with culturally developed tools and symbols, and further negotiating such meaning through cooperative social activity, discourse, and debate.
>
> (Fosnot 1996: ix)

Knowledge is then stored in interrelated networks that expand and become richer as new information and experiences require higher levels of thinking. Different ideas are added and interrelated, causing variations on interpretations (Fogarty 1997; Gijselaers 1996). When learners then encounter new problem situations they more readily retrieve relevant information and seek more knowledge about the situation while expanding their knowledge of content and conceptual background. This cannot be a solitary enterprise. Learning results from negotiating meaning, which occurs when people exchange ideas and thrash out problems. For example, the interpretation and value of information from written sources does not retain the same meaning between people (Smagorinsky 2001). Meaning is culturally derived by consensus. This is why researched materials need to be discussed and analyzed by a group in order to determine meaning (Meacham 2001). Thus, not only does learning occur from shared experiences but it also provides the meaning necessary to work with culturally based tools, such as books.

Main elements of problem-based learning

The main elements of PBL interconnect with the role of the teacher. In all instances the students are active, self-directed problem solvers.

1   The teacher selects the problem scenario based on curricular content, goals, and objectives, matching these with the skills, talents, needs, interests, and cognitive abilities of the students. This is known as curriculum matching, a component of effective teaching. The problem must be relevant to the students so that natural ownership can take place in finding a solution. Problem scenarios often can be artificial;

care must be taken that the problem is plausible so it becomes the students' problem and not the teacher's as most classroom problems remain. For this element of PBL, the teacher becomes a designer or tailor.

2   Students work on the problem, attempting to define the issue and identify those elements of the situation that need research. In this instance the teacher becomes a questioner and facilitator rather than a dispenser of facts. The object is to make the students question their knowledge and understanding of the topic. Often it is hard to watch as they go off on tangents, but this is a normal event in any problem-solving situation.

3   Students then start their research phase, accessing books and experts as they gather relevant facts. The teacher takes on a coaching role, encouraging learning and thinking beyond the facts or information at hand and challenging the students to think beyond a simple problem solution to an understanding of the complexity of the problem facts and situation.

4   The final aspect of PBL is negotiating meaning with the group as all of the members bring their understanding back to the original problem. Here the teacher's role is that of assessor, finding ways to understand the shared meaning of the students.

Becoming a teacher-researcher through problem-based learning

Why should one think about becoming a teacher-researcher? Furthermore, why use problem-based learning as a tool in the endeavor? Current research on how people learn (Donovan *et al.* 1999) identifies the importance of engaging students' preconceptions as a foundation for instruction. Without such engagement, learners may fail to understand the concepts and information taught or they may learn information "for the test" but revert to their preconceptions in dealing with real world issues. The practical implication is that effective teaching gives students the opportunities first to express their initial understandings and then to build on or challenge those understandings (Donovan *et al.* 1999). Problem-based learning affords students and teachers the opportunities to examine initial understandings and "ideas in progress" on the journey to deeper, expert-like understanding.

The teacher as researcher

The problem-based learning approach allows for two critical factors in teaching as research to be realized. The first is *engaging with phenomena* (Duckworth 1987). This step allows students to engage with the real world of the curriculum – to bring to the topics to be studied, in concrete ways, their own understandings and their own questions. Without such engagement, students will not learn in a meaningful way. (We would add that, without such engagement, teaching is far less exciting!) What questions do learners have about the topics in the curriculum? What prior knowledge do they bring to the learning endeavor? How can that knowledge be used as a foundation for the acquisition of the conventional knowledge of the discipline? The teacher's role thus shifts from dispenser of knowledge to one of active listening to learners (Paley 1986) for clues about their understanding of the world around them which, in turn, the teacher uses to guide his or her pedagogical practice. This is where the problems central to PBL come from. Students' preconceptions, ways of knowing, and questions form the basis of meaningful learning problems. The role of active listener thus is complementary to the second factor in teaching as research – *student explanations* (Duckworth 1987).

Students' explanations constitute part of their learning. They achieve clarity, raise questions, and determine what they need and want to understand through their explanations (Duckworth 1987). Thus, the teacher as active listener is not simply an entry-level activity. While it is true that initial understandings must be understood in order to be taken into account in facilitating learning, active listening is critical throughout the learning process. Learners differ in their interpretation and valuing of different sorts of knowledge (Smagorinsky 2001); these differences can be accounted for in learning and instruction if teachers are attentive to and respectful of them. Moreover, active listening is central to teacher research. By listening attentively and curiously to learners throughout the learning process, teachers become engaged in researching their own practice. How do learners respond to challenges to their preconceptions? How do learners represent their current and emergent knowledge? How do they explain themselves to others? These sorts of questions are *research questions*. They form the basis for formulating and testing hypotheses about individual approaches to learning. They provide clues as to methodology.

Although they may not have thought of their role in this way, effective teachers *are* researchers. To paraphrase Eleanor Duckworth (1987: 134), teachers could not possibly learn anything significant about education if they were not genuinely engaged in teaching practice. If we want to learn about our learners, we engage with them in learning and "try to make sense of it as it happens" (Duckworth 1987: 134). This activity is central to both teaching and research, and a critical aspect underlying it is teacher *curiosity* (Paley 1986). If teachers are truly curious about how the learners in their classrooms understand, think, and learn, they will make excellent researchers.

Having engaged with the learners in their classrooms, teachers find their questions "to be the same as those that a researcher into the nature of human learning wants to ask: What do you think and why?" (Duckworth 1987:

134). Teacher research requires, "as researcher, someone who knows ways into subject matter well enough to engage a great variety of learners, and to keep them going as they ask and answer further questions – that is, it requires someone who is a good teacher" (Duckworth 1987: 135). Teacher research requires excitement about the complexity of thinking and learning.

Problem-based learning for the teacher-researcher

Once teachers have laid the foundation for their research by having their students engage with phenomena and listening to their students' questions and explanations, they are ready for a problem-based learning project that will serve both as a teaching strategy and a foundation for research. In Table 14.1, we provide a general guide to the problem-based learning process for teacher-researchers and sample research questions.

Table 14.2 then provides a specific example of how the problem-based learning approach was used to teach and research children's understanding of buoyancy.

Teachers as researchers in the science classroom model the process of scientific inquiry and work collaboratively with the students through each science unit. Students engage in problem solving tasks that provide opportunities to confront the inconsistencies in their understanding. Teachers attend to student struggles to understand concepts by making invisible phenomena (e.g. density) "visible" through experimental investigations that are jointly designed by students and teacher.

Gillian Bickerton (2000) began her teacher research by engaging Grade One students in a discussion of their boating knowledge and experience. The general understanding that "all boats float" emerged. Bickerton now had a lead to follow in investigating the children's understanding of buoyancy. She became the researcher ascertaining her students' scientific knowledge while the students became scientists justifying their beliefs about why boats float. At the end of the discussion, both students and teacher became researchers and jointly formulated the research question: Why do boats float?

The students then became engaged in scientific research. They built different shapes and sizes of boats using different kinds of material. The teacher-researcher provided resources for the students and facilitated the young researchers' direction of inquiry. She drew attention to students' inconsistencies in their thinking or beliefs, and encouraged them to confront their contradictions by experimenting further. Students conducted a variety of experiments – both self-initiated and teacher-designed – to help them develop a basic understanding of what makes a boat buoyant. Children were encouraged to make predictions and provide explanations for why their boat floated or sank. Similarly, the teacher tested, modified, and reconstructed her practice, drawing upon the information she gleaned from the students.

Table 14.1 The problem-based learning process for teacher-researchers

	Problem-based learning: Steps in the technique	Teacher role	Researcher role	Research questions	Sample products
Designing the problem	Curriculum matching: Choose a relevant problem	Active listener Designer – matches student skills, talents, needs, interests, and cognitive ability with the curriculum	Formulate research questions Design research	What do students think about ____? What do students bring to their thinking in terms of skills and background? What relationship does this topic have to the curriculum? What factors keep interest high?	Observational data Annotated notes Checklists Teacher journal entries Student journal entries
Student engagement with the problem	Defining issues; defining elements that need research	Questioner Facilitator Challenges students to question their knowledge	Initial data gathering	What are students' preconceptions? How do other people really think about the problem?* Which ideas build on which others and how?* Which ideas get in the way of other ideas?*	Audiotapes Videotapes Meeting notes Student learning logs Teacher logs
Student research phase	Students access books, experts, and other sources of information to gather relevant facts	Coach Challenges students to expand their knowledge and to think at higher levels	Continue data gathering	What seem to be the critical barriers to their thinking?* How is an idea modified?* How does a firmly held conviction influence how a person reads an experience?"	Audiotapes Videotapes Meeting notes Student learning logs Teacher logs

(continued)

Table 14.1 The problem-based learning process for teacher-researchers (continued)

	Problem-based learning: Steps in the technique	Teacher role	Researcher role	Research questions	Sample products
				What is the range of conceptions covered by a "right-sounding" word or phrase?* In what circumstances is a person confused by/deaf to/helped by another person's thoughts?*	Sample student interviews with experts Sample text-based material First drafts of products (e.g. portfolio, poster, charts, speeches)
Students' Plausible Solutions	Students negotiate meaning	Assessor Understanding the students' shared meanings in their conversations and products	Data analysis	How does a specific representation of one's thoughts influence how the thoughts develop further?* How does a new idea lead to a new question and vice versa?*	Analysis and interpretation of students' products
Pedagogical Practice	Tool for inquiry	Teacher/Researcher: Enacting, reflecting, and modifying one's practice		How do my pedagogical practices enhance or constrain student learning?	Confirmation of some practices Modification of other practices Questions for future practice

* From Duckworth (1987: 134–5)

Table 14.2 Teaching and researching buoyancy in a problem-based framework

	Problem-based learning: Steps in the technique	Teacher role	Researcher role	Research questions	Sample products
Designing the problem	Curriculum matching: Boats are chosen as a way to learn about buoyancy.	To meet the provincial curriculum objectives for the physical sciences, children's understandings are taken as a starting point. Teacher listens actively as children hypothesize about what makes boats float.	Formulate general research question – What is the foundational understanding of buoyancy? Design learning and research tasks.	What do students think about the variables affecting buoyancy (e.g. weight, shape, volume)? How do different experiences with boats affect children's thinking (e.g. rowboats, car ferries)?	Observational data Annotated notes Children's drawings and explanations
Student engagement with the problem	Defining issues. Help students define research question: Why do boats float? In collaboration, formulate a hypothesis. Provide a few teacher-designed experiments to stimulate thinking about what makes an object buoyant.	Questioner Interviewer Use probes to ensure "sense-making" conversations (e.g. Why do you think so? What would happen if ____?)	Initial data gathering	What common understanding do the children demonstrate? How does their background knowledge and experience influence their reasoning and understanding? Do they make connections with different factors? Are there inconsistencies or contradictions in each student's understanding?	Record question and hypothesis for students to use as a guide when designing their own investigations and experiments. Initial data gathering: Students' plans – drawing of boat designs (e.g. shape, size, choice of materials).
Student research phase	1. Planning phase. Small group discussion to plan and design.	Interact and question. Encourage children to make predictions and justify them.	Continue data gathering	Evaluate boat designs. What happened when students had conflicting ideas about what determined a boat's buoyancy?	Observational data Anecdotal notes

Continued…

Table 14.2 Teaching and researching buoyancy in a problem-based framework (continued)

Problem-based learning: Steps in the technique	Teacher role	Researcher role	Research questions	Sample products
Use library resources on boats. Discuss boat construction. List materials. Experiment with different materials and designs. Make a decision on the final boat plan. 2. Boat construction.	Redirect thinking when predictions fail. Raise awareness of conflicting conceptions.		Did other children's ideas influence a student's conceptual understanding? Were students willing to change their thinking when their predictions were incorrect? Did students reflect on their incorrect predictions and come up with an explanation for why they were wrong? Did children change their beliefs to fit the evidence? How do children confront inconsistencies in their thinking? What seems to prevent children from changing their conceptual understanding? Does language present a critical barrier to children's understanding?	
Students' plausible solutions	Students negotiate meaning through hypothesis testing and sense-making conversations.	Assessor Understanding the students' shared meanings in their conversations and products.	Data analysis	Did children become problem seekers as well as solvers? Were children able to raise new research questions to further investigate their understanding of buoyancy?	Analysis and interpretation of students' boats and self-assessments.

continued....

Table 14.2 Teaching and researching buoyancy in a problem-based framework (continued)

Problem-based learning: Steps in the technique	Teacher role	Researcher role	Research questions	Sample products
				Analysis and interpretation of students' responses to questions and their predictions and justifications.
Pedagogical practice	Tool for inquiry into the critical factors offered by children in their explanations for buoyancy.	Teacher/Researcher: Enacting contextual support; reflecting on children's responses, hypotheses, and experiments; modifying resources, questions, degree of support, and teacher direction.	Did my challenges to inconsistency in reasoning further enhance or constrain student learning?	Teaching and learning log: Analysis and interpretation of responses to teacher questions. Analysis and interpretation of responses to teacher challenges to reasoning. Analysis and evaluation of possible alternative pedagogical strategies.

Conclusion

In this chapter, we suggested a tool – problem-based learning – that is useful in addressing the challenge of combining teaching and research simultaneously. There is theoretical support for the technique based on the most current research on how people learn. The table we provided on the problem-based learning approach to teacher research can serve as a jumping off point for stimulating your own thinking as teachers and researchers. Teachers are always engaged in research, even if not formally.

> The school and the classroom become the place where each individual is confronted with the need to explain his own knowledge – first of all to himself – in order to compare it, loan it, exchange it with others. This requires the teacher to be *inside* the context, fully participating, above all because she is curious to understand the various ways that children observe, interpret, and represent the world.
>
> (Rinaldi, 1997, p. 103)

Bibliography

Barrows, H. S. and Myers, A. C. (1993) *Problem Based Learning in Secondary Schools*, unpublished monograph, Springfield, IL: Problem Based Learning Institute, Lanphier High School, and Southern Illinois University Medical School.

Bickerton, G. (2000) *Children's Understanding of Scientific Concepts: A Developmental Study*, unpublished doctoral dissertation, University of British Columbia, British Columbia.

Bruner, J. (1996) *The Culture of Education*, Cambridge, MA: Harvard University Press.

Donovan, M. S., Bransford, J. D. and Pellegrino, J. W. (Eds) (1999) *How People Learn: Bridging Research and Practice*, Washington, DC: National Academy Press.

Duckworth, E. (1987) *The Having of Wonderful Ideas and Other Essays on Teaching and Learning*, New York: Teachers College Press.

Fogarty, R. (1997) *Problem-based Learning and Other Curriculum Models for the Multiple Intelligences Classroom*, Arlington Heights, IL: IRI/Skylight Training and Publishing, Inc.

Fosnot, C. T. (Ed.) (1996) *Constructivism: Theory, Perspectives, and Practice*, New York: Teachers College Press.

Gijselaers, W. H. (1996) "Connecting problem-based practices with educational theory," in L. Wilkerson and W. H. Gijselaers (Eds) *Bringing Problem-based Learning to Higher Education: Theory: No. 68* (pp. 13–21), San Francisco: Jossey-Bass Publishers.

Meacham, S. J. (2001) "Literacy at the crossroads: movement, connection, and communication within the research literature on literacy and cultural diversity," in W. G. Secada (Ed.) *Review of Research in Education, 25* (pp. 181–208), Washington, DC: American Educational Research Association.

Paley, V. G. (1986) "On listening to what the children say," *Harvard Educational Review*, 56: 122–31.

Rinaldi, C. (1997) "A measure for friendship," in M. Castagnetti and V. Vecchi (Eds) *Shoe and Meter* (pp. 101–3), Municipality of Reggio Emilia: Reggio Children.

Smagorinsky, P. (2001) "If meaning is constructed, what is it made from? Toward a cultural theory of reading," *Review of Educational Research*, 71: 133–69.

Chapter 15

Poetic moments in the classroom

Poetry as a tool for teacher research and professional development

Amanda Nicole Gulla

I am a staff developer in a small school district in New York City. This is the story of how writing poetry has helped me to understand my interactions with teachers and reflect on my practice. It is also the story of what has happened when I have shared some of these poems with some of the teachers I've worked with in a professional development context.

Cochran-Smith and Lytle (1993) define teacher research as: "Systematic and intentional inquiry carried out by teachers" (p. 7). I came to do this research as a result of pursuing for the last several years the question of how it is that teachers become teachers. When I began this journey, I was studying my own learning process as a classroom teacher, after having been one for fourteen years.

There must be at least a hundred different ways in which the question of how teachers become teachers could be addressed, and each one would tell part of the story. Where do these impressions of "Teacher" come from? What are teachers drawing on when they take charge of their classrooms?

Over time I narrowed these questions down to the role staff development plays in a teacher's learning process. In the beginning I was interested in studying the staff development experiences I'd had, and trying to understand the role of these experiences in my classroom practice. I thought of professional development as a kind of alchemy of reading, formal and informal study, and interactions with peers and mentors.

This study had brought me through the coursework for a PhD in education. When I began working on this degree, I was a teacher of kindergarten and then second grade. I completed my degree candidacy requirements by writing a paper in which I explored questions about my own professional development in light of what the literature in the field of teaching and learning had to say.

In the midst of this scholarly personal adventure, an opportunity took me by surprise. A small school district, adjacent to the one in which I was at that time teaching second grade, was in the process of creating a new Professional Development Center. A week before the 1999–2000 school year was to begin, I was offered a job as a staff developer. This would provide me with a completely different perspective on the issues that I intended to study. Instead of conducting teacher research on the question of what staff development practices were most useful to me as a classroom teacher, I became involved in researching my teaching practices as a staff developer. In fact, there was really very little difference in the way I defined my new role. I still taught in classrooms, except the students were both the children in the room and their teachers.

There is ample precedent for self-study as a subject of teacher research. Dewey (1904) argued that teachers should be "adequately moved by their own ideas and intelligence" (p. 16). According to Cochran-Smith and Lytle (1993), "Berthoff (1987) puts little emphasis on data gathering and instead asserts that teachers already have all the information they need and should reexamine – or, in her words, 'REsearch' – their own experiences" (p. 9). Margot Ely (1991) tells us that, "All re-search is me-search."

In order to place myself back in the shoes of a first year teacher, I began to reconstruct the memory of my first days as a teacher by writing. I remembered in those first days as a junior high school English teacher feeling totally unprepared to take charge of a classroom. This led me to wonder what sort of magic gave teachers the confidence to at least look like they believed they knew what they were doing. I conjured up an image of my own childhood teachers, which led me to write this poem (Gulla 2001):

> Uncertainty
> As a little girl in the second row,
> hands clasped on worn wooden desk,
> I never guessed that teaching
> was an uncertain profession.
> The crisp woman with planbook poised on palm ...
> Did she ever wonder
> what she was doing there?
>
> I take her place
> in sneakered feet.
> We sit in clusters, circles,
> sprawl on floor,
> not planted like rows of cabbage.
> Sometimes I wish I had
> that big book of certainty
> my teachers possessed.
> I know less and less.
> I am just beginning to know
> the questions.

This poem became the prologue to my candidacy paper. When I shared the poem with fellow doctoral students and faculty members, several commented that they could picture the central figure of the poem, whose authority depended on projecting the image of absolute self-assurance. The more I thought about the idea that one could be absolutely certain of the curriculum and teaching methods before getting to know the students, the more I thought that some degree of uncertainty was an essential part of a healthy classroom. In this case, the experience of writing this poem caused an issue that has become rather important to my work to bubble up to the surface. I began to suspect that there were a lot of teachers who believed that it was their role to project an air of absolute certainty in the classroom.

I saw the role of staff developer as a critical friend (McDonald 1996: 237). As I helped teachers to reflect on their practices, I also needed to reflect on my own practice. Remembering once again the image of the "crisp woman with planbook poised on palm," I made a conscious decision to approach the teachers with whom I'd be working by offering myself as a supportive partner in inquiry, rather than as an expert. In this role, I talked with and observed teachers to determine what their needs were and how I could best help them develop their practice.

During my first week as a staff developer, I met a fourth grade teacher named Darlene[1] who was completely new to public schools. In my observations of her classrooms, and in our conversations, I saw her struggling with issues of control. She would set aside time for what she called journal writing, but she would assign the topic and insist that the children strictly adhere to it. She told me she wanted to encourage class discussions, but she controlled all the talk by asking all the questions and not allowing children to talk except when they were directly speaking to her. Rather than telling her what I thought she was doing and why and how I thought she should do it differently, I thought it might be helpful to find a different way to share reflections on the beliefs that were informing her practice. I started out by asking her to describe what she wanted the children in her class to be able to do. Her initial response was: "To be able to sit and listen to directions, and enjoy the learning." After a pause, she added:

> When I have control, I can see what they can do. I want to be able to put them in groups. I want them to be able to be creative, but sometimes you just have to do what you are told. I'll give them moments during the day to do what they want.

This view of the classroom, that the teacher must maintain control and doles out "moments" during the day, seemed consistent with the idea that the teacher should be absolutely in charge, absolutely certain of what should be happening in the classroom every moment of the day. It made me wonder how she might respond to the idea that there might actually be some benefit to being less certain of exactly what should be going on in the classroom at all times. I wanted to find a way to introduce the idea that a little bit of uncertainty could lead to authentic student engagement in the learning process, not to the chaos she obviously feared.

I decided to take a chance and share the poem *Uncertainty*, with her. I pulled it out of my backpack, and she read it, and had very little to say other than, "You wrote this? It's very nice." I judged from this response that the experiment had fallen fairly flat. A week later, though, I saw her and she said "I was thinking about that poem you wrote." I waited expectantly for evidence of some deep soul searching. "The kids kind of do look like cabbages when they're all in rows like that." Well, it was a response, at least. "You think so?" I asked, not sure where this was leading. "Yeah, I do. I decided to seat them in clusters, to see how it goes for a while." Hmmm. So maybe she really was open to rethinking aspects of her practice. Maybe presenting her with a visual metaphor in the form of a poem helped convince her that change was both possible and desirable.

We continued to develop a working relationship over the next two years. Although many of our views about teaching and learning were at opposite ends of the spectrum, her willingness to engage with me, in discussions, brainstorming, storytelling, and arguments, made working with her a rewarding experience. As long as she was willing to make her beliefs explicit, I would do my best to hold up a mirror for her to examine them. As long as she was willing to share her struggles, I was happy to lend an ear.

I began keeping a field log in order to keep track of the work I was doing with each teacher, and as a way of holding myself accountable for the work I was doing. The field log is essentially a running narrative of conversations with teachers and administrators, observations of teachers, and my plans for and reflections upon demonstration lessons that I gave. The purpose of the log was to enable me to reflect on my practice, and to understand what was working and what wasn't. By having a document that contained a detailed account of my unfolding relationships with teachers and my observations of them over the course of the academic year, I could look at the impact the work was having on classrooms. Over the course of my first year as a staff developer, I filled several notebooks with raw data. At the end of the year I looked back over the logs to see what they told me about the work I'd done. Many of the logs were transcripts of conversations with teachers, or as much as I could remember after rushing to jot them down as soon as I could.

The next poem I shared with Darlene was drawn from a conversation we had, which I had written about in my log. I was so struck by the force of her emotion that I wrote this poem based on direct quotations I'd written down after meeting her during lunch for one of our walks around the block as she smoked and vented her frustrations:

The System[2]

"How can I do something I don't believe in?" she asks,
This child reads at a second grade level,
can be promoted to fifth grade
if she masters thirty five percent of third grade work.
 "How is this supposed to be helping kids?"
The numbers are beginning to weigh her down.
"What good are standards
if they keep promoting kids that aren't learning?"
In the Peace Corps, she got in trouble
for jumping fences into homeless camps to bring food and blankets.
She sat with families along railroad tracks
sharing cans of beans.
"The Washington office got angry,
because they said I was in danger."
Her voice rises and her hand
pauses mid gesture
to push the hair from her eyes
"Until they have really helped homeless people,
they shouldn't be telling me how to do it!"
We stand next to the garbage-strewn lot
across the street from school
She finishes her story and her third cigarette.
She tosses the cigarette into the street and laughs,
"I don't know why I let you keep talking me out of quitting."

I was hesitant to share this poem with her. I had no idea how she'd respond to this portrait, which I had to acknowledge was subjective. Although the words and gestures were authentically hers, by my shaping them into a poem I recognize that I was putting my imprint on the experience. I worried that she might feel I was violating the privacy of our conversation, so I reassured her that the poem could just be between us, if she insisted on that. In any case, I told her, no one would ever know that it was about her unless she told them. As she read it, her eyes widened. "You really got me!" she said, "This is exactly how I feel. And you're right. The numbers *are* wearing me down." "I'm glad you feel that it captures you," I said. But I wanted it to mean more than that, so I asked, "Do you think reading this poem helps you have any insight into the situation?"

She responded that it was interesting that I'd written about the Peace Corps alongside her complaining about what was happening to her student.

I pointed out that she had done that, in the original telling. "Maybe I'm just always going to be frustrated by any system," she said. I asked what that meant to her. She smiled. "Well, I've always managed to get around it before. Maybe I'm always going to be frustrated because I feel like they're not doing the right thing and I could do better, but maybe there is some other way around it." It could just be that this poem helped her to reflect on a situation that might have appeared like a closed door to her before.

According to Margot Ely: "[a poem] encapsulates the essence of an event that many of us have lived in our own way at one time or another ... the intensity and compression of poetry emphasizes the vividness of [a] moment" (Ely *et al.* 1997: 135). For many years, I have made sense of experiences by capturing them in poetic form. Poetry is the means through which I have sought to represent the universal in the personal and the personal in the universal. By carving poems out of the field logs, dialogue journals, and interviews, I am searching for issues that are embedded within the experiences captured in the raw data.

Seeing her story about the Peace Corps juxtaposed against her story of the student being promoted told me something about her perception of herself as someone who was often at odds with "the system." This facet of her personality was central to her identity as a teacher, and it was stripping the dialogue into the bare form of a poem that helped me to see it. It seemed that seeing her own story reflected back to her in the form of a poem helped her to realize this about herself too. The other thing that became abundantly clear was the important role of numbers in her relationship with "the system." The story about the student is full of numbers. It suggested to me that numbers were important data for this teacher. All of this helped me to understand her a bit better, which could in turn help me to be a better critical friend.

This next poem, called *A Meeting in Six Voices* (Gulla 2002), is one I chose not to share with its subjects. It seemed too loaded, and to present them in too unflattering a light. I did not have the sense that any of the participants in that meeting would have been receptive. The eponymous meeting was my initial introduction to the staff members with whom I was supposed to be working. I sensed throughout this meeting that there were some strong but unstated opinions of the children in question, and their capabilities. Writing this poem helped me to tease out these attitudes by making me consciously look for words that were emphasized and repeated, and for ideals that were contradicted or diminished by negatives, such as "nothing beautiful," "they will never be brilliant" and "I can't make them Hemingways." This was important information for me to consider in my staff development work there, since the principal had asked me to work with this specific group of teachers whom she had identified as leaders on developing Writers' Workshops in their classrooms. The first section, which appears in italic, represents my thoughts. The rest of the poem is made up of direct quotations from the teachers who participated. Each different font represents a different staff member of this school:[3]

A Meeting in Six Voices

Surrounded by the principal's peeling peach walls
Five teachers at the long wooden table
Silently wait for me to explain my presence
They are a phalanx of guardians
And I circle their tower
Looking for a way in…

How can I help?
They can't write…
… don't use vocabulary
They don't use vocabulary?
Simplistic sentences
But they have something to say.
How can they write?
They still say "mines"…
I think I see …
…no matter how many times I correct them?
BLACK ENGLISH …
What are you saying?
IT'S A DIALECT.
I want to show them the correct way.
Look, I can't make them Hemingways
They will never be brilliant
I can teach kids like these to write a sentence…
All they can learn is a sentence.
JUST WHO DO WE MEAN BY "THEY?"
You know exactly who I mean.
I just want them to pass the test.
…NOTHING BEAUTIFUL, BUT IT PASSES THE TEST.
These kids have something to say…
If she's got such strong kids…
I KNOW THOSE KIDS.
THEY'RE NOT SO STRONG.

The purpose of this poem was really to help me gain some clarity on what I thought were the subtexts beneath what was being said. I chose poetry as a way of analyzing this particular moment in time because as the meeting was taking place, I was aware of a palpable tension, which I attempted to capture by jotting down what was said.

Writing poetry for me resembles sculpting in that I carve distinct shapes from the larger body of text. These shapes, their meaning and their importance may be entirely subjective. Nevertheless, what I see when I set out to turn an experience into a poem is what I need to learn to move forward in the work at hand. "The poet's business is to … create the semblance of events lived and felt … a piece of virtual life" (Langer 1953: 212).

Poetry may not seem like a natural tool for everyone to use. The raw materials of poems are everywhere, however. Daphne Patai (1988) describes a method of creating poems by using only a person's taped and transcribed speech. The line breaks come from a person's breaths and pauses, the emphasis is theirs; we as the poets are composing a verbal snapshot, leaving ourselves as much out of the picture as possible. At the end of the year, I wanted to gather and record some information from the teachers I'd been working with on what staff development experiences seemed important or helpful to them, and what seemed like a waste of their time. I recorded our conversations with their permission, then later transcribed the tapes. The teachers knew that parts of these conversations might be included in the data I used for my dissertation. As Diane Halaman, a teacher I quoted in my dissertation (2002),[4] said, "Sure, go ahead and quote me. It's about time *somebody* asked us what was helpful." Here is a poem composed using Daphne Patai's method. The teacher's words are in standard Palatino font, with bold for emphasis, and mine are in italics:

Stories I

I think if I didn't have anybody…
or any teacher didn't have anybody to vent to
…I think that is sooooo important! **So** important!
Because…you know
it helped me put things into perspective a bit more.
Um…and not…
you know I was able to sort of control myself a little bit more
when I went back to the classroom.
And that is **so** important.
So just like being able to…to let it out?
Yeah. And share stories
so I know that I'm not the only one that this is happening to,
you know what I mean?
Do you find that stories are helpful?
Absolutely!
Absolutely.
You know…
You don't feel like you're alone.

One of my favorite poets, William Carlos Williams, was a country doctor who wrote his poems on prescription pads as he was traveling to see his patients. He documented patients' narratives about their lives to help him better understand the nature of their ailments. As I travel from school to school, I gather teachers' stories in an effort to understand their beliefs about teaching and learning and the children they work with. From the very beginning, my instincts told me that capturing these stories and giving them back to the tellers would be an important part of encouraging them to reflect on their practices. In this, I can't help but identify with Robert Coles (1989) as he imagines Williams saying: "Their story, yours, mine – it's what we all carry with us on this trip we take, and we owe it to each other to respect our stories and learn from them" (p. 13).

Writing poems and sharing them with the teachers I work with is one way of letting teachers know that someone is listening. Their classroom stories contain a wealth of information, and reflecting on the knowledge they already possess can do more for their teaching practice than any teacher-proof curriculum ever could. The stories we carry can be tools for growth for both the teller of the story and the critical friend who listens to her words and hands them back in a carefully crafted form. Poems are a powerful way of capturing and reflecting these narratives. When I began to write poems about teaching and learning, it was out of a desire to make sense of this world. Sharing some of these poems with teachers has given me a way to get teachers to consider the possibility of change. As one teacher, Odetta James,[5] said:

> When somebody tells me I should change how I teach, that's meaningless to me. I figure I'm the only one that knows what's going on in my classroom, after all. But when you really listen to me and you write it down like that and show me what I've said, it gets me to really think about what I'm doing, and I think that's something that has really made me grow as a teacher and as a person.

Notes

1   A pseudonym. Darlene signed a letter of permission to quote her in my dissertation and in this chapter.
2   This poem was used in my dissertation proposal, and is likely to be included in the final dissertation.
3   Although the poem was not shared with teachers in its entirety, the teachers who are quoted have signed letters giving me their permission to use their words in my dissertation.
4   All teacher names are pseudonyms. Teachers quoted have signed letters of permission, available on request.
5   As quoted in "So I know I'm not alone" (Gulla 2002).

Bibliography

Cochran-Smith, M. and Lytle, S. (1993) *Inside Outside: Teacher Research and Knowledge*, New York, NY: Teachers College Press.

Coles, R. (1989) *The Call of Stories: Teaching and the Moral Imagination*, Boston, MA: Houghton Mifflin.

Dewey, J. (1904). "The relation of theory to practice in education," in C. A. McMurry (Ed.) *The Relation of Theory to Practice in the Education of Teachers* (third yearbook of the National Society for the Scientific Study of Education, Part I), Chicago: University of Chicago Press.

Ely, M. (1991) *Doing Qualitative Research: Circles Within Circles*, London, England: Falmer Press.

Ely, M., Vinz, R., Downing, M., and Anzul, M. (1997) *On Writing Qualitative Research: Living by Words*, London, England: Falmer Press.

Gulla, A. (2001) "A constructive approach to professional development for teachers," unpublished doctoral candidacy paper, New York University, New York.

Gulla, A. (2002) "'So I know I'm not alone:' the use of story in teachers' professional development," unpublished dissertation, New York University, New York.

Langer, S. (1953) *Feeling and Form*, New York, NY: Charles Scribner & Son.

McDonald, J. (1996) *Redesigning School: Lessons for the 21st Century*, San Francisco: CA: Jossey-Bass.

Patai, D. (1988) *Constructing a Self: A Brazilian Life Story*, Feminist Studies, Inc. University of Maryland, College Park, MD.

Chapter 16

Experiences of fear and pain in teaching

A collaborative arts-based inquiry

Susan Walsh

I have lived through survived frequently thought I was
being swallowed up by the mounds of paper on my desk in
my mailbox in the door at home just waiting for my
attention on the e-mail on the phone just waiting and I
don't hear any sirens blaring making me jump going off
telling me that I've goofed up again that I've screwed up
that I've messed up that I've failed I should have known I
could have known but I didn't know beginner's lament
swamped bombarded by the information whizzing
past me I watch people's lips move hear the cacophony of
sounds spewing from their mouths but I don't
hear anything

> stumble bum
> frozen insides
> icy innards
> sunny smile on the outside
> now what?
> stop?
> go?
> energy flow
> out of control out of control
> they know
> they know
> they know
> stumble bum

stumble, like *Alice in Wonderland*
a metaphor for having to fit go through a
keyhole fitting through metamorphosis
having to transform to fit
someone else's image

Figure 16.1

my department head had this
way of teaching that was
totally about rules she wanted
everybody in her mold she'd
come in sit through classes
and then she'd critique you

my principal introduced me
to the staff as someone who
had been out of teaching for
14 years wasn't sure if I
could do this anymore letting
everyone know here's this
person she's been out for 14
years so watch out for
any problems

fear
fear of being a victim in
a corridor war
fear of a drugged
student who kept on

wanting more
fear of what words pushed him
to the edge of hate
to make him dance and
scream I fear I
may be bait

spheres ominous spheres she
just happens to be in the path of
angry spheres they all come
crowding down on her but
underneath in this little
place little hiding hole she
can be safe

Figure 16.2

a colleague has said that the
student's mother is quite
crazy might sue if

all these different little boxes the
fragmentation that nobody really
fits inside of overlapping cutting
off different parts of
the person but nothing really is
there for the whole person who
needs help the teacher trying
to help the maze fragmentation

Figure 16.3

The preceding words and images serve to introduce some of the themes and concerns that emerged over the course of a year as a group of women teachers met to explore their experiences of fear and pain in teaching through writing, painting, drawing, sculpture and other forms of art. Our insights, as we shared our own stories and responded to the stories of others, were both personal and collective. Each woman came away from the group having worked with and through her own concerns: for example, a difficult relationship with an administrator, the fear that ensues from dealing with explosive and unpredictable students, and the uncertainty that comes with learning to teach. Our teacher research was a collaborative inquiry process that enabled us to rewrite our experiences of teaching, to begin to reinterpret what had previously been transparent, taken-for-granted. Through our process of art-making, writing, and talk, we were able to revise personal perspectives as well as to identify collective themes. The purpose of this chapter is to briefly describe our research process and then to outline some of the preliminary themes that emerged.

Nine women teachers participated in the investigation; I was a participant-researcher in the process.[1] My background includes teaching primarily at the middle and high school levels in English, drama, and French, and, in recent years, teaching undergraduate teacher education courses. We all have experience teaching at the secondary and/or tertiary level, and some have also taught elementary school. One member of the group is retired while another is in her second year of teaching. Several have administrative and/or counseling experience. Subject area specialties range from English, French, and social studies, to physical education, health, career and technology studies, art, drama, dance and special education. Some of the members have previous experience as health care professionals, and some have worked in schools as artists-in-residence.

The group was varied in terms of background and teaching experience – though we are all close to the same age.

The work in our group was primarily about bringing to the surface some taken-for-granted notions in teaching – as well as some of our taken-for-granted ways of knowing and being in the world – problematizing what seems transparent. The focus on experiences of fear and pain in teaching provided us with creative opportunities, potential moments when perspectives could be transformed, altered. Through this research, we hoped to explore what Britzman refers to as "the underside of teaching, the private struggles we engage as we construct not only our teaching practices and all the relationships this entails, but our teaching voices and identities" (Britzman 1991: 1). The research design was informed by work in at least three different areas: first, by the solid tradition of women writers who use writing as a means of exploring and transforming fear and pain, both personally and collectively (see, for example, Brandt 1996; Cixous 1993; Wolf 1988); second, by the growing area of arts-based research where different art forms provide ways of exploring, collecting, and representing what was called "data" in a more positivistic research paradigm (see, for example, Diamond and Mullen 1999; Eisner 1997; Richardson 1992),[2] and third, by my understanding of and experience with women's groups as well as feminist theory and practice (see, for example, Christ 1986; Chung 1992; Irigaray 1992, 1993, 1994, 1996; Shildrick 1997; Weedon 1987).

The actual process we followed in our group meetings was influenced primarily, in the early stages, by the research of Haug et al. (1987) and Arelis (1995) and their work with women in groups. Haug's (1987) study centers on the writing and memories of women who explore themes of female sexualization; Arelis' research (1995), which is based on Haug's, explores women's early reading experiences and how they shape gendered identity. While Haug acknowledges the role of storytelling in women's consciousness-raising groups, she goes beyond its circularity where "we could progress no further" and where "no one wanted to listen any more" to a culling of memory through writing and an ensuing process of questioning, contradiction, and rewriting (Haug 1987: 39). This aspect of transformation, of coming to see the experiences in a different way, is particularly pertinent to our work. In Haug's research, a woman would begin by writing an important image related to the theme and then would describe in detail associated images, memories, feelings, and events that came to mind – all in third person as a means of creating distance. She shared her writing with the group, and others responded through discussion. The woman would then rework her story "*against* the interpretations of others" (Haug 1987: 57), adding further detail.

In our group, we loosely used Haug's process as we attempted to rewrite our experiences of fear and pain in teaching. There were significant differences, however. We used spontaneous writing, art, and conversation (consciousness-raising and beyond) as methods for moving below the surface of how we interpreted our teaching experiences. Our initial practice was to begin with some kind of introductory activity – sometimes brainstorming or listening to a reading. We would then write about an experience that somehow connected to fear and pain in teaching, after which one person would volunteer to share her writing. The group listened and sometimes discussed the incident. Next, we responded to the shared piece of writing. Responses took the form of writing, water color painting, drawing in pencil, pencil crayons, pastels, sculpture with playdough and Lego, work with fabrics, and even tableaux – a form of drama. We then finished up with comments and/or discussion.

There are many ways of categorizing the major images and themes that emerged over the course of our work together. For the purposes of this paper, I have divided the discussion into three parts – Eyes, Blood, and Ears – an organization that seems appropriate because it is grounded in physicality. As such, it reminds us that "teacher" is the name given to the lived experiences of real people in particular contexts, a multidimensional construct that occupies space and time. Eyes, Blood, and Ears signal too a dynamic movement through emerging themes and the interconnectedness of these. In a contradictory way, the distinctions of Eyes, Blood, and Ears also sever the body – and thus underline the fragmentation and isolation that "teacher" can also mean.

Eyes

The notion of teacher as a simple and clearly defined role[3] is one that is reinforced through overfamiliarity – almost everyone has gone to school in our society (Britzman 1991: 5–7). Teacher, as role, exists among expectations that often don't fit, that might be conflicting, and that are largely unquestioned. From where do such expectations come? "Expectation" is a word that emerged early in our research study, during a prewriting activity, and one that surfaced a number of times throughout. The tension of living and working in a system of expectations, rules, packages, and boxes that don't always fit either teachers or students becomes evident – as do teachers' discomfort and fear of not fitting, of not doing or knowing what they are "supposed to" – of not meeting amorphous and often contradictory expectations. Britzman discusses cultural myths that surround teaching, the "set of ideal images, definitions, and justifications that are taken up as measures for thought, affect, and practice" and that seem" complete and [speak] for [themselves]" (Britzman 1991: 6). She further suggests that "cultural myths partly structure the individual's taken-for-granted views of power, authority, knowledge, and identity. They work to cloak the more vulnerable condition of learning to teach and the myriad negotiations it requires" (Britzman 1991: 7). The following collage of found poetry culled from the transcripts and images created by the group members over the course of our research serves to demonstrate the lived experiences of teachers living amid the complexity of conflicting and nebulous expectations. As an image, eyes predominate.

> you have to perform in
> front of these people and if
> you stumble you're going to fall
> off and the swirliness
> is like the environment that you're
> in unsure you don't know
> what you're doing if only you
> could get out of this swirling mass of
> all these eyes looking at you

the cool look and
the arched eyebrow

a clown the
performance hoops
and balls and flowers
and all these tricks
that you try to keep
going but we all know
that it's not really real

Figure 16.4

the juxtaposition of
the happy and the sad
I'm not really sure if
it was sadness as much as
feeling insecure about
being able to cope and
the colors the reds and
the yellows are always the
heat all these people expecting
something pulling you in

and the eyes again
always there

you have the eyes of your stakeholders your
community your administrators your everyone your
peers and the kids themselves looking at and
looking at you

and your eyes are
looking evaluating

Blood

Blood – the blood of the teacher – emerged as a striking image when Jessica shared her experiences of teaching grade eight science; violence and physical fear had surfaced a short time earlier with Marie's story of an enraged student. The bloody images have stayed with me; they underline the emotional intensity with which some teaching experiences are imbued – not a topic much explored in educational research – and perhaps not an image that would have emerged without art as part of our inquiry process. In some of these responses, the teacher's blood is leaking while the door is closed – an image that underlines the isolation that teachers can feel in bearing the intensity of some of their experiences – something that can be internalized as one's own inadequacy or incompetence. *And always I looked to, blamed myself. What could I have done differently?*

the class goes on
it's just very quiet
very subtle she's leaking
but the class goes on

Figure 16.5

blood *Lord of the Flies*
one of our teachers had given
up last year this is her
head on a stake now they're after another
teacher who's trying to get behind
the desk she's got licorice sticks and they've
got their little hatchets she's got her books
and she's trying to run away from them and
she's got the clock she's trying to get to
10:30 because that's break time

Figure 16.6

I feel the almost military strength of
the group of 28 of them and that
sense that the door is closed and
the blood is all on their hands to
some degree the police report
we found her body by the door
everyone sitting in perfect order they
all had a little blood on their hands
but we have no idea what the murder
weapon was there's no
murder weapon

Figure 16.7

Ears

The image of ears is important in our work as well, ears that can listen, be present to what is happening. This image is connected to the earlier exploration of eyes and expectation. The word "expectation" comes from the Latin root *spec-tare* which means to look, to see, to await (OED) and is therefore etymologically related to the image of eyes. The idea of looking, awaiting, also signals the importance of moving toward something that is finished, an ideal, something to strive for – a teleological orientation. The image of ears, however, arose in response to Rebecca's story about listening, listening to the screaming of a frustrated elderly woman in a nursing home. Listening and the image of ears signal a different way of being, one not oriented towards the future or what should be, but one that acknowledges what is. A way of knowing and being often infused with uncertainty, ambiguity.

a student was working in a nursing home
and one of the patients would spend
a great deal of time screaming she
took notice of what prompted
the patient to start screaming the lady

was very arthritic could not use her hands
was lying in bed one afternoon the student
wheeled the lady to the unit to sit beside her

screaming just trying to
get someone's attention
someone that will listen

too busy teaching afraid
to look any deeper too
busy with other aspects
of teaching which is
as you find out early
the curriculum and
responsibilities there

I have this wonderful
room at home
a collection of everything
and lots of things not neat orderly
you have to watch where
you step some days maybe I just
need that messiness sometimes because
so many other things have to be
lined up in a row you're supposed
to have the answers you're
supposed to know

Figure 16.8

listening an ear and the things
that are hanging above our heads
pushing down on us and
all this wonderful messiness
underneath that we're not
listening to

Does our discomfort with messiness and not-knowingness and also our inability to trust process emanate from our preoccupation with the future, with expectations, eyes pressing in on us? How can we be comfortable in not-knowing when we are striving towards an ideal of some sort, an expectation that might be nebulous, unclear, taken-for-granted? Following is an excerpt from something Rebecca said about one of her pieces of writing.

> mine was all about fitting in not feeling
> like I fit in there wasn't a fit
> you had to match I wasn't
> included in our curriculum discussions
> I didn't fit into that group I wasn't seen and
> I've internalized all of this as my not knowing
> something not being good not meeting
> expectations of others not having
> the right answer (like there's a right
> answer all the time) and because I
> don't have it it's my fault because I didn't
> study the right thing didn't look hard
> enough or something else
>
> it's not about the process the living and
> being in this world in the way we
> are it's always about knowing
> more knowing enough

The discomfort of not-knowing is a key theme in talking about expectations. Uncertainty doesn't fit – can't be categorized, organized, broken into bits, made discernible – and can therefore cause fear, pain. Many have questioned a way of knowing and being that rests on the objective knowability of things when they are broken down small enough – and hence, the separation between "knower" and what is "known." Theorists from many different disciplines have investigated such assumptions (see, for example, Lazreg 1994; Lennon and Whitford 1994; Shildrick 1997; Stanley 1997; Tomm 1995; Weedon 1987 in feminist theory, Fox 1995; Christ 1986; Chung 1992 in theology; Palmer 1998 in theology/education; Schaef 1998 in psychology) – and have asked important questions about the knower, the "who" – what s/he purports to know – and how. The illusion of objectivity has not served us well as teachers. Britzman, for example, outlines the cultural myth of "teacher as expert" – and the attendant beliefs that knowledge can be broken down into small enough bits that we can transmit it via a set of discernible steps and through a methodology we can learn in teacher education (Britzman 1991: 91, 227–8). In our research process, we delved into difficult teaching experiences, eschewing a subject-object division through working in community and through art-making. Complexity and uncertainty became apparent, though themes emerged. Among these, Eyes, Blood, and Ears serve to foreground the physicality of teaching, a groundedness that juxtaposes seemingly contradictory positions – interconnectedness and fragmentation/separation. As teachers, as researchers, we must continue to work with ways that take us into our lived experiences, find the courage to reinterpret taken-for-granted ways of knowing and being in the world.

it's spiraling partly
protecting yourself but gradually building
building on the knowledge you
got at the beginning building
developing this thick skin as
you gain a great deal of knowledge and then
for some reason a sense of breaking down
a possibility

Figure 16.9

and she surprised the department
head shed her skin performed
magic tricks spoke in tongues and
the department head fainted
dissolved disappeared
and students' faces came
into focus shock imprinted
on every face but they were
totally present

Notes

1 The research described in this chapter is my doctoral research. Though I initiated the questions of the study, the work became more and more collaborative as the process unfolded. The women involved directed the course of the research in various different ways. For more about the collective aspect of the work, see Walsh 2001a.

2 In particular, see Reason and Hawkins (1988), an early arts-based study in which a group of people explored experiences of gender through responding to one another's stories in a language-based way.

3 The tension between teacher role and identity, between living what one "should" do and having the voice to express how one truly feels or sees him/ herself is one that the teachers in a pilot study group I conducted felt keenly (see Walsh, 2001b). Britzman (1992, 1991) makes a distinction between teacher *role* and *identity*.

> Role speaks to function whereas identity voices investments and commitments. Function, what one should do, and investments, or what one feels, are often at odds. The two are in dialogic relation and it is this tension that makes for the "lived" experience of teacher.
>
> (Britzman 1992:29)

Bibliography

Arelis, D. (1995) "Bookmarks: girlhood reading that marked us women," unpublished Master's thesis, University of Lethbridge, Alberta.

Brandt, D. (1996) *Dancing Naked: Narrative Strategies for Writing Across Centuries*, Stratford, ON: Mercury Press.

Britzman, D. P. (1991) *Practice Makes Practice: A Critical Study of Learning to Teach*, Albany: State University of New York Press.

Britzman, D. P. (1992) "The terrible problem of knowing thyself: toward a post-structural account of teacher identity," *JCT: An Interdisciplinary Journal of Curriculum Studies*, 9, 3: 23–46.

Christ, C. (1986) *Diving Deep and Surfacing: Women Writers on a Spiritual Quest* (2nd edn), Boston: Beacon Press.

Chung Hyun Kyung (1992) *Struggle To Be the Sun Again: Introducing Asian Women's Theology*, Maryknoll, New York: Orbis Books.

Cixous, H. (1993) *Three Steps on the Ladder of Writing* (Trans. S. Cornell and S. Sellers), New York: Columbia University Press.

Diamond, C. T. P. and Mullen, C. A. (1999) *The Postmodern Educator: Arts-Based Inquiries and Teacher Development* (vol. 89), New York: Peter Lang.

Eisner, E. W. (1997) "The promise and perils of alternative forms of data representation," *Educational Researcher*, 26, 6: 4–9.

Fox, M. (1995) *The Reinvention of Work: A New Vision of Livelihood for Our Times*, San Francisco: HarperSanFrancisco.

Haug, F. *et al.* (1987) *Female Sexualization: A Collective Work of Memory* (Trans. E. Carter), London: Verso.

Irigaray, L. (1992) *Elemental Passions* (Trans. J. Collie and J. Still), London: Athlone Press.

Irigaray, L. (1993) *An Ethics of Sexual Difference*, Ithaca, NY: Cornell University Press.

Irigaray, L. (1994) "Equal to Whom?" in N. Schor and E. Weed (Eds) *The Essential Difference* (pp. 63–81), Bloomington: Indiana University Press.

Irigaray, L. (1996) *I Love to You: Sketch for Felicity Within History*, New York: Routledge.

Lazreg, M. (1994) "Women's experience and feminist epistemology: a critical neo-rationalist approach," in K. Lennon and M. Whitford (Eds) *Knowing the Difference: Feminist Perspectives in Epistemology* (pp. 45–62), New York: Routledge.

Lennon, K. and Whitford, M. (1994) "Introduction", in K. Lennon and M. Whitford (Eds) *Knowing the Difference: Feminist Perspectives in Epistemology* (pp. 1–14), New York: Routledge.

Palmer, P. J. (1998) *The Courage to Teach: Exploring the Inner Landscape of a Teacher's Life*, San Francisco: Jossey-Bass Publishers.

Reason, P. and Hawkins, P. (1988) "Storytelling as inquiry," in P. Reason (Ed.) *Human Inquiry in Action: Developments in New Paradigm Research* (pp. 79–101), Thousand Oaks, CA: Sage Publications.

Richardson, L. (1992) "The consequences of poetic representation: writing the other, rewriting the self," in C. Ellis and M. Flaherty (Eds) *Investigating Subjectivity: Research on Lived Experience* (pp. 125–37), Newbury Park: Sage Publications.

Schaef, A. W. (1998) *Living in Process: Basic Truths for Living the Path of the Soul*, New York: Ballantine Wellspring.

Shildrick, M. (1997) *Leaky Bodies and Boundaries: Feminism, Postmodernism and (Bio)ethics*, New York: Routledge.

Stanley, L. (Ed.) (1997) *Knowing Feminisms: On Academic Borders, Territories, Tribes and Knowledges*, New York: Routledge.

Tomm, W. (1995) *Bodied Mindfulness: Women's Spirits, Bodies and Places*, Waterloo, ON: Wilfrid Laurier Press.

Walsh, S. (2001a) "Living tensions: collaborative research in a women's collective," paper presented at the Second International Interdisciplinary Conference – Advances in Qualitative Methods, Edmonton, Alberta.

Walsh, S. (2001b) "Opening the underside of teaching: tremblings," *Crossing Boundaries*, 1, 1: 148–63. Available online: http://www.ualberta.ca/GSA/ejournal/vol1no1/front.htm.

Weedon, C. (1987) *Feminist Practice and Poststructuralist Theory*, New York: Basil Blackwell.

Wolf, C. (1988) *The Fourth Dimension: Interviews With Christa Wolf* (Trans. H. Pilkington), New York: Verso.

Part III

Emergent issues in teacher research

Chapter 17

Exploring the nature of teacher research

John Loughran

Introduction

Teacher-researchers bring to bear their expert knowledge and understanding of practice in their research of their practice. They are often attempting to better understand their practice and its impact on their students by researching the complex relationship between teaching and learning in their classrooms. Teacher-researchers then are at the forefront of the challenge associated with better understanding the daily concerns and implications of practice that classroom teachers face. Importantly, as educational practices themselves are the source of the ultimate problems to be investigated in building a science of education (Dewey 1929), teacher-researchers have a "vested interest" in the outcomes and implications of such work.

There are many examples of the new knowledge and understanding that teachers can contribute to education (e.g. Mitchell and Mitchell 1997; Baird and Northfield 1992; Loughran, Mitchell and Mitchell 2002). Teachers researching their classrooms is linked to Schön's (1983) ideas about practitioners reflecting on their work. The extension of these ideas about "learning through practice" is highlighted by understanding the notion of the "authority of experience" (Munby and Russell 1994) and seeing this as a key to the way teachers may better understand teaching and learning. Within this understanding of teachers' work there is also a realization that there is no educational change without teacher change so by focusing on personal practice and experience, teachers can undertake genuine inquiry into practice that might lead to a better understanding of the complexities of, and improvements in, teaching.

The value of the "authority of experience" is that it encourages teachers to place more faith in their own experience and knowledge that, in turn, can help them to meet the demands of teaching. It is through this unique position of being both the practitioner and the researcher that teacher-researchers have so much to offer the educational community. Encouragement of teacher research then offers opportunities for improving professional practice and is a strategy for the professional development of teachers.

Teacher knowledge

Teachers have access to the detail and complexity of the classroom and are in an ideal position to generate knowledge and insights about the implementation of teaching and learning approaches and the impact these have on their students. Teachers begin with comprehensive "big picture" aspirations as they begin to study their classrooms as they often centre on classroom concerns that represent persistent tensions, dilemmas and difficulties. Passive learning (Mitchell 1993), teaching for better understanding of science concepts (Berry and Milroy 2002) and attempting to develop a curriculum of learning rather than content (Wilson 2002) are examples of complex big picture issues of concern to teachers. Teachers are reluctant to focus on more narrowly defined or decontextualized issues, as they remain aware of the uniqueness of their classrooms and the way many factors interact in those settings.

Because teachers focus on their classroom issues, the ability to draw on other related studies (literature in the particular field) and the ability to generalize to other situations becomes problematic. Which literature do we expect teachers to become familiar with in light of the complex concerns they tend to study? How do we make the literature accessible to teachers? Traditionally, literature is seen as informing a study and offering opportunities to build and extend on others' work. In teaching such literature is not so readily available, or if it is, it is not always in an accessible form.

The complexity and uniqueness of teachers' concerns makes communication to others difficult. While reluctant to simplify their classroom concerns, their "stories" are more than subjective accounts of isolated incidents, they are significant for them and are linked to their basic concerns. Teacher stories then are an integral element of the formation of the developing knowledge base (Clandinin and Connelly 1996) in teacher research.

New findings interact with teaching so that teachers feel the need to act immediately on new possibilities. The research focus alters as adjustments are made and new insights emerge and the intertwining of teaching and researching is such that as one alters so does the other. The traditional research notion of *holding the problem in place while it is researched* is not really possible for teacher-researchers as the problem develops, shifts and changes in response to the continual shifts in the teaching.

The impetus for studying a problem is the desire to do something about it. This means that teacher research often includes designing and implementing new approaches – classroom interventions that are intended to achieve change. However, these are not always successful, especially when first tried. For example, it may become clear to the teacher that the students did not see the purpose of the lesson, or that they did not apprehend the links between a practical class and the activities that preceded it, or that the students do not wish to become more actively involved in the task and would prefer to complete routine worksheets. These "failures" may lead to valuable insights and to ways of avoiding such "failures" in the future. However, teachers (unlike traditional researchers) have to deal with the consequences of their interventions as part of their daily routine with the class so teacher research can be a high risk activity.

For many teacher-researchers, the primary purpose in studying their teaching is to teach more effectively in their own classroom settings (Boyle 2002). This is a very personal purpose and is one that is not usually part of the research agenda for a stereotypical academic researcher who may well be researching a range of classrooms and wider contexts. The academic's primary purpose is to contribute to the knowledge base of the academy by publishing to an audience of other academics. For teachers, a wider communication of their findings is difficult to achieve and there are few incentives to publish their work as there is little status or career advancement from publishing.

There are also few outlets for teachers to publish their findings yet when their research is described, the response from other teachers is often positive, for example PEEL (Project for the Enhancement of Effective Learning) (Baird and Mitchell 1986) and PAVOT (Perspective and Voice of the Teacher) (Flack and Osler 1999). Teachers' accounts of their work have increased our understanding of classroom teaching and learning in ways that could only have been achieved through a forum for sharing their perspectives on practice.

Teacher knowledge and the way it is generated, applied and communicated is different from the development and dissemination of more traditional forms of research. To examine this issue I will refer to the work of a valued university colleague and friend, Jeff Northfield, and his return to classroom teaching as documented in *Opening the Classroom Door* (Loughran and Northfield 1996).

Being a teacher-researcher

Jeff spent a year teaching the first year of high school (in Australia) in an effort to embrace "in practice" the principles and understandings of pedagogy which he had been encouraging teachers to employ in their own classrooms. Many of these principles and practices were derived from the work of PEEL teachers and Jeff had a burning desire to do the same.

The impetus for this return to teaching was to better understand, through classroom experience, the tensions, dilemmas and rewards of the PEEL approach to teaching and learning. As he embarked on the task though he immediately became a teacher-researcher as he critically examined issues in his teaching and his students' learning while he was teaching. In this chapter I do not intend to pursue the research in detail as the book documents this process. However, I do think it appropriate to consider how the context of being the teacher inevitably influenced the research conducted and the manner in which it was developed, articulated and communicated.

Jeff was the mathematics, science and home room teacher for a Year 7 class. His main interest was to teach in a manner consistent with that of PEEL teachers, hence his desire was to help his students become more active learners who, through the teaching approach employed would become more engaged in their learning and develop their metacognitive skills. His research effort then was directed towards determining how this teaching and learning agenda could be realized and characterized as a "big picture" study. As an experienced educational researcher he would most likely have advised someone in his position to narrow his focus and make the project more manageable, yet, as a teacher-researcher, he maintained a big picture approach (i.e. attempting to understand teaching through a PEEL approach).

The account of his research purposefully offered the reader sufficient detail to assess the context of the situation. The book contains descriptions from three important perspectives: teacher, learner and researcher. These descriptions were drawn from Jeff's personal journal, from classroom observations by a "significant other," from student and teacher interviews and from triangulation of data sources and analysis. This was designed to invite the reader to consider the issues being raised and to help them identify with the situation in ways that would enhance their understanding. The interpretations of situations and implications of these interpretations are examined and the book describes the research results and the reflections and learning gained from the experience.

Importantly, issues are considered and interpreted in different ways because the data (journal, classroom observations, interviews etc.) descriptions and conclusions are addressed from the three perspectives (teacher, learner and researcher) so the traditional research procedures and assumptions are viewed as problematic. An example of this is demonstrated in the consideration of a particular lesson (the topic was velcro) where Jeff's perspective on the lesson was at odds with those of the students. During an interview with Carol Jones (a research assistant who spent a considerable period of time in the class with the students) Jeff described in detail how he had organized the lesson and why – in terms of encouraging active learning. However, when Carol observed the lesson she "saw" the students acting in ways contrary to this. When she interviewed the students their responses demonstrated a different purpose. Their approach negated the teacher's purpose and demonstrated passive learning styles in their response to the lesson. Hence, Jeff's initial explanations and responses to the situation did not account for the sub-plot (van Manen 1997) which only emerged through triangulating the data and reconsidering the students' responses in light of their perception of the purpose of the teaching approach. The "real" story would not have emerged had it not been for the varying interpretations and a suspension of judgment by Jeff as the teacher-researcher when the situation was being reconsidered.

By including a range of perspectives more possibilities for understanding the real nature of the situation became possible. As an example of this I offer Jeff's personal view of teaching and learning (Table 17.1) and juxtapose it with the students' views of teaching and learning (Table 17.2).

The incongruity of these two perspectives illustrates the importance of eliciting multiple perspectives if problems are to be genuinely understood and responded to. Tables 17.1 and 17.2 are drawn from a chapter on the reflections that Jeff makes when he is reviewing his year's teaching. Clearly, an inability to consider these differing perspectives would dramatically impact on not only an understanding of the teaching and learning environment, but also on the way one might respond to particular situations which could arise as a result of these perspectives.

This issue is an important aspect of teacher research. Jeff's big picture approach (attempting to teach using a PEEL approach), his attempts to articulate what he learnt through his study, and the manner in which that might be communicated to others are all features of researching his classroom. He did not set out to determine what his personal perspective on teaching was, nor to examine his students' understanding of their role as learners. Yet because he studied his classroom and his students as a teacher-researcher, he learnt much more about his practice. Interestingly, the development of these two perspectives, both drawn from analysis of his journal data, classroom observations and interactions and interviews, was informative in terms of beginning to understand what was happening in the classroom in the challenge to teach in a PEEL-like manner and to challenge students to become more active learners. Yet, again, the research did not aim to develop these perspectives, but the articulation of these perspectives helped to explain a diverse array of critical classroom incidents.

The collaborative processes that preceded the publication of Jeff's account of a year of teaching were complex. Drafts of his work were initially developed with Carol Jones (the research assistant who spent considerable periods of time in the school with his class). However, despite this collaboration and internal checks of these issues with his colleagues at the school, Jeff as an experienced researcher was reluctant to publish. It was not until he found that the ideas resonated with me that he was prepared to allow the work to move into a formal writing phase. This was an interesting response from an experienced researcher. In this instance, although his work clearly resonated with his colleagues he was still hesitant because he felt as though he was, "only reporting on his experiences from his classroom."

Before the final manuscript was published, Jeff still had a need to validate the study by asking some of his teacher colleagues to read and comment

Table 17.1 A personal view of teaching and learning

- Where possible students should have opportunities to be active and think about their learning experiences.

- Students should experience success in learning and gain the confidence and skills to become better learners.

- Linking experiences from both within and outside school greatly assists learning.

- Effort and involvement are important and students need to gain credit and encouragement for their efforts.

- Enjoyment and satisfaction with learning are important outcomes.

- Learning involving the above features requires learner consent.

Source: Loughran and Northfield 1996.

Table 17.2: Some student views of teaching and learning

- Learning is associated with gaining right answers and thinking and personal understanding are just different and often frustrating ways of achieving the required outcomes.

- Processes of learning and thinking about learning are difficult to associate with school work, texts and notes are important indicators that school learning is occurring.

- Linking experiences is very demanding and unreasonable when added to the classroom demands for students.

- The final grade is the critical outcome and the basis by which progress is judged.

- Enjoyment is not always associated with school learning – real learning is hard and not usually enjoyed.

- Learning is done to students, and teachers have major responsibility for achieving learning

---

Source: Loughran and Northfield, 1996.

on the book. Had they not responded favourably to the manuscript, he may well have lost a sense of the validity and naturalistic generalizability (Stake and Trumbull 1982) that the work offered other teachers. He was himself asking his colleagues, "Does the situation being portrayed extend to other classrooms?" Fortunately, in this case, the written and verbal comments indicating that "You could have been describing my class" helped to address these concerns. It was this collaboration which encouraged him to see that his experience was of value to others.

His return to teaching demonstrated a substantial effort and commitment as a teacher-researcher. Jeff exposed his own personal vulnerability through the study as he sought to better understand the teaching and learning situations in which he was embedded. Perhaps the best way of demonstrating this is through a quote from his final chapter in the book where he publicly reflects on his learning through the experience.

> ... the return to teaching was often a confusing and unsettling experience. The conditions rarely seemed to be suitable to initiate different teaching learning activities with the class. My journal entries continued to outline disappointments as I searched for understanding of my context. The dailiness of teaching and its unpredictability appeared to dominate my reflections. As I began to understand the student perspective their responses to the demands of their schooling often made more sense than the learning attitudes and outcomes I was seeking. Yet the overall experience with the class was enjoyable and satisfying. What tended to get documented in the journal and discussed with others were the surprises, dilemmas and tensions giving a more negative picture of the experience ... My attempt to analyse and communicate my understanding of teaching and learning at the end of the year was only partly successful ... Very vivid and significant teaching episodes should have been a basis for understanding but it was difficult to separate my own responses and the missed opportunities from any coherent description of progress ... the records of the year's teaching formed a disjointed account of teaching and learning. John was able to examine the records without the personal involvement of teaching in this classroom. His analysis now allows me a clearer understanding of my teaching and learning experience and the nature of teacher knowledge and its generation ... my frustration during the year was in trying to analyse the day to day teaching experiences in a way that might lead to consistent improvement in classroom interactions. I was also struggling to find ways of communicating my "teacher knowledge." I was experiencing the earlier observations made about teachers and their knowledge, yet feeling that I should have been able to better understand and use my experience. I would argue that teacher knowledge has different characteristics in the way it is developed and used ... I [have] developed several insights that emerge[d] from John's analysis ... [these include] contrasting views of teaching and learning [and] implications for teacher education ...
>
> (Loughran and Northfield 1996: 135)

This quotation is indicative of the type of learning possible through teacher-research whilst simultaneously illustrating some of the important dilemmas, issues and concerns that are particular to teacher-researchers.

Conclusion

I conclude this chapter by suggesting that support for teacher-researchers requires certain conditions. If these conditions exist, it is likely that the research findings will help to fulfil the requirements of supporting and improving pedagogical practice. In particular, three important conditions are required:

- *Collaborate and share with others* so that problematic situations may be defined and redefined to move the focus of the research from the personal and specific context of an individual classroom to the "bigger picture" with which others will readily identify. Therefore, although the original problem setting is important, the way it is developed and portrayed to others is critical. Consequently, the ability to move beyond coping with the normal pressures or constraints of the teaching-learning environment so that the development of understanding through genuine reframing might occur will be more likely through involvement of others who are similarly concerned and identify with the situation. Valuable learning is then possible through research as a collaborative venture.
- *Develop one's confidence.*

  > A high level of self-confidence is necessary as "successful" experiences have unintended outcomes and closely held assumptions and ideas are queried. Self-confidence is a most interesting aspect of [teacher research]. One needs to be comfortable with the sense of vulnerability necessary to genuinely study personal practice and the overarching need to learn through [teacher research] will inevitably create personal conflict and a sense of dissonance.
  >
  > (Loughran and Northfield 1998: 14)

  The environment in which teacher-researchers function must support and foster this approach to confidence so that the frame of reference includes positive (successes) as well as negative (failures) outcomes.
- *Communicate findings in ways so that others will identify with them.* The audience for teacher-researchers is initially that of other practitioners, therefore there is a constant need to ensure that the findings are communicated in a manner that encourages others to recognize the value and significance of the research so that it "rings true" with the audience.

Ultimately, a most important outcome of teacher research is to help facilitate a better understanding of the complex nature of teaching and learning so that both teachers and students can benefit from the development of knowledge through the research venture. By highlighting how other practitioners' research is developed, communicated and acted upon, classroom practice and students' learning experiences in "real classrooms" in "real time" become all the more important in articulating a meaningful, useful and valuable knowledge base in teaching. This is more likely to occur when the researcher is also the teacher rather than when an external expert conducts their research in someone else's classroom.

Bibliography

Baird, J. R. and Mitchell, I. J. (1986) *Improving the Quality of Teaching and Learning: An Australian Case Study – The PEEL Project*, 2nd edn, Melbourne: Monash University Printery.

Baird, J. R. and Northfield, J. R. (1992) *Learning from the PEEL Experience*, Melbourne: Monash University Printery.

Berry, A. and Milroy, P. (2002) "Changes that matter," in J. J. Loughran, I. J. Mitchell and J. A. Mitchell (Eds) *Learning from Teacher Research*, New York: Teachers College Press.

Boyle, L. (2002) "Disasters and metacognition in the SOSE classroom," in J. J. Loughran, I. J. Mitchell and J. A. Mitchell (Eds) *Learning from Teacher Research*, New York: Teachers College Press.

Clandinin, J. D. and Connelly, M. F. (1996) "'Teachers' professional knowledge landscapes: teacher stories – stories of teachers – school stories – stories of schools," *Educational Researcher*, 25, 3: 24–30.

Dewey, J. (1929) *The Sources of a Science of Education*, New York: Liverright.

Dewey, J. (1933) *How We Think*, New York: Heath and Co.

Flack, J. and Osler, J. (1999) "We're teachers! We're researchers! We're proud of it!," paper presented at the Annual Meeting of the American Educational Research Association, Montreal, April, 1999.

Loughran, J. J., Mitchell, I. J. and Mitchell, J. A. (2002) *Learning from Teacher Research*, New York: Teachers College Press.

Loughran, J. J. and Northfield, J. R. (1996) *Opening the Classroom Door: Teacher, Researcher, Learner*, London: Falmer Press.

Loughran, J. J. and Northfield, J. R. (1998) "A framework for the development of self-study practice," in M. L. Hamilton and S. Pinnegar (Eds) *Reconceptualising Pedagogy: Self-Study in Teacher Education*, London: Falmer Press.

Mitchell, I. J. and Mitchell, J. A. (Eds) (1997) *Stories of Reflective Teaching: A Book of PEEL Cases*, Melbourne: Monash University, PEEL Publishing.

Mitchell, I. J. (1993) "Teaching for quality learning", unpublished doctoral thesis, Monash University, Melbourne, Australia.

Munby, H. and Russell, T. (1994) "The authority of experience in learning to teach: messages from a physics method class," *Journal of Teacher Education*, 45, 2: 86–95.

Schön, D. A. (1983) *The Reflective Practitioner: How Professionals Think in Action*, New York: Basic Books.

Stake, R. E. and Trumbull, D. (1982) "Naturalistic generalisations," *Review Journal of Philosophy and Social Science*, VII, 1 and 2 (pp. 1–12).

van Manen, M. (1997) Keynote address, Conference of the International Study Association on Teacher Thinking (ISATT), Kiel, Germany, October, 1997.

Wilson, C. (2002) "Open learning: teaching without a road map," in J. J. Loughran, I. J. Mitchell and J. A. Mitchell (Eds) *Learning from Teacher Research*, New York: Teachers College Press.

Chapter 18

Knowledge-creation in educational leadership and administration through teacher research

Jack Whitehead and Jacqueline D. Delong

This chapter explains how teacher-researchers can contribute to the knowledge-base of educational leadership and administration. Jackie Delong is a superintendent of schools who is engaged in an action research enquiry into her own teaching and learning (1995–2001). She is explicating the standards of practice and judgement which can be used to test the validity of her knowledge-claims about her educative influence. Jack Whitehead is a university academic who is researching his own supervision of Delong's research program in relation to the creation of a thesis which demonstrates her originality of mind and critical judgement in contributing to the knowledge-base of educational leadership and administration. We are thinking of a contribution to the knowledge-base that avoids the kind of criticisms made by David Clark:

> The honest fact is that the total contribution of Division A of AERA (American Educational Research Association) to the development of the empirical and theoretical knowledge base of administration and policy development is so miniscule that if all of us had devoted our professional careers to teaching and service, we would hardly have been missed.
>
> (Clark 1997: 5)

In our knowledge-creation we are focusing on the nature of the living standards of practice and judgement we use to test the validity of our claims to know our educative influence. Such standards are a fundamental part of the creation of our knowledge-base of educational leadership which can be related directly to the educational practices of superintendents and other educational administrators.

The developing epistemology of my practice as superintendent: Jackie's story

My contribution to the scholarship of educational enquiry emerges from my storying and re-storying, in my inquiry, "How can I improve my practice as a superintendent of schools in a southern Ontario school district?" One of the issues in my research is that I take much of my political *nous* as natural and so embedded in the way that I do my work that it has been very difficult to uncover. Jack will refer to this below in his analysis of his educative influence in our supervision sessions on my understanding of my "systems influence." My process of learning is as distinctive as finger-prints (MacBeath 2001). My understanding of this process emerges from stories of victory and ruin (MacLure 1996) in my various roles in the school board – in senior management relationships, in my family of schools and systems portfolios and in my relationships imbued with life-affirming energy (Whitehead 2000) and vitality (Tillich 1952) as I contribute to the education of social formations.

Given the constraints of text and space in this form of presentation I will concentrate on my commitment to values of democratic and non-hierarchical relations and improving teaching/learning/schools and school systems. My purpose in doing this is to show that my values are the living standards of practice and judgement I use to test the validity of my knowledge-creation as an educational leader and a superintendent of schools.

Democratic and non-hierarchical relations

Living democratic values

I have a video-clip that shows my family of school principals evaluating my performance. This was coordinated by two veteran principals in the family. In submitting myself to a form of democratic accountability I want to learn from my principals and vice-principals what I could do to improve my practice as a superintendent through a process of democratic evaluation. In addition, I want to contribute to the education of social formations (Delong and Whitehead 2001) by breaking down the hierarchical structures in the system so that principals and vice-principals engage their staffs in creating learning organizations (Senge 1990) where they can learn from their teachers and teachers can share the responsibility for the learning in the classroom with their students. I have lived this process with Cheryl Black, a former secondary school music teacher and presently a vice-principal, who has analyzed evidence in her master's degree of my influence in her learning (Black 1999; 2001).

An earlier paper (Delong and Whitehead 1998) analyzes our response to an imposition of checklist types of performance review procedures that is contrary to my value of research-based professionalism in which teachers take responsibility for their learning and improvement and democratically construct professional standards.

Living values of connectedness to improving students' learning through mobilizing system's influences

Linking policy to practice in supporting parental involvement

Even prior to my being appointed superintendent, Peter Moffatt, Director of Education, and I shared the belief that increasing parental involvement in students' learning would increase achievement. Since 1992 we had been looking for avenues to increase parental and community involvement in schools. In 1996, we published a summary of our activities designed toward "Building a Culture of Involvement in Brant County" in ORBIT Vol. 27, No. 4, 1996. I had just spent a year implementing the new School Councils and brought that recent experience to the article.

Linking action research and provincial test results to improving student learning

By the end of 2000, the year-long project for the Educational Quality and Accountability Office (EQAO) called *An Action Research Approach to Improving Student Learning Using Provincial Test Results* (Wideman *et al.* 2000) was approved by the EQAO. In it, teachers and consultants from my board and the Nipissing-Parry Sound Catholic District School Board explained how they used their provincial test results to inform an investigation of ways to improve their teaching and student learning through an action research process. My role was encouragement, support and editing; my friend, Diane Morgan, educational consultant, was the project coordinator.

There were some important ways in which I was influential in this project. It is important to integrate into accounts those sometimes tense and difficult experiences which are often part of projects designed to improve learning. I insisted on the research questions containing "I" as essential to the process. Against some resistance from the University of Nipissing I persisted in supporting the teachers' views that their names and photos should be included with their work. On the other hand, I was not able to resist a common format to the narratives and my involvement in a separate literature search which seemed to me to be separated from the process of the enquiry. Partnerships are about give and take. The teachers' findings about effective teaching and learning strategies in their classrooms were, to me, inspirational. Several of the narratives have been published in full in the Ontario Action Researcher (http://www.unipissing.ca/oar) and have been presented to the Grand Erie District School Board and at the Ontario Educational Research Council. The teachers recorded their beliefs that having gone through this process their teaching improved, the students' learning improved and that this had a positive impact on the test results the following year. The improved test results tend to support the teachers' beliefs.

*Linking action research and leadership program to improving
student learning*

One way of improving teaching/learning/schools and school systems is to improve the quality of leadership programs. When it became evident to me that Jack's message of accreditation for action research was beginning to take root and knowing that one of the skills essential for being an effective school administrator is the capacity to analyze and use data to improve student achievement I created and implemented (1999–2001) the GEDSB-Brock University MEd program with Susan Drake and Michael Manley-Casimir. Jack and I have also been instructors in the program. One of my priorities in this program was that the research would be conducted in our schools and enquiries focused on improving the learning of our children.

The first cohort of 15 practitioner-researchers graduated from Brock University in November 2001 and have contributed their dissertations to the professional knowledge-base of education.

Bob Ogilvie's (2001) dissertation describes the cohort experience. It is mostly a victory narrative but the idea of the university as vampire, sucking the life-blood of the teacher-researchers (MacLure 1996: 283), became evident in the ethical review process. I mean this in the sense that the institutional power relations worked in ways which pressured the teachers to distort their knowledge. This exerted pressure to conform to scholarly standards of judgement which were not created from the disciplines of educational practice (Lyotard 1984: 63). Geoff Suderman-Gladwell (2001) has presented an analysis of the evidence in relation to this claim in his dissertation.

*Linking my performance appraisals to evaluating my influence on
improving student learning*

Space does not permit the detailed presentation of evidence of this link. My performance reviews by Peter Moffatt (1995–2001) provide some evidence of evaluations of my influence on teaching, learning and school improvement. These reviews have been presented to the School Board. The reviews inform my planning to improve my practice for the following year and over the six years show clearly my own commitment to an action research process and contain evidence, such as that included in the 15 successfully completed master's dissertations, that I am enhancing my educative influence in the system.

*Linking my research and writings to influence the knowledge-base
of educational leadership and school systems*

One of the ways I intend to influence school systems is through my research and writing. In a paper for the 2001 Annual Meeting of AERA in Seattle,

"Knowledge-Creation in Educational Leadership and Administration Through Practitioner Research," I want to get my insider, practitioner knowledge into the knowledge-base of educational administration. I want to do this so that school and system leaders can see that they can create their own living theories of educational leadership and can also develop their own living standards of practice. I want to build the bridge between theory and practice that Joseph Murphy (1999) said no one was interested in building.

The supervisor's influence on Delong's inquiry: Jack's story

One of my pleasures in supervizing doctoral program is at the time when the researcher forms a clear abstract of the thesis which draws attention to the way in which the researcher's originality of mind and critical judgement have engaged with the knowledge-base of the field of inquiry. The standards used in the examination of a doctoral degree in the University of Bath include both originality of mind and critical judgement. Our use of video-clips from our supervision sessions allows me to focus on my influence in Jackie's learning. In one video-clip from the March 15, 2001 I am focusing attention on my frustration in not being able to understand clearly how Jackie's Abstract is defining her originality of mind and critical judgement. In the video I can be heard focusing Jackie's attention on her *system's influences*.

Prior to this conversation Jackie showed me an e-mail she had received, from a teacher in the GEDSB, in which she described being "swept up by the action research SWAT team!" when she expressed an interest in doing some action research.

The e-mail kept coming into my mind as having something significant to say about Jackie's system's influence. So did ideas from Edward Said (1993: xii–xiii) about culture and from Bourdieu (1990: 91) about the habitus which influences the reproduction of social formations. My intuition began working on the idea that this e-mail was showing Jackie's *system's influence* as having pervaded the culture of the board. I mean this in the sense that her influence was being felt through the actions of others who had been directly influenced by Jackie, in face-to-face communications.

In the video-clip I raise the idea of Jackie's influence on a "system." Jackie's story above in the section on "Living values of connectedness to improving students' learning through mobilizing system's influences" demonstrates that an awareness of this influence is now a focal point of her inquiry. Previously it had remained taken for granted. The crucial point about my influence is that I think that I have raised Jackie's awareness of something she has taken for granted and yet which is crucially important for her knowledge-creation in relation to explaining her educative influence as a superintendent. I am thinking of her capacity to hold together, and dynamically relate, two important concerns. These are her focus on improving students' learning through the relationships between teachers and students, and her understanding of how to mobilize the resources of the board in support of the processes of improving student learning.

I now want to focus attention on the "embodied" values I believe that I express in my educative relationships and which can help to explain the nature of my educative influence in the processes of knowledge-creation with Jackie and the other practitioner-researchers whose research program I supervise.

My embodied values as explanatory principles

In my explanations for my educative influence my values constitute the reasons for why I do things. I think of my values as embodied in what I do. They form the goals I set for myself in living a productive life. I often feel a desire to resolve a tension when I experience the denial of values such as freedom, care, compassion, justice and inquiry and explain my actions in terms of my desire to live my values as fully as possible.

Here are some of the values I think I embody in my educative relationships. Let me see if I can share their meanings in a way which enables you to use them as standards of judgement for testing the validity of my explanations of my educative influence.

A life-affirming faith in the embodied knowledge and knowledge-creating capacities of practitioner-researchers

As an educator, supporting the educational enquiries of practitioner-researchers, I hold firmly to the view that the practitioner-researchers already embody much of the knowledge which the research can make public. When I use the term "embodied knowledge" I mean this in the sense that in what I am doing:

> ... there is an infinitude of knowledge previous to all deduction, knowledge whose mediated connections of intentional implication being entirely intuitive have nothing to do with deduction and prove refractory to every methodologically devised scheme of constructive symbolism.
>
> (Husserl 1931: 12)

In saying this I don't want to be misunderstood. I see practitioner-researchers as embodying knowledge (Hocking *et al.* 2001) and as knowledge-creators in enquiries of the kind, "How do I improve what I am doing?"

I think I communicate this value to Jackie, and other practitioner-researchers I work with, as a passionate valuing of their "embodied knowledge" and "knowledge-creating" capacities. With working in education I think the emotional intensity of my commitment carries the additional meaning that in creating publicly shareable knowledge, from and in our practice, we are also creating ourselves.

Communicating a life-affirming energy

In the face of the certainty of death I feel a life-affirming energy which I associate with Bataille's (1962: 11) idea of assenting to life up to the point of death and with Foucault's (1985: 89) ideas on the uses of pleasure. In my educative relationships I feel alive in a way which I believe communicates both a life-affirming energy and pleasure. I am stressing the pleasure associated with my life-affirming energy because I believe that it is crucial in explaining my educative influence in the processes of knowledge-creation with practitioner-researchers. Let me see if the words loving and creative spirit carry any meaning for you. I do believe this pleasure and energy have a spiritual ground in the experience of the state of being grasped by the power of being itself. Paul Tillich's (1952) work in *The Courage to Be* helped me to articulate this point. I don't want to say anything more about this spiritual value, embodied in my practice. I simply want to acknowledge its presence and hope that you can feel this spiritual, life-affirming energy through my educative relationships and, hopefully, through this text.

Engaging with the life-affirming energy of practitioner-researchers

As I engage with the life-affirming energy of others, in my educative relations, I think of education in terms of forms of enquiry through which we create our own forms of life in relation to the certainty of death and other influences. I associate the "giving of form" with my aesthetic values. I think of the art of living in terms of giving form to life itself. I seek to express my value-laden practices as an educator and educational researcher in a way that can be seen to be influencing the educational development of myself and others. When I say this I do not want to be understood as saying that I have educated anyone other than myself. Because I associate education with learning and knowledge-creation I think each individual makes sense of their own experience in a way which is uniquely their own through an engagement with their originality of mind and critical judgment. I do, however, think that I can claim to have an educative influence. I seek to express my values as an educator and educational research in a way that can be seen to be influencing the educational development of myself and others.

As we work at improving our contributions to the knowledge-base of educational leadership and administration we want to share our own insights, in a process of democratic accountability, about both our success criteria and the evidence we use to judge our success.

In an attempt to avoid Clark's conclusion above, we want to offer for your evaluation the success criteria and evidence we use to judge our own contributions to our chosen profession, education.

Jack's success criteria

My criteria are focused on both the reconstruction of educational theory and my educative influence in the learning of other students of education. I want to look back on a productive life in education that I have contributed to the development of living forms of educational theory that can be related directly to the education of individuals and to the education of social formations. I offer, as partial evidence of my success as a supervisor so far, the living theory theses and dissertations in the living theory section of http://www.actionresearch.net.

Jackie's success criteria

I judge my success in terms of my capacity to live my life according to my values which are my standards of practice and judgement. As I attempt to share my embodied knowledge with clarity and elegance, I find that the meanings of my standards are still emerging through the writing of the thesis: the sanctity of personal relationships, the focus on children, democratic and non-hierarchical relations, commitment to improving teaching/learning/schools and school systems, encouraging practitioner knowledge through action research, and professional accountability. And, as I have written every year in my goal package: finding the meaning of balance. I do not want to end my professional life feeling as David Clark did; I do wish to contribute to improving the social order (McNiff *et al.* 1996; McNiff 2002) through the education of social formations.

What is the evidential base that I am living these standards of practice and judgement? First, the answer lies in the data archive of the five years of research that describes and explains the knowledge embodied in my practice. Second, the evidence that the meanings of the standards have emerged through my practice is in my PhD submission to the University of Bath. It is my hope that this PhD thesis can join those in the living theory section of actionresearch.net – soon! (Delong 2002).

Bibliography

Bataille, G. (1962) *Eroticism*, London: Marion Boyers.

Black, C. (1999) "Valuing the student voice in improving my practice," paper presented at Ontario Educational Research Council in Toronto (December 3).

Black, C. (2001) "Managing transitions: how can I improve my practice by valuing the voices of others?," MEd Dissertation, Brock University, Ontario, Canada.

Bourdieu, P. (1990) *The Logic of Practice*, Cambridge: Polity.

Clark, D. (1997) "The search for authentic educational leadership: in the universities and in the schools," invited presentation to Division A at the Annual Meeting of AERA, Chicago, USA.

Delong, J. (2002) "How can I improve my practice as a superintendent of schools and create my own living educational theory?" PhD thesis, University of Bath. Available online: in the living theory section of http://www. actionresearch. net.

Delong, J. and Whitehead, J. (1998) "Continuously regenerating developmental standards of practice in teacher education: a cautionary note for the Ontario College of Teachers," paper presented at the Ontario Educational Research Council, 40th Annual Conference, Toronto (December 4).

Delong, J. and Whitehead, J. (2001) "Knowledge creation in educational leadership and administration through practitioner research," a multi-media presentation at AERA, Seattle (April 14).

Hocking, B., Haskell, J. and Linds, W. (Eds) (2001) *Unfolding Bodymind: Exploring Possibility Through Education*, Brandon, VT: Foundation for Educational Renewal.

Husserl, E. (1931) *Ideas: General Introduction to Pure Phenomenology*, London: George, Allen & Unwin.

Lyotard, J. F. (1984) *The Postmodern Condition: A Report on Knowledge*, Manchester: Manchester University Press.

MacBeath, J. (2001) "Improving school effectiveness," presentation at the University of Bath (February 28).

MacLure, M. (1996), "Telling transitions: boundary work in narratives of becoming an action researcher," *British Educational Research Journal*, 22, 3: 273–86.

McNiff, J. (2002) *Action Research: Principles and Practices*, London: RoutledgeFalmer.

McNiff, J., Lomax, P. and Whitehead, J. (1996) *You and Your Action Research Project*, London: Routledge.

Murphy, J. (1999) "Quest for a center: notes on the state of the profession of educational leadership," paper presented at session 13.53, AERA 1999, Montreal.

Ogilvie, R. (2001) "Cohort story: re-searching and learning together," MEd Dissertation, Brock University, Ontario, Canada.

Said, E. (1993) *Culture and Imperialism*, London: Vintage.

Senge, P. M. (1990) *The Fifth Discipline: The Art and Practice of The Learning Organization*, New York: Doubleday.

Suderman-Gladwell, G. (2001) "The ethics of personal subjective narrative research," MEd Dissertation, Brock University, Ontario, Canada. Online. Available: in the values section of http://www.actionresearch.net.

Tillich, P. (1952) *The Courage To Be*, London: Collins.

Whitehead, J. (2000) "How do I improve my practice? Creating and legitimating an epistemology of practice," *Reflective Practice*, 1: 91–104.

Wideman, R., Delong, J., Hallett, K. and Morgan, D. (2000) *An Action Research Approach to Improving Student Learning Using Provincial Test Results*, Toronto: EQAO.

Chapter 19

Why do teacher research?

Perspectives from four stakeholders

Ian Mitchell

Introduction

Teacher research cannot be disconnected from issues of both professional development of the teacher and of the successful or unsuccessful running of the teacher's classrooms. Moreover, in most situations, as I will argue later, it should not be disconnected from issues of professional development of at least some of the teacher's school colleagues. These strong and unavoidable links between research, practice and professional development imply important differences between research carried out by teachers and much research carried out by university-based researchers. They mean, for example, that any discussion of the value of teacher research as an endeavour must pay attention to the processes, as well as the products, of teacher research.

There are different stakeholders in teacher research; in this chapter I explore the perspective of four: the teacher-researchers, their school level administration, system level officials and university-based educators (hereafter called academics for convenience). These different stakeholders have different reasons for initiating and supporting teacher research, take different risks, face different barriers and potential costs, gain different benefits and have as a consequence, different standards for success and quality.

In this chapter, I explore both the processes and the products of teacher research from the perspectives of these different stakeholders. I argue that all of their perspectives must be attended to if teacher research is to become a widely valued and expected part of education.

My background and sources of data

I draw on 21 years of involvement in teacher research either as or in close collaboration with all four types of stakeholders. I spent 17 years as a classroom teacher-researcher and 14 years leading teacher research groups in my schools in the Project for Enhancing Effective Learning or PEEL (Loughran *et al.* 2002). I have spent 18 years as a part-time and full-time academic supporting groups of teacher-researchers in other schools and collaborating with school level leaders who wished to establish forms of teacher research in their schools. For five years, I had significant leadership responsibilities for professional development in my schools. In the last few years I have been collaborating with system level officials in this area.

An important aspect of most of my experiences in teacher research is that it has not been driven by the desire to get a higher degree. Nor has it been the result of system-funded initiatives. Teachers in PEEL have become involved in teacher research because they were interested in the issues of learning and teaching that drive PEEL or interested in the process of collaborative action research, or both.

Defining teacher research

Cochran-Smith and Lytle (1993) defined teacher research as involving systematic and intentional inquiry. I agree, but this still allows for a range of variations. At one end of a continuum, are teachers whose projects are well connected to relevant academic literature and whose research design and reporting are strongly influenced by concerns of academic rigour. This end is and I believe will continue to be populated almost exclusively by teachers enrolled in higher degrees. Reasons for this assertion are outside the scope of this chapter, but include the inaccessibility and low level of salience of the mainstream academic literature for full-time teachers. The other end of the continuum could be labelled highly reflective practice. The teacher routinely reflects on practice and its outcomes, identifies deficiencies, refines accordingly and looks for improved outcomes. This (very worthy) endeavour has some characteristics of research, but it is done for an audience of one (the teacher), rarely involves the construction of generalizations and does not meet the purposes that concern me in this chapter: promoting teacher research as a widespread and ongoing endeavour.

For this chapter, I include as teacher-researchers teachers who are meeting regularly with articulated concerns about learning and teaching that are the focus of systematic attempts to initiate, sustain and explore change. In the case of PEEL groups, the teachers' goals are influenced by constructs such as metacognition that have come from the mainstream literature, but are accessed from the internal literature of the project. Over time, PEEL groups revisit relevant aspects of this "theory" as they construct generalizations to organize and make sense of their findings. They are developing and sharing new knowledge. Much of this remains within their group, however, they commonly share findings with other teachers in their schools and regularly with audiences outside the school via both conference presentations, PEEL SEEDS, the project journal and a series of books.

The process of teacher research

Reasons for engaging in/supporting teacher research

Teachers decide to engage in research for a number of reasons, but concerns about aspects of their own classrooms are almost always the most important. I argue that concerns of this sort are the only ones that can sustain an involvement in teacher research over several years. This means that improvement in their own classrooms is commonly the most important benefit for teacher-researchers; ranking well ahead, for example, of the generation of new "public" knowledge. This does not mean that generation of new understandings is not a common reason for engaging in teacher research, but, at least initially, the most important aspects are related to personal professional development: better understandings of their own classrooms and the development of new practices.

Over time, the sense of becoming more informed, purposeful and professional about one's practice becomes increasingly important. This results in teachers becoming much more confident about and interested in sharing their new insights. When we began PEEL, I had little conception of how substantial and how rewarding the journey would be in this area for teachers who sustained an involvement over several years.

School level leaders usually see teacher research as a means to achieve one or more ends such as encouraging an aging staff to become more reflective and open to learning more about teaching. It is increasingly common in our system for school leaders to be serious about building a climate of career-long professional development and a culture of greater collaboration and sharing of documented ideas. Increasingly, school leaders are taking the quality of how students approach learning very seriously and are looking for ways of improvement in this area. Teacher research is seen as a way of developing new practices to better deal with problems such as poor retention rates and lack of student engagement.

These concerns overlap with those of the individual teachers, however, school level leaders have responsibilities for the whole staff and whole school and consequently tend to be more concerned about ways of maximizing a school-wide impact of teacher research. A project, however worthwhile, that only impacts on two or three staff is of less value to school leaders than to the individual teachers or academic collaborators. Once again, publication of findings to a wider audience outside the school is not a high priority, if anything (in my experience) lower than for the individual teacher-researchers.

My experiences with system level leaders have been of two types. One is with leaders who want to promote teacher research for its own sake, the other is where teacher research has been seen as a way of achieving centrally determined government priorities; a step that has involved a significant rethink of the roles that systems believe teachers can take on.

In both cases, system level leaders have similar reasons for interest in teacher research to school principals. One difference, however, relates to how new ideas will be shared. Within a school, much of this sharing can be done informally or in scheduled workshops. Sharing across schools increases the need for well-written resources. It also generates a need for teacher leaders who can be used as a professional development resource in other schools.

Compared with the first three groups, academics who are collaborating with or supporting teacher-researchers begin with a much greater interest in the products of teacher research: in documents that report and describe outcomes and new knowledge. For the academics associated with PEEL, teacher research is either the only way, or is the most valid way, of researching some sorts of questions. Research, for example, into the effectiveness of a new teaching approach or product is much more efficient and effective if the teacher has a high degree of ownership of and control over what is being researched. With this ownership, the teacher is likely to react to unexpected classroom events in ways that involve perhaps significant modifications of the approach, but ones that are consistent with its intent. Without it, the teacher is more likely to report what happened to the perceived owner of the research and the critical classroom moment is lost.

The process of teacher research tends to bring out crucial teacher knowledge that is otherwise tacit and hidden. Any research that requires the development of considerable bodies of classroom wisdom needs teacher-researchers. As Wagoner said, teacher research generates knowledge that is qualitatively different from that generated by academic research (Wagoner 1993).

Risks, costs and barriers to teacher research

For teachers, there are some obvious risks associated with teacher research: it is risky to leave one's comfort zone and explore practices whose outcome is unknown. There are also costs of time and energy and teachers' career structures commonly do not provide extrinsic rewards for research. The nature of teachers' working week and the structures of schools also make it difficult for teachers to step back and reflect on their practice.

For school level leaders, the costs and perceived risks associated with having some teachers engage in teacher research are typically lower than for individual teachers. One risk is of creating division in the staff; teachers who are talking about concerns about their own classrooms and teaching are usually at least implicitly criticizing practices that may be common in other classrooms and can be resented as a self-appointed elite. Related to this are sensitive ethical issues that arise if different classrooms are being compared. Any research that looks at an issue or practices across a number of classes is very likely to be threatening and perhaps damaging to some staff. Parental nervousness is a third risk. Many parents regard talk of experimentation with suspicion and have little conception of the extent to which good teachers constantly refine practice. A barrier, rather than a risk for school leaders, is to create time and opportunities for teacher-researchers to meet.

Teacher research can create real challenges for systems that wish to micromanage teachers and curricula (as so many do). The process professionalizes and empowers teachers to critique and perhaps reject or substantially modify system level edicts or initiatives. Teachers engaged in research are less likely to see written curriculum documents as sacred writ and will identify flaws in simplistic solutions to what they know to be complex problems.

Most academics need publication if they are to invest serious time in working with teacher-researchers. However, teacher research is not a fast process and the time period to publication is typically longer than for other forms of research. This can be a risk for academics in tenure track situations – as can the low status of teacher research in some institutions. Another risk for academics is that the teacher, after a year or more of work, may decide to withdraw from the process. While this can result from a breakdown in the relationship, it is also quite likely to occur if the teacher gets a promotion or transfer and decides that this extra role can no longer be carried. The teacher will have already received benefits listed earlier that matter most to them – failure to publish may not be a cost at all – but it is to the academic friend.

Initiating and sustaining teacher research

The preceding discussion provides some guidance and advice about what each type of stakeholder can do to stimulate and support the process of teacher research.

Teachers should begin from concerns that they have about their own classrooms. All my experiences reinforce the value of including a focus on how students are learning and the interactions between teaching and assessment practices and learning. Most other classroom issues and concerns flow from this. Teacher ownership should be maximized: projects imposed by school leaders who have written, with minimal consultation, a proposal in response to a funding initiative are much less likely to be viable than those with genuine participant ownership. If the research will impinge on other teachers not in the research team (e.g. researching assessment practices across a year level) then try and spread at least some aspects of ownership among these other staff.

In most cases a group (even a small group) of teachers will find it easier than an individual to sustain the often-draining process of research.

School leaders need to weave the goals and processes of research and sharing richly into their school's priorities and structures (Burke 2002). Persistence and consistency is required here. School staffrooms can be cynical places and it takes time to build cultures of problematizing apparently satisfactory practice and unselfconscious sharing of new ideas. Both systems and schools need to find ways of capitalizing on the substantial professional growth that commonly accompanies a long-term involvement in teacher research and using key teachers as resources in the school. This is not simple – there are strong traditions in schools that credible expertise can only come from without.

A major challenge for system level leaders, who commonly control some funding, in promoting teacher research is to do this in ways that maximize teacher ownership and minimize opportunistic and hence funding-dependent responses by schools. It is also important to ensure that any funds come into schools in ways that prevent diversion for other purposes. I comment that in the most successful system-initiated experience that I have been involved with, funds have been provided for initial meetings to establish interest, a subsequent in-service for volunteers and for a part-time support person to help document ideas and to organize network meetings, but not for any ongoing payments or release time for teachers. As already mentioned, systems can provide intrinsic rewards for teacher-researchers by using them as a resource and providing them with opportunities to take on new roles as an in-service provider. In my ideal world, career paths would be created in this area.

Much key teacher wisdom is tacit and one key role of academic collaborators is to provide frames that help make this tacit knowledge explicit and to provide teacher colleagues with alternative ways of framing their experiences. Another important role is providing affirmation of the value of the teachers' experiences, ideas and insights. It takes some time for teacher-researchers to accept what Munby and Russell called the authority of their own experience (Munby and Russell 1994). At present, schools and systems often have a limited conception of the potential impacts and benefits of teacher research; academics can help provide them with a vision of what is possible and can provide platforms for teacher-researchers to share their understandings.

The products of teacher research

By products of teacher research I mean new understandings, insights, ideas and advice; things that, at least to some degree, can be documented, although print is not the only way of sharing them. The four stakeholders face different costs and gain different benefits from going public and, as stated earlier, have different criteria for success and quality.

Costs, benefits and reasons for documenting and sharing findings

One cannot neatly separate discussions of process and product and several points have been made already. I described earlier how, over time, teachers develop more interest in going public and referred to the significant impact this can have on their sense of self-worth. A related benefit is that the thinking that a teacher group undergoes when planning to share their work: "What have we found out and how do we know it?" always (in my experience) provides a substantial and rewarding feeling of group progress: "we had not realized how much we had to say." Another benefit of writing is that it helps make explicit previously tacit, but important, knowledge. Teacher research results in a series of contextually specific classroom outcomes; looking back over many of these allows patterns and generalizations to be constructed. The biggest cost for teachers that is associated with writing of course is time, a barrier compounded by the fact that none of the above benefits are apparent to teachers until they have experienced them.

The necessary links between teacher research and professional development are highlighted when one considers the perspectives of school and system level leaders in this area. As discussed earlier, school leaders have legitimate agendas of maximizing the impact of the research across their school. Both they and system leaders want documentation and sharing that will encourage other teachers both to reconceptualize what is possible and to make use of the ideas and findings.

For understandable reasons, system level leaders commonly require documentation for reasons of accountability; the challenge is to structure the documentation process so that the act of writing achieves goals and purposes that are perceived as valuable by the teacher.

Academics, as said earlier, have a legitimate and much greater interest in formal publications of wisdom from teacher research, but this is more than just a need to add to one's CV. Research led and conducted by teachers provides insight into what happens when the inevitably neatened up world of theory interacts with the messiness of practice. It can generate sophisticated understandings of the complexity of practice – not just that it is complex, but how and why change can and cannot be made. For anyone involved in teacher education, this is priceless wisdom.

One, perhaps surprising, barrier for academic friends helping teachers write is connecting with the (academic) literature. A teacher enrolled in a higher degree has signed an agreement, so to speak, to do this. This is useful, but at any moment, only a small proportion of teachers are enrolled in higher degrees. Literature searches are a low gain activity for working teachers – they rarely find (for example) the sorts of wisdom that connect with their concerns. An academic friend can make such connections, but this raises a problem. Cochran-Smith and Lytle (1990) called for the voice of the teacher in the literature. Writing all over (however usefully) teachers' work quickly extinguishes their voice. This dilemma is not easily managed.

Standards of judgment for products of teacher research

Issues of rigour and quality in teacher research are often considered from academic norms. I argue that it is useful and important to consider what other stakeholders find convincing in accounts of teacher research as well as what they want to be included in such accounts.

The concerns of teacher-researchers means that their most important criterion for quality is a personal one: "Did this make a difference to my classroom?" The most compelling pieces of evidence for teachers are relevant changes (compared with previous experiences) in the behaviours and attitudes of their students. These manifest themselves both in unplanned critical incidents that reveal substantial change (Jepperson 2002) and in other, more regular student actions. Consider, for example, an experienced mathematics teacher who begins with the concerns that her students perceive mathematics as a set of pen and paper algorithms to be memorized and are unaware of and make no attempt to search for the big ideas of mathematics behind the algorithms. Successfully addressing these concerns will result in substantial changes to the questions her students ask, the issues they raise, the sorts of answers they demand and the way they talk to each other about the work. These will be profound and convincing changes. For her own purposes, she needs little further evidence – her classroom is better in the ways that matter to her.

The agendas of school leaders mean that they are interested in outcomes that are accessible and convincing to other staff: that will extend teachers' vision of what is possible and encourage other staff to not only try some of the new ideas, but to adapt them to their own contexts. There are four features of written accounts that meet these goals. One is that they are contextually rich – teachers like reading stories that provide windows into classrooms; the same sorts of critical incidents and student behaviours that matter to the teacher-researcher are convincing to their colleagues. A second is that they are "warts and all" – honest in their reflections about what was and was not achieved. A third is that they include insights, causes and frames that allow adaptation and extension, not mere replication. The fourth is that they provide multiple entry points – offering other teachers different ways into exploring change that include different levels and types of risk.

While skilfully written accounts are always an advantage, school level leaders are typically less concerned about quality of writing than other stakeholders. One reason for this is that talking to the teacher can enrich written accounts; a second is that building a school-wide culture of innovation and sharing is not easy and is not helped by setting what will be intimidating standards of excellence. System level leaders have similar agendas and interests to school leaders, but do need accounts more capable of standing on their own.

Academic stakeholders have legitimate needs for quality in the products of teacher research. It is unlikely that teacher research will make any significant contribution to the general research literature unless it meets reasonably agreed canons of excellence. However, the question of the origin of canons is far from resolved. I argue that teacher research should be regarded as a separate genre, should develop its own standards and not have those of other genres imposed.

It is helpful to consider issues of generalizability when seeking appropriate standards. Teacher research must always be contextually framed and is often criticized for not generalizing (Lampert 1997). Our experiences in the PEEL project, which has operated in hundreds of classrooms in a very wide range of contexts, is that teacher research can generalize in important and useful ways. Classrooms are messy, complex and idiosyncratic, but there are recurring themes and features that cross context boundaries and allow for purposeful and effective planning of change (Mitchell and Mitchell 2001).

Constructing such generalizations requires accounts from many classrooms and this leads to two possible characteristics of quality in teacher research. The first is that the research should show evidence of having emerged from a collaborative process, with ideas tested in a number of classrooms. Even a small group of teachers operate in many classrooms and can thus provide quite stringent tests of generalizability, particularly over more than one year.

A second characteristic of quality is evidence of a search for patterns, frames and links between learning, teaching and change that allow the construction of more powerful insights and advice. Generalizations by themselves are of limited value to teachers (and to academics who want to actually use them). They emerge to make sense of apparently diverse collections of practice and lose much of their meaning unless accompanied by representative accounts of the practice from which they emerged. Equally importantly, they need to be accompanied by advice and ideas for enacting them. Quality in knowledge of this sort is more than tips for teachers; it is grounded in the sorts of insights just referred to and includes evidence of seeking to make explicit what are often essential but tacit aspects of sophisticated practice.

Conclusions

I have argued that teacher research occurs in a school and system context and should not be disconnected from these. School and system level leaders are legitimate stakeholders in the process and must be crucial players in any attempts to make research a regular feature of teaching practice. Both of these stakeholders, and often the teachers themselves, see strong links between research and professional development.

The above argument is another way of talking about bridging the theory-practice divide. If any research should be important, accessible and salient to teachers it is teacher research. It follows from this that the academic world should take seriously the criteria that teachers find convincing in accounts of research and the features that they and school and system level leaders need to connect the research to practice.

I argue that, when considering what is important when communicating teacher research to academic audiences, we should reflect on the types of wisdom that academia needs and can best gain from teacher research. One essential plank in bridging the theory-practice divide is the sophisticated practical knowledge referred to earlier. This sort of knowledge is often not highly regarded, but it should be. It can be just as subtle and insightful as other forms of knowledge.

Finally, I argue that being clear about what teacher research can do, for whom and how is an essential precursor to developing appropriate canons of rigour and excellence. The suggestions in this chapter are not intended to be comprehensive, but rather to advance debate in this area.

Bibliography

Burke, D. M. I. (2002) "Principal class leadership – reflective perspectives on long-term management of change in teaching and learning," paper presented at the American Educational Research Association, New Orleans.

Cochran-Smith, M. and Lytle, S. (1990) "Research on teaching and teacher research: the issues that divide," *Educational Researcher*, 19, 2: 2–11.

Cochran-Smith, M. and Lytle, S. (1993) *Inside/Outside: Teacher Research and Knowledge*, New York: Teachers College Press.

Jepperson, P. (2002) "Linking: a strategy for enhancing learning," in J. J. Loughran, I. J. Mitchell and J. A. Mitchell (Eds) *Learning From Teacher Research* (pp. 91–114), New York: Teachers College Press.

Lampert, M. (1997). "Teaching about thinking and thinking about teaching," in V. Richardson (Ed.) *Constuctivist Teacher Education: Building a World of New Understandings*, London: Falmer Press.

Loughran, J. J., Mitchell, I. J. and Mitchell, J. A. (Eds) (2002) *Learning From Teacher Research. Practitioner Enquiry Series*, New York: Teachers College Press.

Mitchell, I. J. and Mitchell, J. A. (2001) "Constructing and sharing generalizable statements of teacher knowledge from context-specific accounts of innovative practice," paper presented at the American Educational Research Association, Seattle.

Munby, H. R. and Russell, T. (1994) "The authority of experience in learning to teach: messages from a physics method class," *Journal of Teacher Education*, 45, 2: 86–95.

Wagoner, J. (1993). "Educational research as a full participant: challenges and opportunities for generating new knowledge," *Qualitative Studies in Education*, 6, 1: 3–18.

Chapter 20

Working on the underbelly of the underdog

Listening for the ring-of-truth in a teacher-researcher's story

Judith McBride

After auditing a summer school course on the topic of educational leadership I wrote:

> Like a tender lavender sprig tugged and slammed by the violent summer storms that we witnessed in Lennoxville this July, I have been whipped through a wind tunnel of intense learning. Two weeks after Summer School began, I was tossed out, stunned, at the other end. Bruised, but not broken. Now, at home, I sit down to write, and try to make sense of it all. I am safe, yet there is a persistent uneasiness, a continuing, stirring draft that won't let me rest, won't let go. It carries a whispered potential. And so I straighten myself up and look at the new landscape in which I have landed. My story may read as an exaggeration, not believable to some. Perhaps it won't be believed except by those who lived it.

Summer school

"What do we hope to learn from the course?" we are asked. I reply with my standard. I am interested in the gap between Theory and Practice, I want to know what's in that space. I suspect it has something to do with experience and interpretation. We've been told we will be learning about research diaries and the validation process. I don't know about the diaries, but, in my head, I hear old arguments about the essentials – Validity and Reliability and Generalisability. I get it. I see the need. If I am going to write a dissertation. Then I hear Jack. Values and Claims and Evidence. And I sense that I am moving into another realm. I am curious. I am surprised that an article that I have been rereading is recommended for the course. Uncanny. Elliot Eisner. I feel at home. "The promise and perils of alternative forms of data representation." This course holds promise for me. Surely, there can be no peril here in Jack's classroom.

We are asked, as professional educators, what we care about in education. What are the standards of practice we live by? How do we hold ourselves accountable? That's easy. I respond as a teacher. I write, "In my work as a teacher I am accountable to my students, for it is the student that I value above all. I can be happy with the job I have done if my student is comfortable, safe and senses that I love and value each and every one. This doesn't happen often. Generally, there is a tension that exists in our classroom that is generated by the needs of the children, and my inability to read them. My inability is a function of many things. I may be preoccupied with issues of curriculum, or bureaucracy, or the politics of the school. Sometimes I just get tired. But because I value the children, and their childhoods, there is a pull that brings me back to them. This it seems to me is the process of accountability in my work. It is collaborative. It drives me, and it drives the real learning – theirs, mine and ours – that takes place."

Jack wrote back to each of us. To me he wrote, "I was struck immediately by the power of your statement, 'I am accountable to my students for it is the student that I value above all.' I'd like to be accountable to similar values where you say: 'I can be happy with the job that I have done if my student is comfortable, safe and senses that I value each and every one' ... I'm wondering if you would like me to help you to construct a story which communicates the values which drive you and to see if we can share an understanding of your claim that these values 'drive the real learning – theirs, mine and ours'."

Jack proposed writing a negative dialectic. Now I am unsure. Where is this leading? Stories could be lurking. Do I really want to know? To tell? Stall. Can I Trust? I answer, "I should like to accept your offer of help to, as you suggested in yesterday's letter, construct a story which communicates the values which drive me, and to see if there can be a shared understanding of my claim that these values drive the learning done by my students, the learning that I do, and the learning that my students and I do together ..."

Jack's classroom is emptied of us from Thursday until Monday. It does not feel safe, and I am glad to leave. A colorless, glass jelly jar, left stark and empty. At home I sift through a decade of files and boxes. Stories, art, journals, tapes, letters, videos, photos, sketches. My family stays away, leery of my tears, my anguish, the cracks ...

Recognizing the ring-of-truth

The task I have set for myself in my doctoral research is a study of the learning of professional educators, and the articulation or embodiment of living educational theories (Whitehead 1993), my own included. I believe that there ought to be paradigmatic consistency between the work of the teacher-researcher and that of the researcher investigating the work of the teacher-researcher, and that the character of most inquiry conducted within practitioner domain is qualitative. Creswell (1998) identifies five qualitative traditions – phenomenological, grounded theory and case studies, along with biography and ethnography. Each offers something to the practitioner embarking on inquiry, and teacher research may present itself as a hybrid, incorporating aspects of conventions, language, and subject matter of each. The teacher-researcher studies the meanings of behavior, language and interactions of members of a group sharing a culture, including him- or herself, colleagues, students in a particular context with a particular problem. Research will usually be driven by purposive sampling, plans tailored by experience, and questions exploring the meaning of that experience. It will reflect contextual, cultural, personal, and institutional themes as witnessed through observation, archival documents, or inter-views, and may include the direct experience of the researcher. Compre-hensive description in the voices of participants will provide explanations and possible multiple meanings through analysis, detailed description, or interpretation. Data may be gathered over a number of years, subjected to specific steps in data analysis, and report a chronology of major events. Ultimately, the process may reveal an image that includes general meanings, a plan for action or a report of change.

Inside a dark, unfamiliar place

At Summer School, I could not see myself as the teacher I believed myself to be. I did not understand the teacher who wrote:

Working on the underbelly of the underdog

This is where I do my work. From the outside, Chambly County High School is unassuming; low, red brick, bad windows, big trees, occa-sional graffiti, space and air. Green Street is suburban and duly quiet. We know little of our immediate neighbors anymore; their children, many Chambly County grads, have grown and gone. It is inside this hard, chestnut shell that the heart beats and breaks. It is inside this school that I have worked hard to become the teacher I long to be.

Most of the time I have taught in Room Two. It is a tiny, teeming space, that I left to begin a year of concentrated study. During my time in Room Two as a special ed. teacher, I have slowly become aware that all in our system is not equal. My kids are treated differently, not always fairly, and the injustices are not always open to view. Along the way I adopted Lewis Carroll's Mock Turtle as our mascot, my metaphor for my kids.

"I only took the regular course," said the Mock Turtle. "What was that?" inquired Alice. "Reeling and writhing, of course, to begin with," the Mock Turtle replied; "and the different branches of Arithmetic – Ambition, Distraction, Uglification and Derision" … "And how many hours a day do you do lessons?" said Alice … "Ten hours the first day," said the Mock Turtle: "nine the next, and so on." "What a curious plan!" exclaimed Alice. "That's why they're called lessons," the Gryphon remarked: "because they lessen from day to day."

(Carroll 1929)

In order to deal with the inequities I perceive, the reeling and writhing, I continually search for knowledge; better knowledge, the right knowledge. Critical knowledge. Liberating knowledge. To that end, I have spiraled in and out of the academic world taking courses, earning diplomas, certificates, and degrees. In my constant and ongoing search for knowledge, teaching and learning have become inseparable for me. There is an enduring tension in my practice, a reminder:

> You are not there yet,
> there is more learning to do,
> you have not yet become the teacher you hope to become.

When I left Room Two in June, I took years of boxed memories home with me, and a certainty that I was a good teacher; hardworking, practiced, sound, accountable. My success with my special needs students has been celebrated. I have been thanked. I have been asked to speak to others. I received an award – deemed deserving by my peers. A good teacher indeed. So, how is it that on the second day of this course I found myself in tears, on my knees? I say:

> I am accountable to my students for it is the student that I value above all. I can be happy with the job that I have done if my student is comfortable, safe, and senses that I love and value each and every one.

My colleague, Annette, understands my work as being to "protect and nurture [my] special education fledglings who have become trapped within an indifferent, if not occasionally hostile, system" (A. Languay, personal communication, 1997).

I nurture and I surrender them to indifference and hostility when they leave. Perhaps I have been caught up in the metaphors; baby birds, mock turtles, sad dogs, and I have lost sight of the real. Or perhaps, I have never known the real. I am confronted by my arrogance. I must think about my value claims, think about my role and my practice, and of how I touch my students. I must do this thinking with and through my students. Still and always mine. I have said that it is my values that drive our learning, that of my students, my own and our shared learning as well. I am questioning this now.

I began to think like a teacher-researcher when confronted with a new teaching assignment, a class of learning disabled students. Discouraged when they came into what was referred to as the bobo class, they were despondent, unruly and most definitely at risk of dropping out by June. I seethed with resentment at a clear lack of interest and support on the part of my colleagues and the administration. I had no sense of myself as a teacher. I was not in control. I became cynical. I spent a summer brooding, rewinding and reviewing the events of the year. I thought:

> You are not there yet,
> there is more learning to do,
> you have not yet become the teacher you hope to become.

By fall I understood a few things. I knew that if those students were to go to grade nine after one more year, I did not have the luxury of time to do a whole lot more remediation. I had to look forward to see what would be expected, instead of looking back to see what had been missed. When I looked for their strengths, I saw kids on the brink of disintegration. When I looked at my strengths, I realized that I could take charge if I opted to. I saw possibilities in basing my teaching on content and ideas that the kids really cared about. With more confidence than I had ever felt before, I returned to school in the fall, and by the end of the school year there was a palpable difference as we engaged in learning together. The kids informed me, I responded to them. We negotiated. Something was working, but I knew neither what nor why. But by now I knew the drill.

> You are not there yet,
> there is more learning to do,
> you have not yet become the teacher you hope to become.

I decided that it was time, once again, to go back to university, where I began a master's degree, and the work of understanding who I am as a teacher, developing a professional metaphor, learning of the value of critical response to my ideas, and of conceptual knowledge made explicit through the study of theory and research. I undertook my first action research project. I wanted to expose some problems posed for our special ed. students. The principal became involved, and when I saw that many of the issues raised by the students and staff were addressed as a result, I began to get a sense of the power of action research. It became clear to me that research was not something that I could do, or not do. Rather, it was becoming a way of thinking, a way of looking at the world, and it was not something that once begun, I could decide to stop. I began to consider myself an emerging teacher-researcher. I reflected. I acted on my reflections. On and on. Still, there was that reminder,

> You are not there yet,
> there is more learning to do,
> you have not yet become the teacher you hope to become.

I began to attend academic conferences. On the two occasions that I heard Elliot Eisner speak, I felt engaged, encouraged, and enriched. He spoke to me, a teacher, with the heart and mind of an artist, and a clear understanding of life in my school. He brought our disparate worlds together in the notion that there are many ways of seeing, and many ways of representing what we see. I was enchanted with the idea of "exploring forms of communication that we do not normally use to represent what we have learned about the educational world" (Eisner 1997: 5).

My camera. My watercolors. Shoe boxes full of photographs, sketches, miles of video tape. Would such work count as a legitimate form of research (Eisner 1997)? And, does that really matter to me? Have I not, perhaps, been more concerned with creating "a visual narrative that displays an array of values, not by describing them, but by depicting them" (Eisner 1997: 6), so that others can see what I see, what my Mock Turtles see? Is it possible that I might use my visual musings to "enlarge our understanding?" (Eisner 1997: 8).

And what about my own understanding? And, yes, how is it that on the second day of this course I found myself in tears, on my knees? I say I am accountable to my students for it is the student that I value above all. Yet, I am credited with trying to protect and nurture my special education fledglings who have become trapped within an indifferent, if not occasionally hostile, system. It is time to return to Room Two for another look, to look through my contradictions, because as a teacher,

> I am not there yet,
> there is more learning to do,
> I have not yet become the teacher I hope to become.

I am looking for the Real and I am seeing Mike. In my work as a teacher I am accountable to him, for it is the student that I value above all. I can be happy with the job I have done if my student is comfortable, safe, and senses that I value each and every one. I know that most of my students feel safe in Room Two. They trust me with their flaws. When I say, "Try this," they do. Tentatively. Willingly. Eventually, automatically. Mostly. I see this trust as a measure of their sense of safety. This doesn't happen often. Generally, there is a tension that exists in our classroom that is generated by the needs of the children, and my inability to read them. The time and energy I need to negotiate with ten, fourteen, eighteen learning disabled kids is huge. Someone always gets less. My inability is a function of many things. I may be preoccupied with issues of curriculum or bureaucracy, or the politics of the school. Sometimes I just get tired. But, because I value the children, there is a pull that brings me back to them. This it seems to me is the process of accountability in my work. It is collaborative. It drives me, and it drives the real learning – theirs, mine, and ours – that takes place. But something is missing here. Have I done enough to justify my claim? There is a world outside our classroom door, indifferent, if not occasionally hostile, that I cannot ignore.

I can see Mike as he hunkers his heavy frame over his work. He is relaxed, and yet the intensity of his attention obliterates all else in a classroom where distractions are many. Room Two is a busy place. It is noisy, cluttered and crowded. But Mike is connected to his story and nothing else concerns him at this moment. He is comfortable. He feels safe.

Figure 20.1

> My best experience I would say of all, Miss McBride's class. One day she came up to me and she told me, like, how good I am, how like, ah, your essays and stuff like, like how I expressed the words in my essays and stuff, how I write and that. She says I use a very good vocabulary and stuff (unpublished raw data).

I know his story will be thoughtful and interesting to read. The hesitation in his speech poses no problem to pen and paper. From the vantage point of my desk in the corner, I am able to read that feeling in the softness of his bearing. There is a certain snugness to the circle created by the curve of his shoulders and arms as he envelops his creation. The features of his face reflect untroubled concentration. The fingers of his left hand splay across the page, defenseless. Not everyone sees Mike as I do. Beyond our classroom his fingers are drawn into tightly clenched fists. He is tall, heavy and imposing as he saunters down the corridor, away from Room Two.

> One thing I would like to change about myself is my behavior (unpublished raw data).

His walk is slow, measured, threatening. He will not be caught smiling unless it is to laugh at another. Mike is a bully. He's looking for his next victim. Last September Mike moved out of Room Two and into the mainstream. Not long after the start of the year there was trouble.

> My favorite song is "When I go away" (unpublished raw data).

Mike was threatening a boy in seventh grade. This accelerated to violence. To terror. No one knew what to do about Mike. No one could understand why it was different in Room Two.

> My favorite movie is *Bad Boys* (unpublished raw data).

No one has been able to stop him. No one can explain why he has been kicked out of class so often, why he has failed his courses, why he appears so unhappy.

> The worst mistake I ever made was going to school (unpublished raw data).

So how can I, his teacher, say that I value, that I love this student? Where can I see my values played out as he experiences our school? Only in Room Two? Perhaps, just perhaps, I did not hear him say he was not ready to leave. Perhaps he did not say it in the right words.

Perhaps he did not say it. He knew I might not hear. Would not hear. My energy was focused on Room Two. The celebrations inside that door. And Mike is not alone out there.

I have not listened. I have not heard. So, that is how, on the second day of this course, I found myself in tears, on my knees. I must spend more time outside Room Two. I must hear my students as they bring me reports of their struggles. Their apprehensions. Their catastrophes. Their failures.Their truths.

The issue of validity

At the end of Summer School I wrote a letter to the professor. I wrote:

Dear Jack,

Ten endless days ago, when I began your course, I had every confidence in my professional ability and integrity. I am well regarded. I have been told that I am good at what I do. I have had no problem accepting this idea. It was easy. It felt good. This morning I am clinging shakily to the underbelly. In claiming educational values which are embodied in my practice and examining the evidence which will decide whether or not my explanation can be regarded as valid, I have had to confront my false assumption that in all I have done as a teacher, my students are at the core of my concern. In the end, I have had to conclude that I have indeed exposed children to risk. Saying that is not easy.

Writing this paper has not been easy either. I have entered and explored new realms and tried new things in your wonderland, in order to make better sense of my work with my Mock Turtles … I'm in a new place. I feel unsafe. I am experiencing first hand what my Mock Turtles do when they leave Room Two. I cut them loose. In writing, I have cut myself loose.

In constructing a story that communicates my values, and strives for shared understanding, I explored the use of images as more than decoration, using them to represent my claim, and as evidence that toppled my claim. I used the watercolor sketch of Mike in this way, and I have used my interpretation to substantiate my belief in the inherent goodness of this child and to add emphasis to the urgency of the need to become the teacher I hope to become. I know now that it is important for teachers to write their stories, to face their contradictions, to break down walls and open doors between class-rooms.

The knowledge constructed by the teacher-researcher holds the pos-sibility of problem solution, direction for future action, and emergent theory. These may be construed as evidence of the teacher-researcher's learning, with learning defined as change in terms of perspective transformation

Table 20.1

Evaluation Criteria

Is there a recognition of a need to reflect on professional practices, in other words, is there

a stated circumstance and purpose for reflection and change

a recognition of a need to act on reflection, or

evidence of systematic inquiry into experience, understanding, alternate theory

evidence of study of meaning of behavior, language and interactions of members of a
    particular cultural group

evidence of reflection on the experience of all members

a plan tailored to the particular experiential phenomenon

evidence of a process of framing of questions, collection and analysis of data

a research question that explores experience

detailed description of a purposive sample

evidence of observation, archival documents and records, interviews

data gathered over a significant period of time

evidence of data analysis organized around themes that may indicate pivotal events

detailed description, interpretation, explanation and possible multiple meanings
    through analysis

a plan for action

an evaluation of subsequent changes to practices, or

a report of the enactment of change

evidence of the view of all members of the group and the researcher's interpretation

evidence of learning in terms of planning, enacting and evaluating change

evidence of general or universal meanings

evidence of emergent living theory

a recognition of a need to share the work of reflecting and acting in a public arena, or

a report which includes contextual, cultural, personal, and institutional themes

a comprehensive, possibly chronological, description of the experience in the voices
    of all involved

evidence of coherence of argument

reason for claims of consensus among researchers and audience

reason for claims of instrumental utility in guiding participants and others?

Sources: adapted from Creswell 1998, Eisner 1991, Elliot 1994, Hamilton 1998, McNiff 1993, Mezirow 1991, Reason 1998, Silcock 1994, and Whitehead 1993.

(Mezirow 1991) as evidenced in the planning, enacting and evaluating of changes to practice. The qualitative traditions coupled with evidence of teacher learning may constitute one set of criteria for determining the validity of the research endeavour, such as those I use when I present my work for public validation.

I am concerned with ascertaining that the report written by the teacher-researcher, my own included, constitutes more than story, and that certain criteria for validation be met. The trustworthiness and usefulness of the work must be established with, and for, others. Eisner suggests that "all experience derived from text is transactive, [and] we can ask what it is about text that is likely to make it believable," (Eisner 1991: 53) using three

Table 20.2

Feedback Frame

Coherence
Does the narrative make sense?
Do the conclusions appear to have been supported?
Is there evidence that multiple data sources have been used to give credence to the
   interpretation that has been made?
What other credible interpretations are there?
What leads you to accept the interpretation offered?
How well does the study relate to what you already know?

Consensus
Do you concur that the interpretations reported are consistent with your own
   experience or with the evidence presented?

Instrumental Utility
Does the story allow you to understand the motives and interests of the students
   and teacher?
What predictions about future events are you able to make?

Source: adapted from Eisner 1991.

criteria – coherence, consensus, and instrumental utility – to determine
whether or not an account has a ring-of-truth. Questions about credibility,
shared meaning and usefulness may thus be addressed. Working with these
ideas implies that "we cannot secure an ontologically objective view of the
world" (Eisner 1991: 60). Rather, the process of knowing is transactional,
and what we know is "mediated by what we bring to the world as we
achieve experience ... [and] what we use to convey our experience" (Eisner
1991: 60).

As an ensemble Eisner's proposed conditions, combined with general
characteristics of qualitative inquiry (Creswell 1998), have provided me
with criteria for public validation, a process that may determine whether
or not the work of the teacher-researcher has value as more than mere
story.

Bibliography

Carroll, L. (1929) *Alice's Adventures in Wonderland*, New York: Everyman's Library.
Creswell, J. (1998) *Qualitative Inquiry and Research Design*, Thousand Oaks, CA:
   Sage.
Eisner, E. (1991) *The Enlightened Eye*, New York: Macmillan.
Eisner, E. (1997) "The promise and perils of alternative forms of data representa-
   tion," *Educational Researcher*, 26, 6: 4–9.
Elliot, J. (1994) "'Research on teachers' knowledge and action research," *Educational
   Action Research*, 2, 1: 133–40.

Hamilton, M. (1998) *Reconceptualizing Teaching Practice: Self Study in Teacher Education*, London: Falmer.

McNiff, J. (1993) *Teaching as Learning: An Action Research Approach*, Bournemouth, UK: Hyde.

Mezirow, J. (1991) *Transformative Dimensions of Adult Learning*, San Francisco, CA: Jossey-Bass.

Reason, P. (1998) "Three approaches to participative inquiry," in N. Denzin and Y. Lincoln (Eds) *Strategies of Qualitative Inquiry*, Thousand Oaks, CA: Sage.

Silcock, P. (1994) "The process of reflective teaching," *British Journal of Educational Studies*, 42, 3: 273–85.

Whitehead, J. (1993) *The Growth of Educational Knowledge*, Bournemouth, UK: Hyde.

Chapter 21

Working it out

When is evaluation not evaluation?

Jean McNiff

Although I have been involved in evaluation work for some 20 years, it was not until one fine morning in October 2001 that I felt the full impact of its power-constituted nature at national level.

We were sitting round the table in the director's office: four of us, the director, his deputy, a senior manager, and me. The meeting had been called to discuss my final project report. The opening gambit by the deputy was not what I expected.

"This is not an evaluation," he said, pointing to the report.

I remember rapidly assessing all of the many responses I could have offered.

"If it isn't an evaluation, what is it?"

He launched into his version of what an evaluation was, and what it was not. My report fitted into the second category. As he was speaking, killer comments came to mind: "Since when did you become an expert in evaluation research? You're only a manager." The adolescent was responding defensively, using the same form of logic he had used, wanting to control, pull rank, and engage in a battle of "who knows?" and "who says?"; because this was what it was about really: whose knowledge was valid and who was to safeguard their status as a legitimate knower. The adult remained silent, thinking about how evaluation, and other concepts, can be appropriated to fit anybody's frame, about how the truth of ideas is communicated and established, and how truths are defended against challenge. I was never so acutely aware of Foucault's images of power and knowledge as the Janus faces of human interests.

I will continue the story shortly. Here, I have to say that the verdict was a shock, but I have learnt to absorb shocks and turn them into opportunities for creative learning. So since that day I have looked seriously at the methodological, epistemological and political bases of evaluation in education contexts, and I can now articulate my own theory of evaluation from my perspective as a professional educator whose work is itself a form of evaluation. I want to use the contexts of the project I was evaluating, as described here, to test that theory. The theory departs from traditional views of evaluation as something performed on the work, after the event. I believe that evaluation is embodied in the work, an organizing principle that transforms the work into a moral praxis. I believe that the idea of evaluation itself needs to be reconstructed as an evolutionary living process of enquiry, part of wider evolutionary living processes of enquiry, as its nature changes through the shifting influences of cultural traditions. Living out this idea of creating our own theories of evaluation, however, involves evaluating the idea of evaluation, in terms of what we believe is valuable in human enquiry and how that value is to be assessed. This also is a developmental process.

Learning about evaluation

I have learnt that different people understand evaluation in different ways, and these ways reflect the values they hold and the logics they use. Different approaches to evaluation have developed over the years, in terms of the objects of the enquiry (what is evaluated), the methodologies used (how evaluation is conducted), and the reasons and purposes of the enquiry (why the evaluation is conducted and how it will be used). Evaluation is to do with the idea that the worth of something needs to be established, and this means setting criteria by which value judgements might be arrived at. As the focus, methodology and purposes of evaluation have evolved, so too have the kinds of criteria identified. Importantly, there is little agreement about these things (as the meeting in the director's office showed), so perhaps people just have to find ways of accommodating their differences and living together reasonably peaceably without aiming for consensus.

Let's look at some of the differences in theories of evaluation. Early formal approaches were located within social scientific enquiry and were premised on a belief that evaluation is a matter of assessing the extent to which people behave as they should. The objects of evaluation were people's behaviours, and outcomes were generally presented as behavioural objectives. Thus we have, for example, the outcomes-based approaches of Tyler (1950), Bloom (1956), and Mager (1962). The values and assumptions communicated here were to do with the wishes of some groups to control others. The history of ideas shows that elaborate protectionist regimes are often put in place to defend the right of some to make decisions about others. These regimes do not usually embody the values of social justice. They are widespread and attractive to many people, particularly those who want to dominate. The situation today is that many people still use traditional social scientific approaches, even though these approaches might deny some of the democratic values those users supposedly espouse. The values of social justice do become manifest, however, in more recent participative models, such as Stake's case study approaches (Stake 1978), the Democratic Evaluation of MacDonald (1987), and the participative evaluation of Cousins and Earl (1995). Here, the object of enquiry has been reconceptualized as the interactions between different groups who are trying to make sense of their practices in the realization of democratically negotiated social goals. The methodology has developed as a form of collaborative enquiry. Questions do arise, however, about the degree of democratic practice achieved, since, while these approaches include participants in the evaluation process, the evaluation itself tends still to be managed and reported by an institutionally authorized "researcher." However, movement is evident towards a form of enquiry that acknowledges the contributions of all. Even more recent forms of evaluation (for example, Kushner 2000, 2001) take the person themselves, in company with others, as the object of enquiry, though there is still ambivalence about who evaluates what and which standards of judgement are used. Hopkins (1989) contains an excellent review chapter on models of evaluation; see also Stronach and Torrance (1996).

Here are my own views about the objects of enquiry, methodologies, and reasons and purposes of evaluation. I believe that the form of evaluation most useful for understanding and improving personal and social contexts is a process of collective personal enquiry, in which the individual comes to make judgements about their own work, through self-study, in the interests of contributing to the development of good social orders. The criteria by which they assess whether they are contributing to good social orders are embodied in their capacity to demonstrate that they are living in the direction of their personal and social values. These ideas are grounded in my own beliefs about the nature of right living, and how this involves a capacity to help others to develop as individuals who also are in company with others. I understand the nature of "right" as in relation to the values that drive one's life. This is a problematic concept, since, if I am true to the idea of pluralism, as I now explain, there is no one "correct" view of "right."

I believe that people are able, and have the right (severe pathology aside), to speak for themselves and be in control of creating their own lives, in negotiation with others. I believe that we should all accept responsibility for what we say and do. And if we want to exercise our capacity for free speech and action, we need to ensure that we speak and act in ways that are right for all, in the interests of developing good social orders. Of course, the idea of "good social order" also is contested. Some philosophers believe this refers to a place arrived at by people acting in ways that are popularly acknowledged as "good." I do not go along with this, because I believe that living in peace with others means recognizing that we are all (not only some) capable of evil as well as good (Alford 1997) – certainly I observe this capacity in myself and others – and, because (probably) none of us is ever going to be perfect, the way we come to live at ease with others is by necessarily recognizing others in ourselves, and ourselves in others (Minh-ha 1989), strengths, faults, and all.

I understand a good social order not as a place, but as a process through which all can come to live together peaceably. This process involves developing an understanding that one person's "good" is informed by the values they hold as "good" because there are no overarching systems of values to make decisions about these things. We act on what we come to believe. However, coercion aside, we do have choices, and choices are exercised in terms of the principles of what is right for a community. We have choices around what, as individuals, we believe valuable and how we think and act, but our thinking and acting always need to be understood as in relation to our communities. I believe that helping people to recognize that they have choices, and can make them in relation to others in their communities, is largely a matter of education. Interpretations of "education" also vary, of course, so we need to be clear about what education means for us. Education, for me, is a context for processes of mental and spiritual growth in the direction of life-affirming practices. I aim to move beyond relativism, because, like Polanyi (1958), I make a commitment to this belief with universal intent. In this view, my work as a professional educator is to find ways to help people develop the kinds of relationships which will help them to understand their work as a process of enquiry that itself constitutes a good order, a process in which we negotiate our identities with one another for mutually reciprocal benefit in the interests of life-affirming practices. To do this, I need to recognize myself as part of that process, a person who is struggling to act in the same way as she is encouraging others to do. This is very hard.

It is also contrary to the traditions of social scientific approaches in general, and to traditional approaches to evaluation in particular, because (a) traditional approaches are premised on values-based assumptions concerning the categorization of people and the inequitable distribution of power; and (b) the very logics used to enquire into personal and social interactions reinforce practices of discrimination and alienation. These logics embrace what Chomsky (1996) has termed "the externalist orthodoxy," that is, the idea that a common body of "things" exists which may be studied and reported by an external observer. The traditional logics of evaluation hold that people's actions constitute a unified body that may be studied, like rocks and trees, and judged in terms of what value the external researcher places on them, rather than evolutionary processes that may be judged by practitioners themselves as potential contributions to good social orders.

These ideas are the grounds for my current understanding of evaluation and other concepts. "This is not an evaluation" shifted my thinking into a new plane. Evaluation, House (1980) rightly says, involves processes of persuasion, and persuasion usually aims to inspire others to change their ways in the direction that the persuader sees fit. Processes of persuasion are embodied in our discourses and practices, as these are communicated through the culture. Traditional social scientific discourses communicate concepts such as identity, race, age, gender, disability, and evaluation as "things," social categories that are communicated as stereotypes, that enable us to "know" what a person is like even without meeting them (Locke and Johnston 2001). I believe new discourses need to be developed, out of an understanding that social categories are manufactured and are continually shifting. We need to be aware of which social practices enable what are discursively created categories to come to be regarded as "givens;" and how the language we use, as embodied most noticeably in our institutional practices, then reproduces and reinforces the stereotypes and categories; and how people become alienated one from the other, not because of any "natural" tendencies, but because we are systematically taught from birth that this is the right thing to do. While we might not be born prejudiced, most of us learn from our first encounters with the culture how to be prejudiced because prejudice is what the culture values.

I disagree with the normative view of evaluation as a "thing," an instrument to be used on categorized people. I see evaluation rather as a discursively created concept that communicates how people come to make choices about the ways they wish to live, personally and socially, and can demonstrate how their ways of living count in the development of what they believe is good. How communities then come to judge their own ways of living as contributing to universal good orders is a wider debate that I explore elsewhere.

Learning about knowledge

The verdict was delivered in October 2001, when the formal project I was evaluating had come to an end. In April of the same year, while the project was still in progress, I had attended the American Educational Research Association Annual Meeting in Seattle. This meeting took as its themes the questions, "What do we know?" and "How do we know it?" The questions took on a special significance for the work I was doing, because they helped me to begin to clarify for myself both the changing nature of the knowledge base of evaluation, and also the political implications of the knowledge base I subscribed to in doing this work. I began using those questions to develop a theoretical framework.

I need to give you some background. I also want to make clear that I am not identifying people here. That would be irresponsible. What I am trying to do is to communicate how I understand approaches to human enquiry as contested, in terms of their epistemologies, methodologies and social purposes; and how these different approaches can be evaluated by the people who are using them in terms of their potentials for developing good social orders. I also want to say that the locations for my learning included not only the peaceful contexts of my living/reading room and the high conceptual ground of AERA, but also the problematic experiential field of institutional contexts like the director's office.

I work in an independent capacity, mainly in Ireland, although I live in England. In November 2000 I had been invited to do this evaluation by a government-affiliated agency in Ireland. This organization had responsibility for implementing a national curricular programme in education, and they wanted it evaluated, though they did not specify by what criteria. It seems that the reason I had been approached, instead of another evaluating agency such as one of the universities, was because my work is now well known in Ireland, in terms of my commitments to practitioner enquiry and its benefits for organizational growth (Collins and McNiff 1999; McNiff and Collins 1994; McNiff et al. 2000). I was invited evidently because the management of the commissioning organization held a vision that the evaluation process might provide a context to begin a programme of sustainable professional education for teachers. In preliminary discussions I made the point that I did not work from an externalist perspective. If the organization wanted a traditional objectives-based evaluation report, they should invite someone else. My work as a professional educator was to help teachers find ways to develop self-evaluation strategies whereby they could come to make professional judgements about their own work. The professional judgements of individuals would then be tested and critiqued by their peers, and this process of negotiated knowledge creation could inform future group practices. In this way, I believed, individuals acting collectively could become change agents in their personal and collective lives. Individual knowledge could transform into collective knowledge, and this in turn might begin to inform institutional practices. Knowledge, in this view, would remain a property of an individual practitioner, but the knowledge that could influence organizational growth would be recognized as embodied within the relationships of people as they negotiated what should count as their truths. The methodology to communicate this epistemological base was action research, a process of enquiry which places the individual "I" at the centre of the enquiry, begins by asking questions of the kind, "How do I improve what I am doing?" (Whitehead 1989, 2000), and follows a systematic action plan to help people learn how to address the problematics of personal and organizational living. This vision of organizational growth through the sustained enquiries of individual practitioners was not an empty pipedream. It had already been realized within the award-bearing courses that I manage and teach in Ireland, with a substantial body of research-based evidence to demonstrate its educational and social potential (McNiff 2000). The possibility of becoming involved in this evaluation work, however, was a first opportunity to try to realize the vision within the broader institutional practices of a national programme and to demonstrate the educative potential of action research approaches for wider educational and social reform.

So I worked with teachers and principals in schools across the country for eight months, helping them to reflect on their work, and produce self-study accounts which embodied their own living educational theories (Whitehead 1989). The research archive contains some 60 self-studies of how teachers have become active participants in curriculum research and development. While I believe I can say that I have helped the teachers to reconceptualize their practice as a form of personal research that contributes to wider organizational development, clearly my influence has not yet engaged all at management level ("This is not an evaluation"). I do recognize this as a difficulty, and am trying out new strategies (see below "Learning about my work").

The project is now part of new writing from the perspective of my own learning (McNiff in preparation). Through doing the work I have come to appreciate the severity with which issues of knowledge are contested, particularly the AERA 2001 questions "What do we know?" and "How do we know it?", and the 2002 questions, "How do we validate and value our knowledge?", because these questions raise other questions about the legitimacy of the objects of evaluation, and its epistemologies, methodologies, reasons and purposes.

Rather than understanding evaluation as an objectivized "thing," I have come to understand it as a developmental process within wider developmental processes of human enquiry. I understand evolutionary forms to be transforming into increasingly mature versions of themselves in terms of their capacity to become ever-life-affirming (McNiff 2000), and I understand action research approaches as more evolved in this view than traditional social scientific approaches. They are more evolved in terms of their capacity to value all people through non-discriminatory practices (and therefore demonstrate their capacity as life-affirming for all), and also in the form of theory used to realize commitments to these practices. Social scientific approaches offer verbal descriptions and explanations, and these can then be incorporated as valuable insights as people come to theorize their own living practice. It is through the experience of living, however, that people actually come to demonstrate what good means for them. As people practise, they identify their values and try to show in practice how these values act as the criteria by which they can make judgements about their own way of living (Whitehead 1999). As they think about these things, their thinking can begin to develop as a form of theory, bringing order to the seemingly chaotic insights generated through the often equally chaotic experiences of practice.

I understand how conflict can arise among people working within different traditions, because they tend to see traditions as categorized "things," rather than as evolutionary processes that are part of larger evolutionary processes. I believe that a major purpose of human enquiry is to understand and theorize processes of enquiry as generative trans-formational processes, rather than as stable states that can be defined in terms of their paradigmatic differences.

Learning about my work

Now, back to the story. Because the report was contested, I withdrew it. I had not claimed payment for this phase of my work, so the issue of ownership did not arise. Therefore, unless I was prepared to do something about it, the findings of the evaluation would remain unshared, and the rich work of 60 teachers would not reach wider audiences and sustain the process of educational reform the teachers had hoped for. In the meantime the organization asked me to write a bland descriptive report, dealing mainly with an account of events and possible implications for schooling. This I did, because I still had a professional responsibility to bring the work to closure. I claimed payment, and my official involvement was at an end.

I now intend to contact all the teachers, in my capacity as an independent researcher, and ask them if I may reference their work in new writing. I hope to produce books and papers that will incorporate the teachers' work and show the processes of collaborative enquiry as a powerful driver of organizational change.

Following the experiences recounted here, I discussed with some of the participants of the project how we might continue to work together. I now work, on an independent unfunded basis, with teachers and principals in three schools, helping them to theorize their practices as self-evaluation and to track how their own improved understanding and practices are contributing to school development. I am monitoring my educative influence as I aim to help teachers improve their school contexts. I am hoping to produce texts to show these processes, in order to contribute to a theory of school development as grounded in the self-evaluations of practitioners, and to the growing body of literature of teacher research for school development (McNiff in preparation).

Evaluating my own work

I believe I have improved my own work as a professional educator. I am testing that claim against the identified criteria of my educational values, as set out earlier, that all people are able, and have the right, to speak for themselves and create their lives in negotiation with others. I am aware of my responsibilities in the workplace for helping teachers to understand their work as a form of self-evaluation that has implications for wider social contexts and for what counts as educational research. I am also aware of my responsibilities as a public intellectual to engage in professional discourses about the nature, uses and purposes of evaluation, and to use my influence to change popular stereotypical perceptions of evaluation in favour of more considered, problematized ones. I ground my claim to improvement in three "warrants" for establishing the legitimacy of research claims (Cochrane-Smith and Fries 2001): an evidential warrant, an accountability warrant, and a political warrant. The evidential warrant is that my work with teachers demonstrates consistently that claims to knowledge are based on validated empirical evidence, that I and teachers have come to modify our practice through self-study in ways that are educationally and socially beneficial for ourselves and our students. The accountability warrant is that we demonstrate how we hold ourselves accountable for our words and actions by testing our emergent theories against the stringent critique of others. The political warrant is that we demonstrate how our personal enquiries have practical significance for policy making in our workplaces and wider contexts. My claim that I have encouraged teachers to develop the kind of practices to fulfil their own criteria of educational excellence, as tested against policy criteria, is grounded in my capacity to sustain the kind of educative relationships through which the values-as-criteria come to life, and to find ways of disseminating reports of the work to contribute to a growing literature on the power of practitioner-based research for organizational and social change.

And the consequences?

It could be that I have burnt my boats regarding any future work in evaluation in some contexts. I have not remained silent, as some people might have wished me to, because I believe that evil flourishes when justice is not lived in the small as well as large contexts of human living. I embrace the Talmudic idea that by contributing to the welfare of one individual we contribute to the wider good of all. I believe that people have the right to engage in public debates that involve their own lives. I believe the people who took part in the evaluation needed to know the findings of my original report, and have their work celebrated and recognized for its enormous educational value, so I am finding ways of doing that. I might have burnt my boats, but I know which boats I have burnt, and why. I also know that, if we are true to our educational commitments, new boats are provided for what we have to do.

Bibliography

Alford, C. F. (1997) *What Evil Means to Us*, Ithaca: Cornell University Press.

Bloom, B. S. (1956) *Taxonomy of Educational Objectives*, New York: McKay.

Chomsky, N. (1996) *Powers and Prospects: Reflections on Human Nature and the Social Order*, London: Pluto.

Cochrane-Smith, M. and Fries, M. K. (2001) "Sticks, stones, and ideology: the discourse of reform in teacher education," *Educational Researcher*, 30, 8: 3–15.

Collins, Ú. and McNiff, J. (Eds) (1999) *Rethinking Pastoral Care*, London: Routledge.

Cousins, J. B. and Earl, L. (1995) *Participatory Evaluation in Education: Studies in Organizational Use and Organizational Learning*, London: Falmer.

Hopkins, D. (1989) *Evaluation for School Development*, Buckingham: Open University Press.

House, E. (1980) *Evaluating with Validity*, Beverly Hills: Sage.

Kushner, S. (2000) *Personalising Evaluation*, London: Sage.

Kushner, S. (2001) "Culture, standards, and program qualities," in A. Benson, D. M. Hinn and C. Lloyd (Eds) *Visions of Quality: How Evaluators Define, Understand and Represent Program Quality*, New York: JAI, pp. 121–34.

Locke, V. and Johnston, L. (2001) "Stereotyping and prejudice: a social cognitive approach," in M. Augoustinos and K. J. Reynolds (Eds) *Understanding Prejudice, Racism and Social Conflict*, London: Sage, p. 108.

MacDonald, B. (1987) "Evaluation and the control of education," in R. Murphy and H. Torrance (Eds) *Issues and Methods in Evaluation*, London: Paul Chapman, pp. 36–48.

Mager, R. F. (1962) *Preparing Objectives for Programmed Instruction*, San Francisco: Fearon.

McNiff, J. (in preparation) *Self Evaluation for School Development*.

McNiff, J. and Collins, Ú. (Eds) (1994) *A New Approach to In-Career Education for Teachers in Ireland*, Bournemouth: Hyde.

McNiff, J., McNamara, G. and Leonard, D. (Eds) (2000) *Action Research in Ireland*, Dorset: September Books.

McNiff, J. with J. Whitehead (2000) *Action Research in Organisations*, London: Routledge.

Minh-ha, T. (1989) *Woman, Native, Other*, Bloomington: Indiana University Press.

Polanyi, M. (1958) *Personal Knowledge*, London: Routledge.

Stake, R. (1978) "The case study method in social inquiry," *Educational Researcher*, 7: 5–8.

Stronach, I. and Torrance, H. (1996) "The future of evaluation: a retrospective," *Cambridge Journal of Education*, 25: 283–99.

Tyler, R. (1950) *Basic Principles of Curriculum and Instruction*, Chicago: University of Chicago Press.

Whitehead, J. (1989) "Creating a living educational theory from questions of the kind, 'How do I improve my practice?'," *Cambridge Journal of Education*, 19, 1: 137–53.

Whitehead, J. (1999) "Educative relations in a new era," *Pedagogy, Culture and Society*, 7, 1: 73–90.

Whitehead, J. (2000) "How do I improve my practice? Creating and legitimating an epistemology of practice," *Reflective Practice*, 1, 1: 91–104.

Chapter 22

The "look" of the teacher

Using digital video to improve the professional practice of teaching[1]

Sarah Fletcher and Jack Whitehead

When Galileo turned his new telescope towards the cosmos he transformed the worldview that placed the earth at the centre of the universe. We are exploring the possibility that, by turning video cameras on ourselves, we can use digital technologies to transform our view of ourselves and thereby transform what counts as educational theory in the academy in relation to the conceptions of visualization, living contradictions and multiplicity of self. We are also exploring the implications of living our spiritual, aesthetic and ethical values as the living standards of judgement to which we hold ourselves accountable and the possibility that we can communicate meanings of our values as standards for testing the validity of our explanations for our own learning.

Fletcher's work is focused on mentoring within initial teacher-education and Master's programmes. Her primary concerns are threefold. She seeks to ensure the competence of entrants into the teaching profession and of mentors in relation to initial teacher-education and the provision and maintenance of educative relationships to enable students to learn.

Whitehead's work is focused on supervision of research students in a range of professional contexts. His primary concern is to ensure that his research students fulfil standards of originality of mind and critical judgement as they create knowledge in enquiries of the kind, "How do I improve what I am doing?"

Introducing ourselves

Sarah Fletcher

When I began teaching in 1973 I found that my educational and educative values, in working with children, could reach a full *creative actualization*. I came fired with a passion that my students should be offered every opportunity to feel secure and "be" to their full imaginative and intellectual potential. Working with others in an educative context has been and remains my driving force. As a keen photographer, I realize the potential of using digital video (DV) to enhance my practice as a teacher educator while I challenge myself to improve my own teaching.

Jack Whitehead

In 1971, while Head of the Science Department at Erkenwald Comprehensive School in Barking, the science inspector provided me with a video-camera to explore its potential in relation to science teaching. I could thereby "see" that I was denying in my practice some of the values I had believed that I was embodying. I was a living contradiction. This offended my sense of integrity but stimulated my creativity to imagine how I could explain my learning as I worked at living my educational values more fully.

Recently, my work has focused on how spiritual, aesthetic, and ethical values and living logics and theories influence the expression, by my students and myself, of originality of mind and critical judgements in enquiries of the kind, "How do I improve my practice?" I am particularly interested in using digital video in multi-media accounts of educational influence to understand the ways in which the experience of embodied values can be transformed into living standards of judgement and practice. I am researching this process through clarifying the meanings of my embodied values in the course of their emergence in my life as a professional educator and educational researcher.

Our social contexts

We see our social role in relation to our work as professional educators and educational researchers in the context of social analyses, which emphasize market forces. We accept McTaggart's (1992) notion of economic rationalism that tends to support devaluation and demoralization and where "economic necessity" is the driving force in decision-making.

As part of our self-education we are seeking to relate our understanding of what we are doing to our influences on our tendencies both to reproduce social formations in the "incorporation of structures" and to transform these social formations in our educational practices. In seeking to extend the influence of the new scholarship in teacher education (Whitehead 1993; Zeichner 1998) we are bearing Bourdieu's point in mind that:

> … practices are always liable to incur negative sanctions when the environment with which they are actually confronted is too distant from that to which they are objectively fitted. This is why generation conflicts oppose not age-classes separated by nature properties, but habitus which have been produced by different *modes of generation*, that is, by conditions of existence which, in imposing different definitions of the impossible, the possible, and the probable, cause one group to expe-

rience as natural or reasonable, practices or aspirations which another group finds unthinkable or scandalous, and vice versa.

(Bourdieu 1977:78)

Educative influence

Our primary responsibility as professional educators is to those we teach, the learners. As practitioner-researchers we have a dual responsibility to those we teach and to ourselves as academics, as knowledge-creators and as learners.

This is how we see ourselves integrating the above responsibilities explicitly within our practices.

Fletcher is learning to clarify and explicate her professional values as they emerge through a synergy of mentoring and action research within educational relationships (Fletcher 2000b). She is investigating how professional values change within multiple expressions of the Self (Elster 1985) and this is the basis of her PhD submission. Whitehead is learning to clarify and integrate values of originality of mind and critical judgement with spiritual values of love and compassion within his accounts of his educational influence on his own and others' education, and on social formations.

Whitehead and Fletcher share values of creative articulation as they form their own lives through education. They also share a strong desire to sustain their own integrity in relationships, while not violating the integrity of others. They are concerned for the well-being of their students as they create and test their own educational theories. They can explain their educative influence with individuals and with organizations and be integrated within their intentions to improve their practice as professional educators.

Researching our practice as professional educators

In this chapter we raise issues concerning the communication of the meanings of our values as standards of practice and judgement in testing our claims to be contributing to educational knowledge. We will do this through an analysis of one video-clip extract from Fletcher's teaching sessions with a postgraduate group on an initial teacher-education programme and from one of Whitehead's teaching sessions with a student about to submit for a Master's degree (Adler-Collins 2000). Finally we turn to the issue of the analyses of evidence we use to justify claims that we are improving our practices.

Revealing ourselves as living contradictions

In this video sequence recorded on February 22, 2000, Fletcher sees herself holding her students at bay, worrying that they will interrupt the flow of her presentation, and thereby denying them the opportunity to engage in enquiry with her. The group of postgraduate students preparing to become school-teachers was participating in a session called "Using Visualization to Enhance Learning." Fletcher has used pre-recorded video sequences earlier in this session to promote discussion about how learners can be assisted in developing their visual skills and she is focusing on developing listening skills. She aspires to enabling shared enquiry with her students, encouraging creativity and valuing individual contributions but in the session she is describing below she begins to close down shared enquiry.

In her planning notes relating to the session she observes
I realize the trainees here may not all support the use of visualization in their teaching but I want them to be ready to experiment. I do not know at the outset how this teaching session will go – I am experimenting too. I will invite the trainee teachers to draw themselves as the teachers they see themselves as being now (Mitchell and Weber 1999) and then as the teachers they wish to become (Markus and Ruvolo 1989; Ruvolo and Markus, 1992). I want to support them beyond mere compliance with imposed standards of competence from the Teacher Training Agency as they develop their own spiritual, aesthetic and ethical educational values to use as their own standards to judge their own educational practice. My educational theory is that such educative values are best developed in a context of shared enquiry as we work together to understand how we can improve our teaching.

I'm drawing on the concepts outlined by Lomax (1999) of "inter" and "intra" dialogues. By inter dialogues I mean I am speaking to the group. By intra dialogues I intend those internally non-vocalized reflections as I am interacting with the group. I depict what I said to the group *in italics* to distinguish it from what is going on in my mind as I seek to show and understand the interplay between vocalized and non-vocalized commentary.

I'm going to ask you to cooperate with me basically by concentrating on just one sense – I'm not sure the group will cooperate; D. is almost certain to interrupt what I am saying.

My group likes to write notes as we go along – but can they do this if they are really involved in this experience? Just tell them what to do, it will be easier in the end!

I don't want you to write or to talk. What I want you to do is just concentrate on listening. Just concentrate on what you are going to hear. Don't anyone talk, please …

Can D. actually do this? – she always seems to interrupt just as we get going – so explain!

Can they do this if they are looking round – maybe suggest they have their eyes closed?

It might help if you close your eyes. Oh no – I can hear the noise of a chair and student moving … that's going to ruin their concentration. I just know

Figure 22.1 Sarah and her group

Figure 22.2 Sarah in didactic mode!

D. will talk now … how can I keep the group's attention focused on listening to the tape? Try telling them.

It's not just yet. Concentrate just simply on what you hear. This is an important point – it needs stressing … *and when you hear* … These are adults – not kids, don't tell – remember, invite them! They have different learning styles – so invite them! *If you can, think what it is that either makes you stay in this room or perhaps reminds you of somewhere else, where you have been.* This tape is too quiet and I need to tell them what to do again. *Think about the sounds around – it's very quiet … you're going to actually be at the level of listening to breathing.* D. ALWAYS interrupts – but this time – she hasn't!!! Great!

How does the video help me to look at my practice?

I see the internal struggling between telling the group what to do and wanting to enable them to engage in enquiry with me. There is suddenly a shift in the detail of my internal dialogue that I recall as I examine the frames of the video one by one. Because my students are adults, I move from a "tell them what to do" approach to one of enquiry. This aligns more fully with my educational values as I engage in teaching. I am sure I would lose an understanding of how my internal and external dialogues interplay without using video as a stimulus to reflection and without its lens to confront me with the reality of my practice.

Jack Whitehead as a living contradiction portrayed on a video of his teaching

Whitehead has similar experiences in viewing his own practice as a supervisor of JeKan Adler-Collins' educational enquiry; he sees himself overriding the compassionate and engaged response with students that he aspires to as he concentrates on the text in hand.

Though the student is clearly in considerable discomfort, Jack apparently ignores this. By so doing he sees himself denying the spiritual and aesthetic values he thinks he embodies.

JeKan   Castaneda excites me from the point of view that for the past five years I have not been able to bring into my writing some experiences because they may be seen to be hallucinogenic or of altered states of mind. I'm irritated that the people who are stopping me sharing my experiences have probably never been a day without a hamburger. They are couch potatoes sitting in front of their VDU screens.

Jack   OK there is also a tendency of yours to disparage: towards megalomania.

JeKan   Megalomania – I'm not a megalomaniac – I'm irritated.

Jack   The other is to disparage.

Figure 22.3 JeKan is feeling unwell

Figure 22.4 Jack is busy reading

JeKan   I'm tired, I'm in pain, I'm irritated. The thing which started this off five years ago was my belief in altered states of consciousness in relation to my complementary medicine. I've jumped through every hoop. I'm now at the last one. But I am so tired. I'm not just mentally tired.

Jack   And I'm giving you tremendous compassion (Laughing).

JeKan   I'm not just mentally tired I'm totally tired. You're saying I'm being disparaging. I'm not. I'm angry.

How does the video help me to look at my practice?

As I analyze my interaction with others frame by frame in a digital video recording I am able to experience how my embodied values can be transformed into living standards of judgement (Laidlaw 1996) for my practice. When I see myself denying my values of love and compassion in this clip of my work with JeKan, I use action research (McNiff 2002) to assist me in improving what I do as a professional educator. I find the assistance of my colleagues and students helpful in the process of clarifying my values in the course of their emergence in my practice. Jean McNiff's work continues to be inspirational and I hope her readers share my enthusiasm and gratitude for her influence for good.

Revealing the meanings of the values which we use as our standards of judgement in our claims to be making contributions to educational knowledge

We both recognize, with the use of DV, moments where we find ourselves as living contradictions of those values we hold as educators. Conversely, we both recognize a shared communication in relation to the meanings of the spiritual, aesthetic and ethical values we use to explain what we do in our educative relationships. But living our values is not sufficient because as educators we seek to clarify, develop and communicate the meanings of our values, such as integrity, freedom and justice, as they are embodied within and emerge through our practice. We are establishing our values as "living standards" of practice and judgement and, by engaging with the politics of educational knowledge, contributing in a small way to a process of social transformation, through a reconstruction of what counts as educational knowledge.

Evidence to justify our claims that we are seeking to improve our practices

Fletcher develops her understanding of the dialogues she holds with her students and how these relate to the dialogues she holds with herself and integrates this understanding back into her practice as she assists her students to engage in creatively and critically forming themselves through education. The evidence for her continuing to extend her professional competence lies in her living a form of research-based professionalism in which she engages in self-studies of her professional practice in enquiries of the kind, "How do I use my understanding to answer questions of the kind, how do I improve what I am doing?"

Whitehead (1999a) is working in a similar way in relation to his valuing the originality of mind and critical judgement of his students as they work together to produce doctoral theses and Master's dissertations. His claim to improvement rests upon his response to past errors (Whitehead 1999a, b, c, and 2000) in his supervision of research students and on the extension of his cognitive range and concern as he integrates the ideas of others within his own learning. As part of her PhD programme D'Arcy (Whitehead 1997) has analyzed these errors in terms of the omission of aesthetically engaged and appreciative responses (D'Arcy 1998). What he would do in his super-vision was to give "Yes-But" responses to her work. He would move much too quickly into a critical stance without focusing on the achievements in the work presented. He is currently researching how to improve the quality of his educational responses with his students and also researching his influence in the education of social formations. By the education of social formations he means that social organizations can learn to live values of humanity more fully in the practices of the individuals constituting the formation, sustaining and re-formation of the organization.

How does Whitehead perceive Fletcher influencing him for good in using DV?

You have provided video-data and a perspective on my educative influence in a way which enhances my awareness of the importance of understanding the antecedents to a particular experience. You have put me under pressure to communicate my understanding of the DV technology as well as the living logics of my educational enquiries. This has stimulated my imagina-tion to think of ways in which I could work with you to extend the influence for good of living theories of professional educators and other practitioners.

How does Whitehead perceive he influences Fletcher for good in using DV?

I see the influence for good in terms of the creation and testing of your own educational theory as you explain your own learning about your educational influences and development. Following Kilpatrick (1951) I see this theory as a form of dialogue that has profound implications for the future of humanity. I think I have helped you integrate my ideas on living contra-dictions within your own of an educational multiplicity of self and within your action research. I have also assisted you in clarifying your educational values as standards of judgement to evaluate the validity of your accounts of your work.

How does Fletcher perceive she influences Whitehead for good in using DV?

I think I am offering you my perspective on what it is to be more fully present when you are engaging in educative relationships and an opportunity to see how you are engaging in educative relationships with others. This can provide you with a focus for targeted questioning of your practice and a basis for dialectical engagement as you seek to improve how you live your values. By my photographing your interaction with students, you now have dialectical perspectives that you would not otherwise have experienced.

How does Fletcher perceive Whitehead influencing her for good in using DV?

Prior to working with you, I was reluctant to use video images to analyze teaching. I preferred stills photography. In using digital video I now have a medium that enables me to see actions unfold and to understand how actions on my part can trigger others from my students. You introduced me to ideas of living theories and living contradictions.

Conclusion

We hope that we have communicated how DV is enabling us to see how to improve our practices as professional educators and educational researchers. Our internal and external dialogues are focused on our experiences of seeing ourselves in video recording as living contradictions, as we experience ourselves negating our aspired educational values. Our learning and explanations about how we live our values are influenced by our creativity, our evolving values, our investigations of our educative influence and our social contexts.

We do not believe that the meanings of our values can be adequately communicated, solely through the medium of written propositional discourse. We believe that we can come to understand and clarify the meanings of our values and how we sometimes negate them in practice by using DV. By analyzing our dialogues with our students and reflecting on how these are shaped by the internal dialogues in our minds as we teach (Fletcher 2000a) we are moving towards an understanding of our educational practice and how we influence others for good as we continue to ask questions like "How do I improve my practice?"

Note

1   An earlier version of this chapter was presented to the British Educational Research Association Annual Conference, September 7–9, 2000, at the University of Cardiff.

Bibliography

Adler-Collins, J. (2000) "A scholarship of enquiry," MA dissertation, University of Bath. Available online: (Living Theory Section) http://www.actionresearch.net.

Bourdieu, P. (1977) *Outline of a Theory of Practice*, Cambridge: Cambridge University Press.

D'Arcy, P. (1998) "Making my own maps" (Chapter 8 of "The Whole Story…"), PhD thesis, University of Bath. Available online: (Living Theory Section) http://www.actionresearch.net.

Elster, J. (1985) *The Multiple Self*, Cambridge: Cambridge University Press.

Fletcher, S. (2000a) "A role for imagery in mentoring," *Career Development International*, 5, 4/5: 235–43.

Fletcher, S. (2000b) *Mentoring in Schools: A Handbook for Good Practice*, London: Kogan Page.

Kilpatrick, W. H. (1951) *Crucial Issues in Educational Theory*, Educational Theory, Vol. 1, 1–8.

Laidlaw, M. (1996) "How can I create my own living educational theory as I offer you an account of my development?" unpublished PhD thesis, University of Bath.

Lomax, P. (1999) "Working together for educative community through research," (Presidential Address to BERA, Belfast, 1998), *British Educational Research Journal*, 25, 1: 5–21.

Markus, H. R. and Ruvolo, A. P. (1989) "Possible selves: personalized representations of goals," in L.A. Pervin (Ed.) *Goal Concepts in Personality and Social Psychology*, Hillsdale, NJ: Erlbaum Publications.

McNiff, J. (2002) "Action research and professional practice." Available online: http://www.jeanmcniff.com.

McTaggart, R. (1992) "Reductionism and action research: technology versus convivial forms of life," in C. S. Bruce and A. L. Russell (Eds) *Proceedings of the Second World Congress on Action Learning* (pp. 47–61), Brisbane: ALARPMA Inc.

Mitchell, C. and Weber, S. (1999) *Reinventing Ourselves as Teachers: Beyond Nostalgia*, London: Falmer Press.

Ruvolo, A. P. and Markus, H. R. (1992) "Possible selves and performance: the power of self-relevant imagery," *Social Cognition*, 10: 95–124.

Whitehead, J. (1993) *The Growth of Educational Knowledge: Creating Your Own Living Educational Theories*, Bournemouth: Hyde.

Whitehead, J. (1997) "The importance of loving care and compassionate understanding in conversations which sometimes become infused with irritation, frustration and anger: conversations and correspondences with Pat D'Arcy," paper presented at the International Teacher Researcher Conference, La Jolla, April, 1997.

Whitehead, J. (1999a) "How do I improve my practice? Creating a discipline of education through educational enquiry," PhD thesis, University of Bath. Available online: (Living Theory Section) http://www.actionresearch.net.

Whitehead, J. (1999b) "Creating a new discipline of educational enquiry in the context of the politics and economics of educational knowledge," paper presented at the BERA Symposium at AERA 1999 in Montreal.

Whitehead, J. (1999c) "Educative relations in a new era," *Pedagogy, Culture and Society*, 7, 1: 73–90.

Whitehead, J. (2000) "How do I improve my practice? Creating and legitimating an epistemology of practice," *Reflective Practice*, 1, 1: 91–104.

Zeichner, K. (1998) "The new scholarship in teacher education," (Vice-Presidential Address to Division K, AERA, San Diego), *Educational Researcher*, 28, 9: 4–15.

Index

Kerri Sackville narrowly missed out on Hollywood superstardom when she came runner-up to Nicole Kidman for the lead role in

, the only

P' ...e has ever been really good at. W....? ¬'N ʳ

Kerri Sackville is now an author, columnist and social media addict. Her blog, *Life and Other Crises* (at kerrisackville.com), details the daily dramas of her life as a forty-something wife, mum, friend, chaos wrangler and owner of an improbably white house.

Kerri has written extensively for mainstream media and online publications, including *The Sydney Morning Herald*, *The Age*, *The Telegraph*, *Sunday Life* magazine, the Child group of magazines, *Notebook*, *Mamamia.com* and *Australian Women Online*. She currently writes regular columns for *Practical Parenting Magazine*, *The Australian Jewish News* and the website *Daily Life*.

Kerri lives in Sydney with her architect husband, their three children and an accident-prone rabbit. When she is not writing, looking after the kids or cleaning the house, she enjoys tweeting, drinking caffeine with friends and lying extremely still on the couch.

Also by Kerri Sackville

When My Husband Does the Dishes . . .

The Little Book of Anxiety

Confessions from a Worried Life

Kerri Sackville

\R^p\

The Robson Press

First published in Australia in 2012 by Ebury Press.

This edition published in Great Britain in 2012 by
The Robson Press (an imprint of Biteback Publishing Ltd)
Westminster Tower
3 Albert Embankment
London SE1 7SP

ISBN 978-1-84954-337-8

10 9 8 7 6 5 4 3 2 1

A CIP catalogue record for this book is available from the British Library.

Set in Sabon by Midland Typesetters
Cover design by Namkwan Cho

Printed and bound in Great Britain by
CPI Group (UK) Ltd, Croydon CR0 4YY

For my parents, who worry about me

Contents

Prologue

My life has been filled with terrible misfortunes, most of which have never happened.

Michel de Montaigne, author

About six months into writing this book I realised it was all wrong. I had experienced the same crisis at about the same stage when I was writing my first book, *When My Husband Does the Dishes . . .* I wrote and wrote, only to hit a point where I thought, No, this is rubbish, I have to start again.

In writing *The Little Book of Anxiety*, I had been trying to describe what anxiety felt like. Well, clearly I was mistaken. What I needed to do, I realised, was to *illustrate* what anxiety felt like: to tell stories from my anxious life, anecdotes from my years and years of worry and stress and panic and nailbiting and all-round crazy-making.

This huge revelation came to me at eleven at night, when I was trying to fall asleep. I leaned over to the notebook that I keep beside my bed and calmly jotted down a few ideas. And then I laid my head back again on my pillow and slept soundly for the rest of the night.

Except that that's not what happened at all.

Yes, the huge revelation came to me at eleven at night. However, I didn't calmly jot down any ideas, and I didn't fall straight back to sleep. I sat up in bed and became incredibly agitated. The book was a mess! I'd got it all wrong! I had to sort it out – immediately!

I need anecdotes, I thought. Anecdotes from my anxious life.

But I couldn't think of any anecdotes.

My husband was just drifting off to sleep. I reached over and prodded him with my finger.

'Tell me about some of the times I've been anxious,' I demanded. 'I need to know for my book.'

T opened one eye. 'I'll tell you tomorrow,' he said.

'But I need to know *now*!'

'Kerri, it's eleven pm,' he said. 'I'll tell you tomorrow.'

My heart started to race. I felt wide awake. 'But what if there are no anecdotes?' I practically yelled. 'I can't remember ever being anxious!'

'There are plenty,' he said calmly. 'I can assure you, there are plenty. I'll tell you all about them in the morning.'

'But I can't sleep!' I shrieked. 'What if this is a horrible mistake? What if I can't think of any times I've been anxious? What if I haven't been anxious enough to write a book about anxiety?'

T propped himself up on one elbow, rolled his eyes and gave me a pitying smile. 'Kerri, if there is one thing I know for certain, you are anxious enough to write a book on anxiety. Now go to sleep!'

I didn't sleep, of course. I sat in bed for twenty minutes, fretting and frowning, before creeping downstairs and spending a bleary hour trying to make notes for the book. Except that I could barely recall anything.

Anxiety is a shocker. It robs you of your ability to think, and your ability to enjoy your life. It is a tightness in your chest. A pounding heart. Intense agitation. A brain clouding over. A mind closing in on itself. And, in its worst manifestations, extreme, blinding panic.

And I couldn't remember a single time I'd felt it. I was way, way too anxious.

I am a mother of three, a wife, a daughter, a friend, a colleague and a writer. My kids are gorgeous and healthy, my husband is nurturing and successful, and I am doing exactly what I love. I am adored by my family and friends, and am reasonably financially secure. I have every reason to be thrilled with my life, and have not one tangible reason for discontent. And yet there is a pervasive issue undermining my happiness, and it comes entirely from within me.

I suffer from extreme anxiety, and it informs every area of my life.

My family and friends are aware of my anxiety, but to people who only know me a little, this may be a surprise. They see the person who chats easily to the school mums, who doesn't panic when her child eats off the floor, who loves public speaking, who makes decisions quickly, who cracks jokes and laughs a lot. And yes, it is true. I am that person. But I am also the person who wakes in the morning feeling ill with anxiety, her heart racing with nerves. I am the person who worries about where the toilets will be, and who holds her breath before the lift door opens. I am the person who still gets unsettled travelling away from home, and whose fears lead her into panic.

No one outside my inner circle has seen this person, and it is possible no one knows that she exists. Except now, as I have made the choice to reveal her to the world.

And that thought makes me very anxious indeed.

A Born Worrier

Anxiety in children is originally nothing other than an expression of the fact they are feeling the loss of the person they love.

Sigmund Freud,
neurologist and psychologist

All I have to do is close my eyes and I am there again, four years old and utterly bereft. I am lying alone under my quilt, sobbing fat tears of distress and missing my mum.

I adored my mother. As a little girl I loved nothing more than to watch her as she got ready for a big night. I would perch on her bath in my nightie, breathing in the sweet, sharp smell of her perfume, fascinated as she applied her eye shadow and mascara, wondering at the silkiness of her dress.

She was beautiful.

My mother was my safe place. She was everything to me. She was my cuddles, my reassurance, my warmth, my love, my everything-will-be-okay.

My mother patted me to sleep. She soothed my worries. She enfolded me and made me calm.

But that night, she wasn't there. I was alone, and frightened, and rapidly becoming panic-stricken. My mum was gone. She had promised me she'd be back but that was *ages* ago and I didn't know how long I could hold out, huddled in my big-girl bed with my baby doll under one arm and my stuffed Doggie under the other.

I stared at my white bedroom door, willing it to open. I visualised my mum walking through, heading over to my bed with her blonde curls and high heels and her sweet mummy smell. But she wasn't coming.

I sobbed harder. My mum was never coming. I needed my mum and she wasn't there! *She wasn't there!*

The thing is, though . . . well . . . that wasn't actually strictly true. My mum *was* there. She hadn't left me at all. She was right outside my door, laughing, greeting guests and carrying plates of canapés. My parents were holding a dinner party, and my mum was simply doing her job, being the perfect hostess. What's more, before the party had begun she had tucked me into bed, kissed me goodnight and told me that she loved me. I had no reason to be afraid or forlorn.

But I was.

I couldn't fall asleep, and I wanted my mum, but at that moment my mum was out of reach. Instead of belonging to me she belonged to my father, and their guests, and the bustle of the party. She was out in the hallway, but she may as well have been on the other side of the world as far as I was concerned, because she certainly wasn't where I needed her to be.

'Mummy!' I cried, my face red and swollen. Tears dripped down my cheeks and onto Doggie's head. 'Mummeeeee!'

I could hear women's tinkling laughter, my father's voice offering drinks, the sound of the doorbell ringing as more guests arrived. Footsteps up and down the hall, music on the record player, glasses being clinked together.

The sounds of the party were a wall between my mother and me. I hated those adults invading our home. I longed for my mum and I was becoming more and more hysterical. When would she be back? Would she *ever* come back to me?

'Mummeeeee!' I sobbed. 'Mummeeeeeee!'

I wanted to go out looking for her, but there were strangers in my house and I was too embarrassed to appear in front of them in my long, purple flannel nightie. So I just lay there in my bed and continued to sob. And sobbed. And sobbed some more. And called out repeatedly, 'Mummeeeeeee! Mummeeeeeeeeee!!!!!'

Eventually, my mother heard my howls. There were hurried steps, and then my doorknob turned and light bled into my room.

'Darling!' said my mother, my beautiful, safe mummy. 'Sweetheart, what's the matter?'

Relief flooded through me, releasing my tension, and I sobbed even harder. 'I . . . missed . . . you!' I cried through gulping breaths. 'I . . . thought . . . you . . . weren't . . . coming back!'

'I didn't go anywhere!' she said, and stroked my forehead. 'I was in the other room with my friends. I would never go anywhere without telling you!'

I nodded. I suddenly felt very sleepy.

'Will you go to sleep now?' she asked. 'I'll come and check on you a bit later.' She kissed me twice and tucked the covers around me. 'See you in the morning, darling.'

As I felt myself drifting off to sleep, I told myself I wouldn't worry anymore. My mum and dad loved me. There was nothing to be afraid of.

And yet somehow, there always was.

• • •

I was a hideously anxious child, and that made life very difficult for all around me. The biggest problem was that I really had nothing to be anxious about, at least not at the age of four or five. I had parents who loved me, and a cute younger sister. It's not like I had to go out to work in the coalmines, or perform in child beauty pageants, or practise violin for three hours a day.

But I was anxious, and that anxiety needed an outlet. And so I worried endlessly about the worst possible thing that could ever befall a small child.

I worried about being deserted.

Night after night, I would lie awake in my bed, alert, vigilant and listening for evidence of abandonment. In particular, I would listen for the sound of cars. My bedroom was at the front of our house, adjoining the street, and my window looked right into our carport. As an unfortunate consequence of this accident of geography, I could hear every car that drove past our house. And every time I did, I would panic that it was my parents, sneaking out, driving away and deserting me.

Car doors slamming made my heart skip a beat. Car engines starting almost made me faint. Time and time again I would bound out of bed, run to the window, lift the heavy green drapes and check frantically to see if my parents' car was still in the drive.

Sometimes the sight of their red Volvo was enough to reassure me. I could trust that they were still at home, and still looking after me; or at least, trust enough to slip back under the covers and go to sleep.

Sometimes, however, even seeing their car wasn't enough to calm my fears. After all, who knew what devious lengths my parents would take to get away from me? What if they had escaped by taxi? What if they had packed their bags and fled by foot? How would I survive? I would be left all alone with my younger sister, with no one to love us or look after us. Or perhaps my parents would leave with my sister in tow and I would be absolutely all alone. I would die by myself, in the scary dark house, because my mummy and daddy ran away forever . . .

By this stage I would have worked myself up into a state of complete agitation. I couldn't sleep – I couldn't even close my eyes – until I had crept out of my room and tiptoed down the hall, to see if I could spot my mother somewhere in the house. I would glimpse her in the kitchen tidying up, or on the couch watching TV, or chatting to a friend on the phone. Once I saw her and knew that she was still there with me, I could quell my anxieties and tiptoe back to bed. And then I would fall immediately into sleep. After all, the panic was utterly exhausting.

I don't know why I thought my parents were going to abandon me. They had never left my sister and me without saying goodbye, let alone left us in the house completely unsupervised. My parents adored us. Neither of them did anything scary, or hit us, or had wild parties, or brought strangers home to stay. They didn't drink, or smoke pot, or engage in other criminal activities, or leave us sitting for hours in a car park while they went to play the pokies. I had absolutely no reason to worry they were going to leave my sister and me in the middle of the night.

I guess I didn't need a reason.

I didn't tell my parents about my abandonment issues when I was a child. I didn't confess my fears to them until I was well into my twenties. My mother, not surprisingly, was devastated at the news.

'But why were you worried we'd desert you?' she cried. 'We never snuck out of the house! We never, ever left you without saying goodbye!' And it was true.

'And you always had lovely babysitters!' she added. Okay, so that part wasn't completely true. Did she not remember Steffie, the ancient, bald woman in grey who made my sister and me sit in the dark so that we didn't 'waste electricity'? Not exactly 'lovely'. However, Steffie wasn't really relevant. Nothing my mother could offer was relevant. There was no reason for my anxiety. Anxiety isn't rational. And neither was I.

Despite my anxieties, I have many wonderful memories of my childhood. I was very close to my family, particularly my mum and my sister. I went to a nice school and had lots of play dates. I did after-school activities like ballet and tennis, had plenty of toys and loved the *Super Friends* cartoons on Saturday mornings. I remember snuggling in bed with my dad reading books, going on family trips to a friend's farm, sitting on the couch with our cat, Sam, and deconstructing every single episode of *Young Talent Time* with my sister.

But wherever I went, and whatever I did, I wore my anxiety like a backpack. I carried it with me to school, to friends' houses, at home, even to bed. Sometimes the pack was heavy, sometimes it was lighter, but it was always with me, day in, day out.

I'd been carrying that backpack throughout my life. Not only did I not know how to take it off, I wasn't even aware that I could.

I worried incessantly throughout my childhood, about matters large and small.

I worried terribly that I was going to get kidnapped while I was walking to school, which was literally one block down the road in a nice suburban neighbourhood, full of families, gentle elderly people and soft, fluffy kittens. I would walk nervously, wary of every man (and some women) who passed, and flinching at the cars that drove by fearing that an arm would shoot out and grab me and drag me into the car. Needless to say I always walked very quickly.

I worried constantly that my parents were going to get divorced. Now, my parents never said that they were going to get divorced. As far as I am aware, they never came close to getting divorced. But they did have arguments, and those arguments terrified me. I would see them in conflict and know for a fact that this meant that they were going to split up, which in turn meant that my world would completely collapse. So I would run between them, crying hysterically and screaming in panic, 'Don't get divorced! Don't get divorced!' My parents would then need to turn from each other to attend to me, sobbing and dishevelled on the floor, which meant that the argument was postponed for another time. So I guess it worked.

I worried a great deal about my friendships. I spent a lot of time fretting that my friend Nat would stop liking me, or that Ella would be angry at me, or that Louise – one of the 'cool' girls – would come between me and Michelle. And to a certain extent my worries were justified. Friendships can be tenuous when you're a kid, and girls in particular can be really mean. In the microcosm of school, minor conflicts can become major issues. There are frequent episodes of 'not speaking' to each other, and there are other girls waiting to pounce from the wings and take your best friend away from you at the first hint of a fight.

Some kids roll with the punches better than others, but I would take these interpersonal dramas extremely badly.

'Julia doesn't like me anymore!' I sobbed to my mum after a falling-out with a close friend. And you know what? She actually didn't. We'd been close for years, but now Julia was twelve, and about to become a teenager, whilst I was a year younger and still very much a little girl. She was wearing a bra, she was interested in boys (really interested, as opposed to being content to admire them from afar), and she occasionally wore lipstick. I was as flat as a board, didn't even have my ears pierced, and wouldn't have known what to do with a boy if he'd approached me with chocolate bars and a ticket to a Young Talent Time concert.

It was natural for Julia and me to grow apart. She moved on to Sarah – another blossoming pre-teen – and I stayed behind with my less mature friends. Still, the rejection was devastating, and it took me a full term to recover. What's worse, a pervasive insecurity remained in my other relationships, an insecurity that lingered throughout my schooldays and beyond.

I also worried a great deal about going on holidays. While I enjoyed going to visit my grandparents interstate, or staying in their holiday house up north, I became highly anxious when travelling anywhere else. I was a child who needed routine and constancy, so any change in my environment would inevitably cause me a lot of stress. This was ironic, because my parents adored travelling and took my sister and me on frequent interstate trips and overseas holidays. Every time, I was an absolute nightmare. I would start to become unsettled in the car or plane, and would be completely out of sorts by the time we arrived at our destination. There was nothing specifically wrong; I just wanted to be home. Home was safe and familiar and easy. Being away was scary and foreign and unpredictable. I hated not knowing where we would go during the day, where we would eat our dinner or where the toilet would be if I needed to wee. I would grizzle and complain and be unhappy and fretful, which must have been delightful for my long-suffering family. I also wouldn't sleep for the first few nights in any new bed, which meant that my parents and sister didn't get a lot of sleep, either.

The general wisdom is that kids are flexible and adapt readily to their lifestyles. In my case, this wisdom proved to be a myth. I never did get used to travelling, and continued to be anxious and unsettled every time I was away from home. Still, my parents persisted in taking us on holidays, and by the time I was twelve, though I had had some wonderful experiences, I had been grumpy and tired all over the world.

My last and most profound childhood anxiety was to worry about infinity.

Actually, I didn't so much worry about infinity as harbour an overwhelming terror of the concept. Infinity haunted me, and I would ruminate on it in bed, night after night after night, until I'd worked myself up into an overpowering frenzy of fear.

I don't do my Infinity Freak-Out anymore, as I've learned to control that particular destructive behaviour. I suspect, however, that if I put my mind to it, I could still use it to induce quite a decent panic attack. The Infinity Freak-Out is powerful and horrifying, and I had it down to a fine art.

Instructions for an Infinity Freak-Out

1. Lie in bed with the lights off and the door closed. Drown out the faint sounds of the TV or your family with your own thoughts.

2. Think about death. Think about dying. Think about YOU dying. Realise that you are going to die one day, that there is no way you can halt this inevitable march to your own doom. You could die any minute. You could die *now*. Immerse yourself in the thought. *Feel* death hovering over you, ready to snatch you up at any second.

3. Once you can feel death nearby, start thinking about what happens after death. Some part of you, the 'you-ness' inside you, the you-ness you can *feel* – your soul,

your spirit – will continue on in some form. It has to. I mean, where else will it go?

4. Once you have thoroughly convinced yourself of this point, reflect on how long this you-ness (soul, spirit) will live on. Forever. It will live on FOREVER. Forever and ever and ever and ever and EVER. Never ending. *Infinity*. Keep meditating on this, for ten, twenty, thirty minutes, until the panic sets in and you start to shake and you have to call your mother in to help calm you down. Assuming, of course, that she is there on the couch and hasn't escaped from the house . . .

In the Box

Don't Panic.

Douglas Adams, author

Growing up, I liked boundaries. They always made me feel safe and secure. I liked knowing how much time I had to get ready for school, and what time I had to go to bed. I liked knowing what we were having for dinner, and what we were going to be doing on the weekend. I liked knowing how I was expected to behave, and what punishments would be forthcoming if I broke the rules.

I liked boundaries. They helped me to stay on track.

Metaphorical boundaries, that is.

Physical boundaries . . . well, they were a completely different matter.

I hated physical boundaries. More than that. I was terrified of them. I was a classic claustrophobe, although I didn't realise this when I was a child. All I knew was that I was deeply afraid of enclosed spaces. It was partly a conscious fear of being trapped and partly a reflexive physical response to being shut in. My heart began to race, my mind started to get fuzzy, and shortly afterwards panic set in. It was not at all a pleasant feeling.

As a claustrophobe, I spent a lot of time checking my escape routes. I would never, ever enter a windowless space and shut the door behind me without first testing the lock to ensure I could get out again. Once I was inside, there was always that niggling thought in the back of my consciousness: what if the lock somehow failed? And in that heartbeat between turning the handle and the door success-fully opening I would experience a momentary rush of intense fear. What if it doesn't open? What if I am stuck in here forever?

Any type of enclosed space made me uncomfortable – internal fire-escapes, cupboards, basements, windowless bathrooms, even toilet cubicles with floor-to-ceiling doors – and I avoided them whenever possible. This caused some problems, espe-cially when I was with other people or really needed to go to the toilet. I recall a particular moment of shame when I was called onstage for a magic show and asked to get into a large wooden box so that the magician could make me disappear. There was no way I was getting into a box, magic or otherwise, and so I ran off the stage in fear. The audience of children laughed and laughed. It was awful.

Still, it's not every day one is asked to get in a box. Or is it?

Well, yes, as it turns out. I was forever being asked to get into boxes – not the kind that sat on the floor, but the kind that travelled up and down in a shaft. And I dreaded it, every single time.

As a child, riding in elevators was one of my greatest fears, and I had to do it, a lot. Several of my friends lived in apart-ment buildings with lifts, my father's office building had one, and my grandparents' holiday apartment was on the twenty-ninth floor. There was no avoiding lifts. And yet they haunted me.

A lift, to me, was like a mobile coffin. You got into the box, pressed the button, the lid (sorry, door) slid shut, and if it did not open again you would be trapped there until you died. And yes, logically I knew that I probably wouldn't die if I was stuck in a lift, logically I knew that I would eventually escape, but I didn't think I'd actually be able to survive until then. I feared my mind would crack under the strain.

As a child, I would step into a lift only if there was absolutely no choice. If I could walk up four or five or six flights of stairs, I would always do so rather than take the elevator. This was hugely frustrating for my friends and family, who were inevitably left waiting for me at the top, but experience had shown them that it was far more efficient to wait for me to walk than to try to convince me to get in the box.

If I decided that the lift was indeed the only option, then I needed some time to prepare for my journey.

It started with my assessment of the lift and the situation. Was the lift modern, or old and rickety? Did I need to travel up twenty floors, or just three or four? Was there a phone in the lift, and if so, was it in working order?

These days, lifts contain an intercom button. When I was growing up in the seventies and eighties, however, lifts were required to have proper phones. My first step would be to check on the existence of the phone, because sadly, not every lift complied. If the lift didn't have a phone, I would take the stairs. If it did have a phone, I would remove it from the cradle to check for a dial tone. If the phone was out of order, I would take the stairs. There was no way I was going to get into a lift that did not have an operating phone. I couldn't risk the nightmare of being trapped in a lift with no means of calling for help. Nothing and no one could coerce me to get into a box without a ready escape plan.

Once the check was complete and I was in the lift, I would remain vigilant. Every fibre of my body would be set on high alert, and with every shudder, every creak, and every pause of the elevator, I would tingle with alarm. Then the lift would stop at the required floor and my heart would contract in anticipation. My breaths would become shallow, there'd be black behind my eyes, the walls would pound, and I would begin my silent chant.

It's not going to open. I'm going to be trapped. It's not going to open. I'm going to be trapped.

When the doors slid open, I'd jump out in elated relief, and decide that next time, I would take the stairs.

Thankfully, I didn't have any terrible experiences in lifts, although for me the very act of being in a lift was terrible enough as it was. Until, that is, the summer of 1983, when I experienced the lift incident I'd been dreading for years.

I was fourteen years old, and was staying up north with my mum and my sister for the school holidays. My sister and I had met up with childhood friends of ours and had spent two weeks racing around with them from the pool to the beach to the games arcade, and back to the pool again. Robert was my age, and tall and tanned and kind of cute. Natasha was twelve, like my sister, and just as pretty and good-natured and cheerful. The four of us got along famously. For a while.

On the tenth day of the holidays, we all hopped into the lift in my grandparents' apartment building. I had stayed there many times before, and it was one of the very few elevators I could travel in without panicking. The phones worked well, the lifts were modern and speedy, and to my knowledge they had never broken down. Besides, our rooms were on the twenty-ninth floor, so I really had no choice but to get used to them. Twenty-nine floors were too many to climb, even for someone as anxious as me.

We stood there, the four of us, towels wrapped around our waists after a swim in the pool, and the lift began its ascent.

'Shall we see if Mum will get us some chips?' asked my sister.

'Yeah, chips, definitely,' said Natasha.

Robert was hovering around the elevator buttons, which usually made me nervous. I liked to be the one standing next to the panel, as it gave me a sense of control. Other people were unpredictable, or fallible, or stupid, and couldn't be trusted to operate the lift correctly. But I liked Robert – I thought I might even like him 'that way' – and so I felt quite safe with him.

'Watch this,' he said, so I turned and watched. With a cheeky smile, Robert deliberately leaned over and pressed the 'Emergency Stop' button. The lift shuddered to a sudden halt.

We were trapped.

OH MY GOD! WE WERE TRAPPED!

'What have you done?' I screeched. I looked around. The space was getting smaller. I couldn't breathe. I needed to get out. 'Make it start!' I screamed at him. '*Make it start!!!*'

Robert laughed and leaned over me. 'Don't worry,' he said. 'It will just start up again when I press another button.' And he pressed a button.

Nothing happened.

Robert frowned for a moment, and then pressed another button. Still nothing happened. He pressed another button, and another, and another, and another. Still nothing. I joined in, and then Natasha and my sister joined us. We pressed every button on the panel, over and over again. *Nothing happened.* In the infinite wisdom of a teenage boy, Robert had thought that pressing 'Emergency Stop' could be revoked with a press of the 'Open Door' button. Well guess what, Robert?

YOU WERE WRONG.

I could feel my clarity draining away as panic flooded my body. I was trapped in a small square box. The walls were closing in on me. The ceiling was descending. There was a rushing sound in my ears. I had to get out. I HAD TO GET OUT!

I screamed and pressed the alarm button. It rang, incredibly loudly, piercing the silence of the apartment building with its bell.

Nothing happened. My mind began to fold in on itself.

'They haven't come!' I howled. 'They're never coming! *We're trapped!*' My sister and Natasha looked nervous, but stayed quiet. I barely noticed. I didn't care about them. I didn't care about anything at all other than getting out of that tiny, tiny box. 'HELP!' I cried. 'HELP!'

I pressed the bell again. And again. And again. 'HELP!' I screamed. 'Please HELP!' And finally, *finally*, after what seemed like an eternity, a voice boomed out of the intercom. I started to cry. We were saved!

'What happened?' the voice was asking. It was male, and it was nonchalant. I vaguely registered Robert explaining the 'Emergency Stop' button to the man, but I kept punctuating their conversation with bursts of screaming.

'Get us out! Please! Get us out!'

'Yeah, yeah, we'll get you out,' said the voice. 'We'll be there in about twenty minutes.'

TWENTY MINUTES! I couldn't wait TWENTY MINUTES!!! The lift was getting minuscule. I was suffocating. My towel was damp, I was shivering (though with cold or panic I wasn't sure which) and I couldn't be there for another second. I had to get out. I needed to get out NOW.

'Help me!' I cried. 'Please, come and get us *now*!'

But the voice had gone.

'Get me out!' I shouted, to no one in particular. '*Get me out!!!*' I threw down my towel and started pressing the alarm button, over and over again. It rang through all thirty floors of the building, into every single one of the 200 or so rooms, filling the ears of the residents with my desperate distress calls.

'They're *coming*,' Robert told me. '*Stop pressing the button.*' My sister and Natasha stood quietly against the wall. They could see I was becoming unhinged, and they didn't seem to know what to do.

I stopped. I backed away for a moment. But the doors were still shut, and I was still in the box, and I had to do something. I had to get out. I couldn't stay there a second longer. I HAD TO DO SOMETHING.

I stepped forward and pressed the button again. Brrrrrrrrriiiiiiii-iiiiiiiiiiinnnnng.

'Kerri!' said Robert sternly. 'Stop it!'

But we were still in the box. We were still in the box! And I was being attacked by the walls and there was no way to escape and I couldn't help myself. I needed to press the button. BRRRRRRRRRRRRRRRRRRRRRRRRRIIIIIIIIIIIIIIIIIIIIIIIIIIIIIIIIIIIIIIII INNNNNNNNNNNNNNNNGGGGGGGGGGG!

'STOP IT!' Robert yelled. 'STOP IT OR I'LL SLAP YOU!'

I looked at him. He looked serious. But I couldn't stop. I HAD TO DO SOMETHING.

I reached forward and pressed the button again.

Robert slapped me across the face. It hurt. It hurt just enough.

I can't remember much about what happened after that. I do believe I stopped pressing the button; I think I was simply stunned into submission. I also recall us being freed from the lift by a couple of blokes in uniform who threatened to charge our parents thousands of dollars and thought the whole episode was the funniest thing they'd seen in a long time. And I recall Robert being very chastened and apologetic, and standing as far away as possible from the button panel during subsequent lift rides, when I dared to ride with him at all.

My fear of lifts was, like all phobias, completely irrational. No stuck lift is fatal, unless it is situated in a towering inferno as it bursts into flames, or in the *Titanic* as it sinks to its watery grave. I was never going to die in an elevator, and at some level I knew that. But it was the loss of control that got to me. Being at the mercy of technology or a technician to get me out of a box was too much for an anxious kid to handle. I couldn't even trust a magician at a kids' party. There was no way I was going to trust a machine.

That episode in the lift was my first real experience of utter panic. And I'd love to say that being stuck in a lift cured me of my phobia. I'd love to say that, having faced my greatest fear, I realised I could survive should it ever happen again. Sadly, the phobia persisted. Still, from then on I was very careful when travelling with fourteen-year-old boys.

And I guarded that 'Emergency Stop' button with my life.

Picky, Picky, Picky

*Nobody realises that some people expend tremendous energy
merely to be normal.*

Albert Camus, author

It was eight o'clock on a school night, I was sixteen years old, and I
was hanging out for a fix. I knew it was there, and I was dying to get
my hands on it, but I was sitting with my family, and I couldn't very
well start with them around. But the frustration was killing me.

We were all on the couch watching *The Cosby Show* – at least, my
family was watching *The Cosby Show*; I was watching *The Cosby
Show* and feeling my chin. There was a small, blind pimple growing
beneath the surface, and whilst laughing outwardly at the antics of
the Huxtable family, I was desperately waiting for my chance to run
to the bathroom and squeeze it out.

I was totally fixated on the state of my skin. Thankfully, I never
suffered badly from acne; I just got the occasional pimple, as did
every other teenager in the world. But whilst others seemed to take

zits in their stride, I worried about them endlessly. I scanned my face every morning and evening for blemishes, fretted horribly if a spot was developing, and smothered acne cream over my entire face as if it was moisturiser. And when a pimple did burst through the surface I was devastated. My self-esteem would plummet, and I'd know for sure that people were staring at my zit. Pimples felt like failure to me, and they looked pretty dismal, too.

Over time, my obsession with my skin grew. As well as spending hours examining myself for blemishes, when I found them I became overwhelmed by the need to get them out of my face. Of course, there was no good reason to get them out of my face, and there was every good reason to leave them there. Picking at my pimples made them much, much worse – I knew that from experience. And on this particular night, this particular zit on my chin was barely noticeable; I had to strain to find it when I looked in the mirror. But its size wasn't at all the issue. The zit might as well have been a boil, or a goitre, or even a parasitic second head emerging out of my face, so greatly did it bother me. I could *feel* it – that tiny bump less than the size of half a grain of rice – and I couldn't bear to have it there.

I can pinpoint the onset of my squeezing obsession to the summer of 1984. It was my summer in the spotlight, my fifteen minutes of fame. For a couple of years, I'd been wanting to be an actress, and finally, at the age of fifteen, my dreams were coming true. After registering with a talent agent, and auditioning unsuccessfully for countless productions, I'd won one of the lead roles in an eight-part television miniseries and was flown up north for six weeks of filming in the sun.

I was insanely excited, and horribly unsettled. I had never been away from home on my own before, and literally did not know how to manage myself in such a strange and adult environment. I had a chaperone on set, but she had several other young charges too, and didn't pay a huge amount of attention to me. What's more, she was often distracted by a rather intimate friendship with one of the older, married male actors, and didn't pay a huge amount of attention to any of the kids on set at all.

I didn't cope very well with my sudden freedom. I was virtually unsupervised with no boundaries to speak of, and I grounded myself the only way I knew how – with food. Film sets serve at least six meals a day, and I availed myself heartily of every single one. I was vaguely aware that I was gaining weight, but I couldn't stop myself. Partly, I think, it was my subconscious way of protecting myself from the rampant sexuality on set. Partly, I think, I just really liked the food.

I returned home from the film shoot around ten kilos heavier than when I left, which posed a considerable challenge to the poor bloke who tried to edit the series. My parents barely concealed their shock when they picked me up from the airport, and my friends didn't even bother concealing theirs when I eventually returned to school.

If I'd expected to be more cool now that I was a bona fide television actress, I'd been very much mistaken.

Still, extra weight wasn't my only legacy from my foray into acting. I had also developed a skin problem during the shoot. Television make-up is heavy and oily, and in the heat of the northern Australian summer my skin literally drank it in. The make-up artist would apply layer upon layer of foundation to my face during the day, until by evening no amount of cleanser could remove it. By the time I returned home I had broken out in huge, blind pimples from my forehead down to my chin. It was not at all the way a glamorous actress was meant to look.

The pimples weren't going away by themselves, so my mother took to squeezing them. It was incredibly satisfying to me to hear the zits explode one by one, and to see the exorcised bumps under my skin settle down to normal. So satisfying, in fact, that by the time my face had cleared up and the squeezing sessions were no longer necessary, I had become totally addicted to the sensation.

Though the huge blind pimples had gone, I couldn't leave my skin alone. I started scanning my face daily, searching for the tiniest of zits to pick and prick and squeeze. Even the least offensive of blemishes screamed to me, begging me to destroy them. I'd try and try and *try* to resist but inevitably, eventually, I'd cave. I'd take the microscopic spot and prod it and meddle with it until I'd made a big, red, squelchy mess.

I knew that picking my pimples just made things worse, but I simply couldn't help myself. I was like an alcoholic being presented with a glass of Scotch. When a spot was there, it taunted me, and I fantasised about squeezing until I finally gave in to the urge. The difference, of course, was that pimples didn't make me drunk. They just made me red and sore.

I despised myself for messing with my skin, but sadly, it wasn't the only focus of my obsessiveness. I'd also been biting and picking at my nails for as long as I could remember.

I'd be worried about an exam, or having a fat day, or think one of my girlfriends was mad at me, or hear my parents arguing, and I'd start tearing at my nails in a frenzy, ripping them apart with my teeth. Sometimes I barely noticed what I was doing, at other times I was perfectly aware that I was decimating my fingertips. Either way, once I started, it was virtually impossible to stop until every shred of available nail was gone.

I hated biting my nails. I was horribly ashamed of my torn cuticles, and of my ragged, chewed stubs. Not only were they ugly, but they were highly indicative of my emotional state: I was basically wearing my neuroses on my fingertips. I longed to have nice long nails like my friend Nat, who was forever complaining about having to file hers down because they grew so fast. How could she complain? I *dreamed* about having to file my nails down!

My nails looked awful, and I didn't know why I couldn't stop biting them – I mean, it's not like they tasted particularly good. But anxiety would generate a rush of adrenaline, and nailbiting was a way I could channel the rush. What's more, biting my nails temporarily distracted me from whatever I was worrying about. Instead of feeling worried, I'd feel angry at myself for biting my nails, which gave me a bit of respite.

After years of biting my nails from anxiety, the behaviour became a habit. All it took was for a teeny, tiny ridge to appear in one of my nails and I would be unable to ignore it. I'd fiddle with it and play with it and file it down until it was smooth. And then I'd keep fiddling with it and playing with it to see if the ridge was still there (which of course it would be, because I couldn't stop fiddling). Before I knew it the crack would get bigger and my nail would start to split. And then I'd give up fiddling and just tear the thing off with my teeth, and curse the fact that I couldn't leave well enough alone.

After that I would make a special effort to be extra careful with my other nine nails. Sadly, however, I was weak and obsessive, and I never could stick to my resolution. Once one of my nails was ruined I couldn't help but systematically destroy the others. I needed perfection, and if one of the set was destroyed then I figured I may as well destroy the lot. And if that doesn't make much sense to you, then know it made even less sense to me.

I had another problem area, a third time-consuming fixation, the evidence of which has been all but wiped from my face.

My eyebrows.

Like my sister, my father, his father, and his father before him, I was born with very heavy, dark eyebrows. They ran across my forehead, meeting enthusiastically in the middle, and were at least two centimetres thick along their length. And they were lush. Really lush. Lush like women long for their hair to be lush. The hair on their *head*, that is. Not the hair on the middle of their forehead.

I didn't want my eyebrows to be lush. I wanted my eyebrows to be skinny and tapered. I certainly didn't want them to look like two hairy slugs kissing across the bridge of my nose. So, as soon as I was old enough to wield a pair of tweezers, I began yanking away at my brows.

I started by pulling out the hairs in the middle, creating two individual brows instead of the monobrow I'd been born with. This pleased me. Unfortunately, my eyebrows kept growing back, so I had to keep plucking as the regrowth appeared. I yanked away frantically, pulling out hair after hair to create two even, perfectly spaced brows. But I wasn't a professional, and I'd end up plucking a little too much from one side, so I'd have to pluck a little bit more from the other side, until the space between my brows doubled in size, giving me the look of a slightly dazed rabbit.

Eventually, I started working on the thickness. I plucked from underneath my brows, taking just enough out to give them a more polished appearance. But then I'd check myself in the mirror, and realise that my brows were very slightly uneven. I couldn't bear for them to be uneven. It was that obsessive thing again. So I'd pluck another hair from my right eyebrow, just to even the two sides up. But no, I'd gone too far, because then it was uneven but on the left side now. So I'd pluck another hair from my left brow. Then it was worse. Much worse. So I'd pluck another from my right, and then another from my left, and then another from my right, in a frenzy of plucking, unable to tear myself away from the mirror, until my once thick eyebrows looked like two drunkenly drawn pencil lines, and my brows were stinging with pain.

I spent hours plucking my eyebrows, trying to get that perfect symmetry. *Hours*. There were mornings when I was late getting to school because I was stuck in front of the mirror plucking, days when I fantasised about shaving the damn things off, just to put myself out of my misery.

But on that evening, sitting in front of *The Cosby Show*, I had other things on my mind. Well, another *thing*. My pimple. That tiny, insidious beast. The second the show was over, and my parents and sister had retired to their rooms, I ran off to the bathroom mirror. I couldn't hold back another second. I took that little zit and I pinched it and I squeezed it until, with a deeply satisfying little *plooph*, it popped. I felt elated for a second, held a tissue to my bruised, bleeding chin, and then despised myself for giving in to the urge. What a total loser I was.

I stared at myself in the mirror some more, glumly examining my eyebrows for stray hairs. I pulled three hairs from my right brow and four from my left, and looked at the results, and despaired. I began tearing at my nails, feeling hopeless and lost, before crawling into bed to worry about infinity.

I couldn't wait to be older. I knew I'd be far more in control. Adults didn't go around picking their faces or biting their nails. Adults didn't spend hours plucking their eyebrows and examining their faces for blemishes. Once I was grown up my neuroses would disappear. I would have nice long nails and clear, glowing skin. I would know when to stop.

I couldn't be this way forever.

Could I?

Teen Angst

*Whether you admit it or not, you are all worried that the
others won't accept you, that if they knew the real you,
they would recoil in horror. Each of us carries with us a secret
shame that we think is somehow unique.*

James St. James, entertainer

It was the eighties, and 'raging and water sports' were the hobbies
listed by every game show contestant under the age of twenty-five.
Well, I was under twenty-five, but I didn't like raging. I also didn't
like water sports, but that wasn't a problem; I could avoid going out
on surf skis and speedboats. But if I wanted a social life – if I wanted
to see my friends – I had to go out 'raging' on Saturday nights. And
that was not my idea of a good time at all.

'Raging' – going out drinking and dancing in pubs and clubs –
was what young people did in the eighties. Come to think of it, they
probably still do. At sixteen, my friends and I were still two years
below the legal drinking age, but most of us had been going out to

licensed venues for at least eighteen months. Many of my friends had fake IDs, and the rest of us got by on a great deal of blue eye shadow, very high heels and our wits.

Ironically, though, we really didn't need to bother. We were virtually never asked for ID, let alone kicked out of clubs for being under-age. There was very little policing of licensed premises, and the bouncers were happy to let in any attractive females, even if we looked like little girls playing dress-ups. Clubbing was what everyone did on a Saturday night, and it was assumed that some under-agers would slip in. No one was concerned, no one was nervous.

Except for me.

'Coming raging tonight?' my friend Ella asked over the phone. Bummer. My stomach started to clench. But I had to go. What else could I do – stay home by myself?

'Yeah,' I said.

'We're meeting at Nat's place, and getting a pizza at the beach, and then heading into Stranded,' she told me excitedly.

The city, I thought. The city at night made me really stressed. There were crowds and drunk people and sleazy men and I just wanted to stay at home. 'Okay,' I said.

'I'm sleeping at Nat's house, so do you want my mum to pick you up on the way there?'

'Sure,' I said, but my heart wasn't in it. I wanted to stay in. I would have way preferred to watch a video at Nat's place and have an early night.

Going to pubs and clubs made me anxious. They felt danger-ous to me, and if there was one thing I tried desperately to avoid, it was danger. I still felt very much like a young girl, and the clubs represented a dark, adult world which I wasn't yet ready to join. I occasionally enjoyed being there once we'd made it through the doors, but the anticipation was nerve-racking, and this caused me a great deal of shame. Teens are meant to embrace danger, not run from it. All my friends seemed so carefree and brave, and yet here was I, scared of my own shadow. I was a total weirdo.

There were a few reasons I didn't like going to nightclubs. Partly, of course, it was the illegality of the exercise, the slight chance, however remote, that we would be caught and hauled off to a police station. I'd never done anything illegal before – I didn't even cheat in Maths tests (really, I didn't) – and the idea of breaking the law troubled me greatly. What's more, I strongly suspected that my parents wouldn't have approved of where I was going, and I hated the thought of letting them down. Of course, I could have told them. I was fairly sure they wouldn't have yelled at me – they probably wouldn't even have grounded me – but their disappointment would have been excruciating to witness. Besides, there was always the chance they would stop me going, and I couldn't risk being alienated from my friends.

And that was the unusual thing about me. Unlike pretty much every teen I knew, I liked to be doing the right thing. I didn't like breaking rules. I didn't like pushing the envelope. I didn't like trespassing, or sneaking into cinemas, or buying alcohol or cigarettes. I didn't even feel comfortable running into a cafe to use the toilet without having first bought a drink. Basically, I didn't like to do half the things all teenagers did almost habitually. I'd like to say it was due to my fine moral fibre. Mostly, however, it was just my anxiety. I really was scared of getting caught.

Still, it wasn't just being under-age that made me anxious at nightclubs. The atmosphere at the clubs – packed and hideously loud – made me deeply uncomfortable. They were generally below street level, and windowless, and dark, and I found them to be intensely claustrophobic. I didn't like being compressed on all sides by dozens of sweaty bodies. I didn't enjoy being closed in by a wall of pumping sound. And every time I ordered a drink, I felt like a fraud, as if a giant 'UNDER-AGE' sign was printed in neon letters on my shirt (instead of the 'RELAX' sign that was already printed there). The bar staff never questioned me, but I knew they knew and felt tense ordering alcohol until I was well past legal age.

The other issue with nightclubs was my concern about men, because I wasn't ready for any sexual advances. I'd kissed a few boys in my time, but nothing more, and I did not feel at all equipped to deal with sexual propositions. At the age of fourteen a nineteen-year-old soldier had tried to chat me up when I was having an ice-cream with my friends, and it had seriously unsettled me. What did he want from me? And why on earth did he think I wanted to give it? I'd felt vulnerable and slightly violated, even though he hadn't laid a hand on me.

By sixteen I was still totally innocent, and had no idea how to navigate the virtual minefield of sexual mores. Some of my slightly older girlfriends seemed fairly open to being picked up, but I just wanted to dance with my friends and go home in time for curfew to my nice pink bedroom. The difficulty, of course, was that I wanted to look good – certainly I wanted to look as good as my friends – but I didn't want to look so good that I would attract the attention of older men. It was a tricky situation, and one that never would have been an issue if we all could have just stayed home together and watched videos.

I never told my friends about how anxious I felt going to clubs. I may have been nervous, and claustrophobic, and uncomfortable, but more than anything else, I longed to fit in. I wanted to be a normal teenager, who loved sneaking into clubs and staying out after curfew. So I allowed Ella's mum to pick me up and I pretended to be really excited. We hung out at Nat's for a while and I touched up my make-up with the others in the bathroom. We made our way to the beach (with our parents' permission), and then headed into the city (without their knowledge or consent). My stomach contracted as I waited in line to get into Stranded, but I acted cool, though I was agitated on the inside.

I couldn't have shared my feelings with my friends. I didn't believe they would have understood at all. And besides, what was the alternative to going to clubs on Saturday nights? Teenagers in the eighties didn't stay home and play Scrabble, or bake cookies, or do crossword puzzles or braid each other's hair whilst watching TV. In fact, I don't think teenagers of any era have ever done that. Teenagers go out together on Saturday nights. They drink and have fun. That's totally normal. Being anxious about it is not.

And I wanted to be normal. More than anything in the world, I wanted to be normal.

In some ways I was a totally normal teen. Because, in addition to my unusual teen anxieties, I had all of the regular teen anxieties, too. In fact, I had most of them in very large doses. When I did 'normal' angst, I really threw my heart into it.

For example, I worried terribly about my appearance when I was growing up. In particular, I worried about my clothes. I never felt that I was wearing the right thing, even when I'd carefully copied the look of some of the trendy girls at school. I'd go out with my mum and scour the shops for the kind of clothes worn by Jenny and Nikki and Robin, who always looked impossibly stylish. I'd put my outfit together at home, change, get dressed again, change again, get dressed for a third time, listen to my mother telling me how lovely I looked, not believe her, change again, and then at last feel pretty good about my ensemble. And then I'd go out to a party and note that Jenny's skirt was slightly longer than mine, Nikki's shoulder pads were slightly wider, Robin's jacket was made of a slightly different material, and they all carried themselves with a haughty confidence I couldn't pull off in a million years. And I would quietly wither away inside, knowing that I would never get it right, that I would never walk into a situation and feel that I was dressed appropriately. I couldn't see myself for who I was, I could only see myself in relation to the other girls, and compared to them, I was a hopeless dag.

My weight was also a significant issue. Now, I wasn't too fat. I was never too fat. At my very largest, I was a healthy rounded teenager. But nothing and no one could ever convince me of that fact, just like nothing and no one could convince me that pimples didn't matter. I thought I was overweight, and I thought that all of my problems would magically fall away if I shed those extra kilos.

Of course, thinking I was fat, and fantasising about being skinny, didn't help me at all to lose weight. It did, however, cause me to spend weeks at a time going on (metaphorically) fruitless diets. (In reality, my diets generally had a lot of fruit in them.) I'd restrict my eating, feel deprived, start craving all the things I couldn't have, and then fall off the wagon, ending up as heavy – or heavier – than when I started. It was a ridiculous, pointless cycle that persisted way into my thirties, when I stopped dieting altogether and finally stabilised my weight.

In addition to my anxieties and obsessions about my appearance, I also suffered terribly from unrequited love. Strangely enough, despite my dagginess and poor self-esteem, I still received my fair share of attention from boys. Unfortunately, however, this attention was all from boys who didn't interest me in the slightest. From the moment I hit preschool, I had a devastating tendency to fall madly in love with boys who would never love me back. It began in Kinder-garten with Leo Whitman (not his real name, but close to it), and ended in the later years of high school with Josh Goldenbum (not his real name, but really should have been).

Josh was the most popular boy in our year, and I pined for him horribly, with somewhat self-indulgent masochism. I watched him go from girlfriend to girlfriend without ever noticing me, despite all my efforts to win him over. I did everything I could to get Josh's attention, sitting near him in the classroom, hanging around him in the playground, inviting him to parties, virtually panting in his face. Nothing worked. I was invisible. He dated half the girls in our class, then began on the year below, and by the time we were in our final year he was dating my younger sister's friends. And he never, ever noticed me. It never occurred to me that maybe I just wasn't his type. I agonised, endlessly, over *why* he didn't like me. What was I doing wrong? Was it because I was too fat? Too pimply? Badly dressed? Was I boring? Would I ever have a boyfriend? Would love ever be reciprocated? Or would I be destined to remain forever alone, unwanted and unloved, as every girl at our school gradually found happiness but me?

I contemplated these questions as I lay in my bed in my safe, pink room. Nights are long when you're a teenager, and my thoughts would race till the early hours of the morning. By then, my Infinity Freak-Outs had become fewer and far between, but they had been replaced by other, angsty musings. Why did Josh not love me? Why was I so weird? What was my place in the world? What was the point of it all?

I began lying awake, agonising over the meaning of life. Why were humans on earth? Was there a God? It didn't seem likely. And yet, if there wasn't a God, how did it all happen?

Who was I, essentially? Where was I going? Why was I born? It was vitally important that I figure it out. I needed to know my path in life, and I needed to know my purpose. I needed to know my reason for being, why I was lying in that bed, why I'd been put on the earth, why the earth was there in the first place. I tried to turn to

God – at one point I prayed every morning for a week – but I didn't get an answer. No matter how hard I searched, I couldn't come up with any clues.

My existential crises deeply tainted my teenage years. I spent countless hours searching for answers I couldn't find. And yet there was one far more prosaic problem I faced, one I never spoke of to another soul.

I worried about using the toilets at school.

Yes, in between worries about the meaning of life, my fear of toilets haunted me, day after day. There were gaps under the stall doors in the toilets at school, and I became terrified that another student would crawl underneath and catch me in the middle of doing a wee. It had never happened to me, but I had heard of it happening to another girl at the school, which is how my phobia developed. I knew that if it did happen to me, it would be the most humiliating thing that could possibly occur, and I had to do everything in my power to prevent it.

Now, I knew I couldn't stop myself from having to wee if the need was pressing enough, so I dealt with things on a more fundamental level.

I stopped drinking on school days.

I didn't drink at breakfast. I didn't drink during the day. No matter how warm the weather, no matter how thirsty I was, I learned to control my intake until I came home in the afternoon. And then, at a quarter to four, I would rush to the kitchen like a crazed person and drink a litre or more of water.

My plan worked beautifully. I virtually never used the school toilets, and I was never, ever caught on the loo. I spent many a hot day being horrendously thirsty, but it seemed a fair price to pay to protect myself from humiliation. In one area at least, I was a success.

• • •

Looking back on those days, I know one thing for certain: I would never wish to revisit my teenage years. I know that the teens are difficult for everyone, but when you add a big dose of anxiety to that mix of adolescent hormones, you can end up with a pretty troubled kid who spends a lot of time being unhappy.

I did not survive my teens unscathed. It took me years to gain any sense of body confidence, and even now, in my forties, it is somewhat tenuous. The feeling of dagginess persisted, latching onto my psyche like a stubborn, dowdy limpet. I'm an adult now, and I know how to dress, and yet I still think of myself as being daggy. Even though I've been complimented enough times to know that I sometimes get it right, even though 'daggy' is no longer in the lexicon, it is still how I see myself, and doubtless always will.

I eventually got over Josh Goldenbum, mainly because I didn't have a choice. Besides, I never really knew Josh, and I certainly didn't really love him. Josh was only ever a teenage crush to me, a symbol of all I couldn't have. He represented coolness, security, acceptance, attractiveness, the knowledge that I wouldn't be forever alone. And, despite finding real, reciprocated love as an adult, I never completely lost touch with my longing for all those things. I still carry with me that anguish of unrequited yearning, for love, for acceptance, for attractiveness, for belonging. More than twenty-five years later, those feelings still surface in my dreams. I think I'll be pining for what Josh Goldenbum represents as I'm hobbling on my walking frame in fifty years' time.

Despite my profound ruminations, I never did discover the meaning of life, but I did, eventually, stop looking. I didn't make a resolution to stop searching. I didn't throw up my hands and decide that it was all too hard. I just got too busy actually living my life to think so much about it, and eventually it stopped being important to know.

As for the toilet issue, well . . . that fear gradually dissipated, when I realised that no one wanted to see my bottom anyway. And then I had three kids, and I got used to weeing in front of a crowd, and now I can barely remember to shut the toilet door.

My teenage self would have been absolutely horrified. Still, despite her angst, she had a fairly good sense of humour, and I suspect she would have found it deeply ironic.

Where Do I Come From?

Worry is a useless mulling over of things we cannot change.

Mildred Lisette Norman, activist

When you first meet my parents you will notice one thing: 'Oh, Kerri's sticky-out ear isn't an accident of fate!' When you've known my parents longer you will notice another: 'Kerri's anxiety isn't an accident either!'

It's true. I was born to be a worrier. Anxiety is in my genes, as much as curly hair, thick eyebrows, sticky-out ears, and the ability to drink scalding-hot liquids very quickly.

Now, the anxiety of my family members is their business and not mine to discuss. But let me just say this: my father and his family are shocking worriers. My mother, on the other hand, is optimistic and calm, but clearly her equanimity is a recessive gene, because I missed out on that trait altogether, and instead got a double dose of angst.

I look back on my childhood and can recall dozens of examples of my father being anxious. Still, although I could list numerous episodes that would illustrate my point perfectly, one particular moment in my earlier life stands out.

My parents had just returned from an interstate holiday and my sister and I, who had been staying with our grandmother, were happily welcoming them home. We looked at photos – *endless* photos (my mother, in her eternal optimism, assumed that we would be interested in shots of every building, monument and tree they had seen on their trip) – and opened our presents (some of which were pretty cruddy, but some of which were actually quite nice). We chatted about their vacation, caught up on what we'd been doing in their absence, and had a cup of tea. And then my father fell asleep in his chair, and my mum jumped to her feet and rummaged around in her suitcase.

'Look, girls,' she said conspiratorially, waving a sheet of paper. 'I saved this for you.'

We scurried over and looked. It was a piece of stationery from the hotel they had visited, upon which the concierge had carefully noted down a phone message.

Your daughter called, it read. *She's just ringing to say hi. Nothing is wrong. Absolutely nothing. She's just ringing to say hi.*

My sister laughed. 'Yep,' she said. 'I dictated it to him. I didn't want Dad to worry.'

My mother smiled wryly. 'You know what your father said when he read the message?'

We looked at each other, and back to her. 'What?'

'Something must be wrong.'

And we laughed and laughed. Because what else can you do?

That's my dad for you. He is a generous, loving, ferociously intelligent man, who has reached the pinnacle of his profession and demonstrates the utmost integrity in everything he does.

Unfortunately, he also has the uncanny capability to perceive the worst-case scenario in every situation.

Our house reflected this worst-case scenario perfectly. I was brought up in a home that had more security than a maximum-security prison, only without the guards and orange jumpsuits (although my mum did have a green jumpsuit in the eighties known as 'The Grasshopper' . . . but I digress). We had bars on all our external windows, *plus* deadlocks, *plus* special locks on all internal doors that could only be accessed from the outside. And if that wasn't enough, we had a complicated alarm system, with sensors, pads and full back-to-base capacity.

Paradoxically, the extreme security of our house didn't make me feel secure. Quite the opposite, in fact. It made me feel vulnerable. The message I received from all those bars and locks and alarms was that the world was a very dangerous place indeed and that I needed to be vigilant at all times. Strangely, though my friends inhabited the same world as me – in fact, many of them inhabited the same *suburb* as me – they didn't see it as dangerous at all. So my world was kind of lonely at times, too.

Since I was such a fearful thing, I became a very obedient teenager. I rarely experimented with boys or alcohol, I rarely broke curfew, and I rarely went anywhere I shouldn't. My younger sister, on the other hand, managed to escape my nervousness, and lived like a normal, experimental, badly behaved teenager. She stayed out late, she drank and smoked, and she partied till the wee small hours of the morning.

My father didn't cope very well with my sister's late-night partying. In fact, he didn't cope very well when she came home on time, or even when I went out to the movies with my clean-cut friends. My dad couldn't sleep until both his daughters were safely home in bed, and that often meant he had to wait up for us for a very, very long time.

Now, my father is a proud man, and he never gave away the slightest hint that he would keep himself awake until we both returned home. He was always fast asleep in bed when we carefully turned the key and pushed open the front door at the end of a big night.

Or so he would have us believe. The man didn't fool us at all.

Whatever our curfew – ten, eleven, midnight, one – my dad would be waiting by the front door at the appointed hour, peering out at the road. (We knew this, you see, because we could see his silhouette, backlit behind the stained-glass door as we approached the house.) Then, as we turned the lock, he would sprint down the hallway and into his bedroom, and bound into bed. (We knew this, you see, because we could hear his footsteps.) My father's footsteps in the hall were a running joke between my sister and me. We loved to giggle together at our dad.

Unfortunately for my father, there were occasions on which waiting by the front door didn't quite suffice. If, by some cruel stroke of carelessness on our part, one of us would be late home (inevitably my sister, as I was too frightened of the consequences), my poor dad would have to go out searching for us. It wasn't that he knew where to look, or that he even thought he had any chance of success – he simply had to stop pacing and *do* something.

My sister would frequently return home at ten past one or a quarter past one in the morning – just a few minutes late – and pass our father's car driving in the opposite direction.

'Oh look, there's my dad!' she once told a boyfriend, as they rounded the corner and saw the Volvo heading down the road. She thought it was pretty funny. So did I, when I heard the story.

Of course, it wasn't quite so funny on the very rare occasions that it was me, and not my sister, being hunted down at night. I vividly recall one balmy evening on a beach holiday when – fifteen years old and just five minutes past curfew – I nervously kissed a boy I liked in the lobby of our hotel. As our lips met cautiously for the very first time, the lift went ping and the doors slid open to reveal . . . my father, standing in his pyjamas and slippers. It was mortifying.

'When did you meet that boy?' he asked me stiffly, as I waved goodbye to my new friend and scurried into the lift.

'Um . . . tonight,' I answered. The boy had been a toga waiter from the nearby Roman-themed restaurant, where I had just had dinner with my girlfriends. My dad shook his head in disappointment. I looked at the floor.

When the boy showed up for our planned date the next day, I wouldn't talk to him. Partly this was because he didn't look quite so good in the harsh light of day without his toga on. But for the most part, I just hated disappointing my dad.

Now, there is no doubt that my father was the most anxious of our immediate family. Still, he was far from the only member of his clan to have issues in that department.

Take, for example, my cousin M, who had a morbid fear of flying. She would require sedatives, relatives and the reassurance of flight attendants just to make it onto the plane. She would then cling to her seat in terror all throughout the journey, giving little cries of alarm when the plane encountered turbulence, or the engines' sounds changed, or the wheels were lowered.

Eventually, after years of therapy, M worked up the courage to enrol in a Fear of Flying course. This involved weeks of familiarisation with aircraft, and desensitisation to the experience of flying, before culminating in an actual return interstate flight. To our pride, M graduated from the course with flying colours (so to speak). Several other participants, however, refused to get back on the plane for the return journey, and caught a train back to their home town. We supposed that meant that they had failed.

Apart from M, there was S, an older member of the family, who picked leaves obsessively from his pool, even in the winter months when no one ever swam. S also became agitated if his lawns weren't watered at the same time every day, and cleaned up cups when they had barely left the hands of the drinker.

J was forever convinced that she had cancer and was going to die (so far she doesn't and she hasn't). P would switch off and unplug all electrical devices before leaving home, concerned that his house was going to burn down in his absence by a rogue spark somehow shooting through the electricity socket. And B was neurotically tidy, getting distressed if her books weren't maintained in perfect alphabetical order, but as I am only related to her by marriage, she probably doesn't count.

These days, knowing where my anxiety stems from is incredibly helpful to me. It stops me from feeling like a complete lunatic, and gives me context and insight into my condition. It also allows me to understand that my anxiety isn't entirely my fault, which in turn helps me to be less ashamed.

Back when I was a teenager, though, it didn't help at all. Living in an anxious family served to normalise my worries for me. Because so many people around me were anxious and obsessive, it seemed totally appropriate for me to be anxious and obsessive, too. I knew I was different from my friends, I knew that I was scared of the world in a way that they weren't, but it didn't occur to me to try to change myself.

I had one sticky-out ear, two very thick eyebrows, and a highly anxious disposition. They made me who I was. I couldn't change any of them.

Unless maybe, just maybe, I could.

Alert and Alarmed

DEFENSE PESSIMISM: [. . .] Rehearse everything that could go
wrong, and devise strategies to avert every conceivable glitch.
This will produce a sense of control and reduce anxiety, helping
you to perform effectively. Or, maybe not.

Jon Winokur, author

During my last year of school I found the cure for anxiety. It was
in a book written by a man called Dale Carnegie, a writer I had
never heard of. (Later I learned that Mr Carnegie was actually quite
famous for a little book called *How to Win Friends and Influence
People*, but at the time I was sure that I'd discovered him.)

Dale Carnegie had written a book just for me. It was called *How
to Stop Worrying and Start Living*, and it contained the answers to all
of my problems. It detailed case histories of people who suffered from
anxiety, and the specific methods that they used to beat their worry.

I devoured *How to Stop Worrying and Start Living* in a day,
pouncing on it like I was my cousin M in turbulence and the book

was the last Valium on earth. I read all of the examples – including the businessman who was being blackmailed, the man with the terminal stomach ulcer who decided to take a trip around the world, and the cigarette manufacturer who died from a 'stress'-induced heart attack (admittedly the book was possibly a little dated) – and I memorised each of the techniques.

There is a huge amount of invaluable material in *How to Stop Worrying and Start Living*, including the idea of living in 'Day Tight Compartments', which I still use in times of stress. However, there is one technique that didn't work for me at all, and unfortunately it was this technique that wedged itself in my brain, doing more damage than all of the other methods did good.

The method is called 'Accept the Worst That Can Happen', and is intended to bring peace of mind to the worrying soul. By accepting the worst, Mr Carnegie explains rationally, we will have nothing more to lose, and we'll be able to work out how we can improve on what we have.

Well, accepting the worst was irresistible to me and I embraced the concept with all of my heart. With every situation that caused me stress, I would determine the worst that could possibly happen, and accept it as if it had already occurred.

Instead of bringing peace of mind, however, accepting the worst created a myriad of problems. I started 'accepting the worst' in the most innocuous of situations, jumping from 'minor issue' to 'utter catastrophe' in one easy step.

If I had a disagreement with a friend, for example, then I would accept that the worst that could happen was that a) she would never speak to me again; b) she would turn the rest of our social group against me; c) this would leave me with absolutely no friends and d) I would be lonely and miserable for the rest of my life.

If I was worried about an exam, I would accept that the worst that could happen was that a) I would fail the exam; b) I would fail the subject; c) I would have no chance of getting into university and d) I would be a failure and miserable for the rest of my life.

If I had to get in an elevator, I would accept that the worst that could happen was that a) the lift would get stuck between floors; b) I would be trapped in it for hours, if not days; c) I would have some kind of brain snap whilst incarcerated and d) I would potentially die of fear.

So you can see, the technique didn't really help so much to ease my concerns.

The correct therapeutic term for what I was doing is 'catastrophising'. (I know this because it's the term my therapist taught me.) I would take a simple problem, blow it out of all proportion in my mind and run with it until it was an absolute disaster. I got so skilled at this technique that catastrophising became my default position. Once I'd practised it for a few months, my perspective was lost forever.

Now, to an objective observer, this catastrophising might seem completely illogical. Who goes from 'elevator' to 'die of fear'? To me, however, it makes perfect sense, and it has continued to make perfect sense as the years have rolled on. For example, these days 'The bank balance is low' proceeds to 'What if we can't pay the mortgage?', which proceeds to imagining us homeless and impoverished in one fluid movement. It doesn't feel excessive, it feels like the appropriate response to the state of our finances. Sure, there is a small voice inside me that acknowledges that not everyone goes from 'low bank balance this week' to 'begging on the street', but I don't listen to it. To me, the voice of disaster is much more compelling.

My relentless tendency to catastrophise makes me sound like I am quite irrational, and indeed I do act irrationally when I am anxious.

However, I am not anxious all of the time, and I remain rational and functional on other occasions. I've studied. I work. I look after my family. I drive a car. I socialise and maintain friendships. I laugh. I love. But anxiety has always been a force over which I have no control. It washes over me. It drains me of my capacity to think clearly, or to deal with my emotions, or to manage my behaviour. It comes and goes of its own accord. And when it visits, it controls me entirely.

I can't even imagine how much richer my life would be if I didn't spend so much time worrying. How much happier I'd be. All the extra brain power I'd have. All the things I would do. All the things I would think! When I consider the hours and hours and hours that I've spent worrying over the years, feeling panicked, distracted and obsessed with negative thoughts, I realise I've lost weeks, if not months, of productive time.

So what is the difference between normal worry and anxiety? After all, everyone worries. Bad things happen all the time, and it's perfectly reasonable to be troubled by that fact, and to brace yourself for the worst-case scenario, right?

Well, I think so, and I spend a great deal of time being troubled by what's ahead and bracing myself for the worst. I get exceedingly troubled and quite seriously braced. Apparently, though, not everyone operates this way. 'Normal' people – people who don't have an anxiety disorder – don't think too much about the misfortunes ahead. Perhaps they don't believe that bad things do happen. Or perhaps they believe that, should things go wrong, they will deal with it at the time.

It's a wonderful way to live your life. Sadly, it's just not how I live mine.

Normal people say things like:

- 'I'll worry about it if it ever happens.'
- 'There is so much good in the world.'
- 'Whatever happens, we'll cope.'
- 'I've had my run of bad luck. Good things are ahead . . .'
- 'Live in the moment. Tomorrow is another day.'
- 'I'm sure it will be fine.'
- 'Let's not worry about things that haven't happened yet.'

I say things like:

- 'Anything could happen.'
- 'The world is such a cruel and unfair place.'
- 'I couldn't cope if something went wrong.'
- 'Two bad things have happened, now I'm waiting for the third.'
- 'Nothing has gone wrong yet, so any minute it will.'
- 'If it happens, it's going to be an absolute disaster.'
- 'What if it's a tumour?'

Being anxious is being alert *and* alarmed. It's also exhausting and demoralising and a waste of time. Worrying about something won't stop it happening, any more than wishing for something will make it come true.

At least, that is what my intellect tells me. My instinct, however, doesn't agree with that at all.

Anxiety is almost superstitious in its nature. I realised this when I imagined my life without anxiety and recognised how vulnerable I would feel without it. There is actually something addictive about chronic worry; it serves a purpose, in a perverse kind of way.

When I sat down to deconstruct my anxiety, I was amazed at my discoveries. I have a number of belief systems attached to my worries, beliefs buried so deeply it took me over forty years to uncover them. My anxiety, I learned, is like a totem of the mind, a form of magical thinking to ward off evil. It protects me from harm, even as it is hurting me, which is why it has been so very hard to let it go.

What I Believe about Anxiety: An Insight into My Subconscious

- If I repeatedly visualise something bad happening, then it won't actually happen.
- If I worry about the worst-case scenario, then I will be far more prepared if it happens.
- If I am well prepared for the worst-case scenario, then it will hurt much less if it occurs.
- If I don't worry, something bad will happen to me without me being prepared.
- If I am not prepared for the bad thing happening, I will be devastated by its impact.
- If I don't worry, I will have to trust that everything will be okay, which is a preposterous thing to think.
- If I don't worry, I will . . . Well, I have no idea. I can't imagine not worrying. It sounds scary.

Now, if I was the heroine of a novel, these realisations would represent a turning point in my life. I would see the error of my ways, throw off the shackles of anxiety, and move forward unfettered by my irrational fears.

Unfortunately, I am not a heroine in a novel. I'm just a very real person with very real issues, struggling to make sense of myself. And, despite my insights into my psyche, I continue worrying. After all, it's not that easy to change. Anxiety is in my genes. It's in my environment. It is comforting to me, in a perverse kind of way. And after forty-odd years, it is an ingrained habit.

But at least I know now why I'm doing it. Surely, *surely*, that counts for something.

The Days My Boyfriend Died

Anxiety is love's greatest killer. It makes others feel as you might when a drowning man holds on to you. You want to save him, but you know he will strangle you with his panic.

Anaïs Nin, author

One of the great tragedies of my life was that Josh Goldenbum never fell in love with me. One of the blessings of my life was that I did find a boyfriend, and he was, indeed, wonderful. T was my soulmate, the very first love of my life, and I knew from the moment I met him that eventually we would marry.

T and I met when I was fifteen and he was seventeen and we were both at school. We finally became a couple more than two years later, when I was doing Arts at uni, and T was a brilliant Architecture student. I loved him desperately, in that slightly unhinged 'You are my world and I would lie down and die if I lost you' way. I was completely immersed in T, was terrified that he would stop loving me, and spent a lot of time asking for reassurances that he still did.

Ultimately, this turned out to be a fairly unattractive quality.

For three years T stuck with me and loved me and soothed my insecurities. Eventually, however, my anxiety about losing my beloved boyfriend became a self-fulfilling prophesy. One night T came to the house where I still lived with my parents, sat down on my bed, held my hand, and absolutely shattered my heart.

Yes, he broke up with me. My neediness had become too much.

I really didn't blame him; after all, I found myself quite unappealing, too. Still, that didn't help with the fact that I was desolate with grief. I honestly didn't know how I could go on living. My worst fears had been realised and now my life was hell. I cried every single night for six weeks, huge racking sobs that were loud enough to wake my mum in the middle of the night. For more than three months I just ached with sorrow. I knew I would never get over the pain.

Interestingly, though, I did. I guess the young heart is much more resilient than I had expected, because after four short months I was ready to socialise again. I went to parties, I spent time with my girl-friends, and after another couple of months, I even started dating. I had a relationship for almost a year and another for several years, and a couple of short ones in between. Still, it was a good six and a half years after T broke my heart before I settled down with the man who would become my husband. And when I did, there was a serious problem.

He kept on dying.

It only began after my husband-to-be and I started living together. Approximately once a fortnight he would be killed in a car accident, or get run over by a bus, or be murdered on the street in a mugging gone wrong. Sometimes it was more frequently, sometimes less, but he died fairly regularly for at least the first year. These terrible trag-edies were exhausting for me, what with all the emotional turmoil and funeral planning. And they certainly weren't easy for him, either, as he was continually coming home to a sobbing girlfriend who had declared herself a widow in his absence.

It was a rough year.

The name of the man who would become my husband began with T, and this was not a coincidence. He was the very same T who had crushed me six and a half years earlier, the one for whom I'd ached with sorrow for months.

Yes, he was back. Turns out T had been pining for me for about six out of those six and a half years – coincidentally, the exact same amount of time that I was not pining for him. Our love was rekin-dled in a burst of romance. We were soulmates once again.

Happily, on our second time around, a great deal had changed in our relationship. I was more confident in myself, and less anxious that T would leave me. After all, he waited six long years for us to be reunited, so it seemed unlikely that he would change his mind now.

The start of our (second) life together was good. We both had jobs we enjoyed, and were reasonably well paid. We moved into a nice flat. We saw our friends and our families. There was really very little to be anxious about.

Still, I was a highly anxious person. And if there wasn't any obvious reason for me to feel anxious, then I had to create my own. I couldn't worry about money as there was enough of that, we didn't have kids, and I tend not to worry about my own health, so the logical thing to worry about was that T would die. Which I did. On an almost daily basis.

Now I'm not sure who would be the ideal partner for a woman with obsessive death fantasies, but I can assure you that T was not that person. He wasn't intentionally insensitive, but he was a workaholic, and little details like informing his girlfriend that he was still alive and well would regularly slip his mind.

T was in the office for long hours at a time, from early in the morning to eight or nine every night. I worked much shorter hours, and would inevitably call T the moment I walked in the door. If he said that he was going to be home at a reasonable hour, I'd hold dinner and eat with him. If he said that he was going to be late, I'd eat early by myself. I never have been great at waiting for my food.

On one particular evening I rang T at six, and he said that he'd be home by eight o'clock. I put dinner in the oven and decided to wait and eat with him. I must have had a big lunch that day.

By eight o'clock T hadn't arrived home. I felt a little worried, but figured he must just be running late. At a quarter past eight I phoned his office. No, they told me, he left ages ago. Okay . . . so why wasn't he home yet? Remember, these were the days before everyone had mobile phones, so I had no way of contacting him at all.

By eight-thirty I was pacing around the apartment in agitation. Now, the apartment was only three rooms, so I really was turning a lot. My heart was racing, and my head felt cloudy, and my thought processes went something like this:

What if T has been in a car accident? What if he's lying on the ground, bleeding and unconscious, the life ebbing from his crushed body? How will I know? Who will come to find me?

What if T is dead? Oh my God – what if he's DEAD??

He's dead. He's DEAD! Oh my God. He's DEAD!!!

Maybe I can see the car accident from the window. I'll go check.

(I run to the window. Nothing.)

NO! I can't see anything! The accident must be further away!

I'll ring his office again. Maybe they'll know where he is.

(I ring the office. They say he left ages ago.)

THEY DON'T KNOW WHERE HE IS!!! He's dead.
He's DEAD!

Okay, calm down. He probably just got held up.

IT'S NINE O'CLOCK!!! OH GOD, HE'S DEAD!!!

There's going to be a FUNERAL! I'll be at his FUNERAL!!!
I'll be wearing my black dress, and I'll be sobbing, like
I'm sobbing now! My parents will have to hold me up!
I won't be able to stand!

Oh, T come back! PLEASE come back!!! Make this
nightmare end!!!! I can't bear it!!!

(I hear a rustle at the front door.)

Oh GOD . . . there's someone at the door. It's the police.
It's the POLICE!!!

I hear a key being inserted in the lock.

Um . . . Hang on . . . That's the sound of a key . . . The lock
is turning . . . That's the handle . . .

(I see my boyfriend walking in the front door.)

It's T!!! He's alive!!! He's ALIVE!!!!!!

'Hey,' he said casually, throwing his keys on the table. 'What's up?'

He was HOME! And he was BREATHING! The hideous dread
drained away, the fog of panic lifted, and I was clear again.

I flung myself at T, bawling in relief and anger. 'Where have you
BEEN? You're so late! I thought you were DEAD!'

T shook his head. 'Why would I be dead? I got held up.'

'But you didn't CALL!' I wailed.

'I was busy and then I just wanted to get home,' he said impa-
tiently. 'Is there dinner?'

'But where WERE you? The office said you'd GONE!'

'I had to stop by a client's office; he called as I was leaving. Okay?'

'But I was so WORRIED!' I cried.

T rolled his eyes and took me gently by the shoulders. 'Kerri, you do this to me *every single time* I am late. I am sick of this. I am an ARCHITECT. What is going to kill me? Tripping over a pencil? A plan falling on my head?'

My sobs were subsiding. I sniffed. 'You could have had a car accident. You're a very bad driver.'

'Oh for goodness sake.' He sighed. 'When was the last time I had an accident?'

'I don't know.'

'*Never*. I have never been in a car accident. Now, when was the last time I was late?'

'Um . . . yesterday.'

'And before that?'

'Monday.'

'So, when are you going to get used to it?' T looked absolutely fed up. And I loved him so much, I couldn't bear to lose him again. If I kept up this behaviour, he really would be gone. But not because he was dead. Because he couldn't stand to live with a crazy person like me.

'I'll stop,' I said, trying hard to calm my breathing. 'I'm sorry.'

T rubbed his eyes in fatigue and frustration. 'Okay. Fine. I'm going to have dinner.'

I watched him walk into the kitchen and help himself to some food. (I'm pretty sure it was chicken. We tended to eat chicken a lot in those days.) I suddenly realised that I was starving too, and, as my boyfriend was alive and well, there was no reason not to tuck in and eat.

I followed him in, grabbed a plate, and we ate together in grim silence.

The next time T wasn't home when I expected him, I talked myself through it. He was fine, I told myself. He'll be home any minute. He just can't get to a phone. There is no problem at all. I remained calm and logical. And I was immensely proud of myself.

For about twenty minutes.

Because after twenty minutes, everything changed. I was flooded with a sickening realisation: this time, T really was dead. I knew it. He was gone. And it was tragically ironic, because I had finally worked out how to stay calm, and now my calm had backfired and kicked me in the guts.

I paced. I cried. I leaned out the windows and scanned the roads. I called work, repeatedly. Nothing. He was dead.

Until he came home, forty minutes later, and rolled his eyes.

'You're nuts,' he said, and stomped past me on his way to the kitchen. And I took a deep breath and realised he was probably right. But what could I do? It was a force beyond my control. And besides, I was scared to let go of my anxiety. Because if I stopped worrying all the time, then something bad might really happen. Mightn't it?

I sat on the floor contemplating these questions for a minute, and then got up to eat my dinner. T was home, so I could relax – at least for the rest of the evening.

And besides, all that panicking had made me hungry.

My anxiety was a source of huge conflict between T and me. He thought that I was unreasonably anxious, which was fair enough, because I thought that I was unreasonably anxious, too. Where we differed, however, was on how to deal with my anxiety. T didn't feel he should have to pander to my neuroses. After all, if I started panicking like a crazy person when he was five minutes late, well, wasn't that my problem? Why should he have to find a phone and call home just because his girlfriend was a bit of a lunatic? And if he didn't call home, if he made me live with my irrational fears, surely I'd eventually grow out of them.

I disagreed. I knew my irrational fears weren't going anywhere. And yes, I might be a crazy person, but then couldn't T be a little more sensitive to my needs? He *knew* I'd be anxious if he was late home. He *knew* I'd be waiting by the window for the police to show up at the door. Why couldn't he be more helpful to me? Why couldn't he work harder to save me from myself?

Luckily we sorted this issue out very early in our relationship.

Except that we didn't. We argued about it for the next seventeen years.

Do You Still Love Me?

We don't see things as they are, we see them as we are.

Anaïs Nin, author

Like many women, and some men, I have always had very intense relationships. From my childhood besties, to my teenage girlfriends, to my boyfriend-who-became-a-husband T, to the beloved women in my mothers' group, I cherish all the people in my life and place a great deal of stock in those friendships.

And when I place a great deal of stock in anything, I worry terribly about losing it.

I am what you might call a little paranoid in my friendships. I scan my relationships like I scan my life, searching for reasons to be anxious, seeking evidence of unrest. I am constantly concluding that my loved ones are mad at me, and will construct entire narratives in my head supporting my thesis.

Just last week, for example, I decided that I'd annoyed my friend Anna, after she'd been forwarded an email in which I mentioned her in passing. Anna had responded to the email in what I took to be a brusque manner, and then I didn't hear anything from her for days. I took that to mean that she was both furious and disappointed, and that our relationship was potentially in danger.

I didn't consider that Anna might not have been angry. The fact that she worked full-time and had two small kids didn't occur to me, either. I jumped to the conclusion that she was very upset, and that she was not going to love me anymore as a result.

I fretted endlessly over how to fix things with Anna. I spoke to my mum and T about how to approach her and what to say. I worried deeply about losing her friendship forever, and was furious at myself for putting it in peril.

I decided to wait a couple of days, then give Anna a call and invite her for coffee. Later that afternoon, Anna texted me about something unrelated.

How are you? read the words at the end of her message.

I looked at my phone and held my breath. She's texting me! I thought. Maybe there's hope for us yet! Maybe, just maybe, she will be prepared to forgive me!

I thought for a minute, and then typed what I felt: *I'm worried about us. I don't want you to be mad at me.*

And I bit my lip and stared at the screen.

My phone beeped its reply within twenty seconds: *Mad? Why would I be mad at you honey?*

Then, in another ten seconds: *If I was mad at you, I'd yell, okay?*

And it was hard to argue with that.

That's the thing about Anna, and my other close friends. They are warm, wonderful women (and a couple of men) who know how much I love them, and who would never allow resentments to simmer without taking the time to talk things over. They give me no reason to doubt them, and they give me no reason to doubt myself. After all, I'm not in school anymore, and I can choose my friends, and these are the people I have chosen to keep in my life.

But as the cliché goes, it's not them, it's me. I'm the one who's always anxious about rejection. I'm the one who needs loads of reassurance. I'm the one who is constantly second-guessing myself. I can be a high-maintenance friend, and I am deeply grateful to the people who love me for choosing to keep me around.

Of course, as much as I can be a troublesome friend, I can be a far more troublesome wife. My friends don't have to live with me, as my husband is fond of pointing out. Besides, the bulk of my relationship anxiety gets channelled into my marriage, and this can make me a difficult partner indeed.

Every couple argues, and T and I are no exception. But whereas most people cope with marital disputes, knowing they are part and parcel of the 'together forever' deal, fighting with my husband leaves me racked with insecurity.

I can't bear it when T is cross with me, whether it's justified or not. I have an immediate, overwhelming, almost Pavlovian response: I see his angry face and I panic. Brain fog sets in, my mind refuses to function effectively, and I catastrophise immediately.

He hates me, I think. He's going to walk out. He's going to divorce me.

If I was able to stay calm and rational, I would know our fight was bound to blow over. After all, T and I have been married for fourteen years. In that time, we've had innumerable fights, and we have made up every time. In not one of those fights has my husband stopped loving me, and in not one of those fights has he considered walking out (although he has occasionally stormed out to the shops, bought a tub of rocky road ice-cream and returned home). And yet I can't be calm or rational because I'm panicking. So almost every time we fight, I think we're going to get divorced.

Knowing T is angry at me evokes my abandonment fears, and my abandonment fears make me irrational. And the only thing that can pull me back from the brink of these fears is for T to soothe me with reassurances of love. Unfortunately, though, that doesn't often happen, because in the midst of an argument, T generally isn't inclined to offer love. I guess when you're cross with someone – when they've been a total pain in the arse – the last thing you want to do is give them a reassuring cuddle.

Being highly anxious can make me extremely needy, and what I want from T isn't always in sync with what he is willing or able to offer. This is never more true than in the aftermath of an argument. Though I need hugs to feel better and move forward, my husband needs time and space. So I will be plaintively asking T if he still loves me, as he is plaintively asking me to leave him alone.

Ultimately, I have to learn to reassure myself, but that's something I have not been particularly good at until now.

Although my husband and I are highly compatible in many ways, we have very different natures. I love staying home. He loves travelling. I love reading. He loves watching TV. I am loud. He is quiet. I want to spend our retirement reading books in the sun and playing with the grandkids. He wants to spend our retirement money on a recreational trip to the moon. See? Different.

What's more, our ways of handling challenging or emotive situations are often poles apart. Take, for example, the time T taught me to ski.

It was 1986, I was seventeen years old, and I had never skied in my life. T, on the other hand, was nineteen, and he'd been skiing regularly since he was two. He wanted very much for me to share his passion, and so he took me on a holiday to the snow.

We drove to the slopes and checked in to our room at the local lodge. I got fitted out with ski gear, and a pair of hire skis, and T managed to haul me over to the kiddie slopes.

'Knees together! Lean forward!' he commanded, as he showed me how to stay upright on the snow.

We had a couple of runs on the kiddie slopes and I thought I might be ready to tackle the mildest run.

'Let's go,' T said, and he helped me onto the chairlift.

'Chairlift?' I asked him. 'Don't we start with the T-bar?'

'We're going on the chairlift,' he said, and we took off into the air.

'Aren't we going a bit high?' I asked him anxiously. We seemed to be soaring right into the clouds.

'It's fine,' he said. 'We're here. Ski to the left!'

We were on the top of one of the highest mountains in the village.

'I can't do it!' I cried. 'It's too steep! Take me down!'

And so T pulled me to the centre of the run, and then he pushed me down the slope.

Now, I would have preferred to learn to ski the traditional way. I wanted to go to ski school till I felt confident on the snow, then start on the junior slopes until I built up to the bigger hills. I would have saved the steep inclines for another year; I was in no hurry to experience falling from a great height. T, however, had other plans.

T's approach to teaching me to ski was symbolic of his attitude to life in general. He did not – and does not – believe in the 'softly, softly' approach. While I like to avoid uncomfortable situations, T believes in facing your fears full on. While I like to take things slowly and steadily, T believes in jumping headfirst into the fire. And while I like to be eased through my neuroses, T believes that pandering to them will just make them worse.

Now, my husband is highly motivated to help me overcome my anxieties. Having an anxious wife is no picnic for him – imagine coming home every night to a hysterical partner who is tearfully planning your funeral. And certainly T's methods of dealing with me are rational. He's right that I shouldn't avoid stressful situations; what I need to do is build up the resources to deal with them.

But what I need and what I want are two different things. I may need to build up my inner resources, but what I want is a partner who will shield me from harm. I may need to confront those things that frighten me, but what I want is to be protected so that I never need to be nervous. I may need someone who resolutely marches me into lifts, but what I want is a partner who will walk with me up twenty flights of stairs, or at least cuddle me and stroke my hair as we travel up in the elevator.

I may need someone with whom I can fight and make up, but what I want is someone who never lets us argue, who tells me he loves me twenty times a day, and who doesn't allow me a moment to doubt myself or feel insecure.

Of course, as seductive as this sounds, I am also totally aware that it wouldn't work. If T had relentlessly protected me and shielded me from all pain, after all these years I'd most likely have become a dependent wreck. And if he'd told me he loved me twenty times a day, I'd most probably feel smothered beyond belief, and be more than a little bored, too. So in fact what I 'need' turns out to look less like my fantasy, and rather disconcertingly like my husband.

Except on the ski slopes, where my fantasy held firm. Because on the ski slopes, my very real partner failed me dismally. I lost control on my way down the slope, fell over backwards almost immediately, whacked my head hard on a patch of ice, and had to be carried down the mountain on a stretcher. I got concussed, was badly shaken, and never attempted to go skiing again.

I learned that skiing is not a metaphor for life. In life, I may need a partner like T, but on an icy, steep slope, I just need a man who will hold my hand.

A Travelling Nightmare

I have panicked unnecessarily in all four corners of the globe.

Jon Ronson, journalist

It's not that I don't enjoy travelling. I do. At least, I *think* that I enjoy travelling. I've certainly enjoyed the places I've visited. I've been to several different countries and to various parts of Australia and I've had some wonderful experiences. But the process has never been easy for me, and sometimes it's extremely tempting to just stay home.

My travel stress begins before I even leave the house, days, even weeks before the trip itself. Packing for a holiday is nerve-racking, to say the least, and puts me in the mood for anxiety long before we hit the airport.

I spend weeks making 'What to Pack' lists, and I fret about them nonstop. Am I packing too much? Am I packing too little? Will I have appropriate outfits for any occasion? Will I have enough shoes? Enough bras? Enough tampons? Enough cosmetics? Will I remember my phone charger, a notepad, my vitamins, a book? Will I remember paracetamol in case of headache, earplugs in case of noise, socks in case of cold feet, and tweezers in case of stray hairs?

I get out the suitcases and calculate how much space I need. Should I take the small suitcase or the large one? I settle on the large wheelie, and lay it open in my room. Then I go on a rampage of my wardrobe and wash all the clothes that I'm planning to take – dresses and tops and jackets and jeans and pants and a dozen pairs of undies. (I may be happy to wear jeans seven or eight times in a row at home, but if I'm placing them in a suitcase they need to be pristine.) I fold my clean clothes with care and put them in the case, along with bags and accessories and four different pairs of shoes. I know that I'm bound to come home with at least five items unworn, but it is better than the horror of being stranded without the right shirt.

And then I look at it all, and decide that I should take the small wheelie, after all. So I take the clothes out, lay them carefully on my bed, and start the whole process again.

Packing cosmetics presents a particular challenge. I want all of my usual products available when I travel – I cannot possibly survive without my special face wash, or toner, or anti-ageing moisturiser – but the problem is determining how much of each to take. I can't take full bottles as I would need another suitcase, so I have to decant the products into smaller containers. Now, I know from experience that I do tend to overpack, but I can't possibly run the risk of being stranded without enough eye serum, or at the mercy of the local pharmacy to provide a suitable deodorant. So I spend a couple of hours painstakingly calculating my requirements, and then meticulously doling them out into the various containers. Seven squirts of night cream into one container, seven squirts of day cream into another, a generous serve of toner, a couple of dozen cotton balls . . . It can take me the better part of an afternoon, then half the time when I'm travelling I don't even end up washing my face. But as far as I'm concerned, when I'm leaving the safety of my home, I can't be too prepared.

Despite my extensive packing lists, I still usually forget something. And even when I do forget something, it is never the end of the world. For one thing, I don't really travel to places without stores in which to buy tampons; for another thing, it's not exactly a disaster to do without eye cream for a week. But it's the *fear* of the forgetting that is my undoing, rather than the consequences of the forgetting itself.

Still, I suspect that my worries are even more fundamental. I believe that packing makes me agitated not because it's difficult in itself, but because it is tangible proof that I'm going away. Getting clothes out of the cupboards, putting toothbrushes into cosmetic bags, buying books for the plane and checking passports are valid all remind me that soon I'll be out of my comfort zone and venturing into the great unknown. And – just as when I was a kid – the great unknown makes me very unsettled.

It's not that I don't like new places. I do. It's just that at home, I know where everything is. I know where to buy the food I like to eat. I know where to find good coffee. I speak the language. I understand the currency. I know my pillow will be firm. I know how much to tip, and how best to hail a cab. I know what my routine will be, and what I'll be doing the next day.

At home, I know where the toilets are. I know that when I need to go, a toilet will be close. I know that the toilet will be clean, have paper and smell nice – or, at the very least, it will have an actual seat. I am literally frightened of hole-in-the-floor toilets; I cannot stand over a filthy sewer and relax enough to wee. For this reason, there are countries I have crossed off my list, because their toilets are famously too horrible to use. And though this may be shameful and princess-like and demented, at least I know my limitations.

What it all boils down to in the end is control. At home, I am able to control my environment. At home, I can predict, and anticipate, and prepare. Overseas is very much an unknown quantity. Overseas I am frequently out of control, and whilst this is exciting and fun for many people, it is highly uncomfortable for a person like me.

Out of all my worries (and clearly, I have a few), I think that my travelling anxiety induces the most embarrassment. It certainly has denied me the most opportunities, as I've never been brave enough to travel extensively. My fear of lifts hasn't actually prevented me from going anywhere; my nailbiting habit hasn't stood in my way. However, I've definitely missed out on overseas experiences, I've never backpacked anywhere, and I've never travelled overseas alone.

The majority of my friends love to travel; in fact, most of them would travel as much as they could afford. I need to be encouraged to travel by my husband, and I always prefer to go somewhere I've been before. That said, even going somewhere I've already been is no guarantee I'll be visiting without anxiety. I still agonise over the planning and packing and preparation, even more so when I am travelling with my kids.

The first holiday T and I took as parents was when we visited Thailand with our five-month-old son. In my normal, anxious state, I became totally obsessed with what I'd feed my baby for the ten days we'd be away. T advised me to just play it by ear but I couldn't possibly deal with the uncertainty; as far as I was concerned, we were going to a foreign country, and I had no idea what I'd be able to find. In the end, I decided to pack a jar of Heinz baby food for every meal my son would require. He ate three meals a day, so that made *thirty jars* of pureed vegetables and fruit stuffed into my case. My suitcase was so full I could barely fit in any clothes, but I decided that peace of mind was far more important than having a change of sarong.

Now, my behaviour may have been reasonable if we'd been travelling to a remote Thai fishing village (although I suspect even remote Thai fishing villages have babies whose parents feed them). We were, however, staying at a Club Med resort in the heart of a major city. And the resort was fully equipped for babies and toddlers, supplying everything from nappies to wet wipes to baby baths to a variety of baby food. Even if they hadn't stocked baby food, they provided buffet meals three times a day, from which I could have found something to mush and feed my son.

I know I would have discovered this if I'd been thinking clearly. I would have contacted the resort, explained that I was visiting with a baby, and asked what provisions they supplied. But I didn't think clearly, I panicked as usual, and came up with a ridiculous scheme to take half a supermarket with me.

Still, once I made the decision, I stuck with it. I'd brought the jars with me, it was done, they were there, and there was no way I was going to schlep the darn things back home again. So I fed my son his ready-made meals three times a day for the duration. By the time we got back home he was so accustomed to the baby food that he'd become addicted to Heinz, crying and thrashing his head when offered anything I'd cooked myself. I had to wean him back onto homemade food over a period of several weeks by mixing small amounts of cooked veggies into his mush. At five months of age, my poor little boy was already a casualty of his mother's neurotic behaviour.

My kids are older now and I don't have to worry about finding them appropriate foods – after all, every country we have visited has served noodles and burgers and chips. Still, I have always found a great deal to be anxious about. Long-haul flights, in particular, make me enormously fretful. Now, I'm not afraid of flying, per se. I don't worry that the plane will plummet into the ocean and that we all will perish in some hideous crash. I don't share that gene with my cousin M. My fears are far more banal than that.

I worry that we're going to misplace our passports, or that we'll be late to the airport and miss our flight. I worry that I'm going to sit next to someone smelly, or scary, or unhinged, or excessively talkative. I worry that there will be a team of rugby players on board who will get drunk and disorderly and open the emergency exits while the plane is mid-flight.

I worry that the toilets will get putrid and revolting and I won't have a choice but to use them. I worry that the meals are going to be disgusting and that none of us will want to eat them and we'll all be hungry. I worry that I'll get that horrible taste in my mouth that you get at the end of a plane trip, and that no amount of toothpaste will brush it out. I worry that the kids will be agitated and not sleep, and that they will keep me awake when I'm exhausted.

In other words, I worry about all the things that will probably happen. And I know that it's my attitude that is the real problem. Other people will say, 'Yes, long-haul flying isn't fun, but it's only fourteen hours of my life,' and get on with joyfully anticipating their holiday. I will dread the flight and plan for those fourteen hours for weeks. I'll pack bags of snacks, and toys, and books, and games that no one will use, because we're all too busy watching movies and napping and eating our horrid meals.

Of course, I don't have to travel overseas by air. There is always the alternative – the old-fashioned cruise. Well, I tried that once, and it didn't exactly work out for me.

As a surprise, my long-suffering husband had booked us a two-night cruise on a giant international ocean liner that was offering discount weekend 'experiences'. And an experience it was. For a start, we all had to go on deck for the safety demonstration, where we were handed our life jackets and shown how to put them on. I immediately took this as a sign that the ship was likely to sink, and spent the rest of the weekend scared to take the life jacket off in case we were called on deck for emergency evacuation.

Still, the fun really started when it was time for bed. Our cabin, you see, didn't have a porthole, just a helpful painting of a window to make us think that we really had a view. I lay awake all night in a claustrophobic panic, clutching my life jacket and trying to visualise dry land. T upgraded us the next day to a room with a porthole (which pretty much negated the 'discount' aspect of the cruise) and, to my great relief, this helped me enormously. I still couldn't sleep a wink the next night, but at least when I lay there on my swaying bed, I could stare desperately at the horizon, and convince myself we weren't going to die.

My husband has not surprised me with a holiday since. For that, I am very grateful.

As T is a keen traveller and I am not, we have come to various compromises. We travel to certain places together, and he travels to places with bad toilets alone. Over the years, we have had some fabulous experiences, but we both know that if we go somewhere new, I'm going to be a little tense.

'You're back!' T said to me after a recent holiday, as we boarded our return flight and settled into our seats.

'What do you mean?' I asked, though I thought I understood.

'It's only now we're going home that you're relaxed,' he observed. 'You haven't been yourself since the moment we left.'

I felt absolutely crushed that I'd failed so badly. I'd tried so hard to be normal. I'd tried so hard to be laid-back.

'But that doesn't mean I didn't enjoy the holiday,' I said plaintively. 'I promise you, I had a wonderful time!'

'I know,' T told me, and kissed my head. 'You did great, I promise. You can't help being you.' And he put his arm around me and we stared out at the clouds, as the aeroplane carried us peacefully home.

Mind-Altering Anxiety

Anxiety is the space between the 'now' and the 'then'.

Richard Abell, politician

I learned a great many things about myself in my twenties. I learned that I should never attempt to cook without a recipe, especially if eggs and/or cream are involved. I learned that a blunt fringe does not suit me, even if I cut it myself in front of the mirror. I learned that I do not enjoy working in an office, as I am not good at pretending people are right just because they are my boss.

And I learned that drugs and me just do not mix.

Now, it will go without saying that drugs have always made me anxious. Even as a teenager I was never one for pushing the boundaries. I tried alcohol, and puffed on a couple of cigarettes, but that truly was enough experimentation for me. I didn't like to be out of control – it was the antithesis of what I needed, and besides, I was highly sensitive to chemical substances. An extra coffee in the morning would make me jittery, a 'daytime' cold tablet would keep me up all night, and an antihistamine could knock me out for hours.

Ironically (or, perhaps, unsurprisingly), my first bad experience with drugs was with a perfectly legal, over-the-counter medication. T and I, newly reunited, had visited New York, where T had lived for several years. We both had suffered from serious jet lag on the way over, and were determined to sleep on the overnight flight back from LA. We popped into a pharmacist and bought some antihistamine-based sleeping medication that is readily available in the United States.

Well, what a fun trip that turned out to be.

T and I settled in our seats, took swigs of water, and slugged back the massive, white sleeping pills. Two of them each. We really wanted to sleep.

Almost immediately, a message came over the PA system announcing that there would be a delay in take-off. A long delay. Around ninety minutes.

T looked at me with big, wide eyes, and pointed to his throat. 'But . . . but . . .'

'I know!' I said. But what could we do? Unswallow the damn things? We had drugged ourselves, we weren't taking off, and we were just going to have to live with the consequences.

Unfortunately, the consequences were not so good. It turned out the over-the-counter medicine was unbelievably strong, and we were both quickly zonked out of our brains. Poor T literally sank to the floor on his knees. He managed to turn himself around so that he was facing his seat, and lay his head heavily in the vicinity of his seatbelt. I looked on in alarm, fearing that he was terribly sick, but was helpless to act, or even ring for help. I could feel myself drowning in a dark, drugged sea. I couldn't speak, I couldn't move, and I kept falling in and out of consciousness. And yet I couldn't shake the horrifying thought from my head: I am going to be stuck like this forever.

As the plane finally got ready for take-off, a flight attendant approached T and asked him to get in his seat.

He can't, I wanted to say. *He's sick. We're both sick!*

But my mouth wouldn't move and my limbs were too heavy. And all I could do was watch with half-closed eyes as he hauled himself into position and then flopped again drunkenly against the window.

I fought sleep for as long as I possibly could, trying desperately to stay focused and awake. I was frightened to leave T, who I feared was dying, and I was very scared of falling into a permanent coma myself. But I am not a big girl, and I am no match against two strong pills, so I eventually succumbed to a deep, nauseating sleep.

I woke up years later as the plane began its descent. I turned to T, who was rubbing his eyes, looking like he'd been dead for a century or more. We looked at each other and smiled grimly.

'I never doin' dat again,' I told him thickly.

'Gah,' he said, and nodded his agreement.

'My bouth feels yuck,' I slurred to him.

'Need dooce,' he agreed, and looked around.

The plane landed with a thump, we collected our bags, and we stumbled back into the land of the living. We picked our luggage off the carousel and dragged ourselves to the cab rank, then sat dazed and confused in the taxi on the way home. Then we slept all through the day, and were awake all that night.

It was the worst jet lag ever.

My next drug experience was also completely legal; at least, it was legal in the country we were visiting. T and I were in Amsterdam, and we were determined to do as the locals did.

We were going to eat a real hash cake.

Despite my intense stress levels when travelling, I really did try to get into the spirit of adventure. I just needed to make sure that the adventure was safe and legal, and that I had taken all of the necessary precautions. So it was with this completely unnatural and somewhat forced spirit of adventure that I joined T in our first experience of hallucinogenic substances. We had been travelling in Europe, to the Czech Republic and France, and Amsterdam was our final stop. We'd been fascinated by the red-light district, quietly overwhelmed by the Anne Frank house, and awed by the magnificent canals. A trip to a cannabis coffee shop was always going to be next on the tourism agenda.

Now, I would never have eaten a hash cake at home. However, I knew that cannabis was famously legal in Amsterdam, and that it was practically compulsory to sample some of the local goods when you were in town. T was even less interested in drug taking than me, but he was a very keen traveller, and he certainly wouldn't have left the country without the quintessential Netherlands experience.

So a hash cake it was. Before we began eating, however, there was some serious planning to be done. I was anxious (for a change) about the idea of taking a mind-altering substance. I knew that hash cakes couldn't be exceedingly dangerous, because they were legal there, and surely the Netherlands couldn't risk tourists dropping dead all over the place. However, I'd never eaten cannabis before, and I had frightening visions of 'lost' hours and waking up in hospital with strange piercings and no idea of my own name. And of course T was inexperienced, and couldn't be relied upon to save me in the case of an unfortunate reaction. I couldn't leave anything to chance.

I scoped out an appropriate-looking coffee shop, as close as possible to our hotel. Then I took a serviette and pen, and carefully mapped out the most direct route from the coffee shop to our hotel.

It was my contingency plan in case we forgot where we were staying once the drugs kicked in, and required a map to get us home again. I also jotted down our names and room number, in the event that we completely lost our senses and required external assistance.

We examined the menu at length, discussed its offerings, and decided to get two hash cakes. The waiter ambled over, and we placed our order, then we quickly changed our minds and ordered one to share. A whole cake each could be far too potent, and we didn't want to be reckless – these were drugs, after all. The cake was set down at our table, we regarded it for a moment, and then we divided it precisely down the middle. We ate it slowly and with caution, before paying the bill, grabbing our serviette map, and practically sprinting back to our room.

And there we lay, on our hotel bed, side by side, waiting for the magic to happen.

Sadly – or perhaps happily – the magic never came. We lay there together for well over an hour, occasionally checking with each other to see if we 'felt anything', but both T and I remained resolutely clear-headed. I was slightly disappointed; after all, it would have been interesting to have had the full, out-of-body Amsterdam experience. Still, I wasn't disappointed enough to try again with a larger slice of cake. I'd sampled it, nothing good happened, but nothing bad happened either, and for that I was secretly relieved.

To this day, cannabis is the only non-medical drug I have tried, and I have never, even momentarily, considered trying anything harder. I wouldn't touch illegal powders or pills with a glove and a surgical mask, let alone a straw and a mirror, or a needle and syringe. I've had plenty of opportunities over the years, but I have never taken one up. If friends asked me why I'd never tried speed, or ecstasy, or cocaine, or their drug of choice, I would tell them that I simply wasn't interested. 'I don't need drugs to have a good time,' I'd say, but that wasn't at all the full story.

The truth about me and illegal drugs is that they absolutely scare me to death. They always have, and I suspect they always will. Even when I was a teenager – and supposed to feel immortal – I still felt like there was danger around every corner, particularly in those tiny little white pills people popped at rave parties, or in the lines of coke they snorted in bathrooms. I never understood how people could ingest foreign substances when they had no idea where those substances came from, the effects they could have, or the damage they could do to their bodies. Partly I was fearful of losing control, that I would do something awful, or get myself into danger. Mostly, however, I was just frightened that I'd have some shocking reaction to the drug and die.

Still, everyone has a line in the sand, and I drew mine at cannabis. Since the little-cake-that-didn't had no effect, I figured I wasn't particularly sensitive to marijuana and tried smoking it on a number of occasions, just to see what all the fuss was about. I reasoned that cannabis comes from a plant that grows naturally, and so falls into a different category than manufactured drugs like cocaine. Further-more, I only smoked with friends, I never took more than a couple of puffs, and I always felt that my anxiety was under control.

Until one fateful night, when my worst fears were realised.

We were hosting a dinner party at my house, and I'd cooked a far better meal than I usually could manage. Before dessert, we passed around a couple of joints, and most of us had a puff. But this was very, very strong stuff. This was cannabis with a twist. Within a minute, my friend D had put her head down on the table, and then stayed there for the better part of three hours. I got totally stoned – as in, sleeping-pills-in-midair stoned – and I knew immediately that it wasn't going to go well.

I rose from my chair with great difficulty and lay myself down on the floor. There were couches available, but I knew instinctively I had to be as close to the ground as possible. I remained there, and willed the fog to lift, but it wasn't going anywhere, and it wouldn't for a very long time.

I could feel the anxiety welling inside me, but my thoughts were scrambling and I couldn't unravel them properly. I knew, however, with absolute certainty, that I was losing my mind. I'd heard of people occasionally becoming psychotic after smoking dope and clearly this was what was happening to me. There was no question that I was unravelling at the seams. My brain was about to snap in two, and I would be a broken wreck of a human being for the rest of my days, condemned to psychiatric wards and sedatives and strait-jackets and padded cells and doctors and a wasted, wasted life.

I was panic-stricken, my heart thumping wildly within my prone, stoned body. But I couldn't move to express my distress and I couldn't call out to my husband or friends. I just lay there mutely as my less drugged friends chatted around me, and D sat with her head resting pathetically on the table. It was the longest night of my life so far – longer even than that night on the plane, which at least included hours of merciless unconsciousness.

I survived, of course, but I never took drugs again. With my anxious nature, I concluded it is simply not worth it. After all, I have a difficult enough time maintaining my tenuous grip on reason when I'm stone-cold sober. Add some drugs to the mix and I become a raving lunatic.

And trust me, that's not fun for anyone.

Pregnant with Concern

We live only a few conscious decades, and we fret ourselves enough for several lifetimes.

Christopher Hitchens, author

It was 1999 and I was lying on a table as two sonographers, a radiologist, and my husband hovered above me. I was freezing cold in my thin hospital gown, and shivered violently as KY jelly was applied to my stomach. The staff were kind but businesslike, and I silently gave thanks for having made it to that day without going completely insane. It had been the most excruciating ten weeks of my life.

I wondered if the thumping of my chest was visible to the others, because I could barely breathe for the pounding against my ribcage. As one of the sonographers fiddled with the ultrasound machine, a sudden rushing sound filled my ears. I tried to indicate to T that I needed help, but I was pulled backwards sharply into the vortex of a tunnel. The room moved further and further away, and I felt myself tipping darkly into nothingness.

I came to sitting on the table with my head between my knees, having fainted for the first and only time in my life. The anxiety had literally overwhelmed me.

I was eighteen weeks pregnant, and I was having a scan to find out if my baby was going to be okay. It had not been an easy pregnancy so far. For a start, it was already my second pregnancy; my first had ended in miscarriage at about seven weeks' gestation. Thankfully, I'd become pregnant again within a couple of months, and the terrible pain of the miscarriage had begun to diminish as the new life grew inside me. However, the experience had been intensely traumatic, and I was left fearful that I would lose this pregnancy, too.

I monitored myself obsessively throughout the first trimester for signs that I was still pregnant. I prodded my breasts dozens of times a day, to reassure myself that they were still sore. I watched my appetite, worrying if I didn't feel nauseous for an hour or two. And I would rush to the bathroom with every twinge or cramp, sure that I was going to find blood, sure that it was the beginning of the end. I spent weeks in a state of almost constant anxiety, and I longed for the three-month mark when the risk of miscarriage dropped significantly.

Then out of the blue, when I was eight weeks pregnant, I somehow contracted chicken pox.

I had no idea where I got the pox; I didn't know anyone at all with the disease. It seemed horribly unfair, and I was terribly sick. What's more, I was desperately afraid. How would this affect my precious unborn baby? Was he going to survive?

I put in a frantic phone call to my obstetrician, who did his very best to calm me down. The risk of damage to the foetus was small – less than one in one hundred, he told me. But when I did my research online, I was overwhelmed by fear. Congenital varicella syndrome, as it is known, can cause abnormalities of the skin, limbs, brain and eyes in foetuses. If my baby was affected, he would be very damaged. And despite my doctor's reassurance, the statistics meant nothing to me. One in a hundred might as well be one in fifty, or one in twenty, or even one in two. The reality was that my baby would either have this syndrome or not.

The syndrome could only be detected for the first time at the eighteen-week ultrasound. At this stage, the radiographers would carefully measure the baby, and determine whether or not he was healthy and viable. I made the decision not to share the news of my pregnancy until then. I was hideously worried, and simply couldn't bear to accept my friends' good wishes until I knew that I really was going to become a mother.

Once I recovered from the chicken pox I began the waiting game, counting down the days until the tell-all scan. Each day ticked by like a week, each week like a month, and it was the most stressful, agonisingly slow ten weeks I had known. I thought about the pregnancy obsessively, unable to focus my attention on anything else. My work suffered, I was distant with T, and I avoided my friends. I refused to allow myself to bond with my baby despite starting to feel him move inside me. I googled *chicken pox in pregnancy* about twenty billion times, torturing myself with statistics, and oscillating between hope and fear.

Finally, finally, the day was here. Once I regained consciousness from my faint, the team began their work. They measured my baby's length and every one of his limbs, twice. They measured his head circumference, his jaw, and the space between his eyes. They checked his internal organs. They consulted each other, and then they gave me the news.

'Your baby looks perfect,' they told me. And I wept with joy.

Getting those results was the happiest moment of my life. The anxiety lifted from me instantaneously, and despite my rounded belly, I felt light, and elated. It was the first worry-free moment I had known in eighteen weeks. It was the first time I believed I was going to be a mum.

I never doubted for a second that my extreme anxiety was an appropriate reaction to my situation. I had contracted a disease which held terrible consequences for one in one hundred foetuses. The odds were poor, and no woman could be relaxed given such a high probability for disaster. Surely there wasn't another way to respond. Or was there?

Several years later I was having coffee in the park with my close friend Jess as our toddler sons played beside us. Jess was around thirteen weeks pregnant with her second, and in between bites of muffin, I suddenly remembered that she would have had her twelve-week ultrasound by now.

'So how did the scan go?' I asked her casually.

Jess screwed up her face. 'The results were bad,' she said. 'A one in 200 chance of having a baby with Down syndrome. I have to have an amnio.'

'Oh no!' I felt sick for her. 'I'm so sorry! Are you still going to start telling people you're pregnant?'

'Yeah,' she said, shrugging. 'I'm sure it'll be okay. One in 200 is still pretty small. And if it's bad, we'll deal with the news at the time. No point worrying about it if it never happens.'

I looked at Jess in wonder, as if she'd suddenly grown a second head. Did she really feel like that? *Could* anyone really feel like that? But she looked as calm as ever, sipping her coffee and passing snacks to her son, Ryan. And as Jess's amniocentesis date approached, there were no anguished late-night calls, no great concern about the risk of miscarriage, no fretting about the possible negative results. She just went to the appointment, had the procedure, and got on with things as usual. Her daughter was born perfectly healthy, and Jess didn't waste her pregnancy being racked with anxiety about something that never happened.

People like Jess fascinate me. To me they are an alien species, a strange breed of almost-humans who look like us but don't worry excessively. I would love to be one of them; their existence seems very peaceful. And I would have loved to enjoy my pregnancies instead of spending so much time being tortured by fear and apprehension. Sadly, however, I'm not built that way.

I found pregnancy to be enormously stressful, particularly the first trimester. I told myself that the foetus inside me was robust. I reminded myself that women in far less ideal circumstances have carried healthy pregnancies to term. I recalled that my friend Sandy went on a (literal) roller-coaster ride before she realised she was pregnant and that her pregnancy was absolutely fine. Still, my anxiety considered all of these to be moot points. My anxiety told me that my baby was highly vulnerable, and that even the slightest wrong move on my part could cause me to miscarry.

I had three miscarriages – one before each successful pregnancy – so in a sense my worries were justified. But worrying about miscarrying didn't prevent it from happening. And besides, each of my pregnancy losses came when I was least expecting it and yet didn't happen in the pregnancies in which I was bracing myself for the worst. This is because I can't influence events with my mind, a fact I am still trying to come to terms with.

My first miscarriage took place when I was seven weeks pregnant. I had been doing everything 'right' for the short term of the pregnancy: eating my fruit and vegetables, drinking my milk, and quite obsessively charting all the nutrients I consumed throughout the day. It didn't occur to me for a moment that I might lose the baby. My whole focus was on doing the best for my child, and ensuring we both stayed healthy.

Well, I did my best, but it didn't help at all. Nutrients or no nutrients, that baby just wasn't meant to be.

When I found myself pregnant for a second time, nutrients were furthest from my mind. All I could think of was miscarrying again, losing this second, desperately wanted baby. I watched for signs of miscarriage, waited for it, and prepared myself. What came instead was the chicken pox, for which I hadn't prepared at all.

If I hadn't been so frantic, I would have found that ironic.

My son was born in May 2009, free from chicken pox scars and looking hilariously like his father. I loved being a mother, so much so that just nine months later I was pregnant again. I was thrilled to bits, and merrily began planning for double prams and day care places. When I started to bleed at nine and a half weeks I was caught completely unawares.

By the time I fell pregnant after this second miscarriage, I was as anxious as I was during my pregnancy with my son. Not only did I worry obsessively about losing the baby, but I worried obsessively about almost everything else. I was terrified of doing something that would harm my unborn child, whether it was touching a raw chicken or inhaling paint fumes.

I craved tonic water one day in my first trimester and drank a satisfying glass, before noticing the ingredient 'quinine' on the bottle. With growing dread, I recalled that quinine cured malaria, which meant that it must be a powerful drug.

I googled *quinine in pregnancy*, and then I googled it some more. I discovered several websites that referred to quinine as an 'abortifacient', which meant that it should be avoided by pregnant women. I felt quite distraught that I had risked my baby's life, and all for the sake of a carbonated beverage. I kept googling, and found dozens of sites that claimed quinine was perfectly safe, but I ignored these, as clearly they were totally inaccurate.

Then I rang MotherSafe, a helpline for pregnant women, and confessed tearfully that I had damaged my baby.

'I've been drinking tonic water!' I sobbed. 'I just realised that it's dangerous!'

'Calm down, dear,' said the nurse on the phone. 'We'll sort this out. How many litres a day have you been drinking?'

'I drank a glass today.' I wept. 'I think it was quite big. Maybe 300 mL?' I sniffed and wiped my eyes.

'You're fine,' the nurse told me kindly, and I could hear the smile in her voice. 'Your baby will be absolutely fine.'

I became very, very fond of the MotherSafe nurses, and I spoke to them quite frequently over the next seven months. I would phone MotherSafe whenever I was worried about my unborn baby, and sometimes I rang them three or four times, just to be sure.

I rang MotherSafe when I used oven cleaner, and then saw on the label that it should be avoided by pregnant women.

'Did you eat it?' the MotherSafe nurse asked in a bright, cheery tone. 'Because if you didn't, then I really wouldn't worry.' So I didn't.

I rang MotherSafe when I cleaned the shower with Exit Mould, and felt a little dizzy from the overpowering smell.

'I know you're fine because you're calling me,' said the nurse. 'You'd have to close all the doors and pass out from the fumes before the chemicals would even get to the baby.' And strangely, almost immediately, I stopped feeling woozy.

I called MotherSafe when I ate a piece of fish one day that turned out to be totally raw in the middle.

'Did you get salmonella?' the nurse enquired. 'Because if not, you're in absolutely no danger at all.' And when I hadn't started to vomit by the next afternoon, I relaxed.

Still, my last moment of pregnancy anxiety didn't come until seconds after my daughter was actually born. It was three in the afternoon, and it had been a long, hard labour. I pushed my baby out with a massive grunt, and the doctor whisked her briskly away.

'Congratulations! She's perfect!' he said over his shoulder. 'She just needs a tiny little whiff of oxygen.'

'Oxygen?' I yelled. 'Is she dying? She's dying!' I thrashed hysterically and tried to climb out of the bed.

My husband appeared beside me and took my hand. 'She's not dying! She's fine! She's beautiful, you'll see.'

'You're lying!' I screamed at him. 'She's dead! You're lying!'

But before he could answer, she was there, in my arms. Warm, slippery, soft. My beautiful girl.

There was nothing to worry about, no matter how hard I tried.

When I tried to get pregnant with my third and final child, the pattern repeated itself again. I miscarried once more in the first trimester, and then went on to carry a viable pregnancy to term.

My final pregnancy wasn't an easy one. My health played up, my back gave out, I had some spotting and cramps, I developed varicose veins and haemorrhoids. And it wasn't surprising, either; after all, I was geriatric. Thirty-nine may not be elderly in human years, but it's pushing the upper envelope in reproductive terms.

Still, the baby, another girl, developed beautifully, right up till the thirty-fourth week. And then, on a routine scan in the maternity hospital, the sonographer casually mentioned that her head was unusually big.

'The rest of her body is in the fiftieth percentile, but her head is in the ninety-ninth,' she said. 'Unusual.'

'Unusual? What does that mean?' I asked. I could feel my body instantaneously tighten with tension.

'It's nothing,' she replied, calmly checking the other measurements. 'It probably just means she has a big head.'

'Probably?' I asked. What was *probably*, for God's sake?

'It's unlikely to mean anything,' the sonographer told me. 'It's just one of those variances that can occur.'

'Unlikely? But what if it is something? What could it be?' I could hear my voice rising in panic, and I was dimly aware that I was shouting.

She sighed. 'Look, you'll have to talk to your doctor, but it's probably just a big head. When are you next seeing your obstetrician?'

I thought for a moment. 'Now,' I said. 'I'm seeing him right now. Can I have the images? Can you print them for me?'

I'd had enough of pregnancy. I'd had enough of anxiety. I'd had enough of the responsibility of growing people in my womb and being terrified that they would come out wrong. My appointment with Dr H wasn't for another fortnight, but I couldn't take the suspense for a minute longer. I grabbed my ultrasound pictures, travelled to the sixth floor of the hospital, and stormed the obstetrics suite where my doctor worked with four of his colleagues.

'I need to see Dr H,' I told the secretary.

'Hello, Kerri!' she said with a smile. 'You're not due for a visit today, are you?'

'I've had a bad scan,' I said, waving the pictures in her face, 'and I have to see him. Now.'

The secretary looked at me for a moment, and I saw my fear registering on her face. 'Okay,' she said. 'I'll slot you in. Just take a seat and Dr H will be with you soon.'

I sat down, tears of relief welling in my eyes. Whatever was wrong with my daughter, at least I would know soon.

After forty-five minutes, Dr H called me into his rooms. He was a warm, bearded man who reminded me of Santa Claus, and made me laugh and feel happy at every visit. On this occasion he greeted me with gravitas. He examined my scans, examined me, called a specialist radiographer, and then sat me down in a chair. I took a deep breath and braced myself for the news.

'I think your baby has a big head,' said Dr H.

'But what does that mean?' I wailed. 'What is a big head? Is she deformed? Does she have a syndrome? What's it called? Are there other symptoms?'

Dr H pulled his chair closer to mine and patted me on the hand. He radiated serenity, and I felt better just being in his presence. 'I think it just means that she has a big head.'

'But . . . but . . . is that *bad*?'

'Kerri,' he said firmly, 'I wouldn't let you think everything was fine if it was all suddenly going to shit. Your baby has a big head. That's all. It really is going to be okay.'

I chose to believe him. My baby was going to be okay. I repeated it like a mantra for the remainder of the pregnancy, though I still occasionally googled *big head baby* out of habit.

Seven weeks later my younger daughter was born. She was beautiful, with huge dark eyes, rosebud lips, and a little round chin just like her dad. She had ten toes, ten fingers, dark hair, and the loudest cry any midwife had ever heard.

And her head, when I noticed, was completely average.

Sometimes, prenatal measurements just turn out to be wrong.

I used to want to have ten children. I used to think I'd have as many kids as T and I could afford. Now I feel exceedingly comfortable in my decision to stop at three. I adore babies and have moments when I feel that tug in my womb, when I long to hold a newborn against my chest one more time. But – aside from the challenges of actually raising another child – there is no way I could cope with being pregnant again. All the uncertainty. All the waiting. All the potential for disaster. All the questions. Am I doing everything right? Is anything going to go wrong? Will my baby be born healthy? Will I survive the birth? No, I know my limitations, and I simply couldn't put myself through that kind of anxiety again.

Besides, one day my own kids are going to make babies of their own. And that will be stressful enough.

Parenting: The Push and Pull

Raising children is an uncertain thing;
success is reached only after a life of battle and worry.

Democritus, philosopher

It is a truth universally acknowledged that when you're pregnant with your first child, you are not supposed to express a preference for one gender. 'As long as it's healthy,' you're supposed to say. 'I just want a baby. Girl, boy, doesn't matter.' 'I'll take whatever God gives me.'

Well, I've never been one for political correctness, and I was quite clear that I wanted to have a girl. I was one of two girls, I loved having a sister, and I longed to be close to a daughter the way my mother was close to me when I was young.

Besides, I didn't know anything about having a boy. My only boy cousins lived in another city, and I didn't have experience with boy babies at all. How would I play with a male child? Was there something special I would have to do to turn him into a boy? How would I raise a son?

I yearned quite fervently for a girl, but despite my yearning, I knew from the earliest moments that I was having a son. I didn't have my suspicions confirmed at the ultrasound; I didn't have to. My body screamed 'boy' all along, and as it turned out, my body was totally right.

I was disappointed that I was having a boy, but I was also strangely relieved. As much as I desperately wanted a girl, I believed that I'd be a better parent to a boy. You see, I knew that I was an anxious person, and I didn't want my anxiety to impact negatively on my child. And in a bizarre stroke of logic I reasoned that it would be easier for me to control my anxiety with a boy, because – wait for it – I would love a boy less than I would love a girl, and so would worry about him less as he grew older.

Looking back, I can see how preposterous this notion was. Not only was it ridiculous to contemplate that I would ever be a 'laid-back' parent, but the notion that I would love my baby less because he had a penis was verging on demented. When my baby boy was born I loved him with a fierce, searing passion that I had never before experienced. Thirteen years later, I still do. (And as a side issue, I discovered that I didn't actually have to do anything to turn my son into a boy. He just became one, all by himself, much like my girls became girls. That seems to be the way it works.)

Still, as misled as I was, my heart really was in the right place. I was determined not to be an anxious parent, firstly, because I was concerned about hurting my baby with my own neuroses, and secondly, because I was also concerned about hurting myself. I knew instinctively that the love I would feel for my child would exceed any love I had known before. And I knew that loving someone that much would make me intensely vulnerable, because the loss of that person would break me completely.

I didn't want to live the rest of my life in fear of being broken. I didn't want the joy of motherhood to be overshadowed by the fear of loss. And I didn't want to be standing at the window at midnight, waiting for my kids to come home, unable to sleep for worry about them. I had to get my anxiety under control before it was too late for all of us.

I made some resolutions before my son was born. I decided to eliminate all anxieties about my baby, to block them from my mind the way you might bar an intruder from your front door. And I succeeded, at least for a period of time. Parenting must be one of the most anxiety-provoking of all human conditions, and yet somehow, I managed to retain my serenity. I suspect that, paradoxically, it was the sheer awfulness of the worst-case scenarios that allowed me to banish them from my thoughts. I could fret about money, I could worry about being trapped in a lift, I could even panic about my husband dying, but to contemplate anything bad happening to my child was just too terrible. My mind shut down when I tried.

I couldn't allow worry about my son to enter my head, because I feared that the worry would take over entirely. So, in a deliberate move, I pushed myself completely the other way. Ironically, I became a far less anxious parent than many other mums I knew, even those who didn't struggle with anxiety in the first place.

I knew, for example, that many parents worried deeply about cot death, putting special breathing monitors in their baby's beds and checking on them constantly throughout the night. I couldn't do that; if I had even entertained the possibility of something dreadful happening, I would never have been able to leave my baby's side for a minute. Instead I blocked off those thoughts completely, put my son in his cot at night, and trusted that he would still be there in the morning, pink and healthy and breathing. It was the only way I knew how to cope.

I didn't worry about a lot of the things that other parents worried about. I didn't chart everything my baby ate, or the number of times a day he pooed. I wasn't off to the doctor three times a week like some other mums, concerned about a minuscule rash or the funny way he cried when he was burping. I breastfed in public, without worrying about what people thought. I allowed my son to be passed around to other people for a cuddle, and didn't make them wash their hands before they picked him up.

I didn't fret about germs like so many others I knew. I refused to purchase hand sanitiser, or to disinfect every surface of my home. I followed the 'three-second rule', allowing my son to eat food he had dropped on the floor as long as it hadn't been there for more than three seconds. (Over the years that gradually extended to three minutes, and my youngest has been known to eat things that fell on the floor the night before.) I sent my son to day care for two days a week when he was eighteen months old, and didn't agonise at all about the threat to his emotional development.

When my second child (Yes! A girl!) was born two years after my son, my parenting workload increased dramatically but my anxiety levels didn't. I was still resolved to be calm and laid-back. And, despite my earlier predictions, if anything I was more relaxed with my girl than I had been with my boy. I didn't bother pureeing all of her food like I had with my son; most of the time, I simply mashed it with a fork. I didn't rush her home to bed for a nap on the dot of noon; if we were out, I just let her doze in the pram. I didn't mark off every milestone in her baby book; in fact, at one point I lost the book altogether.

I was incredibly proud of being such an easygoing parent and couldn't quite believe that I had made the shift so easily. My anxiety hadn't decreased in any other areas of my life, but somehow I had channelled it away from my children. I gave myself a metaphorical pat on the back. I was going to raise them just fine.

Unfortunately, as with all good things, my period of being Not Anxious came to an abrupt end. You see, I had no prior experience of being Not Anxious, so I didn't know how to go about it at all. I wasn't naturally Not Anxious, and I had no instincts for determining when it was appropriate to be anxious and when it was not. This meant that every anxious thought was treated equally and kicked out of my consciousness without evaluation or consideration. So when the day came when anxiety was absolutely called for, I missed my cue entirely, and nearly killed my daughter.

My son was three, and my daughter was eighteen months, and both had caught the chicken pox. I'd actually been pleased when my son was diagnosed, as it proved with reasonable certainty that he hadn't contracted the virus in utero. He came down with only a mild dose, and was barely unwell at all. My daughter, however, became really sick, and was quickly covered in blisters and burning with fever. I took her to the doctor on the Thursday, and then again on the Saturday morning, as she didn't seem to be getting better. The doctor prescribed paracetamol to lower her temperature and various lotions and bath preparations to help with the itching.

'Kids can get very high fevers with the chicken pox,' he told me, scribbling instructions on a pad. 'Don't worry if hers persists for another day or so, but if you're still worried about her on Monday, bring her back in.'

I nodded and thanked him, and carried my little girl back to my car. Obviously it was awful seeing my daughter so ill, but I really wasn't concerned. Kids got the chicken pox all the time. My baby would be fine in a couple of days, and we would all have the pox out of our systems.

The next day, my daughter's temperature soared even higher, to more than forty degrees. I gave her paracetamol and put her in my bed, and she lay there, weak and pale. My husband checked on her and then headed out briefly to the office. 'You need to call the doctor again,' he told me before he walked out the door.

'Nah, it's perfectly normal,' I replied. 'The doctor said that kids can get very high fevers. If it hasn't come down by tomorrow, I'll take her back in.'

My husband looked at me and said firmly, 'Call.'

Worrywart, I thought.

A couple of hours later, my daughter's breathing had become shallow. She was dazed and listless, and barely opened her eyes as I sponged her face with cool water. I still wasn't worried, but I was beginning to feel upset. She really did look very sick.

Suddenly I noticed her neck, which was glowing bright red beneath her ashen cheeks. I pulled up her pyjama top and found a rash covering her entire torso, and snaking down her arms and legs.

It was very peculiar. A rash? Why would she have a rash? Could my daughter have measles as well as the chicken pox? Could it be some sort of allergy to the bath prep? It was strange indeed, but even then, I didn't worry. I wouldn't allow myself to get anxious. I did realise, however, that I needed to get some more information.

Just then, my mum arrived to check on us all, followed closely by my husband.

'I'm on the phone,' I called out to them. 'I just need to find out what's going on with that rash.'

'What rash?' asked my mum.

'On her tummy,' I told her.

My mum hurried to the bed, kissed my daughter's cheek, and then lifted up her pyjama top. She and T both examined the rash for a moment, and I could see the concern on both of their faces.

'Kerri, you have to get her to hospital right now,' T told me.

'I agree, Kez,' my mum said.

At the same moment, I got through to the Children's Hospital Helpline, and explained the situation to the nurse.

'I'd advise you to take your daughter straight to Emergency,' said the nurse, and immediately my brain snapped into gear.

Straight to hospital. Shit. That's bad.

Run!

We quickly wrapped my daughter in a blanket and hurried out the door. My mum stayed behind with our son, who was perfectly happy but still contagious with a few small spots.

'Phone as soon as you know anything!' my mum called after us, as we carried our little girl to the car. I sat with her in the back seat, rigid with fear, as my husband drove. We arrived at the entrance in record time, T parked in a No Standing zone, and we sprinted to the emergency department.

The triage nurses took one look at my daughter and led us straight past the waiting room to a doctor.

This is bad, I thought. This is really, really bad.

The doctor examined my daughter for only a few minutes and sat us down to talk. 'Your daughter is seriously ill,' he said. 'A pox has become infected, and she's gone into toxic shock. She has a staph infection and a strep infection – what we used to call "scarlet fever". That's what's causing the rash. If you hadn't brought her in, she would have been hours from death.'

I was profoundly shocked. *Hours from death?* My precious baby. My beautiful little girl.

'She's going to be fine,' the doctor continued, 'but she'll need to stay in for a while and get some intravenous antibiotics until we know she's out of danger.'

I nodded mutely, too stunned to speak. My baby. I nearly let my baby die.

T stroked my hair. 'She'll be all right,' he said. 'She'll be fine.'

'I did this to her,' I told him. 'It's all my fault.'

I hadn't been anxious enough.

After nine days in an isolation unit in hospital, my daughter made a full recovery. And after nine days of sitting next to my sick child's bed, I was deeply traumatised. I blamed myself for failing to recognise the seriousness of the situation earlier. My unnatural calmness had almost cost me my baby.

Unsurprisingly, my anxiety levels hiked up a notch after my daughter's hospitalisation. I started to fret about the kids' health and wellbeing, and ruminate on all the horrifying possibilities that could have eventuated from my daughter's scarlet fever.

I didn't want to undo all the good progress I'd made in parenting; I was still committed to being the best mother I could be. However, now I was faced with a new dilemma. I couldn't allow myself to be anxious, because that would harm the kids, but I couldn't allow myself *not* to be anxious either, because then I might not recognise when they were being harmed. So I worried about being too worried, and then I worried about not being worried enough. How anybody managed to raise normal, healthy children was beyond my comprehension.

Eventually, I fell into a push-pull cycle which still persists to this day. It is a cycle of anxiety versus calm, fear versus trust. I do my very best to be relaxed with my kids, and give them the freedom that they need to become well-adjusted adults. And then, every now and then, I panic at the freedom I have bestowed, and rush to rescue them from whatever danger I have imagined.

On the weekend, for example, I sent my two big kids outside to play at the park down the end of our road. It is in full view of the street, and right next to a cafe which is always crowded. I told my kids to have fun, and silently congratulated myself on being a laid-back parent who can send her kids unaccompanied to the park. I busied myself in the house, playing with my youngest child, tidying up the kitchen and doing laundry. And then within fifteen minutes, I started worrying about the kids. Were they okay at the park? What if something happened to them? What if someone abducted them? What if they didn't come home – what would I do then?

I realised I had to get to the park *immediately*. As in, five minutes ago. I grabbed my keys and my younger daughter and jogged down the road holding them both. This wasn't easy as my daughter is four years old and quite heavy, but the alternative was to make her walk, and I really needed to run. I started breathing heavily and realised that I'd forgotten to lock the door, but I didn't care – I wouldn't go back, because I had to sight the kids, just to know that they were okay.

As I sprinted along lugging my daughter, I visualised myself turning up at an empty park and having no idea what to do, just staring around at the grass and the vacant swings and screaming because my two precious children were gone. And then I could hardly breathe for anxiety, but I kept going anyway, because I had to see them, I had to know that they were there.

When we rounded the corner I was flooded with relief, for there they both were, sitting at the top of the slide together, chatting and laughing and looking utterly content with the world.

'Oh hi, Mum!' they said, when they looked up and saw me there. 'What are you doing here?'

I was very tempted to bring them back home, because it was just too stressful to leave them there, but I couldn't do that to my two happy children. And I certainly couldn't admit to them that I had followed them to the park out of anxiety, because I don't want them to grow up with a sense of danger and dread. So I said, 'Hi! We've come down to join you!' and put my youngest one on the swing.

Then I spent forty minutes on the grass as my kids played around me, knowing I had a million and one things to do at home, but anchored there by worry.

Worrying about my kids' safety is exhausting, but sadly it is far from my only parenting concern. I also worry about every aspect of my children's psychological, emotional, intellectual and social development.

There is so much to worry about when you're a parent, and the worries never really cease. Little kids have little problems, and big kids have big problems, and adult kids no doubt have bigger problems still. You start off worrying about why they're not playing nicely with the other toddlers, and end up worrying why they're not producing children of their own.

So, in no particular order, here are some of my worries about my kids:

- Are they making enough friends at school?
- Are they spending too much time in front of a screen?
- Are they getting enough exercise?
- Will they develop eating disorders?
- Are they getting bullied or teased?
- Will they end up agonising over their skin and biting their nails?
- Will they experiment with scary drugs?
- Will they fall in with the wrong crowd?
- Will they find their path in life?
- Will they find someone to love them?
- Will they love me when they grow up? (Actually, this last worry might be more about me.)

Still, out of all of my worries about my children, my greatest concern is my own pervasive anxiety, and how it will impact on them. I worry that my children will assimilate my view of the world, and will grow up to be nervous and fearful like me. I worry that they too will believe that the world is unsafe, and will end up fighting the demons I've been fighting for years.

In other words, I worry that I'm worrying about my kids too much. However, the push-and-pull cycle continues, and eventually I talk myself down and begin to gain perspective.

And then I worry that I'm not worrying enough, and the whole damn thing starts over again.

Scanning the Cabin

AMBIENT FEAR: background anxiety of everyday life.

Jon Winokur, author

I was waiting for a taxi outside my friend Kylie's house. I had flown interstate to give a talk, then had stayed on an extra night with her and her family. I would have liked to stay a week, but I had to get back to the kids and T, so sadly it was time to leave.

I'd never been to Kylie's suburb before, so I was relying on her to tell me how long it would take to drive to the airport.

'No more than forty-five minutes,' Kylie assured me, and I quickly did my calculations. I needed to be at the airport by four-fifteen to catch my flight at a quarter to five. I booked the taxi for three-thirty pm, which seemed to me to leave plenty of time.

The taxi rocked up at three twenty-five, five minutes before my planned departure. I hauled out my luggage (I'd been away two nights, so I'd packed half my wardrobe) and kissed Kylie goodbye.

'It's been great having you, hon,' she said, and gave me a hug. 'Have a safe trip.'

I climbed into the taxi and waved farewell. It had been a terrific visit and I felt good; tired but pleased with how things had gone. I thought with happy anticipation about seeing T and my kids that evening, and settled down with my iPod for the duration of the ride.

'Where you flying?' the taxi driver asked me. I pulled an earphone out of my ear.

'Back home,' I answered. The driver had a short dark beard and big kind eyes, and he scratched at his collar as we cruised along.

'Home, good. Boy, this very bad traffic today.'

I shrugged. 'It's not so bad. It's shocking where I live. Nothing like it is here.'

The driver looked around at the road. 'Oh no, this very bad traffic. Very bad indeed. What time you need to be at the airport?'

'Four-fifteen,' I told him. I really wanted to get back to my iPod.

'Four-fifteen?' he asked me, and shook his head. 'Oh dear. This very bad traffic. I don't know you make it.'

I looked at him. Er, hello, Mr Negative! But I wasn't concerned. Kylie had done the airport run a zillion times. She knew how long it would take from her house.

'We'll be fine,' I said firmly. I put the earphone back in my ear.

'I don't know,' I heard him mumble. Well, thanks for that, buddy.

We drove in silence along the busy streets.

'Oh fuck,' the taxi driver muttered. I glanced at him. 'Sorry,' he said. 'Just very bad traffic. I don't want you be late.'

I started to feel uncomfortable. I didn't like swearing drivers, particularly not drivers who swore to themselves. They seemed to be unstable, and I didn't like to be at their mercy.

There was momentary silence, and then the cabbie started up again. 'Shit. Shit. Shit,' he said. 'This bad. Oh shit.'

I took out the earphone again. 'What's the matter?'

'I think we not get there. I think you miss your flight. Traffic bad. Very bad.'

I felt myself tensing up. 'We'll make it. We have to make it.'

He raised his eyebrows. 'Boy, I hope so.' Then he sighed dramatically.

It'll be fine, I told myself. It'll be totally fine. We still had twenty minutes to get there. But I could feel myself tensing up more. The man was a stress machine. And, possibly, a little psychotic.

Another red light.

'Fucking shit,' said the taxi driver, and I started to do some deep breathing. 'This so bad. Oh my God. Bad, bad, bad.'

Now I really was becoming nervous. I had no idea why this man was so anxious about my flight, but he was starting to get to me. He was the driver. He knew the roads. He said there was bad traffic. And if he didn't think I was going to make it, then it seemed pretty clear that I needed to start worrying, too.

I tore both earphones out of my ears and threw my iPod into my bag. 'Are we nearly on the freeway?' I asked fretfully. 'How much further can it be?'

'Two more lights,' he said. 'But traffic, it so slow from school holiday, you know?'

I thought for a minute. 'But it's not school holidays yet!'

'Tomorrow,' he said. 'So maybe people they don't go to last day of school?'

Okay, so that made absolutely no sense at all. But his anxiety was infectious, and I was well and truly descending into the madness with him.

There was another red light. 'Fuck,' said the taxi driver.

'Oh *God*,' I replied.

We drove grimly along at a snail's pace. The taxi driver glanced at the clock. I glanced at the clock. Time passed extraordinarily quickly, the minutes racing by as we ground to a halt on the endless road.

'You must be back tonight?' he asked me suddenly. 'You cannot change your flight?'

'No!' I practically screamed. Just get me there, I pleaded silently. We're not going to make it. We're not going to make it.

After an eternity at the lights, we hit the freeway.

'How much longer now?' I asked him urgently. It was three minutes past four. I had twelve more minutes.

'Nine or ten minutes,' he said. Well, that sounded positive. 'But traffic very bad. I don't know. I just don't know.' We slowed down momentarily behind a four-wheel drive. 'Fuck,' he said. I plucked my T-shirt away from my sweaty armpits and stared out the window, determined not to look at the clock.

Finally, we pulled up outside the airport. It was eleven minutes past four.

'We make it!' the driver said cheerfully. 'I start to panic there for minute!'

I looked at him incredulously. 'You reckon?' I asked. I was exhausted and headachy.

I didn't leave a tip.

Anxiety, to me, is highly contagious. I don't just carry the burden of my own worries, I also pick up on other people's worries and magnify them a thousandfold. If T is stressed, I start to feel super stressed. If my mother is anxious, I'll feel horribly anxious as well.

And if a taxi driver panics, I will start to panic too. I can't objectively assess the concerns of those close to me; I just take them on and make them my own. This may seem unreasonable, but it makes perfect sense in the flawed logic of anxiety. You see, when someone whose opinion I value is worried about something, then by definition there is something to be worried about. And when there is something to be worried about, then clearly I need to be worrying about it, too.

This particular rationale is what I think of as 'Aeroplane Logic'. Imagine that you are on an aeroplane and the flight is calm. You are comfortable and peaceful in your aisle seat. Suddenly, the passenger sitting next to you looks out the window, jumps up in alarm, and urgently presses the call button.

Immediately, your heart skips a beat. Your neighbour looks scared, so obviously there is something to be scared of. Maybe he can see smoke coming from the engine. Maybe he can see another aircraft heading towards you. Maybe a piece of the wing has fallen off. Maybe you are all about to crash and burn.

You want to look out the window, but you can't see anything, and you don't wish to seem like a fool. So what do you do? You scan the cabin and look at the other passengers. If they look relaxed, then obviously it is reasonably safe to stay relaxed yourself. If they are biting their nails and praying, then you can be pretty sure it's time to panic.

Now along comes the flight attendant. The passengers aren't relevant anymore because the flight attendant is the authority; she is higher in the pecking order, and you will be guided by her response. She talks to your neighbour and looks out the window. If she smiles and says something reassuring, you can rest easy for the remainder of the flight. If she gasps and runs to the cockpit screaming, you know that you'd better assume the brace position.

I spend my life scanning the faces of flight attendants, both literally and metaphorically. I am constantly on the alert, looking for signs from those around me, checking to see if there is anything to worry about.

If someone is worried about something that doesn't relate to me, I can be helpful and unbiased and give wonderful advice. If I am affected by what they are worrying about, I will lose all perspective and become a panicky mess.

When it comes to the worries of those I love, I cannot filter them to see if they're reasonable or just. If T says money is tight at the moment – even if I know that we have plenty in the bank – I'll absorb that and morph it into anxiety about losing our house. If my father is worried about my mother's health, I'll start planning her funeral and my life without her. If an expert says that overpopulation is a problem, I'll be visualising my children in a world without food.

On the other hand, if a girlfriend is having issues with her partner, I can offer words of wisdom with both insight and compassion. It is only my own problems that I cannot see clearly.

Unfortunately, my anxieties have made me rather gullible, and my default position is to believe most alarming things I hear. Predictions of social decline, recession or impending global catastrophe seem probable to me, even if others can assess them with a critical eye. Of course I don't want to be scared – I want to believe in goodness, and justice, and prosperity, and peace – so I will work passionately to persuade myself that the opposite is true. Ironically, this can make me present as highly argumentative, batting for the positive team with all I have. It may look like I'm trying to convince other people to believe in good. In reality, though, I'm just trying to convince myself.

I don't want to be always scanning the cabin of life. I don't want to be so finely attuned to other people's anxieties. It uses up a huge amount of my emotional energy, and frankly I've got enough worries of my own to keep me going for years. Still, I wouldn't want to relinquish this quality altogether. Being sensitive to other people gives me insight and empathy. These are nice qualities to have, if they don't eat me alive first.

I guess I just have to learn when to get out of the taxi.

Awake Again . . . Naturally

The worst thing in the world is to try to sleep and not to.

Unknown

I love my sleep. For someone who has so many reasons for being awake – three gorgeous kids, a loving husband, an exciting career – I really do adore being unconscious. I wouldn't want to sleep all the time, mind you, just eight to nine hours a day. Ten on weekends. Eleven when I'm really tired. Twelve hours absolute tops.

And yet, despite my love of sleep, I have had sleeping problems for as long as I can remember. Even after I had ceased contemplating the nature of infinity, I experienced enormous difficulties dropping off at night. Once I was asleep I tended to stay asleep, but it was getting to sleep that was the challenge. It didn't matter how exhausted I was; once I got into bed my brain would shift into gear and I'd be unable to switch it off. I'd feel my heart begin to pound violently within me as adrenaline surged through my veins. And although I did my best to push the thought from my consciousness, it would flash inside my head like a mocking neon sign: *You are not sleeping, Kerri. You are* never *going to sleep.*

The sign tormented me, night after night. It tortured me because it was right: I wasn't going to sleep. And I longed to sleep more than anything in the world.

As a child, I would call my mum to comfort me when I couldn't sleep. She would sit by my bed and stroke my hair and tell me that it was okay.

'It doesn't matter if you don't sleep,' she would say. 'Resting is just as good.'

It's the best (and only) thing you can say to an insomniac and I say it to my own kids now. Unfortunately, however, it is just not true. Resting is nice but definitely not as good as sleeping. The only thing that is as good as sleeping is sleeping. And I need to sleep. A lot.

I know people who can function perfectly well on minimal sleep, and I envy these people immensely. The less time you sleep, the more time you have to be awake, and I'd love to have an extra two or three hours a day to work, hang out with my family, or simply eat chocolates and watch TV. Unfortunately, I become fuzzy and cranky without a full eight hours' sleep, and feel at my best with eight and a half to nine hours, or even more. With anything less than seven, I become depressed and dysfunctional, and I need a nap during the day if I am to focus and cope.

Sleep is absolutely vital to my wellbeing and my sanity. And because it is so important, I worry terribly about losing it.

There is very little worse than lying in bed at night craving sleep, yet finding sleep out of your grasp. It creates a type of desperation that is unparalleled in the daytime hours. In the quest for sleep, unlike nearly any other endeavour, you cannot work, you cannot push to make it happen. The harder you fight to become unconscious, the more elusive unconsciousness becomes.

Throughout my childhood, teens and twenties, I tried all sorts of things to fall asleep.

My favoured technique was called 'Clearing My Mind', and it involved a complex series of thought processes designed to lead me into slumber:

I want to go to sleep now. I have to clear my mind.

Right, I'm going to clear my mind.

Okay. Clearing the mind. Imagining a broom sweeping away all the thoughts in my head.

No, that's stupid. I can't think about a broom. I'll just imagine the thoughts blowing away with the wind.

What do thoughts blowing away with the wind even look like?

This isn't working. What about just noting thoughts as they roll in and letting them go?

Yep, I'll try that.

I'm not asleep.

That was a thought! Let it go.

I'm still not asleep.

That was another thought! Let it go.

I'm still not asleep. What time is it? It must be late.

Don't think about not being asleep. Just relax and let your thoughts clear.

Shit. It must be at least eleven, and I have to get up at six-thirty. There is no way I'm going to get enough sleep.

I need to go to sleep!

I have to clear my thoughts. Clear my thoughts!

What am I thinking? I don't know what I'm thinking!

I'M NOT SLEEPING!!!

• • •

Needless to say, this technique was not especially effective.

The second technique was called 'Relaxing My Muscles'. I would lie in bed and talk myself through a detailed physical relaxation exercise, with the aim of getting my body so completely calm that my mind would inevitably follow. My nightly routine went a little like this:

You are going to relax your whole body, starting with your toes and working up to the tip of your head. By the time you have relaxed your whole body, you will be so relaxed that you will fall asleep.

Okay, concentrate on your toes. Can you feel your toes? Yes? Now relax your toes.

Concentrate on your feet. Can you feel your feet? Yes? Now relax your feet.

Concentrate on your legs. Can you feel your legs? God, this is boring.

Concentrate! Now, can you feel your legs?

Yes, I can feel my legs, but is this going to help me sleep? I don't feel sleepy. I just feel bored.

Just concentrate. Focus. Okay, relax your legs. They're relaxed? Good. Let's move on.

Now, concentrate on your pelvis. Can you feel your pelvis? Yes?

Well, yes! How can a pelvis not be relaxed? Can you carry tension in your pelvis? Anyway, who cares? This isn't getting me to sleep. It's stupid.

Just keep going. Relax your pelvis. Is your pelvis relaxed?

Yep. Still can't sleep. I'm bored. And I'm hungry. What's the time? Oh my God. It's so late! Why aren't I asleep yet? I CAN'T SLEEP!!!

So that didn't work either.

The final technique was called 'Repeating a Mantra'. I had read in a newspaper article that the best way to relax was to choose a soothing mantra and repeat it to yourself, over and over again. Eventually you would fall into a trancelike meditative state, from which sleep was sure to follow.

My problem was that I could never settle on a mantra. Every mantra I tried sounded foolish to me, and I spent more time deliberating on a new word to chant than I spent actually chanting the word. My attempts at a mantra were rather pathetic, and sounded a lot like this:

Okay, I am going to start chanting my mantra now.

Um . . . which one did I decide to use again? Was it 'Peace' or 'Let go'? Or was it 'Calm'? Nah, I think it was 'Peace'.

So . . . Peace . . . Peace . . . Peace . . . Peace . . .

Yep, well, I don't feel very peaceful.

Stop it! You can't give up yet. You have to keep at it. Peace . . . Peace . . . Peace . . . Peace . . .

Nup. This is stupid. Maybe it's the mantra. It doesn't resonate with me. I need to choose a different one.

What about 'Let go'? Let go . . . Let go . . . Let go . . . Let go . . .

Nah, that's not specific enough. What exactly am I supposed to be letting go of, anyway? Nope, I need another one. Maybe 'Calm'? Except that 'Calm' is too short, and it's too much like 'Peace', and 'Peace' didn't work at all. I need something better, something punchier . . .

What about 'Release'? Release . . . Release . . . Release . . . Release . . . No, 'Release' makes me think of doing a wee.

What about 'Sleep'? Sleep . . . Sleep . . . Sleep . . . Sleep
. . . No, that's too desperate. It will just upset me when
I don't.
Oh, for God's sake, I don't know. I can't do this. I just want
to go to sleep! Why can't I go to sleep?
AM I EVER GOING TO GO TO SLEEP???

I'd suffered from insomnia before I became a mum, but after my first baby was born my sleep patterns really became dire. My newborn son slept like a baby – a normal baby – which meant he needed a lot of settling and was up every four hours of the night to feed. I didn't put him on a rigid schedule but he fell into a pattern pretty quickly: I would feed him around six pm, then again at ten pm, then he would be up at two am, and then again at six.

I knew this would happen. I'd read the books. I was ready for night waking. But nothing could have prepared me for the fatigue that my baby brought. Nothing could have prepared me for the crazed longing I would feel for sleep. And nothing could have prepared me for the way my anxiety would destroy the precious hours I had remaining for rest.

Every single night I would feed my son at ten pm, burp him, change him, and pat him back to sleep. By ten-thirty or so I would be lying in my bed, and that's when the problems would start.

I have to go to sleep, I would think in agitation. I only have three and a half hours before the baby wakes up again. I would lie there under the covers, willing myself into unconsciousness, in a race against the clock to get myself to sleep. The minutes would tick by, and I'd still be wide awake, and I could feel my desperation growing by the second.

Sleep! I would tell myself. Time is running out! I only have two hours and forty-five minutes to go! I'd become more and more anxious, knowing that I would be woken in two short hours, and that the cycle would start all over again. Often I would fall asleep in the half-hour before my son woke up, sometimes I would be awake the entire three and a half hours. It was infuriating and depressing and extremely distressing. There were many nights during which I would get up to breastfeed and burst into tears of exhaustion.

'I can't do it anymore!' I would sob to my husband. 'I'm so ti . . . red!'

T would prop himself up on one elbow, rub his eyes, shrug sadly, and then point to his chest. 'Unless I start lactating, I can't do it, either.'

I had always intended to exclusively breastfeed my son for the first few months, but after ten weeks of torment, I tried giving him a bottle. I needed to hand him over to my husband, so that I could break from the grip of insomnia and get some much-needed sleep. Sadly, though, my son did not cooperate with my plans. He didn't want a bottle. He refused to drink from it. He screamed and thrashed and cried and vomited and eventually fell asleep from sheer exhaustion (a feat I envied enormously, as I was still unable to do it).

I tried everything. People said he would take a bottle when he was hungry enough, so I waited until he was starving. No luck. They said to try with formula instead of breastmilk, so I tried that, too. No luck there, either. They said to try handing him over to someone else to feed him, so I gave him to my husband, my mum, my sister and a friend. None of them had any luck. The child wanted me.

My son slept through the night at just four months of age, which is remarkably early by normal baby standards. For me, however, the damage was done. My sleep patterns were utterly destroyed, and they would remain destroyed for the next eight years.

I couldn't sleep. It continued to take me hours to drop off every night. I coped by taking naps during the day – whenever my baby slept, I would sleep, too. It helped, for a while. But when my first daughter was born a couple of years later, it became even harder. She and her brother were on different schedules during the day, which meant that at least one of them was awake for most of the time. It became even more important for me to sleep well at night, which meant that it became even more impossible for me to drop off.

Dark circles developed under my eyes and I sank into a serious depression. Everything looked grey. I couldn't enjoy my babies. I couldn't love my husband. I woke up in the morning wondering how I would get through the day. Insomnia is a leech: it sucks the light from your life and the joy from your soul. I needed to fix it. I needed to sleep.

I tried all of my old tricks and more. I tried taking relaxing baths before bed, but all they did was frustrate me that I was wasting time bathing when I could have been in bed. I tried listening to soothing music, but I couldn't focus, and my mind wandered to more worrying matters, such as why I hadn't fallen asleep.

I did an evening course in meditation to learn to clear my mind, as I couldn't stop it churning at eleven at night. The meditation classes were held in an old school hall, and were attended by a motley group of twelve lost souls. We sat at classroom desks and closed our eyes and focused on the calming, monotonous drone of our instructor's voice.

'Inhale . . . exhale,' he would intone. 'Focus on your breath. In the mouth, out the nose.'

The meditation classes worked wonders for me. I fell asleep in every single session and woke refreshed forty-five minutes later, head down on the desk, in a pool of my own dribble. Unfortunately, however, I still couldn't sleep at night. When I tried to do my meditation whilst horizontal in my bed, I failed dismally, and lay awake till the wee small hours.

To add insult to injury, the meditation instructor caught me dozing one evening. He firmly informed me that meditation can only be practised in a state of full consciousness, so the fact that I was sleeping whilst focusing on my breathing was a sure sign that I wasn't doing it correctly. Well, quite frankly I didn't care if I was doing it correctly. I really just wanted to be falling asleep.

I didn't re-enrol for a second term.

Eventually, I resorted to the herbal schmerbal option. I bought every kind of herbal insomnia preparation I could find, each promising to give me a full and restful night's sleep. Most of the pills were as big as my thumb, and as brown and uninviting as rabbit droppings, but I swallowed them dutifully, night after night, praying for the calm and slumber they promised. None of them worked. They were huge and expensive and absolutely useless. And to be honest, I knew that they would be.

Possibly my most desperate moment came over a glass of wine. Not any old wine, mind you. This was sedative wine, a special herbal alcoholic concoction I'd purchased at my local health food store. The wine was made of sherry, included the natural calmative valerian, and had a flavour like stale malted vinegar. It was horrid. I downed a glass every evening and tried to convince myself that really, it wasn't too bad. As nasty as the stuff was, if it had helped me to sleep I would have drunk an entire bottle. Sadly, though, it didn't help at all. I may as well have been drinking a nice cab sav for all the rest it gave me.

Ultimately, what saved me were good old-fashioned sleeping pills. I got a script from my doctor and took them every night for a week and had the most wonderful, restorative sleep I'd had in years. And from that week on, I rationed my sleeping pills. Conscious of the addictive nature of sleep medication, I allowed myself three sleeping pills a week, so that if I was wakeful Monday, Wednesday and

Friday, I could sleep well Tuesday, Thursday and Saturday. Magically, the routine did the trick. Once I had the safety net of my pills, I didn't need them as often. Just knowing the pills were tucked away in my bathroom cabinet decreased my anxiety sufficiently for me to sleep most nights.

Even so, the end of my insomnia didn't come until 2007, with the birth of my younger daughter. And it wasn't hormones, or a change in attitude, or a sense of fulfilment that did it. I was, quite simply, shattered beyond comprehension. Having three kids pushed me to my limits. By the end of each day I would collapse into bed and become instantly unconscious, usually without washing my face, often without even brushing my teeth. I became one of those mystical people who fall asleep anywhere – on the couch, on the floor, at the movies, on trains. It was miraculous and marvellous and astonishing all at once. My third child restored to me the powers of sleep, and four and a half years later I am still grateful for my rest.

My challenge now, of course, is staying awake during the day. I can barely settle myself into a seat without nodding off, which is a problem when driving a car, having a work meeting, or being called into the principal's office for a 'chat'. And it's certainly a problem for my husband, who occasionally would like me to stay awake in bed for more than twenty seconds so that we can . . . well . . . talk.

Still, as he knew when he married me, I've never been one for a happy medium.

Wake in Fright

Your nightmares follow you like a shadow, forever.

Aleksandar Hemon, author

The dream is always the same, and it is maddeningly frequent. Some of the details change slightly, but the theme and plot are identical, and, weirdly, so is the setting. I'm standing in a university campus, and I know it intimately. In real life I've attended two universities, and my dream campus doesn't look like either of them, but it has elements of both, with some of my old school mixed in for good measure.

The dream campus is large and set on a hill. There is a cluster of classrooms at the top, and a long walkway leading to a dark, square building at the bottom of the slope. Usually in the dream I am trying to climb up to the classrooms from the lowest point of the grounds; generally it is night and I can't see very well. Occasionally I am in the street outside the university trying to find my way home, going round and round the block, circling the campus, recognising with growing horror that I am completely lost.

Whatever the variation, in every dream there is a crushing sense of anxiety. It is always the middle of the year (never the end, and never the beginning), I have just realised that I've forgotten to attend any of my classes, and I know that I am going to fail.

My Failing University dream has haunted me for years. There are periods when it has visited me once or twice a week, and periods when it has come to me every night. It shadows me, like a parallel existence that hovers beside my real life. It is vivid, and utterly pervasive, and leaves an enduring sense of agitation. Sometimes I become confused as to whether I did finish uni or not, so thoroughly does the sense of incompletion in the dream linger in my consciousness.

Now, it's not exactly shocking to me that I have anxiety dreams. I'm a highly anxious person and it is natural that this will play out in my psyche. What surprises me is the subject matter of my dreams. For a start, I didn't have any trouble with university when I was actually there. I enjoyed it, attended all my lectures, and always handed in my assignments on time. Secondly, well . . . let's face it, I'm a writer, not an astrophysicist. I mean, it's great that I completed a Bachelor of Arts, and it has certainly helped me in my writing, but it's not like I'd get kicked out of the profession if I hadn't finished my degree. And yet this is how my anxiety plays itself out. This is the metaphor it chooses.

I have tried many techniques to rid myself of my dream. I have tried reminding myself before I go to sleep that I have completed university. I have tried visualising my dream whilst awake, and walking myself through an alternate ending, one in which I am attending my graduation ceremony. I have tried exploring the meaning of the dream, aiming to determine what is unfinished or unresolved in my life. Nothing has ever worked. The dream persists.

About five years ago, in desperation, I posted my degree on the wall next to my bed. It wasn't that I was so proud of my fine achievement (as I said, it was an Arts degree, not a doctorate in Astrophysics), but my dream world was taking over. I needed something to ground me, something to look at when I woke in fright, sweating and shaking, panicking that I was about to fail.

Hanging the degree on the wall helped. It didn't stop the dreams, but it did bring me back to reality quickly, with physical evidence that I'd studied for my tests, and that I wasn't going to be in trouble after all.

I rely on posting things next to my bed, because the person sharing my bed isn't helpful at all. My husband used to be very comforting, stroking my head and telling me everything would be okay after I woke from my uni nightmare. Sadly, however, after years of reassuring me, T seems to have used up his reserves of sympathy.

'I had the dream again!' I said the other morning, and a wicked look flashed across his face.

'Oh no!' he said. 'Did you forget to go to class? You know exams are coming up. You're going to fail!'

'Stop it!' I said plaintively. 'You have to make me feel better! You have to tell me everything is all right!'

T sighed and shook his head. 'I can't!' he said. 'It's terrible news. I can't believe you didn't study!'

I hit him with my pillow.

Of course, I haven't always dreamed about failing university. As a child, I hadn't yet been to university, and so I dreamed about houses in the air.

My Floating House dream was my recurring dream throughout my childhood and teens, and despite its innocuous title it was really very frightening. I would be standing outside in my street, totally alone, I would look up at the sky, and there would be a house suspended in midair. The house never moved. No one went in and no one came out. It was huge and empty and utterly still.

On occasion there would also be other inanimate floating objects – chairs and tables and the odd car – but for the most part it was a solitary house.

Back then, I had no idea what the Floating House dream meant. Now, I can see that it reflected a lack of control, a sense that everything was terribly out of order in my world. It was sinister and disturbing and deeply upsetting, and I was always grateful to wake up.

My Floating House dream and my Failing University dream have been my most persistent anxiety dreams, but they are far from the only ones. After all, my subconscious is creative, and has come up with numerous other ways to torment me over the course of my life.

I frequently dream that I am moving in slow motion, which is a most unpleasant sensation. I am frantically trying to get somewhere, but my body feels like it's mired in quicksand and I can only move at about one hundredth of my usual speed. It is exasperating and frustrating and no doubt reflects some deep fear in me that I am not moving forward in life. Or perhaps that I am bogged down in the quagmire of my existence. Or perhaps I'm just really unfit. Whichever way, it's uncomfortable.

I have dreams in which I'm about to launch off a cliff in a car. Either the vehicle has failed in some vital way, and I'm trying desperately but unsuccessfully to keep it on the road, or *I* have failed in some vital way, and am driving really, really badly on the road to disaster. I go faster and faster, heading for imminent catastrophe. I cannot stop the car as it races towards the precipice, and I feel my death approaching with a dreadful sense of doom. And then I'm airborne, sailing over the edge, about to crash into the water. My body screams as I soar through the air, and then I awake, tingling horribly all over, with a sinking sensation in my stomach. It is not a very nice way to start the day.

I suspect that the Out of Control Car dream is not regularly experienced by people who are relaxed and easygoing. It is the kind of dream had by people like me, who feel a desperate need for control and are terrified of losing it. It seems cruel of my subconscious to taunt me with what I most fear, but I guess that's just how the subconscious rolls.

Happily, I don't ever dream about appearing in public naked. I would be horrified to do so, but evidently my psyche doesn't find that scenario particularly frightening. I do, however, have a different version of this anxiety dream, which is far more disconcerting and worrisome. I dream that I am talking to someone I wish to impress – perhaps a celebrity, a work colleague, a new friend or a stranger – and I realise halfway through the conversation that I am wearing a shower cap on my head and a pore cleansing strip across my nose. The other person doesn't seem to notice, and certainly doesn't comment, but I am utterly mortified, and carry the shame with me long after I have woken.

Finally, and unsurprisingly, I have anxiety dreams about my children. I dream about all three of my children, but primarily my youngest – ironically, the one about whom I consciously worry the least. I dream that I have lost her, or that I've forgotten to pick her up. I dream that I hear her calling and can't determine where her voice is coming from. Or I dream that I have entrusted her to someone close to me, and they tell me that they have left her alone, and I rush frantically to find her.

Sometimes I dream that she is tiny, the size of an egg, and equally fragile. Sometimes I break her when I hold her in my hand. Once I dreamed that I found her in one of those little plastic bubbles that are inside some chocolate novelty eggs. She was about three centimetres tall and wearing miniature fairy wings, and we were standing together in the Arabian desert. Even in the midst of the dream I realised it was fairly odd.

I have long believed that dreams are deeply significant. I see my dreams as my psyche's way of working through my issues, of exorcising some of the demons I don't deal with in my conscious hours. And I can see the correlation between my anxiety levels and the nature of my dreams. When I am particularly stressed, I dream about failing university and flying off cliffs. When I am in one of my rare, calmer moments, I dream about food and sexy men.

Still, as much as I appreciate the importance of dreams, and am grateful to my mind for dealing with my issues while I'm asleep, sometimes I do wish I could speak to my subconscious harshly. I have long since graduated from university. The only houses I can see are firmly anchored to the ground. I don't drive near cliffs, I've never left the house in a shower cap, and my daughter is as healthy and robust as a four-year-old could be.

I'm aware that my dreams are metaphorical in nature, but I do wish they would update a little, and let me move forward in my sleep.

The Worry Pit

I finally know what distinguishes man from the other beasts:
financial worries.

Jules Renard, author

I was standing in front of a construction zone with my husband and the kids. T's chest was puffed out with pride; this was the moment he'd been waiting for. He was about to give us the very first walk-through of what would be our new family home – the first house that he, the architect, had designed especially for us. The kids jumped around in anticipation as T took out a bunch of keys and unlocked an enormous padlock. We climbed through the narrow entranceway, made our way over the rubble, and entered the foundations of our house. It was a special moment for all of us.

Well, it was supposed to be a special moment. It *should* have been a special moment. But I ruined it. I couldn't enjoy it. To be honest, I didn't even want to be there.

• • •

Anxiety tends to make one very risk-averse, and I am certainly no exception to that rule. Quite frankly, if I'd had my way, we would never have bought a new house in the first place. I was perfectly happy where we were, in our first marital home, where we'd lived for almost a decade.

Our house was a suburban duplex built into a cliff side, with a gorgeous view of the district, a large living area and an eat-in kitchen with modern appliances. It was light and breezy and I loved it. Of course, the house did have its limitations. For one thing, it was accessible only by sixty-seven steps. Yes, sixty-seven, which is an awful lot of steps to be climbing several times a day. The steps were outdoors and fully exposed to the elements, so I spent a great amount of time getting cold and wet (although on the upside, I was quite outstandingly fit).

What's more, the house was set in the wet rock face, so it was constantly damp and full of mould. There was no outdoor garden, just a narrow, concrete courtyard barely wide enough to fit deck chairs. And there were only three bedrooms, with no real possibility of expanding, so my 'study' was a corner nook next to our bed. As I worked from home, I would spend up to sixteen hours a day in my bedroom, which was hardly ideal for my mental health.

Still, the idea of moving was way too anxiety-provoking to me. I was comfortable in our home and we were relatively unburdened by debt. I would have happily given up the chance to move us all into a bigger, drier house with no stairs if it meant not having to worry about money. What's more, moving houses involved both change and uncertainty, and these were two things I dreaded more than anything in the world. I liked stability, and security, and knowing what was ahead – even if it was a tiny study nook in my permanently damp bedroom.

Despite this, after nine years my husband decided it was time to sell, and reminded me of three important facts:

1. The market was strong and we would get a good price;
2. He was an architect so we could build a new house for a very low cost; and
3. We were expecting our third child, and didn't have enough space for a large family in our current home.

T's arguments were absolutely logical and made perfect sense and didn't persuade me in the slightest. After all, anxiety shouts louder than any logic, and fear rules rationality every time. However, T is a very determined man, and eventually he managed to convince me to proceed. He contacted the real estate agent, we signed the contracts, and I braced myself for the rocky road ahead.

The road indeed was rocky. Building a house may be torturous, but selling a house is its own special kind of hell. We spent a fair amount of money getting the place into shape – painting and doing repairs and buying some new furniture – so I became committed to the idea of selling the property, if only to avoid wasting our investment. And then once I committed to the idea of a sale, I became racked with anxiety about whether anyone would want our home, let alone for the price we were asking.

T, being an expert in the field, set a reserve that he felt was reasonable. I, being a writer with no knowledge of housing prices whatsoever, felt that this reserve was way too high. I worried and fretted and pleaded and cajoled and spent the entire campaign trying to negotiate a lower figure with my husband.

T wouldn't shift a single dollar.

Just before the end of the campaign, we received an offer slightly less than what my husband was willing to take. The agent and I both begged him to accept it – the agent, because he wanted his commission, and me, because I was certain it was the last offer we would ever see. T flatly refused. I nearly fainted with despair.

A week later, to my astonishment but not my husband's, we sold the house for ten per cent above our reserve. It seemed that I had been proven wrong.

'Didn't I tell you?' T asked me, with undisguised pride. 'If we'd been led by your anxiety, we would have missed out on thousands of dollars. Do you see how your worry affects our lives?'

'I do,' I said, still glowing with the thought of all that money. And I really did. I shouldn't have been so stressed. I worried too much. 'I won't do it again,' I promised. 'I'll relax next time, and trust you. I will.'

'Good,' said T, 'because I really have earned it.' We hugged, and I knew that everything would be okay.

And then four months later, T found a new house to purchase, and I tried to stop him again.

We had decided on a figure that we would spend on a new house, a figure I shall call X, for 'eXcruciating'. X was far too large for my comfort – I would have been nervous spending half of X – but to be honest, any level of debt was uncomfortable for me. T had identified a property we were interested in buying, and he went to the auction alone. This was partly because I couldn't deal with the strain of an auction, and partly because T didn't tell me when the auction was, as he knew I couldn't cope with it.

That night, T came home triumphant. He'd bought the property. For more than X. He'd bought the property for ten per cent more than X. He'd spent *110 per cent* of our budget, and I thought I would have a coronary arrest.

To be fair on me, X was already a very substantial sum. To be fair on T, most people go slightly over budget, so his decision wasn't exactly unprecedented. What's more, the property was in a great location and was bound to appreciate over time, so no doubt it was a wise move in the long term.

Still, the thought of 110 per cent of X made me start to hyperventilate. I argued with T and begged him to rescind on the contract. I threatened to go into the bank and withdraw all of our money, so that the cheque he had signed would bounce the next day. I told him I'd never forgive him if he honoured the deal and bought the property. But T remained resolute.

The deal went ahead, the plans for our new house were submitted to council, and my anxiety levels soared. Now, most people find buying and renovating a property to be stressful, but for me, it was torture. I managed the situation in the only way I knew how: I disconnected completely from the process. I couldn't cope with the anxiety of debt and of construction, so I pretended that it wasn't happening. I went about my life, looking after the kids and our new baby, trying hard not to think about the house taking shape just a couple of suburbs away.

Life wasn't easy for the eighteen months we were building. We stayed in a tiny rental apartment, the five of us on top of each other, and it probably would have helped to look forward to the day we would be living happily in our spacious new home. But I couldn't do that; my nature wouldn't allow it. Every time I looked to the future, I saw the looming threat of debt and disaster, the foreclosure and/or site shutdown that could eventuate if we continued along such a reckless path.

Looking back on the period of construction of our house, I am overcome with profound guilt. I was so concerned about the impact it was having on me that I didn't even consider the impact it was having on my husband. T visited the site every morning before work, and again every evening before coming home. He coordinated every aspect of the building process, from liaising with the tradesmen to choosing materials. He made all the decisions about the design and fittings, pricing everything from taps to shower screens to balustrades. The project was his responsibility, and I did nothing but write the occasional cheque and fret endlessly in the background.

Now, partly I was content to leave things up to T because he was the architect, and his taste was far better than mine. (Actually, I wasn't even sure that I had 'taste', given that every piece of furniture I'd owned before him had been from the same pine warehouse.) Mainly, however, I distanced myself because I couldn't cope with being involved. The more I knew about the development – about the myriad of tasks that had to be accomplished every day, the innumerable choices that had to be made, and the number of people who had to show up for work – the more I worried. There was so much that could go wrong, and, in my mind, surely would. There could be delays due to rain and materials lost in transit and incorrectly measured windows. There could be tradesmen who went AWOL and objecting neighbours and council restrictions and cost blowouts. The possibilities made my head threaten to explode; I couldn't think of the house without my imagination running wild and worst-case scenarios bursting in. The only way forward was to shut out those thoughts and focus on the kids.

I am certainly not proud of my behaviour that year. My husband was building us our dream house, and I barely even acknowledged it. He would come home energised and try to chat with me about his day – share information about the colour of a wall, or an interesting light he'd tracked down – and I would respond briefly and steer the conversation around to something less emotive. I never asked questions and I never looked at pictures, let alone visited the site or took friends around. Whilst other people I knew who'd built homes had eagerly anticipated each new development and tracked the progress of their house with daily visits, up until that moment I had done everything in my power to stay well away from ours.

T thought that I had no interest, which really wasn't true. It's just that my anxiety overwhelmed my interest and crushed my pleasure, stamping out the happy anticipation I should have been feeling.

On the day of that first tour, when I couldn't stay away any longer, I felt like I couldn't breathe. Facing the house was like staring at my executioner. I was burdened, stifled by the weight of the mortgage, and by what I saw as the potential for financial disaster. The kids explored excitedly and shouted with glee as, one by one, they found their rooms. I followed T, rigid with tension, as he led me through the kitchen. I struggled, but I couldn't even give a word of praise, much less gratitude.

'You don't like it!' T shouted. 'You don't even care!'

But I did care. Of course I cared. And I so wanted to be there, celebrating with my family, enjoying my husband's achievement and such a wonderful milestone in our lives. But I was locked in my own head, trapped by the anxiety that screamed to me words like, 'Money!', 'Debt!', 'Foreclosure!' and 'Danger!' and I couldn't experience the joy at all.

We were standing in our home, and everything had gone perfectly, and all I could think of was what could still go wrong.

At this moment, I am sitting at my stylish desk in my gorgeous office in our beautiful home. Behind me is a sloping roof with a view out to the garden; beside me are three bookshelves set against a picture window. I love this space. It is the very first time I have had my own home office, and – two years down the track – I still get a small thrill every time I sit in my chair.

Already we have created many fond memories in this home. We have entertained friends around the poolside barbecue, shared innumerable family dinners at the dining table, and hosted giggling kids for sleepover parties. We have played games of charades on the couch, and curled up together on the balcony lounge. We have laughed and argued and had earnest conversations within these fresh white walls.

This construction zone has truly become a cherished home.

I wish I could have enjoyed the process of building. I wish I could have supported my husband, and thanked him for all he was doing for the family. But instead I was held captive by my fears about the future, and so ruined all the good things that were happening in my present.

I will never be able to get those two years back. I will never again be able to explore my new house for the very first time. I will never have another chance to stand next to my husband and marvel at our work in progress. All I can do is enjoy my home now, and try not to worry endlessly about what might never happen.

And hope that in the future I won't make the same mistakes again.

Ruined Day Out

When you suffer an attack of nerves you're being attacked by the nervous system. What chance has a man got against a system?

Russell Hoban, author

Sometimes my worries fall neatly into a category. Other times I get anxious for not much reason at all.

It was a Sunday morning, and my husband proposed that we take the kids to Chinatown for an excursion. 'We'll drive into the city, go for yum cha, and then wander through the markets,' T said.

It seemed like a good idea – I'm always pushing for us to spend more time together as a family, and the children enjoy going somewhere a little bit different – and so I agreed. Still, his words triggered an immediate anxiety response in me. Well, not all of his words, just the main ones, you know: *drive*, *city*, *yum cha*, *wander*, *markets*. They meant we'd be going out of our suburban area (*drive*) and out of my comfort zone (*city*), to an unfamiliar restaurant (*yum cha*) in which we'd eat foods the kids don't usually eat, then spend an indefinite amount of time (*wander*) in a crowded, open space (*markets*).

My body jumped to high alert and the tension set in. And though I could feel it happening, I didn't know how to halt it in its tracks. I was setting us up for a disastrous day yet I didn't have the resources to stop it.

We climbed into the car, and T drove us into the city. I worried about where we were going to find a parking spot, as it is notoriously difficult to find a park in the city, not to mention prohibitively expensive.

'Where are we going to park?' I asked T fretfully.

'Don't worry about it,' he answered. But I did.

'Don't park illegally,' I told him anxiously.

'Why on earth would I park illegally?' he asked.

'You always park illegally,' I said. That was, perhaps, a slight exaggeration – T always parked legally around me, but we'd had many a parking ticket sent to our home after he had parked in No Standing zones for work.

'Have I ever parked illegally except for work?' he replied.

'No, but I know you do it all the time, so . . .'

'Are you trying to start a fight?' he asked.

'No, but . . .'

'Do you want to drive?' he asked.

'No, but . . .'

'Then be quiet.'

'Okay.'

I sat back in my seat, chastened, as the kids stared at me reproachfully (at least, I assumed they were staring, I was too chastened to turn around). Five minutes later, my husband parked in a free, perfectly legal spot, an easy seven-minute walk from Chinatown, and we were all set to go.

We marched through the streets of Chinatown and started checking out the restaurants, searching for a suitable place to eat.

'This one looks good,' I said to T.

He perused the menu and peered inside. 'Nah,' he said. 'I don't like it. Let's keep going.' He continued walking, the kids chattering together happily behind him. I felt agitated.

'How about this one?' I asked, two seconds later.

T stopped and considered it. 'No, not this one,' he said. I tried to breathe deeply, but I was rigid with stress. I wanted to choose a restaurant. I wanted us all to sit down for lunch.

'This one?' I asked, indicating the next restaurant. My husband shot me a sharp look.

'Do you actually care where we go or do you just want to make a decision?' he asked. 'Because this place looks pretty crap.' I looked inside. Ew. It wasn't good. I guess I did just want to make a decision.

'The kids are starving,' I said. 'They need to eat.' But the kids weren't starving. They didn't need to eat. They were relaxed and giggling and absolutely fine. It was I who was the problem, and I wasn't even particularly hungry. I just couldn't bear the uncertainty of not knowing.

We eventually agreed on a huge yum cha restaurant, and to my relief were seated quite quickly. We settled ourselves as trolleys bearing a variety of dishes were wheeled in every direction. We grabbed some dumplings and spring rolls, but I became fixated on the idea of getting rice for the kids.

The kids like rice, I thought. Get some rice. We need rice!

I frantically asked for rice from every staff member who walked by, but none was forthcoming, so I just kept asking. In my quest for rice I accosted a drinks waiter, the maître d', and several bewildered-looking trolley pushers who didn't speak a word of English. And yet, no rice.

'Can you calm down?' my husband asked.

'We need rice!' I hissed at him.

In the end, the rice appeared on our table, provided by the designated rice dealer. And of course, after all of that, none of the kids wanted any rice. Why would they? They had dumplings.

I put some rice in my own bowl, and told myself that this was my cue to relax.

Apparently, I didn't listen.

My son was eating well, but my daughters were barely touching their plates, and I became agitated that so much of the food was being wasted.

We're wasting so much food! I thought with distress. We're spending lots of money on a lavish lunch, and nobody is eating it! We're haemorrhaging money in a Chinese restaurant on tiny plates full of uneaten spring rolls!

It was unbearable.

'This is such a waste!' I cried, indicating our laden table.

'Relax,' said T. 'Can you at least try to enjoy it?'

'But no one's eating!' I shrieked.

'Then eat!'

And so I ate. I ate as much as I could, just so I didn't have to feel stressed at the sight of all that uneaten food. I ate and ate and ate some more, and then I felt hideously full, because I had grossly overeaten. I was going to gain heaps of weight, and it hadn't saved me any money or got the girls to eat any more.

So far the day was going *really* well.

We paid the bill and left the restaurant, the kids skipping merrily ahead, and me waddling behind with a belly full of spring rolls. I was still upset about all the money we'd spent, even though I knew I was being quite unreasonable, as we ate out fairly regularly and frequently spent more money than that. Eventually I stopped thinking about the money, but I couldn't shake the anxiety. It weighed on me like an enormous, heavy bag slung across my chest.

By the time we entered the markets I was uptight, unhappy and radiating discomfort for all to see. The point of the outing was to browse through the stalls, and yet I couldn't tolerate my family doing just that. When I found one or more of them lingering too long at a particular stall, I worried that they were falling behind, and hurried them along. And yet when they marched too quickly ahead of me, I worried about losing them in the crowd, and pulled them back again.

I was tense and controlling and snappish and miserable, and I could not shake myself out of my state. I had enough insight to know that I was ruining the outing for everyone, but not enough insight to know how to bring myself back. The anxiety was in control, not me. It didn't want me enjoy myself, it was selfish and stubborn, and would not relinquish its hold until we were all back home and the chance for fun was over.

The excursion was cut short after less than an hour, when my husband could cope with me no more. And once we were back in the car and heading for home, my anxiety slipped away. I looked at my silent kids and their tight-lipped father, and I understood that I had trashed their day, and I was flooded with mortification and shame.

Days like that Sunday happen all too often. Of course, we do have family outings that go fabulously well, and we also have outings that are wrecked by someone else's crappy mood. However, I regularly get anxious when we venture out somewhere new, and that anxiety can impact negatively on the people I care about.

I don't fully understand where my daytrip anxiety comes from. It's a free-floating anxiety, not grounded in a particular concern, which makes it all the more difficult to justify. Why am I so agitated when all we are doing is driving somewhere for lunch and a wander?

I can't pinpoint what I'm afraid of but I do know that I get tense in situations that are open-ended or uncertain. I function much better when I know exactly what is going to happen and when. I like to know where I'm going, and how we will get there and back. I don't like to 'walk around and find a restaurant'. Phrases such as 'we'll see', 'let's play it by ear' and 'whatever we feel like doing at the time' are impossible for me. No wonder I never backpacked around the world as a teenager; I can't even wander around the city for a day as an adult.

I suspect the whole issue boils down to one of control. My anxiety makes me feel out of control in many new environments, and feeling out of control is remarkably uncomfortable for me. So I become stressed and uneasy, which causes me to behave badly, which causes me to become angry at myself, which causes me to become even more stressed. It's a vicious cycle which I can only break by forcing myself to relax. Relaxation, however, doesn't come easy to me at all. If it did, I wouldn't be writing this book.

The worst part of a ruined day out is the self-flagellation which follows. I become distressed at the waste of precious family time, and am stricken with remorse. I don't want my kids to suffer because of my neuroses, and I don't want my family life to be limited because of my irrational fears. So I make resolutions to turn over a new leaf. I promise myself that I'll embrace fresh ideas and fresh experiences with positivity and calm.

But then the weekend comes, and it's sunny outside, and my husband looks up from the paper and says, 'Hey, why don't we take the kids to this festival down south? It looks interesting,' and my stomach clenches into a fist, and my shoulders go rigid, and I know this is going to be a difficult day . . .

All Worked Up

Anxiety is the handmaiden of contemporary ambition.

Alain de Botton, author

It had been fifteen minutes, and so far the blind date was going well. I was sitting in a cafe with a lovely young woman who'd invited me for lunch. We'd met online; R was an aspiring writer whose work I had read and admired.

'It's so great to meet you,' R said after we'd ordered.

'It's great to meet you too,' I told her. And it was. R was funny and smart and highly articulate, as interesting in person as she was in cyberspace. I was genuinely enjoying her company.

'I was really nervous,' she admitted. 'You're so talented and successful. I'm very happy you agreed to come.'

'Talented and successful'? Oh dear. Suddenly, I wondered if R wasn't so smart after all. She seemed to be a little bit deluded. I started to feel uncomfortable.

Later that week, I had breakfast with my friend L, and told her about the meeting.

'I really liked R,' I told her over scrambled eggs, 'but then she called me "talented and successful". It kind of put me off.'

L made a face. 'Why on earth did that put you off?'

'Because I'm not talented or successful!' I exclaimed. Jeez. Wasn't it obvious? 'I mean, what have I done? I've written one little book . . .'

'. . . and you're writing another . . .'

'Yeah, but that hardly makes me a success.'

L put down her latte. 'Okay, so what *would* make you a success?'

I contemplated the question. 'I don't know. Writing seven books? Hitting the bestseller lists?'

'But your book's been published, and it's selling really well. It's been sold overseas. It's had great reviews. How is that not successful?'

'I don't know. It just isn't.'

'But wouldn't you think someone else who'd published a book like that was a success?'

I thought for a moment. 'Yes,' I admitted.

'So then why aren't you?' she asked me pointedly.

'Because I'm a fraud and they're not.'

L shook her head sadly. I shrugged and went back to my eggs.

I have loved to write for as long as I can remember. As a child I wrote poetry and won story competitions, and I kept personal diaries for most of my life. I was a voracious reader, as writers tend to be, and studied Arts at university, majoring in English Literature and Linguistics.

Still, it never occurred to me that I could choose writing as a career. Arts was simply a stopgap measure, to keep me busy whilst I worked out what I was going to do with my life.

After two years of Arts I switched to a Social Work degree, which was never a comfortable fit. I finally finished my Arts degree after my son was born, and a couple of years later began my freelance writing career.

I enjoyed freelance writing, but I never thought of myself as a 'real' or 'proper' writer. Though I was published regularly, particularly in parenting magazines, I never considered myself to have accomplished anything of significance. I had a couple of minor successes – a double-page feature in a Sunday magazine was a particular highlight – but these seemed to me to be exceptions, rather than the rule. I thought of myself as a chronic underachiever, and had no reason to believe that would ever change.

For a long time I told myself that my mediocre career didn't matter, that I didn't really care about achievement. I told myself that I simply wasn't ambitious, that it was a lifestyle choice I was happy to make. But gradually, it dawned on me that I was lying to myself. As I grew older, I realised that I *did* care about achievement, I *was* ambitious, I *did* want to succeed. But I had shied away from ambition, because ambition generated anxiety about failure, and I would do anything in my power to avoid anxiety.

This massive realisation was like a key in a lock. The ambition I'd kept tightly under wraps for most of my adult life came flooding out with a vengeance. I decided that it wasn't too late to live to my full potential. I started blogging, and gained a steady following, and soon became motivated to write a book. At the time I was forty-one years old, and had never written anything longer than 1000 words in my life. Suddenly, I was filled with energy and bursting with ideas, and I knew that finally I was on the right path.

I wrote *When My Husband Does the Dishes* . . . in about a year, and it made me very proud. My only goal was to see it in print; to me, becoming a published author was the pinnacle of success.

I had an agent, the lovely P, who had discovered me through my blog. I knew that she was going to try to sell my manuscript to a publisher, but what I hadn't counted on was having to show it to her first. No one had read my book – it was my own personal project – and revealing it to the world was the most terrifying thing I'd ever done.

My fingers literally shook as I composed a rather abbreviated email to P (*Here is the manuscript. Let me know what you think.*). As I attached the document, and pressed 'Send', I thought I might collapse with nerves. Instead, I shut down my computer and went to the shops. I couldn't bear to be in email contact when she received the file.

The next few days were agonising as I waited for P to respond to my email. At last, she did, and to my delight and disbelief, she announced that she loved my book. P sent *Husband* out to a number of different publishers, and told me she'd keep me posted about the feedback.

Once I knew I was in with a chance, I wanted that deal with every fibre of my being. And I hated wanting it, because it made me demented with anxiety about whether or not I was going to get it. The waiting period was unbearable. I was constantly worried about how my manuscript was being received by the publishers, and kept hounding P for reassurance about my prospects and the outcome.

'Why are they taking so long?' I'd ask P. 'What does it mean? Is it bad?'

'It's fine,' she would tell me. 'These things take time. They're going to love it.'

And I'd feel calm and reassured . . . for about a minute.

Eventually, some good news came through. Several publishers had given extremely positive feedback, and at least two were planning to make an offer.

Oh. My. God. It was happening! I was going to publish a book! I told my husband, my parents, my closest girlfriends. It was a dream come true! I was overwhelmed with excitement . . . for about a minute.

Then I started panicking. What if P was wrong? What if all the publishers decided they didn't want it after all? What if they realised, after closer inspection, that it was utter rubbish?

The deadline for the offers was two weeks away, so I tried to keep busy and not worry constantly. I wasn't very successful. I jumped every time the phone rang, and became immediately deflated when it was just my mum. My heart pounded madly every time I booted up my computer, or a little ding indicated that an email had come through. I lived in a state of crazed expectation, hovering on the brink of hope and despair.

What's going on? I emailed P. *Why hasn't anything happened?*

Don't stress! she responded. *These things take time. They are really keen, they're just putting their offers together.*

I felt a huge surge of relief . . . for about a minute. And then the doubt crept in, as it always did. What if P was wrong? What if the publishers were just finishing off their rejection letters? What if they were taking their time to let me down gently?

Time ticked by slowly as the end of the fortnight approached. P reminded me once again that the deadline was Friday, and told me to sit tight until then.

Well, I thought that was completely ridiculous advice. How could one 'sit tight' when one was waiting for important news? I couldn't 'sit tight'. I didn't *do* 'sitting tight'. Quite frankly, I was so stressed I couldn't 'sit' at all, let alone do it 'tightly'. All I could do was worry about whether my book was going to be sold. I couldn't concentrate, I couldn't sleep, and two possible scenarios played out in my head on an incessant, relentless loop:

1. My book is rejected for publication. I am a complete failure. My hopes and dreams are crushed for all eternity, and I return to menial labour in an unfulfilling job; or
2. My book is sold to the highest bidder for a huge sum of money. It hits the bestseller charts, I become a huge star, and my life is perfect from then on.

Anxiety can make one very dramatic, and I can see that my projected outcomes were a little extreme. Still, it felt like a make-or-break situation to me, and the tension was absolutely torturous. For days I paced and cleaned and drove to the shops and roamed aimlessly around looking at nothing in particular and then drove home again and checked my emails and paced and cleaned some more.

Finally, at the end of the week, the email I'd been waiting for came through. *When My Husband Does the Dishes* . . . was going to be published. My dream was coming true.

My book was in print just six months later, a remarkably quick turnaround by publishing standards. I was ecstatic to see it on the shelves, and was on a massive high for the first couple of months after publication. This is what it feels like to know success, I thought. This is what it feels like to achieve.

It was about two months after publication when things started to go downhill. I hadn't given much thought to what life would look like after I wrote my book, other than that I would feel like a complete success, and that it would be perfect in every way. I honestly believed that once I attained my goal, my anxiety would drop away, and I would enjoy my accomplishment.

Well, once again, I was wrong.

For one thing, to my great surprise, I didn't actually feel like a success. Before *Husband*, I had compared myself unfavourably to every published author. Now that I was published, I simply switched gears, and compared myself unfavourably to every author who was more accomplished. 'More accomplished' authors included those who had written more than one book, those who had written best-sellers, and those who had written books I felt were better than mine. I'd only written one book, and it hadn't hit the bestseller list, so I felt like an abject loser.

For another thing, my anxiety about achievement didn't dissipate once the book was sold. It wasn't, as I had anticipated, the culmination of my ambition, it was simply a transition to the next stage of my career. A new, and equally insidious, anxiety took over, in the form of 'How many books am I going to sell?'

I began ringing my publisher every week, asking how many copies of my book I had sold. 'What are the figures?' I'd ask him nervously. 'What does Bookscan say?' (Bookscan records the number of copies of every book sold in Australia per week, and allows publishers to judge the success of their titles. It also allows publishers to judge the neuroticism of their authors, by seeing how frequently and how fretfully they call asking for Bookscan reports.)

My Bookscan figures were healthy, and my publisher seemed pleased. Still, no matter what number he reported to me I wasn't satisfied, because I didn't really know what I was hoping to hear. I wasn't even sure what represented 'good' sales, or at least, what represented good sales to me. Was it a hundred copies? A thousand copies? Ten thousand? A million? It was irrelevant anyway, because I was never content for long. I was only ever as good as my next Bookscan report, and that was only ever a week away.

Eventually I stopped asking for my weekly sales figures, as the whole routine became way too stressful. And the pressing anxiety about how many books I'd sold gave way to a more enduring anxiety about the status of my career.

Writing a book hasn't made me feel like a writer. Writing a book has made me feel like a fraud. I'm like a sixteen-year-old again, sneaking into nightclubs with a fake ID and a terror of being caught. I'm just waiting for someone to come along and say, 'You reckon you're an author? Who on earth do you think you're kidding?'

I try very hard to come across as an authentic author, but frequently, the facade comes crumbling down and I realise that I'm not an author at all.

'When do you write?' I am often asked in interviews.

'Well, I write whenever I can,' I answer, 'during the day, or at night, or in snatches when the kids are watching TV.'

'Oh really?' comes the response. 'Because most writers have some sort of routine – you know, they have to write first thing in the morning, or only within office hours, or late at night after work.'

And I start to worry, because I don't write according to a schedule, which means I'm obviously not a real writer at all.

'Do you need to write in a special place?' the interviewer asks.

'Well, no,' I answer. 'I'm a mum, so sometimes my kids kick me out of my office, and I have to write in the kitchen or on the couch.'

'Oh really?' comes the response. 'Because many writers can only write in certain areas of the house.'

And I start to worry, because I don't write in a particular area of the house, which means I'm obviously not a real writer at all.

'You write unbelievably quickly,' an author friend said, when I mentioned how many words I'd written in one day.

And I started to worry, because I'd been writing pretty quickly, which means I'm obviously not a real writer at all.

If you ask me who a real writer is, I'll tell you it's anyone who has published a book.

As for me, well, I'm just someone who keeps pretending.

When My Husband Does the Dishes . . . was sold to the publisher as a completed manuscript. However, my second book – the one you are reading now – was sold before completion. I submitted an overview, an outline and a couple of sample chapters, and my publisher bought it as an unfinished manuscript.

This was, and is, utterly nerve-racking for me. Of course I am thrilled to have sold another book, but my anxiety levels have soared yet again. I worry that my publisher's faith in me has been misplaced, and that the completed manuscript won't live up to their expectations. I worry that I'll be exposed as a talentless fraud, and bring shame to my publisher, my agent, and my family. I worry that this book will never be published, and I'll be a one-hit wonder forevermore.

Of course, if you are reading *The Little Book of Anxiety*, then it means it actually went to print. It means I'm not a failure after all, and perhaps I am even a real author.

But still, I'll be worrying about how many copies I've sold, and comparing myself to writers more successful than me. I'll be anxiously reading my reviews online, and obsessing over any negative comments. I'll be fretting about what my next book will be about, and whether I'm going to be a two-hit wonder.

I'll be tense and stressed and insecure and anxious.

But aside from that, life will be absolutely perfect.

Nervous Tension

We shall probably never attain the power of measuring the velocity of nervous action; for we have not the opportunity of comparing its propagation through immense space, as we have in the case of light.

Johannes P. Muller, scientist

This may surprise you, given the calm and easygoing disposition I have demonstrated throughout this book, but I tend to get nervous. A lot.

Nervousness is a milder form of generalised anxiety – not the full catastrophe, but irritating nonetheless. It's all of the uncomfortable physical symptoms of anxiety without the terrible mental anguish, a sort of decaf anxiety, or anxiety lite.

I get particularly nervous in new situations, and since I wrote my first book there have been many. The first time I was interviewed on radio, for example, I was an absolute quivering mess.

The producer had arranged to call me at home at eleven, and I spent the entire morning rehearsing what I was going to say. I paced around the house composing sound bites in my head and practising, 'Hi, great to be on the show' in 1000 different ways. Finally the clocked ticked eleven, and then eleven o'clock passed, and I decided dramatically that the station was never going to call. I collapsed despondently in my chair, texted my publicist to say there was a problem, and sent a tragic email to my husband explaining I'd been stood up. Of course the station called, at exactly three minutes past eleven, but by then I had completely run out of steam. I got on air and fumbled my way through the entire interview. I forgot to say, 'Great to be on the show', said none of the gems that I'd planned to say, and blurted out something totally inappropriate about marital sex that I hadn't planned to say at all.

Then there was my first author talk, which had given me nervous jitters for days. It was supposed to be a 'casual, relaxed chat' about my book, but quite frankly I would have been far more relaxed sitting a calculus exam, or having a tooth extracted. I kept worrying that I wouldn't remember what *Husband* was about, despite having written it, and having re-read it around twenty-seven times. I jotted down some notes in point form to help jog my memory, then fretted that I wouldn't remember what the notes were referring to. So I wrote an entire twenty-minute speech that ran to several pages, which I studied so often I practically learned it by rote. During the talk I ended up ditching the speech and just chatting to the audience, but the speech sat in my bag like the security blanket it was, and knowing it was there made me feel much better.

Still, none of those nerves compared to the first time I appeared on live TV.

It had long been a dream of mine to be interviewed on morning television. To me, that epitomised the pinnacle of success, which is ironic considering I've now been on TV many times and still don't feel in the slightest bit successful. I was tense for a week before my scheduled appearance, waking up super early every day with a thumping heart and adrenaline racing through my veins. I wasn't scared of being interviewed at all – I'd done several radio spots by then and felt pretty sure I could handle any question – but I had no idea how I would react in front of the cameras. Would I remember to look away? Would I feel compelled to stare right into the lens? Would I hiccough, or sneeze, or cough mid-sentence? Would I get tongue-tied or fumble my words? Would I accidentally use a naughty word like I did occasionally in front of the kids?

It took me hours of deliberation to choose my outfit, and after trying on a dozen ensembles I settled on a short, multicoloured dress. I laid out my outfit the night before, set the alarm (and a backup, just to be safe), then went to bed early to get a good night's sleep.

I lay in bed for a couple of hours, and then at around midnight a thought flashed through my head.

My legs! My hairy legs! I'd forgotten to shave!

It was the middle of winter, and I hadn't shaved for months. It was a disaster. I couldn't possibly go on national TV with fur on my legs. I leaped out of bed, grabbed my phone to use as a torch, so as not to wake T, and searched for stockings that could disguise my shame. To my dismay, there were no stockings to be found. Not surprising, as I hadn't worn stockings in years.

I knew exactly what had to be done, and so I trudged into our ensuite and grabbed a razor. By the light of my phone I dry-shaved my legs on the edge of the bath. I checked quickly for blood, rubbed on some cream, and then crawled back into bed to try to sleep.

I must have dropped off eventually, because I woke up the next morning, half an hour before the alarm and shivering with nerves. I hopped straight in the shower before the kids woke up, then stepped into my carefully chosen outfit. I glanced in the mirror to check that it worked, and jumped up in horror when I saw my reflection.

My legs! My bright red legs! They were stripy from the dry-shave!

It was an absolute nightmare. I literally had red-and-white striped legs from the knees to my feet. The hair on my legs would have been less noticeable; in fact, leprosy on my legs would have been less noticeable. There was no possible way I could wear the dress, and yet I was in far too agitated a state to choose something else. I didn't have stockings, so what to do?

'What can I do?' I wailed to T.

'You woke me!' he complained.

'Look at my legs!' I cried.

'Ew,' he said.

In the end, I grabbed a black pair of pants, and wore them under the dress. It wasn't ideal, but then neither was my emotional state, and I couldn't afford to be late.

The kids were awake, so I went down to the kitchen, and tried to help them with breakfast. But I was frantic with nerves, and I couldn't focus on my family. I barely could hear them over the rushing in my head.

'Mummy, can I have my milky?' my youngest child asked sweetly.

'Huh?' I answered and walked away from the fridge, then found myself by the sink, where I stood wringing my hands.

'Mummy, I want *milky*!' my daughter cried again. I'd been stuck in a trance, but I immediately jumped to attention.

'Okay!' I yelled, and headed back to the fridge, where I stood wondering if it was possible to faint on camera. I held onto the fridge door and gazed at the laden shelves.

'Mummy, my *MILKY*!'

It was all too hard.

'Can you get her that thing she wants?' I called to T. I clearly just wasn't up to the task.

I went into my bathroom to put on my make-up. This posed a problem as my hands were trembling so powerfully that I got into serious difficulties with the mascara wand and my cheek. With the aid of some wipes I managed to make myself look passable, and I eventually made it out the door.

I travelled to the studio by taxi, which was helpful; if I had driven myself, in my delicate condition I may have run off the road. I was quickly ushered into the make-up room, where I apologised for my mascara and tried very hard not to stare at the famous people.

On set I coolly feigned nonchalance, as if I gave television interviews several times a day. To admit to my nerves would have been a sign of weakness, and I wanted to appear smoothly confident and professional. Still, my faux nonchalance actually worked in my favour; I did genuinely calm down slightly, although it's possible I was simply numb with nerves. I was quite composed as I was hooked up with a microphone, shown to my place, and seated on the couch. I was introduced to the hosts as the show ran to a commercial break, and I responded as if they weren't famous at all. Only my heart gave me away, thumping so loudly beneath my chest I felt like I'd smuggled a metronome under my dress.

I'd love to report how I went in the interview but I really have no idea. The entire segment was an absolute blur, and passed in about three seconds flat. I was unhooked from my mic and ushered from the set, and I wandered dazed into the sunlight. I made it to a taxi and fell into my seat, and then my insides melted away. I was as physically exhausted as if I'd just run a marathon, and as emotionally drained as if I'd just been to a funeral.

And in addition to being exhausted and drained, my multi-coloured dress was soaking wet.

You see, when I get nervous I tend to sweat a lot, which is both infuriating and kind of gross. Now, normally I'm not a very sweaty person. I might work up a gentle sheen while exercising – although given the rareness of me exercising, this is fairly hypothetical – but under regular circumstances it's not an issue at all. Most days I could easily forgo deodorant entirely, although I do tend to use it, just to be safe.

When I'm nervous, however, my glands go into overdrive. My armpits become veritable rainforests of perspiration, drenching me in rivulets of sweat. It doesn't matter whether the day is warm or cool, whether I'm wearing cotton or polyester, or whether I have long sleeves or none. I will just drip, drip, drip until the nerves have passed, at which point the tap will magically turn off, and I can raise my arms again.

This stress-induced sweating is the bane of my existence. It's just not a good look to have circles of sweat under your arms, so I have to be careful about my choice of clothes. I never buy clothes that will turn dark when wet, so I wear a lot of white, and black, and loose-fitting patterns.

Even if the world can't see my sweatiness, I can feel it under my clothes. And, being driven away from the TV set that day, I felt sticky and clammy and horrid. Happily, I just headed straight home and got changed, but it isn't always that easy. There are times when I am out for the day and suffer an attack of nerves, and don't have a spare layer to change into. I can't bear being stranded in a damp top, and so will go on a mission to find a new one.

This leads me to Post-Traumatic Stress Shopping Syndrome, the compulsion to buy new clothes to replace the sweaty ones I am wearing. PTSSS is not an addiction; it is a response to a situation, and differs from therapeutic shopping, which is an end in itself.

PTSSS has greatly added to my wardrobe, but sadly, not always for the best. Occasionally I will buy myself a nice new top, but I'm usually in far too much of a rush to browse. If I'm wearing something simple, I'll match the top I was wearing, which is why I now have four sets of identical T-shirts hanging in my wardrobe. Usually, however, I'll just grab something cheap and nasty, and wear it until I can get home to change. This explains my bulging pyjama drawer, which holds around three pairs of pyjama pants and approximately 7000 tops.

My nervousness has, quite literally, cost me dearly.

Nothing smells as bad as the scent of stress, and no ordinary perfume will mask it. Stress smells worse than exercise and socks and rubbish bins and unwashed dogs combined. My friend L once commented that the manufacturer of Xanax should market a deodorant, and I think the idea is pure genius.

Xanax roll-on! Extra strong! Fresh scent!

Double action AND relaxing!

An emotionally soothing antiperspirant to keep you calm, dry and fragrant all day.

I would buy it in bulk without checking the price. No matter what it cost, I'd be saving a fortune in tops.

Thinking of sweat makes me recall my wedding (which is a phrase possibly never, ever written before). It was a beautiful evening, and I have many special memories, from the weight of the flowers in my arms to the smiling faces of my guests. I remember walking down the aisle to where T was standing and seeing the gathered crowd for the first time. I remember laughing at all of the hilarious speeches and seeing T laughing at mine. I remember cutting our almost-impenetrable cake and dancing for the first time as a married couple.

What I most vividly remember, however, is a little scene that took place before we even left for the ceremony.

I was all dressed up in my cream bridal gown, which unwisely included full-length sleeves. It was a cool day, but I was understandably crazed with nerves, and began panicking about how sweaty I was getting. Nothing is worse than a perspiring bride (which is probably not true, but I was catastrophising, too). I couldn't get changed, and I couldn't calm myself down. So, as the photographer arrived to take my photo, and the hire cars began to gather outside, I pulled my dress to my knees, crouched down on the toilet seat, and began blowing my armpits with a hairdryer.

It wasn't the most glamorous way to get in the mood for my wedding. I'd originally planned on relaxing with champagne.

I wish I could report that I only get nervous in new situations, but sadly this isn't true. I also get nervous in many situations I've been in 1000 times before.

I get nervous before parties, for no particular reason, and the more formal the party, the more nervous I'll be. If the party is casual, I'll be a little bit edgy; if it's a black tie event, I'll be pacing around the room. I also get nervous before big functions, whether it's a concert, a play, a festival or even a fete. I tell myself I'm actually worried for a good reason: that we're going to be late, lose the kids, or not know where the toilets are. But the truth is I'm generally just nervous with no cause. Big functions give me butterflies, and that's all there is to it.

Happily, on these occasions, my jitters don't make me sweat. Unhappily for those around me, they make me atrociously tight and snappish. I am not a nice person before we go to an event. I can yell at people to hurry up, pick fights for no reason, and radiate tension from every pore of my body.

Fortunately I recognise my pre-event jitters, and respond to gentle prompts from my husband to relax. Unfortunately, however, I don't respond well at all. In fact, God help T if he tries to point out that I'm uptight, as it is the worst possible thing that he can say to me when I am anxious. I will explain quite vigorously that he is totally wrong, wonder out loud why he's picking on me for no reason, slam doors shut, and yell that the problem is *him*.

And then we go to the function, the jitters pass, and I apologise profusely for having been so tense. Usually he forgives me. Sometimes . . . not so much.

Still, there is something worse than getting nervous for no good reason, and that is getting nervous for no reason at all.

There are days when I am physically overwhelmed by nerves, without anything consciously bothering me. I will wake up every couple of hours throughout the night with a pounding heart and extreme agitation and be baffled as to what I'm anxious about. The day stretching ahead is filled with school runs and laundry, but my body is telling me that I'm being interviewed for my dream job, then presenting an Oscar at the Academy Awards.

I feel very resentful of these bouts from the blue, but I do suspect that they serve a purpose. They are nerves being released from a pressure valve, the result of bottled-up anxiety that has burst from the surface after I've tried to suppress it for too long. I try to run, but I catch up with myself eventually, and I guess that I always will.

There is a Yiddish phrase that perfectly describes that edgy feeling of nervousness: to be 'on *shpilkes*' – literally, on pins and needles. A rush of adrenaline pumps relentlessly through my body, leaving me restless and unsettled and unable to focus.

I hate the feeling of being on *shpilkes*; it's like caffeine and sugar highs and red cordial all at once. I hate that sensation of bouncing out of my skin, I just want to be calm and serene and peaceful and still. However, being on *shpilkes* gives me enormous energy, and sometimes I can channel that energy into good instead of evil.

Nothing puts me on *shpilkes* more than waiting for news, whether it's a test result, an important work-related phone call, or a friendship or family issue. Waiting, for me, is completely unbearable; I simply don't deal well with uncertainty. I can't work, I can't chat, I can't sleep, I can't read, I can't do anything that requires concentration.

On the other hand, the adrenaline surge from *shpilkes* gives me an almost-superhuman ability to complete mindless tasks. My brain stays focused on the news that I'm awaiting and my body goes onto autopilot as I race around finding things to do.

I have accomplished an astonishing amount when I have been on *shpilkes*, often without even realising I'm doing it. I once scrubbed all my windows without pausing for breath whilst waiting for a doctor to phone with a test result. I spent an hour in a trance cleaning a grotty white couch whilst waiting for my agent to call me back. I spent two hours in a frenzy rearranging a disordered pantry whilst waiting to hear back from a friend after a fight. And I have polished and wiped and swept and ironed and washed dishes and done innumerable loads of laundry whilst barely even registering that my hands were moving.

Of course, the problem with nervousness is the toll it takes on my body. If being on *shpilkes* isn't emotionally wearing enough, the hours of vigorous activity leave me physically worn out. Eventually the news arrives, and the period of uncertainty is over, and I am inevitably hit by a wall of exhaustion. If the news is bad, I'll feel tired and depressed; if the news is good, I'll feel too drained to celebrate.

Even so, my house will be gleaming and the cupboards spotless, which is a very rare event in my home indeed. And if that's the outcome of feeling nervous, I can almost say that it's worth it.

Panic: Drunk on Fear

Panic is a sudden desertion of us, and a going over to the enemy of our imagination.

Christian Nestell Bovee, author

The last time it happened we were in New York City. My husband and I were travelling alone for ten days, and we were having a wonderful time. Of course, I was my usual unsettled overseas self, but there was nothing seriously bothering me. I was slightly anxious about leaving my youngest child for so long, and was a little uncomfortable being so far away. Also, I was seeing some high-powered publishers in New York and I had been fairly nervous about those meetings. And finally, we were staying in a minuscule hotel room, which was fine in the light of day, but extraordinarily claustrophobic at night. Yet, I was genuinely having a ball, and had no inkling of what was to take place that night.

We'd had a great day and I had fallen asleep easily. But at around one in the morning I woke with a start, filled with blinding, mind-destroying panic. It was sick, hot dread, starting in my chest and radiating outwards. My heart was pounding so violently I found it hard to catch my breath, the air felt stale and thick and I feared that I was suffocating. Around me, the walls of the tiny room were closing in on me, the blackness threatening to swallow me whole. I felt an overpowering urge to flee the room, though I had no idea where I wanted to go. Into the hall? Down to the lobby? Out into the street? To Central Park? I was drowning in fear and I couldn't reach the surface.

My saving grace was that I recognised the anxiety attack for what it was, as I'd had a similar episode once in the past. My mind had hijacked my body, and though it felt like I was dying, I knew that I was experiencing pure panic.

I sat there on the bed in the dark hotel room as wave after wave of dread rolled over me. The desire to run from the room became almost overwhelming and I knew I had to wake my husband. I didn't want him to be woken by the sound of a slamming door and find me sprinting down the corridor in my pyjamas.

'Help,' I said, as I shook T awake. 'I don't feel well. I think I'm having a panic attack.'

'Why?' he asked sleepily, and snuggled in close. 'What's wrong?'

'I don't know,' I told him. 'I feel bad. I feel really, really bad.'

T rubbed his eyes and sat up in bed.

'What are you thinking about?' he asked.

'Nothing,' I told him. 'I just can't breathe. I have to get out of here.'

'Come on,' he said. 'It's okay.'

I shook my head. 'Can you turn on the light?' I asked him. 'I need light.' T switched on the light, but even the brightness didn't lift the panic.

'Turn on the TV,' I said. 'Maybe that will help.' T turned on the TV and put his arm around me, and we sat together on the bed watching late-night talk shows. I tried to focus on what the people on the screen were saying, but they seemed very far away and I couldn't shrug off the nauseating fear.

T stayed with me and stroked my back, and in time the panic began to subside. I lay down and tried to sleep, but I was still far too agitated. Eventually I remembered the sleeping pills I had brought for the flight, took two, and finally fell asleep. When I woke up the next morning I was shaken and tired, but could put the whole hideous evening behind me.

That episode was one of the most excruciating experiences of my life – as distressing as the most intense physical pain I have known. The panic took on a life of its own and threatened to engulf me, with no obvious cause at all.

I have only ever had two full-blown anxiety attacks, but I do frequently panic in certain triggering situations. And in those circumstances, my body seizes up in alarm, my mind clouds over and I think I'll die of fear.

When to Panic

- During that horrible second after the lift comes to a halt and I'm not sure whether the doors are going to open
- When the aeroplane levels out and the engine noise changes and it sounds like it's stopped and we're going to all crash into the ocean
- When I'm being followed by a car as I walk down the street (although the car could quite possibly just be travelling at a very slow speed behind me)

- At the sight of a mouse on the floor of a holiday house, particularly if there is no chair to jump on
- If T phones and his first words are, 'Kerri, there's a problem . . .' (even though he might just be referring to our restaurant booking, or the fact that the newspaper didn't arrive on our front lawn that morning)
- At the sound of a scream
- At the sound of a siren
- At the sound of a loud clap of thunder
- At the sound of the phone ringing in the middle of the night
- If I can't immediately spot my kids in a shopping centre, park, beach, or even at home

When I panic, logic flies out the window. Adrenaline surges through my body, my heart pounds, and everything around me blurs at the edges. I scream, jump, gasp, gulp, and generally re-enact every slapstick routine of a startled person you've ever seen. The panic passes quickly, but I'm sure it takes months off my life. If I continue panicking at this rate, soon I'm going to be in arrears.

Though there are many triggers for my panic reaction, sometimes I don't need a trigger at all. Panic is always hovering nearby, and it can descend on me without warning or cause. I will experience a profound and unshakeable sense of imminent disaster – that something catastrophic is about to happen in my life. Perhaps one of the kids is going to be abducted by a psychopath, or T is going to get lung cancer and die, or my parents are both going to go down in a light plane crash, or I'm going to be paralysed in a horrible car accident and will only be able to communicate by blinking my eyes.

The ideas come out of absolutely nowhere (after all, T doesn't smoke, and my parents don't often travel by light plane), but they play out in my mind as vividly as in real life. I can actually *see* T pale and thin in his hospital bed, I can *see* my parents' tombstones laid out next to each other, and I can *see* myself in my wheelchair, using a fine pole attached to my eyelid to spell out letters on a board.

When these terrible visions befall me I try to remain sensible and rational, and remind myself that all is well in my world. Still, it is impossible to shake the sense of dread and vulnerability; it has a life of its own, and lasts for as long as it chooses to stick around.

It can be particularly hard to keep panic at bay on those occasions when there are portents of doom all around me. Of course, it is possible that they are not portents at all – that the significance of the events is completely in my interpretation – but they feel very real to me.

'Mummy, what will happen if you get dead?' my four-year-old will ask cheerily over breakfast, and a shudder will run down my spine.

'Why? Did you have a dream? Did you see something?' I'll demand, wondering if she has experienced some eerie prescience of my demise.

'Have a safe flight,' I'll tell my parents as they head off to the airport, and then I'll pause for a moment. Should I have said that? Have I jinxed them? What if they never come back?

The fears are illogical, but that doesn't make them easier to dispel. Anxiety, you see, correlates with a person's belief about the world. A 'normal' person believes the world is safe, and that – whilst bad things happen – they are unlikely to happen to them. A person like me – a person with anxiety – believes that the world is perilous, and that anything bad can happen to anyone at any time. So the benign question of a four-year-old, or a simple farewell, is as likely as anything else to foretell tragedy, because tragedy can befall us at any time.

Anxiety and our beliefs about the world are fundamentally linked, but, like the proverbial chicken and egg, it is hard to know what comes first. Believing that the world is unsafe will create deep anxiety; however, anxiety also feeds the belief that the world is a dangerous place.

I see my anxiety as a dynamic condition, which has periods of remission, and long periods of relapse. There are times when I feel quite emotionally robust, and can see the world around me in a balanced and realistic light. And then there are times when I feel extremely vulnerable, and the world seems deeply scary to me, filled with endless possibilities for disaster. My husband has a theory that I am particularly anxious when everything is going well in my life. It is possible, of course, but it's hard to shake my negative view of the world when every newspaper and TV abounds with evidence of misfortune all around.

When I am feeling particularly fragile and stressed, I know that I have to protect myself. There are times when I simply can't read newspaper stories about war or child abuse or accidental death, or watch anxiety-provoking shows on TV. Even frightening fiction can make me anxious during periods like these; I will start inserting myself or my kids into the storyline of the novel or film and the next thing I know we're all dropping dead of sudden brain haemorrhages or falling victim to drug abuse or being held hostage by crazed terrorists.

Over the past few years I've realised that I need to accommodate my anxiety, much as one would have to accommodate a condition like diabetes, or high blood pressure. I have to manage all the stressors in my life and try to minimise my triggers for fear and panic. Sometimes this is as easy as taking some time out for a massage, or ignoring the newspapers for a week or so. Sometimes it's not easy at all. Sometimes it's not even remotely possible. I have three children and a career and a husband and a mortgage and I can't always elimi-nate all of the problems in my life. And even if I could eliminate all of the problems in my life, I certainly can't eliminate all of the problems in my head.

There are occasions when a panic wave hits me hard, and all I can do is ride it out till it passes. Then, like a diabetic after an episode of hypoglycaemia, or a migraine sufferer after a day in a darkened room, I regroup. I might look back on the attack and try to work out what caused it, and whether I could have done anything to keep it at bay.

Mostly, however, I'm just grateful that it's over, and that life can return to normal programming.

And I hope that, for a while anyway, the panic stays at bay.

Worryingly Inconsistent

Worry is a complete cycle of inefficient thought revolving about a pivot of fear.

Unknown

This morning I went to my GP, as I've been having a run of headaches. The doctor looked at my file, confirmed some details, asked lots of questions about my symptoms, and then did a thorough physical examination. She looked in my ears and my eyes, performed a series of neurological tests, said, 'Hmmmm' a lot, and made some notes.

Then she sat down in her chair, typed a few things into the computer, swivelled round to face me, and began to speak.

'I think your headaches are very likely to be the result of neck pain,' she said. 'The fact that they worsen in the evening indicates that. It still could be migraine, but the pattern suggests otherwise. It's unlikely to be anything more sinister, but we should do some blood tests just to rule that out, and then possibly an MRI further down the track.'

I only heard one word out of the dozens she said. *Sinister*. It could be something sinister? SINISTER? Oh my God. What could it be? Did I have a brain tumour? Did I have some neurological disorder? Was I going to die? Go blind? Have my head shaved and surgery performed on my brain?

'What do you mean, "sinister"?' I asked her. 'Like what? What could an MRI show?'

The doctor looked at me reprovingly. 'No, I said it's *unlikely* to be anything more sinister. I said it's very likely to be the result of neck pain.'

'But "unlikely" doesn't mean "impossible",' I cried. 'I might have something sinister!'

'I really don't think you do,' she said.

'But I might! What could it be? Is it going to kill me? How long do I have?'

'Kerri, you need to calm down,' she said firmly. 'You're not going to die. You're going to be fine.'

'I'm going to die?' I gasped, and fell to the floor. 'I don't want to die! Please don't let me die.'

The doctor looked pityingly at me as I lay on the floor. It was a tragic scene indeed.

Except that it wasn't at all. Nothing of the sort ever happened. The doctor told me her neck pain theory and it made perfect sense to me. 'Cool,' I said, and calmly took the order form for blood tests. And then I picked up some paracetamol from the chemist, and went about my day.

I don't worry about my health. I never have. And I don't know why I don't worry about my health, considering that I worry so much about so many other, less important things. It's certainly not that I am unnaturally healthy – I've actually had several significant health problems – but I always presume I'll be fine until I'm proven wrong.

Several years ago I found a lump in my breast that required ultrasound and mammography. I was concerned about it, and was relieved when I got the all clear, but I handled it very well. I didn't catastrophise and assume it was cancer, nor did I start planning for chemotherapy and imagine myself hairless and ill. I took it one step at a time, and thankfully, there was a happy ending.

I've had hepatitis twice (once from glandular fever and once from an allergic reaction) and I was hideously sick, but I always knew I'd recover – I didn't worry about the possibility of permanent liver damage. I've had skin spots and back injuries and arthritis and cysts and taken each and every one of them in my stride. I was even diagnosed with lupus after an illness, and instinctively didn't believe the doctor, and was proved right when the diagnosis was found to be mistaken.

When it comes to my health, I err on the side of optimism.

Even when I do have health problems I deal with them very well. I have a couple of medical issues that I manage day to day, but I don't waste time worrying about them, or railing about my misfortune. I figure that neither of them are lethal, and if they're not lethal, then I've got absolutely no right to be anxious. After all, everybody ends up with one health issue or another eventually, and this is just my lot in life.

All of this positivity is completely discordant with the rest of my thinking, and I can't quite explain it myself. But I am far from anxious in every area of my life; instead, I am incredibly inconsistent in the things I worry about. I agonise over things that many people consider trivialities, but am not fazed by certain experiences that others find terrifying.

Though I get nervous before parties, it is not the socialising I am worried about, because I never get anxious about meeting new people. I am genuinely interested in other people, and feel confident in my ability to make them like me. My anxiety doesn't kick in until I care very deeply for someone, at which point I become my alternate, insecure self. I will fret that I have offended or disappointed them, or let them down, or that they will realise I am not worthy of their affection. I'd be far less anxious if I just stuck to acquaintances. It's unfortunate for me that I adore my friends.

I'm not at all anxious about public speaking, which is the number one fear of a vast majority of people. In fact, I will take any opportunity to grab a microphone and show off in front of a crowd. I also love being in front of a camera, and since that very first appearance on TV rarely ever get nervous beforehand. And yet many people are horrified by the idea of being filmed; I know many other writers who would rather eat their toenails than appear on live TV. So why does it not bother me? Why am I, the anxious one, so comfortable in a potentially fraught situation?

I don't know. It is simply not where my worry is channelled. There are many areas in which I am incongruously calm, when by rights, I should be highly anxious. For example, I really should have a phobia about flying – after all, I am terrified of lifts, feel immensely uncomfortable in boats, and am intensely anxious about travelling generally. However, I quite enjoy aeroplane trips, if only for the fact that they afford me a few hours of enforced time off. I am able to completely relax once I get in my seat, to the point where I often fall asleep midair and dribble on my own chin. Perhaps I just exhaust my anxiety quota before take-off and after landing, so I can use the flight to rest and recharge. Or perhaps my cousin M – she of the fear of flying – did enough worrying for both of us. Either way, I'm very grateful, because the last thing I need is more tension on a holiday.

What's more, I never stress about my house being messy, despite being extremely stressed in other areas of my life. I have many friends who are incredibly obsessive about their homes, and who become agitated if there are crumbs in the carpet, clothes on the floor, or coffee cup rings on the table. I don't worry about those things in the slightest. If I have time to do the dishes in the morning it's a bonus, but quite frankly if I can find my keys and the children's shoes, then I am perfectly satisfied with the state of my home. My untidiness is a perpetual source of wonder to my very neat mother, who wouldn't ever leave her home without making her bed. It is also, no doubt, a source of wonder to many of my friends, who thankfully are too polite to comment. And it is a tremendous source of angst to my husband, who feels that just a little anxiety about mess would not necessarily be a bad thing.

I am also strangely incongruent when it comes to phobias. I find mice and rats to be utterly petrifying, and yet other small creatures don't scare me at all. My reaction to mice is purely visceral – I know logically that they are less threatening than dogs, and far less dangerous than spiders – and yet they invoke in me an imme-diate fight-or-flight reaction. I will scream dementedly at a mouse like a woman in a Charlie Chaplin movie, and though I know I am being totally ridiculous I would rather hug a lion than get down from my chair.

On the other hand, when it comes to insects and spiders I am absolutely without fear. I will happily catch a rogue spider in my hand, or trap it in a cup if it is a giant, hairy monster. I will chase a cockroach and squish it with a tissue, or grab a moth in my fingertips and release it in the garden. I quite enjoy playing the role of Brave Spider Hunter in my family. It's nice to be thought of as a superhero now and then.

In terms of my parenting, I am also oddly inconsistent. Though I worry deeply about many aspects of my children's psychological and emotional development, I am very relaxed about certain elements of their upbringing. I know many parents, for example, who obsess about their kids' diets, banning 'treats' and fast food, and insisting on three veg with every meal. I don't ban junk food – given my own proclivity for chocolate, it would be fairly hypocritical – and I don't force-feed my kids vegetables, either. I figure that everything is fine in moderation, and that if they don't want to eat brussels sprouts, well, that probably means they have good taste. What's more, I am pretty easygoing about the amount of TV my kids watch, the amount of time spent playing electronic games, and the amount of time in front of the computer. It is certainly not a free-for-all, but I do consider myself to be flexible and relaxed. And so far, touch wood, despite all the television and computer and chocolate and occasional fast food and lack of broccoli, my kids have been wonderfully healthy.

Possibly my greatest inconsistency is in my attitude to major disasters. I fret endlessly about the little things in life – bills, deadlines, my fingernails, whether or not I'm wearing the right outfit to a party – and yet I don't worry much about Armageddon. Obviously I'm concerned about global warming, but I don't fret about the possibility of tidal waves, or earthquakes, or world war, or meteors hurtling towards earth. I suspect I don't worry because they are such universal catastrophes; if the world ends for whatever reason, we're all going down together. Furthermore, I only worry about what I believe I can control on some level, however distorted my belief might be. And even I know I can't possibly control the world. I can't even control my own children most of the time.

Unusually for someone as anxious as me, I don't agonise over decisions. I make decisions very quickly, whether it's choosing a dishwasher, or deciding where to go on holidays. I don't do my research, weigh up the pros and cons of every option, and then carefully make my choice. I just look around briefly, pick what looks good, and go for it, without doubts or second guesses. Still, as free and easy as this makes me appear, it is actually misleading. I don't rush through decisions because I am so laid-back; I actually rush through decisions so as to avoid the period of uncertainty that provokes so much anxiety in me. I would rather decide quickly, and risk choosing the inferior option, than take my time and live with doubt. That said, one would have to know me pretty well to figure this out, so for all intents and purposes I am an extremely relaxed decision-maker.

Not only am I inconsistent in terms of what I am anxious about, I am also inconsistent in terms of *when* I am feeling anxious. There are times when the slightest problem causes me stress, times when my shoulders are permanently knotted, my temples are constantly throbbing, and my life feels utterly overwhelming. Yet there are other times when I am calm, when I feel on top of my workload, when I laugh and have fun and am full of energy.

And this is an important point: I am not anxious all the time. Just as 'happy' people aren't gleeful every minute, and 'intense' people have moments of levity, there are times when even I am totally relaxed. Yes, I am anxious, but I am not anxious about everything. Yes, I worry, but I don't worry every moment of my life. Remembering this gives me confidence. It gives me hope. It reminds me that there are situations I can handle without stress, which means I do have the capacity to manage my life differently.

It reminds me that, one day, the little calm part of me might prevail.

Therapy

Those artists who say that somehow therapy or analysis will thwart their creativity are completely misinformed. It's absolutely the opposite: it opens closed doors.

Paul Schrader, director

I've always been a very strong advocate of therapy. I think that nearly everyone can benefit from it at some stage, except for those people who have no problems. Which means that absolutely everyone can benefit from therapy, as I don't believe a person without problems exists.

Still, I never sought therapy to address my anxiety issues. I knew it could be a useful tool for people with anxiety disorders, but I genuinely didn't think my anxiety stemmed from a disorder. I was quite sure that everything I worried about was justified, and that anyone who didn't worry about such issues was unreasonably laid-back.

I did seek counselling many years ago, but it wasn't for anxiety. I was in my late twenties, about to get married, and felt my career was floundering, when I consulted a psychologist I'll call Michael (which wasn't his name). Michael was a boyish, pleasant-looking man in his late thirties, who thankfully wasn't handsome enough to be distracting. He specialised in short-term, focused therapy, and I saw him on and off for about two years. We plodded along, talking about relationships and my career, until one day I complained that I couldn't sleep for worrying. Michael listened for a while as I began outlining the myriad of issues I was anxious about. Then, as time was running out, he suggested that I write down all my concerns and bring the list to our next session.

I sat down with a biro and a piece of foolscap paper, and thought about all the things I was worried about. Within two minutes, the page was full. My list was quite comprehensive. Turns out there were ten separate matters that were bothering me, covering everything from finances to my family to my lack of friends.

My Worry List

1. I'm worried that it will rain on our wedding day.
2. I'm worried that we're spending so much money on the wedding and I'm not earning enough and we haven't invested our money wisely.
3. I'm worried about my career.
4. I'm worried about my sister's health.
5. I'm worried about the toll my sister's health is taking on my parents.
6. I'm worried that T isn't happy in his job and that he won't have the motivation to leave.
7. I'm worried that T works so hard and that it will become a big problem for me.
8. I'm worried that I don't have enough friends.

9. I'm worried that I'll never be able to have a baby.
10. Most of all I'm worried that I'm not worried enough at the moment and we'll have nothing to talk about in this session but in another week or month or three months I'll be totally neurotic again.

Now, if points one through nine weren't convincing enough, point ten really put the icing on the cake. I was actually worried that I wasn't worried enough. Only a true master of anxiety can wrangle that one.

Needless to say, Michael did not share my concern.

Michael's biggest achievement with me was to help me to look inwards instead of outwards. I came to him with a long list of issues that I obsessed about, and learned that perhaps they weren't really the problem. Perhaps the problem was the way that I was thinking about the issues. Perhaps there could be another approach.

Michael helped me to gain some insight and perspective, but he wasn't the person to help me to change my life. He was skilled, and personable, but the chemistry just wasn't there. Choosing a therapist is much like choosing a life partner, and while I liked Michael, he and I never truly clicked into place. There was a distance between us, and whilst professional distance is appropriate, I could never completely let down my guard with him. In therapy, you need to be able to let down your guard. If you can't allow yourself to be open and vulnerable, then there's no point in the process.

I finished up with Michael and went solo for a while, then, some years later, stumbled upon my next therapist almost by accident. I found Susan (also not her real name) when I wasn't looking at all, which is often how the best relationships begin.

Susan was a softly spoken psychologist who specialised in child and family therapy, and I got her name from our family doctor.

T and I had been concerned about the behaviour of one of our kids, and we consulted her specifically to give us some advice. We had a couple of very productive meetings as a family, and then I scheduled a final, one-on-one consultation.

Susan and I outlined the issues that had been discussed in the sessions, and the strategies that had been set in place. We were reviewing the progress that had been made when I startled myself by beginning to cry. I felt utterly mortified, but Susan wasn't fussed; no doubt every second person starts to weep in her office.

'You're obviously very distressed,' she said gently. 'What is it that's upsetting you?'

I shook my head, tears dripping off my nose. 'It's not related to the kids,' I told her guiltily. Susan was a child psychologist. It seemed as inappropriate to discuss non-child matters with her as it was to discuss my gynaecological health with my dentist.

She smiled and handed me a box of tissues, the prop of psychologists around the globe. 'I deal with adults too, you know,' she explained.

'Really?' I asked, and wiped my eyes. 'I thought you only dealt with children.'

'Well, children tend to be attached to adults, so it's hard to deal with one without the other. Now, do you want to tell me what's bothering you?'

So I started talking. I talked about my anxieties, my fears, my insecurities and my inability to sleep. I talked about the problems I saw looming large in my life, and the worst-case scenarios that hijacked my thoughts. I talked about the worries I harboured for my marriage and my kids, and the low self-esteem that hindered my career. I talked all through the session, made another appointment, and came back the following week to talk some more. I ended up seeing Susan two or three times a month for more than six years of my life, and she helped to get me where I am today.

I trusted Susan on many levels and believed from the beginning that she was able to help me. She came highly recommended, and had given us excellent advice about the kids, which had naturally engendered my respect and confidence. But it was more than the recommendation, and it was more than the advice that allowed me to click with Susan on a deeper level. I instinctively felt safe with her as my therapist, and could sense her genuine concern for my welfare and growth. In every session I was aware of her commitment to me as a client, and that gave me the security to open myself up to change. With hindsight, I realised that my ex-therapist Michael hadn't demonstrated the same level of commitment. He had done his job, and was professional and courteous, but he wasn't as invested in the outcome. In me.

Susan talked to me, a great deal, which was incredibly important. I couldn't go to a therapist who sat in silence, scribbling notes on a pad as I lay on a couch. After all, I could talk to myself alone, and I often did, when I was driving, doing housework, or standing in the shower. What's more, I'd kept diaries for years, which were really me talking to myself on paper. I wanted a therapist who was prepared to ask me questions, to challenge me, and to tell me how to change. I wanted someone who would engage in a dialogue and unravel my tangled thought processes. And I wanted someone who could unpick my anxieties and make me carefree and relaxed.

Sadly, not even the most skilled therapist on this planet could make carefree and relaxed. But Susan did a truly commendable job with all the rest.

For the first few months of my therapy with Susan, I couldn't stop talking. There was so much to say, so many years of bottled-up angst, that I could have talked solidly for a month. The initial intensity eased, but I still found things to talk about, week after week, month after month, and eventually year after year. Sometimes I felt I didn't need my therapy session. Sometimes I thought I wouldn't have anything to say. Sometimes I even contemplated cancelling my appointment. Still, whenever I entered that office and sat down on that chair, the words would flow out of me, fifty-five minutes' worth, words I didn't even know I was going to say.

Susan helped me to understand the triggers for my anxiety, and to deconstruct the thought processes that impeded my peace of mind. I would talk to Susan about my life and my beliefs, and she would point out my habitual catastrophising, and my tendency to put myself down.

'I've done a terrible job,' I'd tell her despondently, after a particularly difficult week with the kids. 'I am screwing them up for the rest of their lives.'

'Do you hear yourself?' she would ask. 'Why are you assuming you're such a bad parent? Look how much thought you've put into it and how well your children are doing. What else could a good parent do that you're not doing?'

And I'd pause and realise that, maybe, there was another perspective.

Or, 'I totally messed up this weekend. I overreacted to something T said and now he hates me and everything is a complete disaster.'

'You're catastrophising again,' Susan would point out evenly. 'Has he actually said he hates you?'

'No,' I'd say. 'But I know he thinks it.'

'Are you sure?' she'd ask, and raise her eyebrows.

'No,' I'd say. 'But I'd hate me if I was him.'

'Really?' she'd ask. 'So if he ever made a mistake you'd hate him?'

And I'd pause and realise that, maybe, there was another perspective.

Or, 'I'm so lucky,' I'd say. 'I've just been asked to give a talk interstate. I can't believe they chose me. They must be a bit deluded.'

'Are you listening to yourself?' she'd say. 'You're a talented writer and an experienced speaker. Why wouldn't they choose you?'

And I'd pause and realise that, maybe, there was another perspective.

Susan helped me to sort out the muddle in my head when I felt overwhelmed by life, bogged down by my worries, or unsure of which turn to take. She was neutral but not uncaring, able to advise without being directive. She challenged the perspectives that I had never before questioned, the negative way I viewed myself, and the negative way I viewed the world.

Susan worked with me to understand the genesis of my anxiety in my childhood, and in my genes. This was an incredibly important process, for very practical reasons. Firstly, it helped me to overcome my worries, as I could recognise where my irrational thought processes originated. Secondly, and just as importantly, it helped to ease the burden of guilt and shame I carried, that so much of my life, and so many of my relationships, had been compromised by my anxiety.

'I'm so pathetic,' I'd tell Susan, recalling a recent attack of nerves.

'You're not pathetic, Kerri,' she'd say firmly. 'You have an anxiety disorder. And you're doing really well.'

For more than six years, Susan was my voice of reason, quietly pushing her way into my stubbornly unreasonable thoughts. I never became carefree and relaxed – nor did I ever really expect to – but I did eventually incorporate her point of view into my thoughts, where it now lies alongside my own. It's not my point of view, but I respect it, and I listen to it, and it's there in my head every day, even though I no longer see Susan on a regular basis.

I will be racing to worst-case scenarios, or putting myself down, and suddenly she'll be there, her words in my ear.

'You're blowing things out of proportion,' I'll hear, as if Susan was perched on my shoulder, a mini-therapist in bird form.

Or, 'This is your anxiety talking,' she'll cheep to me in the middle of a panic, and I'll realise I'm not being rational, and that I need to question my thought processes.

Or, 'Why did you just insult yourself?' she'll chirp as I tell myself I'm useless, and I'll notice I'm being disparaging to myself.

Susan has given me the tools to deconstruct my fears and negativity, and replace them with a more constructive approach. I'm incredibly grateful to her, not only for all she helped me to achieve, but because she helped me to achieve it without her. I finished therapy a couple of years ago, and whilst I occasionally visit for top-ups, I've been doing pretty well since. Susan didn't cure me, because I'm not going to be cured; anxiety is something I'll live with forever. However, she's helped me to manage my condition far better, and live an easier and happier life.

I proselytise for therapy now like some people proselytise for religion. Willpower is great, and positive thinking is wonderful, but to truly change one's thinking, you need a skilled, committed therapist.

Just never make the assumption that you're not worried enough for therapy. You'll walk in that door, and you'll sit on that chair, and fifty-five minutes later, you'll be astonished at what has come out of you. And, hopefully, much of it will be out to stay.

'No Secret'

If you listed all the reasons for your faith, and all the things that make you cry, it would be essentially the same list.

Robert Brault, writer

I really should stop complaining about my anxiety. After all, it's exceptionally easy to cure. I know this because there are dozens of websites and self-help books that will allow me to overcome worry in just three easy steps. (Or five steps. Or ten. It depends on the website.)

All the strategies boil down to the same basic principle: I just need to change the way that I think. Er . . . yup. I kind of figured that out for myself. The question is *how* I manage to change the way that I think, when I have been suffering from anxiety for the past forty-odd years.

Well, there are many helpful suggestions, from the simple to the rather complex. For example:

- Think positive.
- Listen to music.
- Dance in my lounge room (my personal favourite).
- Smell the flowers.
- Chat to a friend.
- Visualise everything going well for me.
- Squeeze a stress ball.
- Do yoga.
- Meditate.
- Remind myself that this is a 'First World problem'.
- Engage in a written debate with my anxiety.
- Tap on my forehead repeatedly whilst chanting, 'I am calm and happy' (and yes, I really did read about this one).
- Laugh for no reason.
- Keep a gratitude journal.
- Take up a hobby (gardening seems to be the popular choice).
- Exercise for an hour every day.
- Buy a pet.
- Become a vegetarian (and no, I don't really understand this one, either).

Now, don't get me wrong; there is value in each of these techniques (with the possible exception of forehead-tapping, which has only ever made me feel silly). Unfortunately, however, it's not quite that simple. These practices may well assist a normal person to deal with the normal experience of anxiety. But for someone like me, with an anxiety disorder, they just aren't strong enough to cut it. Prescribing a dance to a person having an anxiety attack is like prescribing aspirin to someone who's been decapitated. It's a little bit too late. They can't actually swallow.

A certain amount of work needs to take place before these strategies can become effective. I would have loved to have 'changed my thoughts in three steps' at the age of seventeen, but it was never that easy for me. I did need to change my thoughts, but it was a long, hard process. After all, anxiety is the inability to control your thoughts – your thoughts take over, as you helplessly watch yourself being carried away to places of dread and fear. You can't change your thoughts if you can't control them. First you need to learn to take them in hand.

Telling me that 'thinking positive' will solve my worry problems is like telling an athlete he can win next week's race by running thirty seconds faster. Well, DUH. He *knows* he needs to run thirty seconds faster, but he is already running as fast as he can. To run any faster, he needs an understanding of his running style, and of the barriers preventing him from running to his full potential. And then he needs to practise running, day after day, with his newly learned techniques. He will make small gains, and have days when he feels like he'll never run any faster. He'll have days when he runs slower than the day before. But if he keeps on training with a great coach, he will eventually run as fast as he is physically able to run.

Anxiety – genuine, crippling anxiety – can't be alleviated by pat solutions. There is a place for pop psychology in the marketplace, to assist people with normal levels of worry, but I've never found that they offer anything to someone with anxiety as profound as mine.

And yet, I'd love to have been helped by simple philosophies, instead of having to do all of the therapy I did. A philosophy that seemed particularly attractive to me is the one I will call 'No Secret'. The premise of 'No Secret' is that the universe is based upon the 'law of attraction', and that a person will attract people, events and experiences to match those of which they are thinking. If you think thoughts of prosperity, you'll attract money to yourself. If you think thoughts of babies, you'll attract a child. If you think thoughts of love, you'll attract romance.

'No Secret' would be the perfect answer for someone like me. It implies that nothing in the universe is beyond my control, and if I just think positive thoughts all the time then nothing bad will happen, ever again. There will, therefore, be no more need for anxiety, because if I can control everything, what could I possibly be anxious about?

Sadly, however, it seems utterly implausible.

For a start, 'No Secret' begs the obvious question: how can there be a universal law of attraction that only works for part of the world's population? Can we solve world hunger by getting all the starving people to visualise food, or solve drought by getting people to visualise rain? Nice thought, but I suspect it's pretty unlikely.

What's more, I've more or less disproved the principles of 'No Secret' in my everyday life. Each of my miscarriages, for example, came when I was least expecting it. I'd been visualising giving birth to my baby, planning for our lives together, feeling fertile and well and happy. I hadn't had grim thoughts of loss, or worried in any way about losing my baby. And when each of those pregnancies ended in tragedy, it hit me out of the blue. Then, with each of my three successful pregnancies I was filled with negative thoughts, anticipating disaster at every turn. And yet the outcome was perfect: I had three beautiful, healthy children, despite sending the universe portents of doom.

And that's just my pregnancies. If 'No Secret' really worked, and I attracted those things I visualised, then I'd be a broke, homeless woman who was stuck in a lift with no career. Happily, I can say that is not my reality.

The brilliance of 'No Secret' is that it is objectively irrefutable; it's a totally circular argument. Imagine you have cancer, for example, and you visualise yourself healthy and in remission. If you survive and thrive, it means you've done your visualisations properly. But if you get sicker and die, then clearly you haven't. In other words, if it works, you've done it right; if it doesn't, you haven't. The fact that it may not actually work can never, ever be tested.

Still, it would be very helpful to believe in 'No Secret', and occasionally I have toyed with the idea. But every time, I come up against the starving Africans, and the droughts, and my miscarriages, and I realise that I can't. Though my logic isn't strong enough to banish anxiety, it seems it's far too strong for sending out positive messages to the universe.

The other philosophy to which I'd love to subscribe is that 'everything happens for a reason'. It would be incredibly comforting to believe that there is order and meaning in the universe, instead of believing that things happen at random and that essentially there is chaos. There would be no need for stress and anxiety if I knew that things always worked out for the best. I would know that a run of misfortune – even a terrible catastrophe – would be certain to work out in the end. Good would come out of bad, lessons would be learned, and it might even be the best thing ever to happen to me.

Unfortunately, however, this way of thinking also feels intuitively wrong. Sure, people learn lessons from terrible experiences, but they might have learned equally important lessons without such suffering. And sometimes dreadful things happen that simply don't lead to anything good. Nothing good can come from the loss of a treasured child, at least nothing that is equal to the pain. Nothing good can come from war or natural disaster that is commensurate with the tragedy they wreak.

Despite this, I want to believe in order and reason, which is why I fervently want to believe in God. A belief in God would solve most of my worry problems, because it would mean that everything was always going according to God's plan. If things went well for me, it was because it was God's will. If things went badly for me, well, that was God's will, too.

But my problem again is one of logic. A belief in God mirrors the circular argument of 'No Secret' – it cannot be proved or refuted. The one important difference is that 'No Secret' confers all responsibility on the individual, whereas faith confers all responsibility on God.

I'd pray quite happily if I thought it made a difference, but I really can't believe that it would. If there is a God, He seems to have His own agenda, and is pretty much unswayed by human requests. After all, good things happen to pretty nasty people, and some deeply religious and deeply moral people experience shocking tragedy and loss. And though they will supposedly be rewarded at the gates of heaven, it still won't make a difference to pray about what happens in this earthly life.

I have often been genuinely perplexed by some displays of faith, when people pray for 'God's will to be done'. If it *is* God's will, then He'll *do* it, right? God is omniscient and omnipotent; it's not like anything is stopping Him. And if it's not God's will, then presumably He won't do it, and no amount of human begging will convince Him.

Now, this doesn't mean I have a problem with religion, because I don't. I am Jewish, and I deeply love and respect my Jewish culture: the chicken soup, the challah bread, the sense of community, the Friday night dinners, and Yiddish words like *shlep* and *meshugena* and *broigas*. But my respect for my Jewish heritage hasn't conferred on me a belief in God – it seems that the culture and the faith are two very different things.

Even so, I'm encouraging all of my children to believe in God as I feel it would add enormously to their lives. My girls are a little too young to decide, but so far my son is unconvinced.

'If God was real, He'd come down right now and help out all the starving people,' he said to me one day, and it was virtually impossible to argue with that.

Still, faith is not logical, which is why it's called 'faith'. You either have it or you don't, and sadly, I don't. And I'm sure I don't, because my lack of faith has actually been tested. They say there are no atheists in foxholes, but I was once in a foxhole, and I didn't find God – and if I ever was going to, that was the time.

I had just given birth to my third child, by caesarean section as I'd had complications. I was lying in my hospital room several hours later when the concerned faces of the nurses alerted me to the fact that something was wrong. Turns out that all the pressing on my stomach wasn't standard post-op behaviour – I was actually bleeding into my uterus at quite an alarming rate. What's more, I was gushing blood vaginally, which definitely wasn't normal. Pretty soon afterwards they told my husband and me the news.

'We're going to call in your doctor. You're haemorrhaging internally and externally and you'll need to go back to theatre straightaway.'

I panicked, as one does when the word 'haemorrhage' is mentioned.

'I'm bleeding?' I cried. 'What does it mean? Will I be okay?'

'Just hang on,' the nurse said. 'The doctor will be here soon.'

'Hang on'? *Hang on?* I knew then that it was bad. What on earth was I supposed to hang on to?

A couple of minutes later a registrar walked into my room with a syringe. By then T was outside calling my mum, and I could feel myself drifting in and out of consciousness.

'I don't want to die!' I begged the registrar. I thought of my children living without their mummy, and began screaming, 'You can't let me die! Please! You can't let me die!'

'Calm down!' the registrar ordered. 'I need to do this procedure that may save your life.'

May? *MAY???* That did me in. I began sobbing hysterically, whilst trying frantically to stay awake. I was dying. This was it. I was thirty-nine years old and I was dying. I didn't want to die. I didn't want to leave. My poor husband. My poor kids. My poor parents. The fear was utterly overwhelming.

Suddenly, my doctor walked in. 'I'm here,' he said briskly. 'Let's get you into theatre.'

'Am I going to die?' I asked him.

'No. I won't let you.' And then everything faded to black.

I survived the surgery, of course, but I had looked death in the face and seen nothing but an abyss. I didn't see God, and I didn't pray, because I couldn't feel a God to pray to. It was the most frightening few hours of my life, and I had nothing at all to help me get through.

Not believing in God, or a Secret, or the universe, is like walking a tightrope without a safety net. When you fall the whole impact is absorbed by you, and you alone. If I could flick a switch and have faith, I truly would. If I could 'change my thoughts in three steps', I'd do that, too. Hell, if I could tap myself repeatedly on the forehead and rid myself of anxiety, I'd do it in a second.

Unfortunately, though, that's not how my brain is wired. The only thing that has ever significantly helped me is therapy, and lots of it.

Having said that, I do like to dance in my lounge room occasionally. Those internet sites were right. It is actually very therapeutic.

Getting Through

To suffering there is a limit; to fearing, none.

Sir Francis Bacon, philosopher

The emergency surgery after the birth of my youngest child was far and away the most terrifying experience of my life. But there was more to that story, and it began three weeks to the day before I checked into hospital to have my baby.

I was thirty-eight weeks pregnant when the phone call came. My sister – my only sibling, and my closest friend – had died. She'd been ill for years, but her death was sudden, and deeply shocking. Though I knew how sick she was, I had never allowed myself to believe that she could really die. And so I was plunged into bereavement completely unprepared.

I'd always imagined that a grieving person would behave in a particular way. They would howl, wail, moan, perhaps even collapse in despair. And yet when I was faced with the loss of my darling sister, I didn't do any of those things. I didn't cry. I didn't collapse.

I didn't feel an aching chasm of grief. I was blank. I was numb. I couldn't feel much of anything.

I did, however, feel profoundly guilty. I was concerned that I wasn't feeling enough, and that my relatives and friends wouldn't understand how deeply I loved my sister. I felt that I should be honouring her life by demonstrating how shattered I was. On the other hand, I worried that she would walk in the door and be horribly embarrassed by all the fuss being made, so clearly I wasn't quite ready to mourn.

I understand now that I was completely in shock. Perhaps it was the pregnancy, or the fact that the death was so sudden, but I hadn't processed the loss at all. Grieving, as it turns out, comes in all different shapes and forms.

Three weeks after my sister's death, I gave birth to my baby, and then haemorrhaged and was rushed to theatre. And finally, forty-eight hours after I nearly lost my own life, the full impact of my loss hit me. As I lay recovering in my hospital bed, the floodwaters broke, and I began to feel it all. A black, thick grief descended on me, taking away my reason, my clarity, and my ability to think. I became utterly distraught, crying deep, guttural sobs that seemed to come from the place my baby had just vacated.

I know now what it feels like to drown in grief, as wave upon wave of sorrow engulfed me and I couldn't keep my head above the pain. As the hours rolled by, I continued to cry, and the kindly nurses attempted to soothe me. Those who didn't know my story would assume I was having the post-baby blues, and would pat my leg under the sheet and smile understandingly.

'It's normal to feel weepy after having a baby,' they'd say, and I'd shake my head and continue to cry.

Those who did know my story were awkward, but caring. 'You poor, poor thing. You've been through a lot.'

Still, I sobbed without pausing for more than sixteen hours. I phoned my husband at midnight, convinced that I was losing my mind, but he was unable to calm me down over the phone. I rang my grieving mother, and talked to her, but nothing could penetrate the searing anguish. At around one am, the nurse on duty gave me some sleeping pills, but they didn't work, and I continued to cry in a disoriented, groggy state. In the early hours of the morning, I slept for a short time, and then woke up and continued to weep.

For the first time in my life, I had literally fallen apart.

This is what worst-case scenario really looks like. This was the realisation of my darkest fears. I couldn't function. I couldn't care for my baby. I couldn't hold myself together to speak to my kids. I felt nothing but despair, and I thought that I would never, ever, stop crying. And I didn't. For about twenty-six hours.

But eventually, I did.

I cried endless tears for those twenty-six hours, and then over the past four and a half years I have cried endless tears more. But I got through those initial devastating hours, and I have never again cried for a full day at a time. I survived the loss, and I continue to survive. I live my life, I love my family and friends, I work and I care for the household, and I smile and I laugh and I learn and I grow. I have lived through tragedy and survived. And I know that, despite all my anxieties, if tragedy was ever to befall me again, I would continue to survive in the future.

Prior to my sister dying, the most intense emotional pain I had endured was the break-up with T when I was twenty years old. I loved him then as I love him now and was utterly distraught when he ended our relationship. I had spent months living in fear of losing him, and genuinely believed I would never survive our break-up. I think I imagined I would somehow just die of a broken heart, like a tragic heroine in a nineteenth-century novel. (Though in reality, of course, the tragic heroines most probably just died of consumption.)

When the worst happened, and he left me alone, it was excruciatingly painful. Unexpectedly, though, it also came as a relief. That terrible anxiety about losing T had gone, and I could get on with actually dealing with the loss. As it turns out, it was easier to face the reality than to live with the fear of what might be. I grieved, I cried, and I eventually got through it – far quicker than I had anticipated. Within six months of the break-up, I started seeing another boy (and, if I remember correctly, had rather an excellent time with him, too).

Like anyone else, I've had some challenges in my life. I've had bouts of illness, friendships that have ended, career setbacks, periods of financial strain. And yet, as difficult as they have been, I've got through them. They were generally much worse in my imagination than in my reality.

Even my pregnancy losses were more manageable than I would have expected. They were hard, particularly the first, as I longed so desperately for a child. And there were devastating moments; moments when careless friends asked when we were going to start a family, or speculated as to whether I was feeling clucky. However, I survived. I still functioned. I still went to work every day and saw my friends and ate and read books and watched TV and talked to my husband. I still lived my life. I was sad, but not defeated.

What's more, as much as I dread T going through difficult times, because his pain is my pain and his worry is my worry, when the bad times hit – as they do occasionally for everyone – I cope. In fact, I do more than just cope. I can actually be quite supportive. I manage to disconnect from my own anxiety and offer my husband reassurance and advice and love, showing him that I believe in him and that everything will be okay. And eventually, it always is.

This is the principal irony of my anxiety. I spend so much of my time – no, I *waste* so much of my time – worrying about disasters that will never happen, and yet when something bad does happen, I deal. Initially I cry, I grieve, I am filled with despair or disappointment, but then after a while, I simply get on with living.

So why haven't I learned my lesson? Why do I still experience anxiety when I know perfectly well I can cope with misfortune? I should be one of those wise people who 'don't sweat the small stuff', who operate on a serene, higher plane. I should be one of those people others refer to as 'inspirational'. But alas, nobody refers to me as 'inspirational'. At least, nobody who's seen me stressing out whilst trying to get ready for a party.

Now, don't get me wrong – I'm not the poster girl for surviving tragedy. I have known great loss, but many people have been through far worse times than me. I am constantly aware of how fortunate I am. I have three beautiful children, a wonderful husband, parents who adore me, and a career I love. I live in a prosperous, peaceful country with a democratic government. So why am I wasting so much of my blessed, First World life being worried when I should spend my time being thankful? There are millions – probably billions – of people who would give anything to swap lives with me, to live in peace and financial security and (relative) good health in a wonderful country.

There are people who are persecuted for their religion. People who can't afford to feed their family. People whose children are dying of preventable diseases. People whose countries are at war, and will be for generations. These are the people who have a right to be anxious. I don't have a right to be anxious. I am insulting all of them by being anxious. I should respect their genuine hardship by not manufacturing my own. I should be content every minute of my life.

And I am content, right now, as I write these words. But in a day, or an hour, or ten minutes, or even three, something will pop into my head – maybe the mortgage payment is due, or T and I have a squabble, or there is an ambiguous email from my publisher – and my contentment will be replaced by anxiety in a second.

I can't be content every minute of my life. Contentment is not my natural state; it is something I experience in fleeting moments, in between long bouts of worry, brief periods of panic, and occasional episodes of elation. Anxiety is my default position. It is part of me, like my eye colour, or my love of oranges. I can't shake anxiety permanently from my psyche. The best I can do is manage it, and try to prevent it from impacting too deeply on my life.

No doubt everyone's experience of anxiety is slightly different, but anxiety as I experience it is a fear of future pain. There are rational fears and irrational fears, and fear of future pain falls firmly into the latter category. For a start, fear of anything in the 'future' is fairly irrational, as it hasn't happened yet, and probably never will. And even if it is going to happen, there's no point fearing it now; may as well wait until it's actually happening to be afraid.

Secondly, when pain does occur it is generally finite and manageable. It is the fear of pain that can linger on indefinitely. I have spent far, far more time being proactively distressed by bad things that haven't happened to me than by the few bad things that have. I am constantly frightened of the pain that will never come, whilst resolutely facing the pain that does.

Irrational.

Of course, I'm not alone in being irrational. Most of us have one irrational fear or the other. My mum, who travels around the world and catches mice in her bare (well, gloved) hands, is horrified by spiders. My friend A, who rides motorbikes and is one of the most rational people I know, has a deep-rooted fear of hospitals.

My friend M has a morbid fear of sharks, even though she's rarely by the ocean and has never come near one in her life. And my friend H is terrified that her son will be kidnapped, despite not being in the Mafia, the government, royalty, or even very rich.

Irrationality is part of the human condition, like needing love, searching for meaning in our lives, and coveting our neighbour's ox. My particular irrationality is fear of pain, and I know now that it's okay. As my therapist Susan would say, 'You have an anxiety disorder. Do you think you can give yourself a break?'

And these days, that's just what I try to do.

Calm

There are times when you can only take the next step.
And then another.

William Gibson, author

For the record I don't pick my face anymore. The urge stopped. I still bite my nails but I dealt with that by getting acrylics. And I got electrolysis on my eyebrows so they're not an issue anymore, either. Sometimes you just have to think laterally.

As I write this final chapter, I am sitting at my dining room table with my laptop, looking out of our large glass windows onto the tree-lined street outside. It's a cloudy Saturday morning, and the roads are wet from an early rain shower. T has taken our son to his softball match, the girls are curled on the couch watching cartoons, and I am happily into my second cup of coffee. Later today we are all going to my parents' home for brunch, and then tonight the baby-sitter is coming and T and I are meeting some friends for dinner. It is shaping up to be a good weekend.

Over the ridiculous, interminable theme song of *SpongeBob SquarePants*, I hear a siren. I strain to see where it's coming from, and within a few moments it's in view – an ambulance, racing down our street. Suddenly, a vision flashes in my head: T skidding on the wet road in his car, he and our son crashing into a tree, the ambulance coming to the rescue, the police coming to our house, their solemn faces as I open the d–

STOP.

No, I won't do it. I shake the vision away. I tell it to get lost. I rise up from my chair and go and sit with my girls for a moment, remind myself of what's real. I snuggle next to my ten-year-old, pretend to eat a piece of plasticine 'dinner' that my youngest offers me, and clear my head.

I won't do it. I won't go there.

For years anxiety has been an intruder in my mind, barging in without invitation, causing misery and chaos. I've rarely even tried to kick it out, feeling that somehow it keeps misfortune at bay, and I don't have the strength to defeat it anyway.

But recently I've learned that I'm stronger than I think. Recently I've learned that I can make my life easier.

I will never entirely banish anxiety from my life, and I will never be 'carefree', 'laid-back' or 'easygoing'. I have, however, started to fight for my peace of mind.

I try to use discipline to push catastrophic thoughts from my mind. I refuse to entertain them, kicking them out as they knock on my door. I read books, I watch TV, I focus on my kids, I surf the internet, I do anything to distract myself from the fears bubbling beneath the surface. And the more I distract myself – the less I allow those fears to rise and take hold – the less power they have over me. It's a long, slow process, but I'm on my way. If I continue at this rate, by my eighties or nineties I might even be able to call myself 'calm'. Or if I can't call myself 'calm', then at least, 'not agitated'.

I try very hard to recognise when I'm being unreasonably anxious and to talk myself down. It's not easy, because my default position is to believe my own propaganda, so that when I tell myself things are dire, I trust in that. But I have the voice of my therapist in my head, and I have T in my ear, and I try to listen to them both. Often it takes me a while to hear them, and occasionally I still choose to ignore them, but I'm definitely getting better at meeting them halfway.

In times of great stress – of which there are many – I resort to taking my life one day at a time. I don't think about tomorrow, or next week, or next month; I just focus on getting through the day. When that doesn't work, I focus on getting through the hour. And when that doesn't work, I take things ten minutes at a time. Sometimes, it's how I get through.

I keep myself extremely busy. The devil finds work for idle hands to do, and in my case, the devil is anxiety. So I take on as much work as I can get, and when there isn't enough, I generate my own. I raise three kids, and I look after the finances, and I cook (occasionally), and I clean (sporadically) and I do the laundry (when I absolutely have to). I do school runs twice a day and drive my kids to after-school activities and spend countless hours at the supermarket. I am so busy that I literally *never* do nothing, because if I ever have a moment free during the day I am asleep before my bottom hits the couch. I am always tired, and I go through bottles of under-eye concealer, but it's a small price to pay to keep panic at bay.

I look after myself emotionally. Life is so hard, in so many ways, and I try to be as kind to myself as possible. Every day I do something nice for myself, even if it's as simple as putting aside ten minutes before breakfast to read the paper and have a coffee before starting the morning rush. I love books and read them in five-minute snatches, whilst eating lunch, waiting to pick up the kids, even sitting on the toilet. I spend time online, in the fascinating virtual world. I phone my friends, who nurture me in 1000 different ways, making me laugh, boosting me up, calming me down, and supporting me. I lie in bed with my husband and watch silly TV and laugh. And I make time to cuddle up with my kids, away from homework and chores and Nintendo games, just to breathe in the wonder of these three beautiful people I made. This is what it is all about, I remind myself. None of the other stuff matters.

I am honest about how anxious I am. I don't try to pretend that I'm coping when I'm not, except in front of my kids. I don't put on a brave front or pretend to be the perfectly together career woman. I ring friends in tears. I turn up on my mum's doorstep asking for reassurance. I talk to my husband about my latest worries. I allow the people I care about to comfort me, and generally they do an amazing job.

I exercise every day, as I know that a healthy body is a healthy mind. Or at least, I *think* about exercising every day, and I plan to start an exercise regime really soon. Or rather, I know I should be planning an exercise regime, and I feel guilty that I haven't started one yet. But I also know that guilt is a useless emotion, and my anxiety is more than enough useless emotion for one person, so I let the guilt slide, and figure I'll start exercising when I'm ready. Which will be soon. Really soon. I promise.

I try to focus on all I have to be thankful for. I don't keep a formal gratitude journal, as that feels a little forced to me, but I feel thankful for my good fortune every single day.

When my kids are driving me to distraction, as they are wont to do, I remind myself of how lucky I am to have them. In a world filled with kids with disabilities and illnesses, in a world in which parents lose children every day, or are unable to have them at all,

I have an extraordinary son and two magnificent daughters, and I feel profoundly blessed.

When I get worried about the state of my marriage – when T and I fight, and I feel like it's all a disaster – I remind myself of the good times. I think of how we laughed the night before over a private joke. I recall him taking the kids out on the weekend so that I could stay home and work on my manuscript. I remember how much we love each other, and how lucky I am to have a life partner. And I realise that marriage is hard, and the fight will pass, and I just bide my time until it blows over.

When I feel stressed and anxious about my career – that I'm not successful enough, that I haven't written enough books, that I started too late and now time is running out – I give myself a reality check. I am a published author, which would have seemed unbelievable just a few short years ago. I am paid to write for several publications, which also would have seemed unbelievable up until recently. I pick up *Husband*, and I turn it over, and try to recall the elation of seeing it in print for the first time. I achieved my goal, and now with this second book I'm achieving another, and I am a very lucky girl indeed.

When I feel anxious about finances, I try to put things in perspective. I have a home, a car, food in the fridge and clothes on my back. Everything is relative, and with a home usually comes a mortgage and with a mortgage usually comes financial strain, but I know that I will never starve or be homeless. Compared to most of the world's population, I live in the lap of luxury, and I am deeply grateful for the stroke of good fortune that saw me born into a country in which this lifestyle is possible.

Now, this all sounds very Pollyanna-ish, and yes, feeling grateful is a wonderfully positive emotion. Unfortunately, however, gratitude doesn't completely negate anxiety. The opposite of anxiety isn't gratitude, it's serenity. In fact, gratitude can theoretically coexist with anxiety, as I can feel lucky for my tremendous good fortune, and then start worrying about all that I have to lose. In reality, however, it is hard to balance the two sensations simultaneously. Feeling grateful grounds me firmly in the present, and whilst I hold on to those feelings, I can't be focused on what might happen to me in the future.

Of course, I still have times when my anxiety gets the better of me. I still have days when I run around in circles like a frantic puppy, fretting about absolutely everything and accomplishing absolutely nothing. I still have moments when I experience a failure to cope, when I need to run to my bedroom, lie on the bed and check out for a little while. And I still have the rare anxiety attack, from which it is simply impossible to talk myself down, and all I can do is take a Valium and go to sleep.

This, however, is as bad as it gets. I know that there are people who have complete nervous breakdowns, and end up emotionally disabled and requiring care. I also know that I will never be one of those people. I might cry, I might yell, I might chase my own tail, I might curl up in the foetal position for five minutes, or fifty, but eventually I will always get up again. I will haul myself up and go back to my life, in all its complicated, anxiety-producing glory.

Most of all, I will forgive myself for being such an anxious person. My worry is part of me – it's in my genes and in my nature – and I have accepted myself for all that I am. I can laugh at myself, and my life filled with crises, those that are real, and those born purely of my imagination.

Even that is a big step. And maybe, even that is enough.

What a wonderful life I've had!
I only wish I'd realised it sooner.

Colette, author

Acknowledgements

To the team at Curtis Brown, for looking after me so well;

To Iain Dale and all at The Robson Press, for bringing this book to the UK, and to Namkwan Cho, for the amazing cover art;

To Kylie Ladd, whose daily messages keep me sane;

To Michael and Melanie Spiller, who I adore, and not just because of Simon;

To Gabrielle Reid, who I could not live without;

To my parents, for all the support and love;

And to Tony, Arkie, Saachi and Calliope, for the joy, the laughter, and for putting up with me as I wrote this book;

THANK YOU.

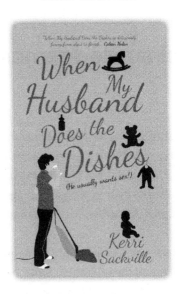